C0-CBU-981

B

UNIVERSITY OF WINNIPEG
LIBRARY
Portage Avenue
Winnipeg, Manitoba R3B 2E9

DISCARDED

Business Communication
Theory and Technique

5718
.H293
1983

RICHARD HATCH
San Diego State University

Business Communication
Theory and Technique

SRA
®
SCIENCE RESEARCH ASSOCIATES, INC.
Chicago, Palo Alto, Toronto, Henley-on-Thames, Sydney
A Subsidiary of IBM

Acquisition Editor	John T. Maloney
Project Editor	Sara H. Boyd
Manuscript Editor	Douglas Becker
Designer	Paula Schlosser
Cover Designer	Joseph di Chiarro
Compositor	Graphic Typesetting Service

Library of Congress Cataloging in Publication Data

Hatch, Richard A.
  Business communication.

  Includes index.
1. Communication in management.   2. Business report writing.
3. Commercial correspondence. I. Title.
HF5718.H293   1983   808'.066651021   82-21519
ISBN 0-574-20660-4

Copyright © Science Research Associates, Inc., 1983
All rights reserved
Printed in the United States of America

Some of the material in this book was adapted from the author's earlier work *Communicating in Business*, © 1977, Science Research Associates, Inc. Appendix C is reprinted from *Typewriting: A Mastery Approach* (Advanced Course) by Mitchell, Mach, LaBarre, ©1978, Science Research Associates, Inc.

5 4 3 2 1

Contents

To the Instructor

This text is designed to meet the needs of business-communication instructors who wish to base their writing instruction on the psychological principles of communication. *Business Communication* integrates communication theory, writing principles, and writing practice in such a way that the student can understand the practical relevance of the theoretical material. The psychological principles of interpersonal communication are not isolated in a self-contained unit or an afterthought appendix; they are emphasized throughout the text. As a result, students learn about the psychology of communication as they work on their writing skills.

The theoretical principles stressed in the text are fused into a single consistent conceptual model of interpersonal communication that is relevant to the communication problems of people in business. Earlier theory and practice texts have presented an overview of the principal schools of thought on communication rather than a unified and functional conceptual model; students exposed to such texts were often completely confused either about what they were supposed to learn or about how they were to apply what they did learn to actual communication problems. The model of communication in Chapter 3 integrates all the theory material into a single perspective and shows the student how to apply it to real-life situations.

The psychological principles presented in the text are related to three major areas of communication: the psychology of perception (especially as it relates to the problem of assessing the reader's frame of mind) is discussed in Chapter 4; symbols and their meanings are covered in Chapter 5; common psychological barriers to communication are discussed in Chapter 6. Chapter 3, which provides a conceptual integration of all these areas, could be restudied as a valuable review following Chapter 6.

The purpose of studying psychological principles is better writing. Ideally students should begin writing very early in the course. The first student writing problems are presented in Chapter 2.

Basic communication principles and writing techniques are covered in the introductory chapters and Parts I and II (Chapters 1–11). In Part III (Chapters 12–16), the student is asked to apply these skills to letters and intra-organizational memos (so often ignored in business-communication texts). In Part IV (Chapters 17–20), the student learns the basic principles of report writing and oral presentation. Short, manageable practice pieces give students a chance to apply what they have learned.

The basic writing skills and principles covered in Chapters 7 through 11 are designed to be studied *at the same time as* the theoretical material in Chapters 3 through 6. In this way, students can improve their writing skills through regular practice while they are deepening their understanding of the communication process. For the instructor's convenience, student writing problems for Chapters 7 through 11 are clustered at the end of Chapter 11. These problems are carefully designed to provide good practice at any point in the early chapters. As students become more sophisticated, they will produce increasingly better solutions to the problems.

A major difficulty for students in business-communication courses is that the writing problems they're asked to solve make it necessary for them to imagine themselves in a variety of unfamiliar environments and situations, and their imagination (or lack of it) is often a major determinant of their success as writers. This book contains two continuing cases that allow students to write messages throughout the course in the same organizational setting. As students continue to solve the problems in the ABMC Case or the Education and Training Case (both following Chapter 11), they will develop an increasingly sophisticated understanding of the organizational context of their messages. Thus they spend more time learning about writing and less time trying to figure out the realistic complexities of a whole series of situations. The Forms Design Minicase (also following Chapter 11) lets the student assume a variety of identities in a developing communication situation, with many of the same advantages.

Additional practice problems—a total of 230 in all—are provided at the ends of Chapters 12 through 20 for instructors who prefer a variety of practice settings or who wish to supplement the two continuing cases with additional problems.

The process of writing—planning, writing, and revising—is emphasized throughout the presentation of basic writing principles. (Also emphasized is something rarely dealt with in other texts—how a good writer works.) In addition, Chapter 11 discusses dictation and the use of word processing in message production. Students explore efficient working methods in depth and are shown the advantages of using them.

In Parts III and IV, writing instruction focuses on two major areas of communication. The first area, informational messages, includes both brief informational messages (often called good-news messages) in Chapter 12 and business reports in Chapters 17 through 20. The second area deals with the special problems of messages in emotionally charged situations (bad-news and persuasive messages); this material is covered in Chapters 13, 14, and 15. By concentrating only on these basic message types, the book avoids overwhelming students with detailed instructions for extremely specific types of messages (such as the various kinds of acknowledgment letters used in wholesale and retail trade) which meet the needs of only some students. Varied examples and writing problems help students understand how to adapt these basic approaches to all kinds of specific situations.

Experienced teachers recognize that students learn intensively by studying a wide variety of good examples. This text provides nearly a hundred such illustrations, most of them complete messages rather than just isolated fragments.

Instructors who wish to emphasize report writing can go directly to Part IV of the text after covering the introductory chapters (1–11). Instructors who want to concentrate on letters and memos should go directly to Part III.

Whatever the emphasis of the course, most instructors find that students react positively to the material on job applications and résumés. Chapter 16 serves a dual purpose; it shows students how to write a good résumé and application letter and gives them an opportunity to apply all the principles, both theoretical and practical, presented in the book.

I would like to thank the following reviewers for their helpful comments and criticisms:

Dorothy A. Anderson
Foothill College

W. E. Gentzel
Pensacola Junior College

Jean Johnston
University of Akron

David H. Kane
Foothill College

Jon Loff
Allegany Community College

Kenneth R. Mayer
Cleveland State University

Rosemary Piserchio
College of San Mateo

Charlene Schou
Idaho State University

Andrea Word
Central Texas College

I am greatly indebted to Ann, Karen, and Kevin Hatch, whose support made this project possible. I thank Douglas Becker for his thorough editing of the manuscript. Michel Lipman provided especially useful example and problem material. Jack Maloney's encouragement kept the project moving through the rough spots, and Sally Boyd made the editing and production process very smooth and pleasant.

San Diego
November 1982

Business Communication
Theory and Technique

1

The Importance of Communication in Business

Language serves three functions.
The first is to communicate ideas.
The second is to conceal ideas. The
third is to conceal the absence of ideas.
Otto Jespersen

How forcible are right words!
Job 6:25

We're at Tribune Square, Chicago. We're in the well-appointed office of the president of WGN-Continental Broadcasting Corporation—'the most powerful broadcast medium in the Midwest.' He [Ward Quaal] has been battling a slight sinus condition, but his presence is, nonetheless, felt."

Ward Quaal Speaks

"I'm responsible for all its [CBC's] broadcasting properties. We have radio and television here. We have a travel company here. We have a sales company here. We have Continental Productions Company here. We have radio and television in Minnesota and translator systems in northern Michigan, Wisconsin, as well as Minnesota. We have cable television in Michigan and California. We have television in Denver. We have sales companies in New York and Tokyo. I operate sixteen different organizations in the United States and Japan.

"My day starts between four-thirty and five in the morning, at home in Winnetka. I dictate in my library until about seven-thirty. Then I have breakfast. The driver gets there about eight o'clock and oftentimes I continue dictating in the car on the way to the office. I go to the Broadcast Center in the morning and then to Tribune Square around noon. Of course, I do a lot of reading in the car.

"I talk into a dictaphone. I will probably have as many as 150 letters dictated by seven-thirty in the morning. I have five full-time secretaries, who do nothing but work for Ward Quaal. I have seven swing girls, who work for me part-time. This does not include my secretaries in New York, Los Angeles, Washington, and San Francisco. They get dicta-belts from me every day. They also take telephone messages. My personal secretary doesn't do any of that. She handles appointments and my trips. She tries to work out my schedule to fit these other secretaries.

"I get home about six-thirty, seven at night. After dinner with the family I spend a minimum of two and a half hours each night going over the mail and dictating. I should have a secretary at home just to handle the mail that comes there. I'm not talking about bills and personal notes, I'm talking about business mail only. Although I don't go to the office on Saturday or Sunday, I do have mail brought out to my home for the weekend. I dictate on Saturday and Sunday. When I do this on holidays, like Christmas, New Year's, and Thanksgiving, I have to sneak a little bit, so the family doesn't know what I'm doing.

"Ours is a twenty-four-hour-a-day business. We're not turning out three thousand gross of shoes, beans, or neckties. We're turning out a new product every day, with new problems. It's not unusual for me to get a phone call on a weekend: 'What are your thoughts on it, Mr. Quaal? Would you speak out on it?' I'm not going to hide my posture on it. I'm going to answer that. This may mean going into the studio to make a recording. Or I may do a tape recording at home. Or maybe I'll just make a statement. I am in a seven-day-a-week job and I love it! . . .

"When I come to Broadcast Center, I'll probably have about five or six different stacks of mail. One stack is urgent and should be acted upon before I make any phone calls. Once I handle that, which usually takes about fifteen, twenty minutes, I start the important phone calls. In-between these phone calls and others of lesser importance, I get into the other mail. On a typical day we'll get thirteen hundred pieces of first-class mail addressed to me personally. Every letter is answered within forty-eight hours—and not a form letter. There are no form letters. If they write to the president of the company, they don't want to hear from the third vice-president. They hear from the president. Mail and the telephone, that's the name of the game in this business."[1]

As you can see, communication is important to Ward Quaal. It's what he does for a living.

WRITTEN COMMUNICATION IS VITALLY IMPORTANT

Communication is important to you, too. As a future manager, you too will be a professional communicator.

Textbooks commonly define a manager as someone who plans, coordinates, organizes, controls, and supervises the work necessary to carry out a given task. All these activities are largely communication activities. And many studies have found that managers spend 75 percent or more of their time in communication activities: listening, reading, talking, telephoning, writing, and dictating. They do their jobs by communicating. Good managers are very skillful communicators.

Although managers communicate in a variety of ways, their written communications are particularly vital. In most organizations, the most important messages are written ones: policies, plans, proposals, and reports. These messages allow the organization to grow and prosper.

Written messages are important in every functional area of an organization. In the marketing area, some of the most important messages pertain to promotional campaign plans, product descriptions and catalogs, sales forecasts and reports, and procedures for handling incoming orders. In finance and accounting, the major written messages include annual reports, financial plans, justifications, procedures, and explanatory material to accompany all the various printouts produced in the accounting process. In production, written messages include plans, procedures, directives, production reports, proposals for changes in methods, and quality control reports. In information systems, written messages include system and program documentation, manuals for users and operators, and requests for proposals from vendors.

---

1. Studs Terkel, *Working: People Talk about What They Do All Day and How They Feel about What They Do* (New York: Pantheon Books, 1972), pp. 390–91. Used by permission.

Besides this documentation is the heavy flow of correspondence between all parts of the organization and users of its products or services. In addition to that is the virtual avalanche of day-to-day interdepartmental memos, requests, opinions, summaries, advisories, and other routine messages.

Your Written Messages Improve Your Image of Competence

In your own department, your boss and others assess your competence and industriousness through their experiences with you. But other people learn more about you from your writing; they don't see you often, but they see your written messages often. As a result, the influence that you build in your organization rises largely on the foundation of your writing.

Exposure through writing is especially important at promotion time, when your boss must persuade his or her superior to promote you, because most of the superior's knowledge of you is based on your writing. Skillful and competent writing can really pave the way for advancement.

In fact, one of the best reasons for studying writing in school is that you can learn—and make the inevitable mistakes all learners make—in a safe environment. If you write a course assignment that communicates poorly, the worst that can happen is that you'll recognize its flaws and have to rewrite it. But if you communicate poorly on the job, you can establish negative images in people's minds that will take quite a while to erase. Having to learn on the job can be very expensive!

Your Writing Allows You to Influence Events

Once you develop confidence in your writing, your willingness to write will give you the opportunity to exercise influence in your organization.

When issues affecting your job are being discussed, you can contribute your arguments in writing, a form that people take more seriously than speech. When you express your ideas aloud, people can get distracted just as you reach a key point. And when they summarize your ideas for others, they'll seldom say them as clearly or forcefully as you did. But they can take your written statement back to their offices to read carefully, and they can show it to others, allowing your ideas to come through clearly and strongly. In fact, your ideas often carry extra weight simply because you felt strongly enough about them to write them down. Writing shows that you really care about an issue, and it suggests that your points are carefully considered and not just mentioned off the top of your head.

Your writing will help you influence events in other ways, too. If you're willing to write the first draft of policies and procedures, then you'll be the one to work out all the details; the fine points will be the way you think they should be. After you finish your draft, others will surely change certain points, but typically three-quarters or more of your draft of a new policy will remain after all the changes are made. Even as a junior member of your department, you can exert strong influence in this way.

Your Boss Will Value Your Writing Skill

When your boss discovers that you can write well, he or she will begin shifting to you some of the heavy writing load that all managers carry. The fact that you can handle such assignments successfully makes you more valuable to your boss and gives you an opportunity to demonstrate the quality of your work in a very visible way.

Furthermore, such writing can be the best possible training for the day when you take over additional responsibilities. Writing for your boss helps you to see your boss's viewpoint—to see beyond the limits of your own job. That kind of broad view will be valuable as you progress through your career.

WRITING CAN BE FUN

Perhaps most important of all, once you develop confidence in your writing ability, the writing part of your job will become fun. Typically, the first two or three years of a career are spent largely on carrying out routine procedures devised by others; thus writing assignments are often the most interesting and creative parts of your job. At these times, your ideas and your special qualities can make a difference. That's fun!

YOU CAN LEARN TO WRITE WELL

Some people are born with more writing talent than others; that's certainly no secret. What's often overlooked is that people with only average writing talent can become very good writers.

When we say "writing," we mean several different things. Sometimes we mean getting ideas down on paper in grammatically correct form, with all the words spelled correctly and all the punctuation in the right places. And many people think that that's what good writing is. But good writing, as we'll discuss it in this book, is a very different thing: it's writing that gets ideas across. And that's much more a matter of paying attention to your reader than of paying attention to your English.

Please don't misunderstand; good English mechanics are important. They're important because, to many readers, good English suggests good thought. Such readers tend to disregard messages with misspellings and punctuation errors, assuming the ideas in them are probably as sloppy as the mechanics. Whether or not that assumption is correct, we must recognize that many readers believe it's correct; thus we help them believe in our messages by taking care with the mechanics.

But at the same time, we also recognize that effective written communication is largely a matter of good planning. What makes good writing good is the writer's decisions on how to approach a particular reader and how to explain the ideas. These decision-making skills can definitely be learned, even by people with only average natural writing talent.

You'll be learning about these skills as you study this book.

HOW THIS BOOK IS ORGANIZED

This book is divided into four major parts. In Part I, you'll learn about the communication process itself, which is valuable background for any working communicator. You probably agree that knowing science and literature makes you a better citizen, even though you may not be able to specify a given piece of scientific knowledge that helped you vote more wisely in the last election. In the same way, knowing the fundamental nature of communication makes you a better communicator. It helps you think about communication more wisely and plan messages more effectively.

In Part II, you'll learn the basic writing principles that experienced business writers use. By studying how good writers work, you'll capitalize on their experience, thus avoiding some of the mistakes that everyone who learns the hard way has to make.

In Part III, you'll apply the basic writing principles by planning and writing various kinds of short messages, including memos and letters. Here you'll not only learn generally accepted message plans, but you'll also learn how to adapt them to your special situation.

Finally, in Part IV you'll learn some special techniques that good writers use to compose longer messages, such as reports. Since the ideas in reports are more complicated than those in short messages, special planning is needed to help the reader understand them. And since report writing is often particularly critical to career success, you must understand the techniques that have worked well in the past.

THE WAY TO LEARN TO WRITE IS BY WRITING

As you study the material in this book, the most important thing to remember is that no amount of reading and study can improve your writing—unless you practice what you're learning. You must practice your writing to improve it. And the more you practice the techniques discussed in this book, the more your writing will improve.

So even if you're studying this book for a course in which the instructor will assign practice writing, do your own practice writing besides. This book contains about 200 writing problems, many more than any course can use. But you can use them. After every study session, pick two or three practice problems in whatever section of the book you're in and plan how you would write those messages. Then write one or two of them. When you finish, set your practice draft aside and come back to it two or three days later. By that time, you'll be able to look at it objectively and evaluate it critically; you may even be able to spend five or ten minutes improving it. In this way, you'll make the best use of your practice time.

FURTHER EXPLORATION

Talk to a manager in an organization (or review your own management-related experience) and explore the importance of communication, especially writing, in that manager's career. Specifically, what kinds of writing does that manager do? How important is writing skill in that manager's job? How much difference would it make to that manager if he or she were a better writer? What makes "good" writing good, in that manager's view?

2

Basic Concepts of
Business Communication

*Talk of nothing but business, and
dispatch that business quickly.*
Placard on the door of the Aldine Press,
Venice, established about 1490

*Vigorous writing is concise. A
sentence should contain no
unnecessary words, a paragraph no
unnecessary sentences, for the same
reason that a drawing should have
no unnecessary lines and a machine
no unnecessary parts.*
William Strunk

E ven though communication is clearly a vital factor in personal and organizational success, another question remains: Why study English again? You've probably been studying English almost constantly since you began school at age five. Now, at least fourteen years later, you're asked to explore it one more time. Will you really learn that much more in one more term of English?

If that question were truly relevant, it would be very hard to answer. But it isn't, and here's why. There are many kinds of communication, and your English and speech courses had to cover them all. But business communication is one particular kind of communication with special characteristics that distinguish it from most kinds of communication you've studied before. In the next section, we see how.

HOW BUSINESS COMMUNICATION IS DIFFERENT

Business communication differs from other kinds of communication in four important ways that form the basis for this book's approach to the study of communication.

Business Communication Is Goal-Oriented

People communicate in organizations to accomplish specific goals, such as imparting some information or persuading a co-worker to do a job in a certain way. The purpose of business communication is to achieve the communicator's goals.

Many other kinds of communication are not goal-oriented in this way. Songs and poetry, for example, are often communicated for the sheer enjoyment of the experience itself and not to accomplish some practical goal. You exchange small talk with friends for the simple enjoyment of it, not to accomplish some practical goal. But in business you're calling a meeting, announcing a new policy, evaluating a proposal, or selling a product. To succeed in your job, you must make these messages work by accomplishing their goals. All the kinds of communication situations we'll consider in this book involve specific practical goals.

Once communication goals have been stated, success or failure can be determined very simply (at least in theory). Did the message accomplish its communicator's goals? If it did, then we say it was effective. In evaluating a business message, effectiveness is the single most important criterion. If the message was effective, then it was a good message. If the message was ineffective, then regardless of its other merits, it wasn't a good message.

This point doesn't mean that other criteria are unimportant. Good grammar, spelling, and punctuation, for example, are very important characteristics of effective business messages. They're important not only because they make the message correct, but also because a grammatically phrased, correctly spelled, and conventionally punctuated message is more likely to communicate successfully. Let's face it, if every third or fourth word in your memo is misspelled, then your readers may begin to wonder if your ideas aren't as sloppy as your spelling.

Business Communication Takes Place in Real Time

Not only is business communication oriented to specific goals, but it also takes place in specific situations. Business messages are written not to edify future generations of mankind, but to meet the immediate needs of here-and-now situations. The time scale in business differs from many other settings, and that makes the messages different.

This textbook was written at least two years before the date you're reading it, and it was composed to help students over the next decade or so learn about communication principles and techniques they'll apply over careers spanning half a century into the future. That's one kind of communication. Somewhere, at this moment, an organization's department head is drafting a memo requesting an additional employee in the department to cover next quarter's work load, and that memo will be typed, sent, read, and decided upon in the next three or four days. That kind of communication is typical in business.

One of the most important differences between these two situations is the need for efficiency in communication. In business, the typical reader is an extremely busy executive with a heavy daily reading load. He or she may receive a three- or four-inch stack of mail and interoffice messages every day, perhaps even twice a day. (If you think you have a lot of reading to do in college, just wait!) In that setting, a message must communicate quickly and efficiently.

To begin with, a message that can be quickly read and easily understood is more likely to be read. If your message is awkwardly stated and hard to follow, or twice a long as it needs to be, the reader may pass on to something else without giving your message full attention. After all, many other issues compete for a busy reader's attention, and some of these may be more important than your message.

In addition, an efficient message is more likely to leave a good impression in the reader's mind. It meets the reader's needs better by letting him or her absorb the necessary information, take whatever action may be required, and move on to something else in a timely manner. That's the way executives like to do business.

The first step toward making a message efficient is to get right to the point. A message that starts right out by saying what it has to say is an efficient message. In conversation, the listener often expects some initial socializing and small talk (as Figure 1 illustrates), but in written communication, the reader expects the message to get right down to business. In your early practice writing, concentrate on getting right to the point, saying what you have to say (in a friendly and relaxed way), and then quitting.

```
DATE: July 19, 1983

TO: Willard Muñoz, Purchasing

FROM: Hyland Foster, Warehouse 5

SUBJECT: Need for J-45 Sealing Tape


                          Poor

      How are things going, Will?  How's your family?  It sure
was nice to get a chance to sit and talk with you and your family
at the company picnic last week!  Give my best to Jerry when you
see him again.

      I checked over our supply of J-45 tape, and it looks like
our consumption in the last quarter has been about average.  If
you put us down for the usual five cartons in your next order,
that should do it.


                    Right to the Point

      I checked over our supply of J-45 tape, Will, and our
consumption in the last quarter has been about the same as usual.
Please order us the standard five cartons again for next quarter.

      I really enjoyed our chat at the company picnic.
```

Figure 1 Getting right to the point

The Communicator, Not the Audience, Is Responsible
for Successful Communication

As we've seen, people in business communicate to achieve certain goals. Almost every time you communicate at work, you're the one who will profit or lose from the communication. Audience members reasonably assume—and you should, too—that making the message easy for them to grasp is your responsibility. The communicator does the hard work of communicating; the audience shouldn't have to work hard to understand.

In some nonbusiness settings, communicators don't make this assumption. Unfortunately, some college teachers, and even a few textbook writers, make the opposite assumption. They assume that, if they make a message available, then digging out the meaning is the student's responsibility, no matter how hard that is. Certain literary messages contain several levels of meaning, not all of which are accessible to the ordinary reader. For example, over the last few decades, scholars have spent literally thousands of hours studying the meanings in James Joyce's *Ulysses*. But if you force a business reader to spend even two hours digging out the meaning of a report, the report is a failure.

This point is important because communication requires someone, either the communicator or the audience, to do some real thinking. Since no two people view the world alike, the communicator views the subject one way, and the audience views it another. Either the communicator or the audience must translate one of these viewpoints into the other. In business, the communicator must do that job.

A Business Message Should Present the Communicator and His Company in a Favorable Light

People in business recognize that future promotions and raises depend upon the impressions that others (particularly managers) have of them. These impressions, in turn, depend largely on how well they communicate. In the same way, when business representatives communicate with people outside the company, their messages should encourage the audience to think favorably about their company. The image-building goals of every message are essential; they shouldn't be overlooked.

One way you can achieve these image-building goals is to cultivate a writing and speaking style of relaxed friendliness and enthusiasm (as Figure 2 illustrates). The attitudes expressed in your writing and speaking style come through very clearly. In fact, a perennial complaint about the U.S. government is that many government communications are written in a stuffy, pompous style that not only is difficult to understand, but also suggests that the writer feels superior to the audience. Businesses, however, spend enormous sums on writing and speaking programs to help employees avoid an obscure communication style.

Writing in a friendly and relaxed style is a skill you can learn through practice, just like any other skill. Writing in this style may be very difficult at first, but, once learned, it becomes an almost automatic response that requires very little effort. Before long, you'll find it difficult to write any other way, and then you'll have a writing style that will be good for a lifetime. In this book, you'll learn ways to improve your writing, and you'll see many examples. But to make your own style friendly and relaxed, you have to practice hard, for a while. This is one place where hard work will pay off.

Besides cultivating a good writing style, communicators accomplish their image-building goals by thinking carefully about communication situations and maximizing the effects of whatever positive factors are present. If you're telling the audience something to its benefit, carefully phrase the message to maximize the good effects. If you must tell the audience something unpleasant, try to stress the positive aspects of the message (Figure 3). Of course, you should do these things simply because they're courteous and tactful, but do them also because the image-building goals of messages are so important.

TRUAX–VEHLOW INVESTMENT SERVICES

10 KEARNEY DRIVE
KEARNEY, NE 68847
(402) 554-6314

March 23, 1983

Ms. Adrienne Gulik
Office Products, Inc.
433 LeMonge Avenue
Selma, AL   36702

Dear Ms. Gulik:

     Thanks for sending such complete information about your
AmburSam forms system. I appreciate your quick response.

     I've passed your materials on to Harley C. Berlo, our
treasurer, who will be evaluating whether this system can meet
our needs. Mr. Berlo will be in touch with you in about ten
days.

Sincerely,

Raymond C. Johnson
Purchaser

Figure 2 A relaxed, friendly writing style

Poor

Dear Ms. Gustav:

After your interview with us, we at Fedderson and Associates have carefully evaluated your qualifications for the position of expediter. As you agreed in the interview, your background has some deficiencies in relation to the qualifications ideally needed in the job. Although you did work in an expediting department for a period, you aren't familiar with the materials used in our industry, and you have no experience in working with foreign vendors.

After due consideration, we've concluded that we can only offer you the position on the condition that you agree to spend the month of August at our company training center in Memphis before joining our office here in Beaumont. For that reason, the earliest date we can accept as your starting date would be August 1. In addition, we must have your firm commitment that you'll extend yourself to become familiar with the problems of dealing with foreign vendors as quickly as possible.

If you wish to accept these conditions, please respond immediately so we can terminate our recruitment for this position.

More Positive

Dear Ms. Gustav:

Fedderson and Associates is happy to offer you the position of expediter, beginning August 1.

As we discussed in your interview, we would like you to begin work on August 1 by spending the month at our training center in Memphis. As you suggested in our conversation last week, you'll probably find the training period extremely interesting and challenging.

When you arrive in our office in September, you can anticipate further challenges in learning to cope with the special problems of expediting with foreign vendors. We're looking forward to helping you get started in this area as quickly as possible.

Please give me a call in the next few days so we can arrange for your visit to Memphis and take care of any necessary details.

Figure 3 Making the most of positive factors

Every message, no matter how trivial, can contribute to the long-term image-building goals of the communicator and the company. In fact, the maximum effect comes when a whole series of messages repeatedly reinforces good images that have been established before. Just as advertisers establish an image by repeating ads day after day on TV, you can establish the image you want to project in message after message.

THE BASIC THEMES OF THIS BOOK

Anyone who sets out to explain a subject as complicated as business communication must analyze it, that is, break it down into components, to make it understandable. This book does that.

If a subject is only moderately complicated, then analyzing it in one dimension, that is, breaking it down into a set of parts that permits a clear explanation, may suffice. For very complicated subjects like business communication, however, one dimension of analysis may not be enough. You may need to examine the subject from one viewpoint and break it into one set of parts, then examine the subject from another viewpoint and break it into another set of parts, and so on. In such a case, no one dimension of analysis permits a complete understanding of the subject, but each contributes to the full picture.

This book analyzes business communication in four major dimensions.

Theory and Practice

Nothing in this world is as practical as a good theory. In communication, a firm foundation in theory allows us to see day-to-day communication problems as specific cases of general problems that human beings have faced over thousands of years. Often, ways have been found to solve the general problems—ways that can be used in the specific cases.

The practical value of a good theory is that it helps us solve problems better. Some ways of viewing problems and asking questions about them often help us find good answers, and other ways often lead us to bad ones. A good theory gives us good questions to ask ourselves about problem situations, and simply being able to ask the right questions is often half the battle.

Chapters 3 through 6 explore business communication from a theoretical viewpoint, identifying the basic problems of human communication. The remainder of the book concentrates on practical devices for solving specific problems of written and oral communication that often arise in business.

Technique and Application

Over the last 50 years, many excellent business communicators have analyzed how they managed to communicate so successfully. From such analysis has come a body of how-to-do-it knowledge about communication techniques. Chapters 7 through 20 are about such techniques.

Certainly, being able to pass a test on techniques is not the same as being able to communicate well; you also need opportunities to practice these techniques and perfect your skills. Therefore, this book includes practice problems throughout the material on techniques. Stop at each set of problems and write several of the practice messages on your own to firm up your knowledge. Unless you use the techniques, you won't really know them.

The time to begin practicing is right away. When you finish reading this chapter, do three or four of the practice problems at the end, and work on making your messages friendly, relaxed, and right to the point. Later we'll study specific techniques for doing that, but right now just rely on your own experience and judgment. A little extra practice now will pay big dividends as you continue to develop your writing.

Routine and Nonroutine Messages

Most people's written messages are of two types. One type is easy and straightforward, composed in a single draft with little or no revision and completed quickly. Only if the writer has formed good writing habits are such messages well done, because they're written with little analysis or forethought. These are messages the person perceives as routine.

The other type requires more time and thought. Messages of this type can't be treated as something to be finished off in five minutes, because they require careful analysis and planning beforehand, and plenty of time for revision and polishing afterward. These are the person's nonroutine messages.

Some messages are nonroutine simply because they're long or complicated. Many others, however, are nonroutine because of some specific problem in the communication situation that must be overcome. When you answer complaints, for example, often the reader's mind is already set against you, and that makes the writing more difficult. Most writers treat such messages as nonroutine.

Right now, many written messages are probably routine to you. A quick note to your instructor requesting an office appointment, for instance, is something you probably expect to write in a couple of minutes without much analysis or extensive revision. But very likely most business messages are now nonroutine to you. As you progress in studying business communication in this book and in your career, you'll seek to broaden the number of messages you can treat as routine. Certainly you'll never reach the point where all your writing is routine—to most people, formal reports never become routine. But in time, you'll be able to compose a wider and wider range of messages quickly and seemingly effortlessly.

The reason for such progress is that you'll be developing good habits. More and more often, your automatic responses to situations will be good ones, and with time your confidence in your ability to write simple messages quickly will increase. A major part of your study is building good habits. Therefore, in this book you should treat all the practice problems as nonroutine messages, even if they seem fairly simple and straightforward. Sometimes you may intentionally overextend your analysis far beyond the level that would be called for in a real situation. In this way, you maximize the improvement in your writing habits and enlarge the scope of your routine messages.

When you enter your career, your superiors will expect you to write quickly and effectively the messages they define as routine. Therefore, you must build writing habits that will carry you through this critical period. A principal benefit of studying business communication is that both the scope and the quality of your routine messages will improve. At the same time, as you practice your analytical skills, your ability to produce nonroutine messages will improve, too. If you can't analyze communication situations, you must treat all messages as routine; you don't know how to do anything else. Studying business communication will give you a solid foundation for improving your skills with nonroutine messages.

Short and Long Messages

The difference between short messages and long ones is far greater than mere length. Short messages are easy to write and read because they convey relatively simple ideas that people can hold in mind at one time. Long messages are harder mainly because they convey much more complicated ideas that people must understand part by part, since they're too complex to be comprehended all at once. In one sense, long messages consist of a series of short messages, with each one communicating part of the whole picture. But before the writer can think in terms of such a series, he or she must put a great deal of effort into organizing the material and selecting the best sequence of parts to provide a clear overview of the subject. For this reason, a five-page message isn't just five times as hard to write as a one-page message; it is ten or twenty times as hard. Organizing is hard work.

Most of the practice problems you'll do in this book will involve fairly short messages. In Chapter 19, you'll learn to write longer analytical reports. Although most people write relatively few long reports in their careers, the ones they do write are extremely important, and the basic principles of report organization are worth knowing.

YOUR FIRST PRACTICE

It should be perfectly clear from this chapter that practice is the key to improving your communication skills. And the time to begin practicing is now. That's why your study of this chapter ends only when you've done several of the practice problems. Afterward you'll have a big head start in your skill development.

In this chapter, we've looked at the main goals of written communication. You can begin aiming toward them right away.

1. Since your message is goal-oriented, identify its goals and try to achieve them.

2. Since your reader is probably a busy person who expects efficient communication, your message should get right to the point and not waste words.

3. Since it's your responsibility (not your reader's) to assure successful communication, make your message perfectly clear.

4. Since you seek to create a favorable image of yourself and your company, your message should be pleasant and at least mildly friendly.

For each of the practice problems you work on, then, first figure out what the writer's goals probably were or should be. Then rewrite the message to achieve those goals. Concentrate on making your message clear, pleasant, and right to the point.

FURTHER EXPLORATION

1. Are there any circumstances in which an effective business message (one that achieves its main goals) might not be a good message? Could an ungrammatical message, for example, ever be a good message? Could a discourteous message ever be a good one?

2. Does the responsibility for successful business communication always fall on the communicator? Is the listener or reader sometimes more responsible for successful communication than the speaker or writer? Try to think of examples.

3. Do image-building goals sometimes not apply in business messages? Try to think of specific examples.

4. List some kinds of written messages you can reasonably treat as routine. Then list kinds of messages an employer will probably expect you to write as routine messages as you begin your career. How accurately do you feel you've predicted his or her expectations?

WRITING PROBLEMS

1.   Revise the following first draft of a memo to make its style friendly and relaxed.

```
DATE: August 5, 1983
TO: Helmers
    Pedersen
FROM: Orin Thompson
SUBJECT: Inspection of Pendleton Facility
```

Inasmuch as Helmers, Pedersen, and myself have undertaken the obligation of conducting the on-site inspection of the Pendleton facility on Monday next, and seeing that no company vehicle has been rendered available for such purpose. Therefore, I direct that Helmers and Pedersen present themselves at the north gate at 9:30 a.m. sharp. Whereupon I will drive Helmers, Pedersen, and myself to the site. Return may be expected at some point in time following the hour of 4:00 p.m.

2.   Here's a letter from the assistant to the Director of Word Processing at Central Industries, Inc., to the sales representative of a paper supplier. Try to accomplish its goals more efficiently.

Dear Cynthia:

Just this morning Arlen Gates and I were talking about the delightful afternoon we spent with you and your family out at Indian Lake last month. You folks certainly do have a pleasant place for a cabin out there.

I'm dropping you this note because we just may have a little order for you, if you can supply the stock we need. What we need is some paper with pin-feed holes up the side for automatic feeding through a printer. The sheets should measure 17 inches from top to bottom and 11 inches wide—that's after you tear off the little strips that have the pin-feed holes in them. I think that's what you folks call 12 inches wide, tear-size 11 inches.

We do have a bit of a time problem on this order. If we can't get delivery within about 20 days from today, we won't be able to wait.

The paper stock should be 18- or 20-pound plain white stock. It should be bond stationery quality, if possible, or at least very good quality white paper.

Our requirement at the moment is a bit small, but we may use larger quantities later if the project we're working on is accepted. Right now we could use about 10 cartons, but if the project succeeds we should be taking about 30 or 40 cartons a quarter like clockwork. I am assuming each carton has the usual 3300 or so sheets.

If this sort of thing is up your alley, Cynthia, how about jotting down the figures and giving me a call? Hope we can do some business!

Cordially,

3. The following notice is included every six months in paychecks to all employees. Company policy requires that these facts be presented. Can you say them better?

NOTICE

Pursuant to policy 44–391, all employees are hereby notified of their rights and obligations regarding correctness of periodic compensation. All inquiries regarding such compensation, the time and attendance reports upon which it is based, the federal and state tax amounts withheld, the Social Security tax withheld, the state employment insurance tax withheld, and deductions for payments to insurance benefits and other purposes must be presented in person or by a legally empowered representative of the employee within ten days of issuance of such compensation to an employee payroll adjustment representative in Room 2667, Administration Office Building, during the hours of 9:30 to 11:00 a.m. and 2:30 to 4:00 p.m. on any Tuesday through Friday, excluding official company holidays. In the event such inquiry cannot be resolved to the satisfaction of the inquirer and the EPAR at the time of initial inquiry, this policy requires a written response by the employee payroll adjustment representative to the inquirer within five official workdays. Should the inquirer determine that such response is not acceptable, notice of appeal of payroll adjustment response must be filed with the Director of Payroll within eight official working days of the date of response.

Suggestion: Once you figure out exactly what the policy is, try to explain what the employee is supposed to do and what the company agrees to do. Would it help to use "you" and "we" to refer to the employee and the Payroll Department? Even though your version of this message will be less stiff than this legalistic version, be specific and precise to avoid misunderstanding.

4. Revise the following memo to achieve a more appropriate style.

DATE: October 30, 1982
TO: Superintendent, Assembly Line 3
FROM: Quality Assurance
SUBJECT: Rejected Parts

It has been brought to our attention that nearly 20 percent of the total reject rate on Assembly Line 3 is engendered by consistent failure of certain assemblers to assure

```
that parts 2598-G and 402384 are seated firmly and securely
in their respective sockets. Such failure allows high current
to pass to a number of other components when test power is
applied, leading to irreparable failure of the assembly under
test. Pursuant to this finding, you are hereby notified to
instruct assemblers to expend all necessary effort to seat
the aforementioned components per assembly directive
Q-490.71.
```

5.   As administrative assistant to the Director of Production Engineering, you have been handling the preparation details for the Plant 5 conversion project. A major step in the project is next month's three-day meeting among your department's seven-person project team, the Plant 5 Production Manager and five supervisors, four representatives of the contractor who will remodel the plant, and five representatives of the supplier of the new process control devices.

Since your department has no conference room large enough to accommodate this meeting, you telephoned the secretary to Gladys Schlutermann, the Director of Training, who has reserved her department's seminar room for you on Wednesday, Thursday, and Friday of the second week of next month. Check your calendar for the dates. She agreed that the room would be available from 8:00 A.M. to 5:00 P.M. on Wednesday and Thursday and from 8:00 A.M. to 12:00 noon on Friday. Since you've learned that such agreements should be confirmed in writing to prevent later misunderstandings, write Gladys Schlutermann a memo to establish a written record of the conversation. You'll want to include all the relevant details. Perhaps the message could be phrased as a thank-you note.

6.   As Director of Sales in your company, you're planning a season's greetings goodwill letter to the company's high-volume customers. The letter will convey holiday greetings, thank them for their orders during the year, and wish them well in the coming year. Each letter will have a personalized inside address and salutation, but the bodies of all letters will be identical. Your company's word processing department can produce and mail such letters economically. So he can schedule production, write a memo to Winston Bates, Word Processing Supervisor, telling him that you're planning this letter. You expect to provide copy for a two-page letter late in October, and you want the finished letters in the mail in the first week in December. The high-volume customer list, which is fairly stable, has 2155 entries right now.

7.   The small company you own occupies half of the fourth floor of the Koster Building, which contracts with a security service for alarms and nighttime guards. You've just purchased a $30,000 word processing system, which will be installed in your office early next month. Since such equipment is a prime target of burglars, write Linda Montes, building manager, asking her to inform the security service of the addition. As far as you can see—and your insurance inspector verified this—the building is well protected, and you want to be sure the new equipment is also fully protected.

8. As Supervisor of Nurseries in the Buildings and Grounds Department, your job includes supplying approximately 100 Christmas trees for display in various offices and public areas in company buildings. Because of the current interest in ecology, several people have suggested that live potted trees be displayed. These could be returned to the nursery after the holidays rather than being discarded as cut trees are.

As a matter of curiosity, you've assembled some figures showing that live trees could be moved into offices for about the same amount of money that the company now spends on cut trees. The trees themselves would be free, since you already have hundreds of potted live trees of all sizes growing in the nurseries, and the cost of moving the trees into buildings and later removing them would roughly equal the amount now spent on cut trees. Nursery trees could easily be trimmed and cleaned up to be quite presentable in offices, and suitable containers would be inexpensive and could be reused from year to year. Because of past chemical waste disposal problems, the company's image among local environmental groups could be improved. Make your suggestion in a memo to Edith Watson, Director of Buildings and Grounds, offering to provide cost figures if she's interested.

9. As Director of Health and Safety for your company, you're responsible for a project to ensure adequate lighting at each work station in the company's administrative offices. Checks of each desk and other work stations in Office Building 3 were completed last week. Of the 936 work stations in that building, 914 were found to have adequate lighting. The latter figure includes all 47 of the stations that have special lighting requirements because of the nature of the work carried on there. The 22 work stations with inadequate lighting exhibited various kinds of problems; you've compiled a detailed list showing locations, lighting problems, and suggested solutions. Convey your findings to Joey Bisero, manager of Office Building 3. Indicate that the problem list is attached. Incidentally, the average percentage of lighting deficiencies found in the company's office buildings has been 7.2, so Office Building 3's low 2.35 deficiency rate is commendable.

10. A list of employees who've been granted merit raises or promotions effective next quarter has been distributed, including 15 members of the Accounting Department. Current company-wide cost cutting has drastically limited the number of such increases, making each of these persons' accomplishments more impressive than usual. As administrative assistant to the Comptroller, draft a congratulatory message that could be individually addressed to each of these 15 persons for the Comptroller's signature.

11.   The following memo was addressed to the Director of Purchasing by the Vehicle Maintenance Supervisor. Rewrite it to make it clear, pleasant, and right to the point. Before you revise, be sure you've identified the message's goals.

```
DATE: July 17, 1983
TO: Jacob Furley, Director of Purchasing
FROM: Robert Smith, Vehicle Maintenance Supervisor
SUBJECT: Vehicle Maintenance
```

I am in receipt of your memo of March 9 in which you stated a request for any and all information pertaining to maintenance costs of the Vinsen motorized messenger vehicles relative to maintenance costs on the Saihatsu units we have put into operation in the past two years. In response to your request, I spent several hours this morning checking over all figures relative to every motorized messenger vehicle maintenance transaction for the last two years, as you prescribed. The results follow.

During the period in question, the company purchased four Saihatsu motorized messenger vehicles, two at the beginning of this period, one 8 months into the period, and one 14 months into the period. The Vehicle Maintenance Department has processed 26 maintenance transactions on these vehicles in the last 24 months. Since that figure is quite high, I believe the company should seriously consider a return to the Vinsen motorized messenger vehicles which were selected for purchase prior to that time.

During the identical period, the Vehicle Maintenance Department processed a total of 31 maintenance transactions on the Vinsen motorized messenger vehicles. Of course there were five of the Vinsens in operation throughout this period. The last Vinsen we had to retire from service was over three years ago, and it had been in operation for just over seven years. The average time out of service for the Vinsen units during maintenance was less than one eight-hour shift.

We have been experiencing a great deal of difficulty acquiring replacement and maintenance parts for the Saihatsu vehicles. In consequence average time out of service for these units during maintenance was 3.7 work days, with a top of 62 days out of service waiting for a part which we finally had to fabricate in the machine shop.

The Vinsen units that we operate are all older machines, but they seem to hold up better for us. Parts are available immediately here in the city.

I
Communication Theory and Business Communication

The purpose of studying this book is to increase your skill at communicating. To do that, it's important to understand how the process of communication works, which is the subject of Chapters 3 through 6.

Nearly everyone has commonsense ideas about how communication works. Yet when many such ideas are carefully analyzed, difficulties appear. Usually the problem is not that the ideas are completely wrong, but that they're too unsophisticated for use in serious business communication. In studying Chapters 3 through 6, you should revise your picture of the communication process to make it more accurate and complete. You should also improve your powers of analysis to approach real-life communication situations more effectively.

3

The Communication Process

It takes two to speak the truth—one
to speak, and another to hear.
Thoreau

"Where I use a word," Humpty
Dumpty said, in rather a scornful
tone, "it means just what I choose
it to mean—neither more nor less."

"The question is," said Alice,
"whether you can make words
mean so many different things."
Lewis Carroll

Communication is a process. Processes, unlike objects, are difficult to define and describe. For example, communication between people involves a communicator, an audience, and a message. But the communicator, audience, and message by themselves are not communication; we haven't really described communication by pointing at these people and objects. As a process, communication is the set of relationships between communicator, audience, and message.

COMMUNICATION MODELS

Communication consists of a whole series of related actions and reactions, which together may result in the sharing of meanings between individuals. To understand how communication works, we must be able to describe each part of the process and concentrate on each specific detail without losing track of the whole process.

To make things easier, communication theorists have developed a simplified model, or mental picture, of the communication process. The model tells us what the individual parts of the process are and demonstrates how they're related to one another. The model lets us concentrate on one detail of the process and at the same time remember how that detail fits into the whole process.

Besides aiding our study of communication, a communication model helps us think about real-world communication problems and figure out how to deal with them. It identifies the crucial points in the process and guides our analysis and planning. For example, when most young managers sit down to write their first quarterly report to the boss, they simply don't know how to begin—what questions to ask about that communication situation. A model helps them ask good questions.

Finally, a communication model helps us focus on the important factors. Communicating, especially in writing, is a very complicated activity. We must keep many things in mind at once, some vitally important and others not so critical. A model helps us keep our priorities straight so we're sure to pay attention to the important things and not get bogged down in the many details.

To be most useful, both in learning about communication and in solving problems, a communication model should be simple and easy to remember. We don't need to carry around a lot of excess theoretical baggage; we just want to remember things that are actually useful. The model we'll develop here is both simple and easy to remember.

A Commonsense Model

If you tried to construct a model of people's commonsense ideas about communication, you'd probably arrive at something like the oversimplified model in Figure 1. In fact, nearly all of us think about communication in roughly this way when we're not thinking carefully—even communication experts do, in weak moments!

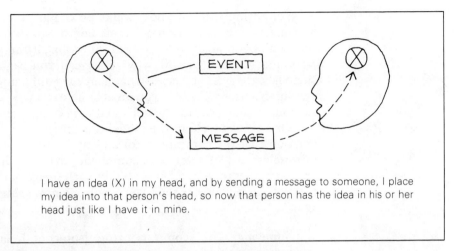

I have an idea (X) in my head, and by sending a message to someone, I place my idea into that person's head, so now that person has the idea in his or her head just like I have it in mine.

Figure 1 The steam-shovel model of communication

Nearly everyone can identify the elements that are necessary for communication to occur. There must be two or more people; there must be a message; and there must be something to talk about, which we're calling an "event." But most people have difficulty putting these elements together. They tend to think of communication as a steam-shovel process in which some great steam shovel reaches down and lifts an idea out of one person's brain and carries it over to another person's brain, dropping it into place as complete and intact as it was when it started out.

Of course, the steam-shovel description of communication is hardly adequate, but it does describe a great many everyday communications. For example, a typist asks a boss when a certain letter needs to be ready to mail, and the boss answers, "By the end of the day." The steam shovel reached into the boss's head, picked up "end of the day," and dropped it into the typist's head; now the typist understands the idea pretty much the same way the boss does.

The steam-shovel description of communication is good enough for many simple situations. But we don't need help in simple situations. And the times when we do need help are precisely the times when the steam-shovel model breaks down. In these situations, we need something more.

A More Sophisticated Model

The basic problem with the commonsense steam-shovel model is that it ignores the fact that each participant perceives the communication situation differently. The communicator has one set of perceptions, and the audience has another. In the simple situations in which the steam-shovel model seems to work, the two sets of perceptions are enough alike that communication does occur. But in problem situations, differences in perceptions prevent effective communication.

For example, if your boss walks up and gives you instructions and the conversation is fairly predictable and reasonably cordial, then little communication analysis is needed. But what if the boss suddenly gets angry and you don't know why? How can you begin to figure it out? Obviously, the boss perceives what happened differently than you do, but how? In situations like this, you must be able to analyze these perceptions, and a more sophisticated model should make such analysis easier.

One aid is to add to the model the "images" of the communication situation that the communicator and the audience have in their heads. This inclusion adds a degree of complexity to the model but doesn't make it much harder to remember. Actually, each image of the communication situation simply repeats the basic people-event-message model itself. (See Figure 2.)

Someone   The communicator ($someone_1$) and the audience ($someone_2$) are the active participants in the communication process.

Perceives an event   "Event" is used here in a special way to refer to what the communicator is talking or writing about. Your typewriter could be an event; the business meeting you attended yesterday could be an event; the history of the United States from 1620 to yesterday could be an event. An event is anything someone might talk or write about.

When $someone_1$ perceives an event, he or she develops a mental representation, or image, of the event. This image forms part of the set of images that $someone_1$ brings to the communication situation.

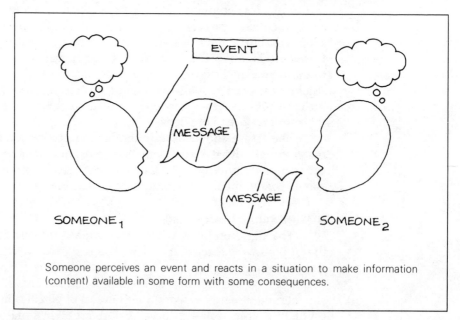

Someone perceives an event and reacts in a situation to make information (content) available in some form with some consequences.

Figure 2 The image model of communication

And reacts in a situation　For communication to take place, someone₁ must do something with his or her mental image of the event. Someone₁ must take some action in response to that image. The action is affected not only by the image of the event, but also by his or her images of the whole communication situation. The communication situation greatly influences how someone₁ acts.

To make information (content) available in some form　To put it simply, someone₁ reacts by sending a message. The message symbols in Figure 2 are divided into two parts to remind you that a message has two important attributes: form and content. Everyone realizes the importance of a message's content. But the form is important, too, because it shapes and limits the content. A message in the form of a conversation about some business event will have different content from a formal oral presentation about that event, even though all the other elements of the communication situation remain the same.

With some consequences　All things that happen as a result of a given communication are consequences of it. Some—but not all—consequences of a given communication may be desired. The particular consequences the communicator hopes to achieve are called "effects," and when these occur we conclude that the communication has been effective.

Feedback

One effect that someone₁ normally hopes to achieve by communicating is that someone₂ will perceive the message and form the mental image of it that someone₁ is trying to communicate. Since someone₁ can't see into the mind of someone₂ to determine whether or not the message has been perceived effectively, he or she must wait to see what someone₂ does as a result of the message. Anything the communicator perceives the audience to do as a result of the message can be labeled feedback.

Feedback is one of the key concepts in communication. Feedback is important because it provides the only way to determine whether or not communication has been effective. When someone₂ perceives the message, he or she may reply by sending a message back to someone₁ or may react by gesturing or by making some other change in behavior. All these forms of feedback provide clues about whether the original message was effective or not. If effectiveness is the communicator's goal, then feedback is the measuring instrument for determining success or failure.

THE IMAGES IN PEOPLE'S MINDS

Now that we've identified the elements of the communication situation and have at least a preliminary understanding of how the process works, let's look further at the participants' mental images.

Figure 3 The images in the communicator's mind

As Figure 3 indicates, when you communicate you have four important mental images: (1) your image of yourself; (2) your image of your audience, including your image of the audience's mental processes; (3) your image of the event; and (4) your image of the message you're transmitting.

Your Image of Yourself

No doubt you realize that your self-image and other people's images you may differ considerably. Certainly the image you see in the mirror and the images other people see when they look at you aren't the same. And your image of your behavior is probably even less objective.

Your Image of the Audience

Just as your self-image differs from what you're really like, your image of another person differs from what he or she is really like. Your perceptions of your audience probably differ in important ways from that person's self-image. Incidentally, whose image is correct is not a very important question. In fact, none of the images is altogether objective and complete; having a totally accurate image of anything is probably impossible. The important thing is that your images and your audience's images are definitely different from each other.

Your Image of the Event

As we'll soon see, what an event means to you is not something that comes from the event itself; the meaning comes from inside your head. Since your perceptions of an event are selective and are heavily influenced by your past experiences and expectations, your mental image of an event is bound to differ in important respects from the event itself.

For the same reasons, your audience's image of the event differs from both the event itself and your image of it. In some situations in which persuasion is needed or complaints are responded to, most people expect differences in images. But even in more normal communications, you should expect such differences. You and your audience are never talking about quite the same event.

Your Image of the Message

As we've noted, the two aspects of a message are form and content. In the purely physical sense, a message must take one of two forms: a pattern of sound waves in the air or a pattern of light waves reflected from some surface, such as a piece of paper. Because your eyes and ears are imperfect receptors, the physical form of the message undergoes a good deal of systematic distortion before it reaches the brain. Therefore, your image of the message's form differs from the real message, and since the audience's aural and visual distortions differ from yours, the audience's image is bound to differ from yours.

But the message's physical form is only one aspect. The patterns of sound or light carry meanings, which evoke a second kind of image of the message. Your image of the meaning of a message, based on your distorted perceptions of its physical form, is almost certain to differ somewhat your audience's image of its meaning.

The interesting thing is that, even though you know your images aren't totally accurate, you act as though they were. You have to. You have no other information to act on. The only pictures you have of what's going on are those mental images, with all their imperfections. So you proceed just as though those images were correct.

The Imaginary Participants
in the Communication Process

Images give rise to an interesting situation. When you communicate, you have a certain image of yourself as a communicator. That image is not "the real you" but "your image of yourself." The person you're talking to is listening to a message from "his or her image of you," which is still another person. In the same manner, you're communicating with "your image of the other person," but the message is received not by "the real other person," but by "his or her self-image." Since you're each reacting to your own set of images, the four imaginary people are just as real in the communication process as if they were standing there in flesh and blood.

When you and your audience are communicating, these are the participants:

1. The real you
2. The real other person
3. Your self-image
4. Your image of the other person

  5. The other person's image of you

  6. The other person's self-image

  For the moment, we'll set aside some other ghostly participants who might sometimes be important, such as "your image of the kind of person he or she thinks you are." Of these six participants in the communication process, the two least important are the real you and the real other person; these two have only an indirect influence upon the outcome. In a much more real way, the four imaginary participants determine the outcome of the communication. They're the ones who are really communicating.

  Let's look at the simplest possible communication situation, namely two people talking. We see all of the following.

  Reality: the real you talking to the real other person about the real event using the real message.

  You see: your self-image talking to your image of the other person about your image of the event using your image of the message.

  The other person sees: his image of you talking to his self-image about his image of the event using his image of the message.

  Notice that at no point in the communication process are you and your audience using the same perceptions. It's as though you and your audience were communicating through a tiny hole in a thick wall. You can't see each other at all; you can only see the pictures in your own heads. The only point of contact is the physical message—just the patterns of sound waves or light waves that come through that hole. You don't know what the other person perceives, nor does that person know what you perceive. It's a wonder that anybody ever succeeds in communicating at all!

  One reason we do manage to communicate despite all these difficulties is that we're constantly exploring each other's images. Although we can't look inside others to see their images directly, we can infer things about their images from the feedback we receive. By studying this feedback carefully, we may be able to make a passably good guess about the nature of other people's images.

  That's exactly what you do nearly every time you communicate. For example, imagine talking to a friend. You say something or make a suggestion, and your friend reacts by commenting or gesturing. Your mental computer goes to work: What's my friend really thinking? Should I say anything further, or would that be useless? Does my friend agree or disagree? How does my friend perceive this subject?

  When we talk about getting to know someone, we mean developing more and more accurate mental images of how that person sees things and reacts to ideas. We get to know someone by talking with him or her—bouncing opinions and ideas back and forth, studying the feedback we receive. Slowly we piece together an image of that person's mental processes and use it to predict future reactions: "If I say such and such, I think I know how my friend will react." People who've developed very close relationships, such as many husbands and wives, can often predict each other's reactions quite accurately.

Company images People have images of companies, just as they do of individuals. And when people deal with a company, they approach it in the ways their images direct them to. If they perceive the company to be pleasant and easy to deal with, they'll take a friendly approach to it. If they perceive it to be hostile, they'll probably take a particularly aggressive or defensive approach toward it.

People's images of companies are affected most heavily by their personal experiences. But when people have had little personal contact with a company, its communications may be their only source of images. Thus a company must pay careful attention to the images it conveys in its advertising and other public communications. For most people, these messages are the primary source of images.

The employees of a company, too, have an image of it that shapes the way they respond to one another and to outsiders. If they perceive their company to be extremely cost-conscious, for example, they'll probably weigh cost considerations very heavily in dealing with each other, and they'll make decisions affecting the company and outsiders with this image in mind.

USING THE COMMUNICATION MODEL
TO SOLVE COMMUNICATION PROBLEMS

As we noted earlier, our model of communication is useful both in understanding communication and in solving problems that may arise in the planning and communicating stages. Here's how it can help. When you face a difficult communication problem, think about the goals you're trying to reach by communicating. That is, start at the end of the process and work backward.

Step 1. Start by trying to define the ideas you want to plant in the audience's mind (Step 1 in Figure 4). Be sure to include any secondary goals—for instance, goodwill. If your goals include getting the audience to do something, be sure to include that. Then consider what kind of feedback will tell you whether or not you've effectively communicated these ideas. Now you probably have a better idea of what you're trying to accomplish.

An employee performance review is, for most managers, one of the most difficult communications. In a performance review, you'll write or talk to the employee, reviewing the employee's quality of work over the last year and suggesting goals for improvement for the coming year. Because such a message has great potential for good or harm, it requires careful planning.

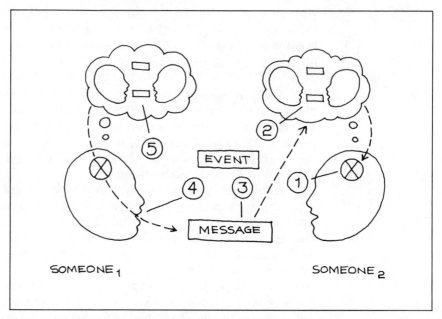

Figure 4 Using the communication model to solve problems

Thus you'd begin planning by making quick notes on what you want to accomplish in your message—your goals. What are the employee's strong qualities? Weak qualities? What realistic improvement goals should the employee consider? What rewards may there be for improvement in these areas? What penalties may there be for continued weakness?

Step 2. Now consider the other person's images—his or her mental processing patterns (Step 2 in Figure 4). How does that person look at the world, at you, at himself? In the past, how has that person "processed" ideas like the one you're trying to communicate? How is your message likely to be modified and reshaped by that person's perceptions of it?

In planning for a performance review, consider how the employee has responded to praise and criticism in the past. Is this person discouraged easily or offended quickly, or is he or she filled with self-confidence? In the latter case some bluntness may be required to convey the point that certain areas need improvement. What potential rewards may stimulate this person to try to improve?

Step 3. Now you're ready to do something concrete (Step 3 in Figure 4). Ask yourself, "What kind of message can I send through that person's particular set of images so that, when my message is processed, he or she will grasp it? In other words, "How can I shape my message to get the right result in my audience's mind?"

At this point in your performance review, you'd be ready to begin planning the shape of the message—not writing it down, just planning what you'll say. Based on your previous analysis, how should you approach this person? What, for example, should you say first? With most people, beginning a performance review on a positive note is effective; is that the most effective approach for this particular person? How should you introduce the weaknesses? How can you stress the value of improvement? How should you bring in each of your main points? Be sure your planning includes each one of the goals you've set.

Step 4. The next step (Step 4 in Figure 4) is very practical. Ask yourself, "How can I produce the message I need in this situation? Do I have the necessary skills? If not, what compromises should I make to bring the needed message within the range of my practical communication skills and still have a good chance that it'll work?"

Based on your planning for a performance review, you now know what the ideal message would be like. But probably some parts of the message you've designed will be very difficult for you; you may justifiably doubt that you can communicate them effectively. Thus you may need to think about ways to communicate those parts so you can approach them more confidently.

If the employee has been easily offended in the past, for example, you may want to think through the message and identify places where offense could be taken. In those places, you may seek the least offensive ways of stating your points. By the time you communicate the message, you'll have planned these parts so carefully that you've maximized the chance of saying them effectively.

Step 5. Finally (Step 5 in Figure 4), think about changing the way you look at the situation to make communication with this audience easier. Of course, as you've been applying the model up to now, you've been changing your image of the situation—that's what the model is for. But in many situations, the key to improving communication is to find some more effective and workable viewpoint for yourself. Often that viewpoint will help you communicate better almost automatically.

Changing your image of the audience often helps to improve communication; negative or unrealistic attitudes toward the audience can block communication completely. Sometimes the relationship between you and your audience should be reexamined. If, for example, you see yourself and the other person as equals and that person sees you as an inferior, then communication may be blocked. To improve communication in such a case, you should reconsider your image of that relationship. Whose image is correct may be less important than finding a way to communicate successfully. In other cases, your image of the event you're talking about can be simplified or clarified to improve communication. In all these cases, once you've readjusted your images, improved communication should follow automatically.

In a performance review, one of the most sensitive issues is the kind of relationship you suggest between yourself and the employee. If the employee feels fully qualified to take over your job and perceives that you're treating him or her as a very junior employee, then there's bound to be friction. On the other hand, the employee may undergo a great deal of stress just in fulfilling his or her present duties. If you treat such an employee nearly as an equal, your approach may be highly complimentary, but it may suggest demands the employee isn't confident of fulfilling. This matter certainly should be thought out carefully before you compose the message.

Most people begin thinking about a communication problem by trying to compose a message that will work. By now you should realize that you're much more likely to be effective if you've thought about some other things first. Only after you've defined what you want to accomplish and considered how your audience's mind works in relation to your ideas are you ready to begin thinking about specific messages.

TRANSACTIONAL COMMUNICATION

One of the current buzzwords in the psychology of communication is "transaction." To the business person who must communicate effectively, it's an important idea.

When we say that communication works best when it's transactional, we're reminding ourselves that one-way communication is seldom very effective. In the long run, at least, you can't affect upon another person's perceptions and behavior much if you refuse to allow that person to affect your own perceptions and behavior. Talking *at* people doesn't work as well as talking *with* them.

Your communication becomes transactional when you take the other person's ideas and feelings into account as you communicate. To do so, try to listen carefully to what the other person says—the feedback—and think carefully about his or her viewpoint. Try to imagine how he or she sees the events you're talking about. Do this not only to win that person over to your viewpoint, but also because his or her viewpoint might be just as valid as yours. You allow that person a chance to win you over. Of course, thinking about other people's viewpoints too carefully can be a little scary; you may begin to think they make sense! You may even have to change your message, because seeing the situation from another's viewpoint can make you look at it differently yourself.

Most company-to-employee communication is clearly not transactional. It's one-way. The company sets a policy, someone writes a policy directive, the personnel department tacks the directive on each bulletin board, and the managers tell their employees to read it. The company has communicated to its employees, not with them. And most company-to-employee communication is not very effective—just ask personnel managers. Communication is one of their favorite topics. They wish their companies were more effective at it.

UNIVERSITY OF WINNIPEG
LIBRARY
515 Portage Avenue
Winnipeg, Manitoba R3B 2E9

The key to making communication transactional is paying attention to feedback. If you really think about what your audience is saying to you, then you're communicating with it, not just to it. When you write to someone, however, you lack that feedback. How can you communicate transactionally then? The answer is that you have to work much harder to imagine what the probable feedback will be. When you write, instead of getting feedback through your eyes and ears, you get it through your imagination. And if you don't keep your imagination alive and acute, you won't get any feedback at all.

Writing a letter without thinking carefully about the other person's viewpoint costs a lot more—in misunderstandings, in needless additional communication, and in the bad will you create for your company—than the time it takes to use your imagination. Thinking about the other person's likely reactions gets results!

FURTHER EXPLORATION

1. Think of a simple case of misunderstood communication from your own experience, or imagine one, and trace through it step by step using the commonsense model of communication in Figure 1. Apply the model to each statement and try to describe what happened in terms of the model. Were you able to account for the misunderstanding?

Analyze the same situation using the "image" model in Figure 2. As before, apply the model to each statement and describe what happened in terms of the model. Were you able to account for the misunderstanding?

2. Watch two people talking for a few minutes and try to notice all the kinds of feedback that pass between them. After a while, move to a place that's out of earshot and concentrate on the visual feedback. How many kinds of feedback can you identify?

3. Think of a recent simple communication between you and another person and guess at the differences among the two real and four imaginary participants in that process. For example, how do you think your image of the other person differs from his or her self-image?

4. For a simple communication situation that you'll face in a day or two (such as dealing with a sales clerk in a store), apply the problem-solving model of communication in Figure 4. Make notes of your conclusions for each of the five steps. Will you approach the situation any differently because of this analysis?

5. Recall a recent disagreement you had with someone. Spend a few minutes trying to "see" the situation through that person's set of images. First analyze that person's viewpoint until you understand it intellectually; then try to feel the way that person felt during the disagreement. Did your role-playing reveal new explanations for that person's behavior?

6.   Analyze your interaction with one of your instructors or with your boss. How transactional is that communication? Provide specific examples to illustrate your conclusions. Should such communication be completely transactional?

7.   Can written communication ever be completely transactional? Why?

4

Perception, Images, and Communication

*If you're not able to communicate
successfully between yourself and
yourself, how are you supposed to
make it with the strangers outside?*
Jules Feiffer

In Chapter 3 we saw the vital role that images play in the minds of communicator and audience. These images give the communicator the ideas that he or she tries to communicate to influence the audience's images.

Mental images are formed through the process of perception, the process by which people take in and organize information from the outside world. A clear understanding of perception is one of the keys to effective communication.

THE PERCEPTUAL PROCESS

Our knowledge of events in the world around us is not directly connected with the events themselves. We find out about them only indirectly. In fact, there are three intermediate steps between an event and our conscious perception of it. In these steps, each person unconsciously impresses his or her individuality on the perception of an event.

The three steps of the perceptual process can be called (1) the nervous system, (2) the mapping system, and (3) the selecting system.

The Nervous System

Before a sensation can be perceived, it must be translated from whatever form it takes outside the body by the various kinds of nerve endings inside the body. The nervous system receives and processes stimuli in the following ways.

1. *Vision.* Light waves in the outside world strike your retina, and nerve endings in the retina translate the patterns of light waves into patterns of nerve impulses.

2. *Hearing.* Sounds waves strike your eardrum, and nerve endings in your inner ear translate the patterns of sound waves into patterns of nerve impulses.

3. *Touch.* Pressure and temperature changes on your skin are translated into patterns of nerve impulses.

4. *Taste.* Certain chemicals stimulate special nerve endings in your mouth, and they transmit patterns of nerve impulses.

5. *The Other Senses.* The other senses include smell and senses of body conditions, such as hunger and muscle tension (proprioception). They work similarly; in response to some condition outside your nervous system, nerve endings transmit nerve impulses. The information you can perceive takes widely varied forms outside your nervous system. Inside the system, all such information is translated into one form—patterns of nerve impulses.

The nervous system and the real world The translations from external to internal information are generally accurate enough for most purposes. We do, after all, manage to live reasonably secure lives with the information our brains receive through these nerve impulses.

But the nerve translators can be fooled, and in fact commonly are.

Stereophonic sound systems, for instance, trick our ears so that we seem to hear things we know aren't really there. Most people have listened to a stereo and "heard" a singer's voice coming from a place between the two speakers. Our knowing where the sound actually comes from doesn't change where we perceive it to come from. And anyone who has lived in a cold climate has come indoors on a subzero day and washed his or her hands in cold water that felt very hot. Similarly, dry ice "burns" if you touch it.

We need to understand that there's a discontinuity, a disconnection, between events outside us and the patterns of nerve impulses that signal our brain about these events. All we really experience is a complex series of nerve impulses generated inside our bodies. And the impulses that reach our brain may not have any direct connection with events themselves.

What your brain "sees" An amusing way of making the perceptual process seem more real is to imagine that you're a tiny person imprisoned in a windowless little room inside your head. You can't see out; you can't hear anything; you can't feel anything. The only information that reaches your dark room comes through an enormous panel of flashing lights on the wall. Day and night, summer and winter, millions of lights on that huge panel flicker on and off in endless response to the nerve impulses in your body.

As an infant, after months of terribly frustrating trial-and-error experience with these flashing lights, you began to recognize that some patterns of flashes led to pleasant outcomes if you made your body react in certain ways when they occurred. Now, after 19 years or more of watching those flashing lights, you've become a real expert at deciding how to make your body react to various patterns of flashes. You still don't know for sure what's going on outside your little room, but you've managed to react to the patterns of flashes in ways that got your body food and shelter and a good deal of pleasantness in life. In fact, you've become so good at making your body react to those flashing lights that you think you've figured out what's really going on outside. But of course there's no way to be sure; all you can really see are the lights.

Certainly we're not conscious of perceiving a pattern of nerve impulses; we consciously perceive pictures of events, images, and meaningful sensations. So let's consider how meanings get attached to the patterns of impulses our brains receive.

The Mapping System

Consider for a moment the patterns of nerve impulses that would reach the brain of someone near a burning house. Neural patterns would be produced by light striking the retina, by the crackling and roaring sounds striking the eardrum, and if the person were standing close enough, by the heat waves striking his or her face. Mentally, the person would put these patterns together and come up with the meaning "burning house." Where did that meaning come from?

According to authorities in this field, an easy way to understand what happens is to imagine that you have a map of the world in your head.[1] This map contains all the meanings that you know—all the things you know about—and shows you which meaning to attach to a given pattern of nerve impulses. When you're watching a burning house, for instance, your brain receives a complex pattern of nerve impulses from your eyes, ears, and skin, and your map supplies a meaning, "burning house," that matches that neural pattern.

Think what would happen if you'd never seen or heard of a burning house. What would those patterns of nerve impulses mean to you then? Probably nothing. Only because you already have the meaning "burning house" in your head can you perceive the actual event of the house burning down. The meaning "burning house" is part of your map of the world.

Maps of the physical world   Some parts of our maps of the world are very much like regular road maps. For example, part of your mental map tells you about your neighborhood. If you suddenly found yourself walking on a sidewalk a few blocks from home, how would you find out where you were? First, you'd examine your surroundings. Then you'd search your mind—your map of the world—for a place that has the same configuration as this one. And your map would tell you how to get home.

Maps of social relationships   You also use your map of the world to make sense of your relationships with other people. Your mental map of your close personal relationships is very complex. When you're talking to your boss, your husband or wife, your best friend in the next office, you can read a thousand subtle shades of meaning into comments that another person might take at face value. A great deal of the territory in your map concerns attaching meanings to the actions and statements of people who are important in your life.

And another large section of your map provides the meanings you need to maintain casual relationships. Applying at the security gate for a pass, requesting information about a new product, asking directions in a strange company—in all these situations your map helps you to interact meaningfully with other people. It tells you how to identify the appro-

---

1. Alfred Korzybski, in *Science and Sanity: An Introduction to Non-Aristotelian Systems and General Semantics* (Lancaster, Pa.: Science Press, 1933), discussed "maps of the world in our heads" in a way that is similar, but not identical, to the way this text uses the term. S. I. Hayakawa popularized the map concept by using it extensively in his widely read *Language in Thought and Aciton*, 3rd ed. (New York: Harcourt Brace Jovanovich, 1972).

priate people to talk to and how to interpret their answers. A person lacking experience with these routines wouldn't have them mapped and would be quite mystified by their complexities. To you, they're very simple.

The important thing to remember about the mapping system is this: the meanings you attach to events are not inherent in the events themselves. The meanings come from inside you. What you call a thing isn't part of the thing itself; its name and what it means come from your mind.

The Selecting System

One more aspect of the perceptual process is quite important in communication: selectivity. The fact that perception is selective creates a perennial problem for the communicator.

Filtering So much goes on around you all the time that your brain would be overwhelmed with sensations if you perceived it all. It's just too much. You must somehow filter this flood of sensation to a manageable trickle.

The first filtering occurs in the nervous system, where weak and usually unimportant kinds of impulses get low priority. Signals from these weak sensations are simply overridden by much stronger impulses that succeed in reaching the brain. At 6:00 A.M., for example, you can hear a robin chirping in a nearby tree. By 8:00 A.M., when sounds of traffic and neighborhood activity have increased, you can no longer hear the robin. The chirp is still there striking your eardrum and creating nerve impulses, but now those impulses are overridden by stronger ones.

Even when impulses reach the brain, however, few are ever consciously perceived. Consider for a moment the room you're sitting in right now. Look around you and see how many things you hadn't noticed. Your eyes have been generating nerve impulses in response to these things all along; now you've selected these impulses to be perceived. Listen for a moment to all the sounds you can hear where you are. How many were you conscious of a minute ago? Feel carefully. Feel the pressure of your clothing on your skin. It was there a minute ago, but you selected perceptions from your reading instead.

You "see" what you're programmed to see Occasionally someone will summarize the idea of selective perception as "You see what you want to see." Unfortunately, that's not an adequate summary. The problem is that your selective perception is only partly under your conscious control. If you could control your selective perception, then you could easily study in a noisy place; you could simply screen out the noise. But it's not that simple.

Yet your conscious interests and preferences do contribute importantly to the selections your brain makes. Perhaps a better way to summarize the concept, though still a bit oversimplified, is "You see what you're programmed to see." Such programming is determined by a very complex equation involving past experiences, present expectations, interests, physical needs, psychological needs, the relative strengths of the sensations competing for attention at a given time, and your conscious efforts to pay attention to a given thing.

How selective perception affects behavior Selective perception makes more difference in the way people "see" the world than most of them would ever dream. The teenager looks at a car and instantly "sees" what make and model it is. He doesn't decide to notice; he can't look without "seeing." In the same way, when you look at this page, you can't stop yourself from "seeing" what the words mean. Your selective perception won't allow you to look at words as just interesting designs and shapes. It forces you to read. Right now a hedge probably looks like a hedge to you; if you've seen one, you've seen them all. But landscape your own property, and right away you'll find yourself noticing barberry, euonymous, and forsythia when you look at hedges. Your habits of selective perception are among the most important parts of your identity.

Not only does selective perception affect what you notice, but it also affects how you act. A great many of your actions are reactions to events around you, and the events you notice are the ones you react to. As a future manager, if you're programmed to notice when an employee has done a particularly good job, then you'll probably pay compliments when they're deserved. If you're programmed to notice your readers' probable reactions to what you write, then you'll communicate better. Much of the material in this book is intended to help you tune up your selective perception for better communication.

In addition to becoming aware of your own selective perceptions, you, as a future manager, must become sensitive to the selective perceptions of the people you're communicating with. What do they perceive in the communication situation? They may be selecting a whole different set of perceptions from those you're trying to get them to notice. Often your success or failure in communication will depend on just this point: can you get the audience to perceive the same things in the communication situation that you perceive in it?

AUDIENCE ANALYSIS: PREDICTING AUDIENCE REACTION

Learning about people's mental maps can help you predict their reactions to your messages and thus compose messages that work.

Actually you make predictions continually about how people will react to what you say and do. Otherwise you couldn't lead a stable and secure life. When you instruct a secretary to type a memo, request a demonstration of a new office copier, or ask where the business reference books are kept, you assume that the people you're talking to will react predictably. You make predictions without thinking particularly about them, because you've learned through years of experience that certain reactions are predictable. You predict almost by intuition. And for most purposes, that works well enough.

Sometimes, though, communications are so important that you want to be able to predict better than you can by intuition alone. For example, when you prepare for a job interview or when communication with a boss has broken down, you may want to analyze in detail how the other person may react. That's what this section is about.

The audience analysis method presented here certainly isn't 100 percent effective. It's obviously impossible to predict with complete accuracy what someone else is going to do. This sort of analysis can, however, increase the probability that your predictions will be correct. Your predictions are a matter of guesswork when you make them by intuition, and they remain a matter of guesswork—educated guesswork—when we make an explicit analysis. The analysis helps you make better guesses.

Our approach to analyzing people's likely reactions consists of asking questions about the communication situation. No set of ready-made answers could possibly fit all situations; we must analyze each situation as it comes up. Thus we need questions that are useful and productive in most situations.

In What Situation Will the Reaction Take Place?

Earlier, in our model of communication, we found that the situation in which a person reacts is an important determinant of his or her reaction. We saw that a person may react to the same message differently under different circumstances. To analyze possible reactions, the first important question you can ask is "What's the situation in which I want to influence the other person's reaction?" The answer to this question is often very easy when you and the other person are in the same place at the same time and you expect to get an immediate reaction. Under such circumstances, you already take the "situation" factor into account intuitively, and you don't have to think about it explicitly.

But when you communicate in business, you're often separated from your audience in space and time; you nearly always are when you write. Then you're not automatically compensating for the audience's situation, and you have to plan accordingly. Sometimes the problem is even more complicated: not only are you writing to someone who will read your message in another place at a later time, but even worse, you're asking that person to behave in a certain way at yet another time and place. You might, for example, be writing instructions that your assistant will read at home next Tuesday evening and carry out in a client's office on the twelfth of next month. Then you must plan your message very carefully to fit the situation in which the assistant will react.

You'd like to know, then, what situation your audience will be in when it reacts to your message. If you know that situation, you can shape your message to fit it.

How Would I React in That Situation?

Very often you can complete the formal analysis at this point by asking yourself, "How would I react to this message in that situation?" That is, you look inside yourself, and you predict that your audience will react as you think you would.

Looking inside yourself, or introspection, is often a very productive way to predict audience reaction, especially in everyday situations in which the very best predictions aren't absolutely essential. Introspection works because in many ways people are similar, and in many situations they do react alike. At its simplest, introspection means assuming the other person will react the way you think you would.

In some respects, however, people do react differently to certain situations. In many situations you'd react much like a corporate president, but in others you'd react differently. Even in these cases, though, you can use introspection if you do it thoughtfully. You can say, "I don't think this person would react to this message the same way I would. But I believe I can predict what the differences would be, and I can take them into account." This is an entirely legitimate line of reasoning, and it often works.

If you're satisfied with the results of your introspection, then your analysis ends here. But what if you're not satisfied yet? What's the next thing to look at?

What Patterns Exist in the Audience's Behavior?

Over the past 75 years, social scientists have devoted much research to predicting human behavior. Researchers in psychology, sociology, education, market research, and other fields have taken this as a central task. And their findings often allow them to predict exactly the kinds of things that you as a communicator want to predict.

In their research, these scientists have found that there are patterns in the ways people react. If you know what patterns to look for, then you can often make accurate predictions. Often you can identify key reaction patterns from a very small amount of information. Of course, you won't always be right, but you may be right more often than if you had just guessed.

It's obvious, even to the layman, that some kinds of information are extremely helpful in predicting people's reactions. If you intend to communicate with someone and happen to know that that person is three years old, then you have an enormous amount of information about how he or she may react. In that case, knowing the audience's age is crucial. Age, however, is a good predictor only within certain ranges—the very young or the very old. In the middle, age may not make such a great difference. Yet one piece of information is often all you need to make accurate predictions. If you know, for example, that Lois Haber simply couldn't raise $80,000 to spend on a car, then you can predict accurately enough (with hardly any other information about her) how she'll react to a sales pitch for a Rolls Royce.

Some kinds of information, however, are useful in a very broad range of situations. Social scientists have found three kinds of behavior patterns of this sort: (1) psychological patterns, (2) cultural patterns, and (3) social patterns. These are patterns you can use in improving your predictions.

Psychological patterns We all tend to attach labels to the people around us—labels that reflect their individual personalities. One person is gregarious and enjoys meetings and working with others; another person is introverted and prefers solitary work. One person is easygoing; another is nervous and high-strung. One person is meticulous and careful; another lets well enough alone and doesn't worry about the details. Nearly every time you meet someone and talk to him or her, even just for a minute or two, you form impressions about that person's personality. Social scientists make more detailed analyses than the average person can, but the goals are pretty much the same. Psychological patterns have value as predictors of people's reactions, and you can learn to use them.

To do this, you must overcome, to some extent, your early training against prejudgment. You learned, perhaps too well, not to rely on first impressions but to get to know people before you draw conclusions. Sometimes, you learned, first impressions can be misleading. No doubt that's true, but much more often your first impressions of someone turn out to be entirely valid. After working with someone for twenty years, you're often even more convinced that your first impressions were correct. When you remember that all predictions about people are guesswork, taking advantage of your well-developed ability to make quick guesses about people's personalities is a little easier. Guessing on the basis of first impressions, if that's all the information you have, is more likely to be productive than guessing with no information at all. Sometimes the differences between these two kinds of guesses can be very significant.

Cultural patterns Nearly every middle-class American holds certain values or beliefs about how people should behave: for example, a nation should be governed by laws that apply equally to everyone, a person should be rewarded for working hard, and owning a family car is a normal part of life. There are thousands more. (Of course not everyone acts on these beliefs all the time, but the important thing is that people feel strongly that they ought to be acted on.)

Put together, such shared values are the culture of middle-class American society. Although we believe in these cultural values very strongly, they're hardly universal. For every value mentioned above, we can point to an opposing value held by another society. Values vary from society to society.

In general, our cultural values permit a range of acceptable beliefs; they don't restrict us to one specific belief. For example, our society specifies a range of clothing that's considered appropriate for a college classroom. As you look around a college classroom, you realize that the range is quite wide; usually a variety of clothing is considered acceptable. But there are limits: a person who comes to class stark naked—or in a ball gown—would be considered inappropriately dressed by nearly everyone.

Many areas in our maps of the world are determined almost entirely by middle-class American culture as transmitted to us through our parents and teachers. Our knowledge of appropriate sexual behavior, patterns of dress, even our language and communication patterns, come to us through our culture. Cultural patterns are very important determinants of the ways people are likely to react.

Most of us spend most of our time talking to middle-class Americans. Therefore, knowing the cultural values of someone raised in Japan or Nigeria, though interesting in itself, is probably not very useful in planning day-to-day messages. What's useful to know is that in any society, including ours, subcultures of various kinds have specific values that differ slightly from those of the main culture. In the United States, for instance, we have subcultures based on race, religion, and ethnic background. We even have subcultures based upon age, of which the college student subculture is the most visible example. As you become sensitive to subcultural consistencies, they can help you predict how someone may react to your messages. It's often easy to ascertain what subculture someone belongs to. Sometimes this single piece of information can give valuable clues about that person's consistent patterns of reactions, thus helping you both to communicate.

Social patterns   As we've noted, in many areas our culture allows us a whole range of possible values. For instance, our culture permits quite a range of attitudes toward labor unions ranging from strongly prolabor to strongly antilabor. Within that range, we each hold some specific attitude toward labor unions. Where do these specific attitudes come from, if not from the culture?

An important source of such values is the people in our lives who are important to us—our parents, spouses, very close friends, and coworkers. Social scientists call these people our reference groups. They're the people we compare ourselves with, the people we discuss our values and beliefs with, the people who influence our lives. Consider for a minute how much your values have been influenced by the people who are close to you. Perhaps you can identify the areas they influenced. Since a person's patterns of values are strongly influenced by reference groups, knowing about that person's family, friends, and coworkers can tell us something about him or her.

We use information about an audience's psychological, cultural, and social patterns to improve our guesswork about how that audience may react. We realize that informed guesses are more likely to prove correct than wild guesses are. But even informed guesses are still guesses. Our analysis, we hope, increases their likelihood of proving correct.

Audience Analysis Reviewed

In this chapter, we've examined in detail two of the most important parts of the communication process: perception and prediction. We saw that the meaning someone attaches to an event depends on that person's mental map, which is the way he or she conceives the world. We also saw that the meanings people attach to events come from inside; the meanings aren't determined by the events themselves.

In addition, we examined how to predict the shape of someone's mental map and how to predict, as a result, how that person will react to our messages. We developed the following questions, which can be used to analyze formally how an audience will probably react:

1. What's the situation in which I hope to influence this person's reaction?

2. Can I predict this person's reactions in this situation accurately enough by introspection? (If not, then answer Question 3.)

3. What kinds of consistencies can I predict in this person's normal behavior patterns? Can I find:

   a. Consistencies based on personality?

   b. Consistencies based on membership in a subculture?

   c. Consistencies based on the kinds of people who form his or her reference groups?

   d. Other useful patterns of consistencies?

Using Audience Analysis

The above questions assist in the audience analysis you'll perform in the planning stage of nonroutine messages. In Chapter 11, you'll study the audience analysis process in more detail and add further steps to your normal audience analysis. Although the questions listed above are firmly based on communication theory, they're reminders of highly practical points. In a difficult or sensitive situation, answering these questions helps you communicate better.

The way to develop your audience analysis skill is to practice predicting people's behavior and then test your predictions. If you aren't already doing it, try making predictions before you communicate with someone you know well. Test yourself: see how accurate you can be. Be aware of the predictions you make about people's reactions. The more you're aware of your predictions, the more control you'll have over the consequences of your messages. By paying just a little more attention to predictions you've been making half-consciously, you'll improve your batting average almost automatically—and probably improve it a lot.

If you're a very good predictor of people's reactions, then you're probably already a very good communicator.

FURTHER EXPLORATION

1. I wrote this question in my office in San Diego, California, in the summer of 1980; you are reading it in your place and time. How are those two situations different in space and time? What effects do you think these differences might have upon communication? How should a message be adapted to minimize communication problems resulting from these differences?

2. As we've seen, if a person is very young or very old, information about his age may tell us a lot about the way he is likely to perceive and react to messages. What are some other facts we might know about someone that would let us predict that much about the person's behavior?

5

Symbols and Their Meanings

Words differently arranged have a different meaning, and meanings differently arranged have different effects.
Blaise Pascal

There is one stylistic development which most people seldom notice in themselves or others, but which should be watched. As we grow older, we use more and more abstract nouns and adjectives: we move up the semantic ladder. The man who at 25 would have said "tough nut to crack" will when he is 55 say: "Conceivably that might be a problem which admits no solution."
Gilbert Highet

One of the richest and most detailed areas of our maps of the world is the part that contains our language. The symbols we use affect our communication in two ways: they carry our messages and influence our perceptions of events. The complex relationship between our symbols and their meanings in our mental maps is very important.

MEANINGS DEPEND ON THE WHOLE COMMUNICATION PROCESS

In real life, the meanings of symbols are quite dependent on the whole communication process; we can't consider them apart from it.

For example, the message "Our production dropped by 2 percent last quarter" could mean "I've been telling you all along we were in trouble, and I was right." It could mean "What are your suggestions for solving this problem?" It could mean "I knew it; I just knew if we implemented those new policies we'd have trouble!" Or it could mean "Wonderful—only a 2 percent drop during conversion to the new system." But what does it actually mean? We don't know.

To know what a statement means, we have to know:

- Who said it
- To whom it was said
- In what situation it was said

If we know these things, we have a fair chance of understanding the meaning the symbols convey.

A message is understandable only in the context of the whole communication process. The message is only one of four key parts. The communication process includes (1) someone who reacts to a set of circumstances (the event) to produce (2) a message, which (3) someone else perceives in (4) a situation in which the meaning is interpreted.

Of course, in most everyday situations we do perceive messages in the context of the whole communication process. When someone tells you, "Our production dropped by 2 percent last quarter," you subconsciously consider all the circumstances of that communication as you interpret it. You do consider the person who said it and the situation in which it was said as part of the meaning.

EVERY STATEMENT IS A STATEMENT ABOUT "ME"

We often forget that the message itself is only one part of the communication process, because messages appear directly connected to the outside world. When I say, "Our production dropped by 2 percent last quarter," I appear simply to confirm something that already exists in the outside world. And yet the real meaning of that statement pertains much more to something that's going on inside my head than to anything that's happening outside. The real meaning is about "me" much more than about the state of the business. My statement really means something more like, "I've noticed that our production dropped by 2 percent last quarter, and I think there will be such-and-such consequences because it did."

Let's look at another statement. When I say "John is a poor worker" or "Sue is a good worker," I seem to be reporting the fact that "poor worker" and "good worker" are characteristics of John and Sue. But what I really mean by such a statement is something more like, "When I perceive John's behavior on the job, I'm disappointed, irritated, or frustrated." The statement I use to express my perceptions and evaluations of these events is "John is a poor worker." Therefore, when I say, "John is a poor worker," I'm saying more about myself than about John. I've just forgotten to get the I into the sentence.

Actually, when I talk about John, most of what I say refers to "my mapping of John" rather than to John himself. Certainly my mental map is what supplies the meaning "poor worker," and my reaction is based on all the events I've perceived that John participated in. John acted this way on this occasion, and that way on that occasion, and "I" have perceived those actions and supplied the label "poor worker." When I say, "John is a poor worker," I'm really talking about something I've done.

SYMBOLS ARE OUR LABELS FOR PIECES OF OUR MAPS

Symbols usually refer to pieces of our maps of the world rather than to things in the real world. In this section, we see how that's true.

In this chapter, the term symbol means any label we apply to a piece of our mental map. All words are symbols. But not all symbols are words. For example, the U.S. flag, a company emblem, and a picture of a hungry child are symbols. A smile, a shrug, or a wink can be a symbol. But normally we find a word, or invent one, to symbolize a thing we want to talk about. Most of our symbols are words.

Symbols and Their "Pointing" Meanings

Part of the meaning of most symbols lies in their reference to some object, action, or quality that we could (in some sense) point at. The symbol "chair," for instance, has as part of its meaning a reference to a chair or a number of chairs that we could indicate by pointing at them with our fingers. We call this kind of meaning the denotative meaning of a symbol.

Concrete denotative meanings The denotative meaning of some symbols is very easy to specify. "This book," for instance, is something you can easily define: you can point to the book and everyone can see it. You can easily clarify your meaning in the same way when you use the symbol "the chair that I'm sitting on." When you use a symbol to refer to a specific thing you're looking at or doing, the relationship between the symbol and its meaning can be extremely clear. The symbol points at something everyone can see and understand. This kind of meaning is called concrete denotative meaning.

But as soon as we leave behind the small group of symbols for the specific things we can point to, we encounter difficulties in defining the relationship between a symbol and its meaning. The symbol "this cat" (if you can point your finger at a specific cat) is one everyone can understand; people can look at "this cat" and see what it is. But the symbol "cat" is more difficult to define.

Abstract denotative meaning   Let's consider for a minute how we can reasonably say that the symbol "cat" refers to something in the outside world that we can point to. What can we point to that corresponds to "cat"? We could begin by pointing to a particular cat and saying that what we mean by "cat" is the set of things that resemble this thing. But suppose that particular cat happens to be a short-haired, gray, female alley cat with one torn ear and two claws missing from its right hind paw. Surely a thing doesn't have to be just like that cat to warrant the symbol "cat."

Let's look at it another way. We can imagine that at the dawn of time a man saw one little wild furry animal and then another one something like it and another and another, and he invented the word "cat" to mean those four animals. When he saw a fifth cat, of course he included that one in the meaning of "cat," and so on, until he had seen thousands of cats. At some point, he began using the symbol "cat" to refer not only to the thousands of cats he'd actually seen, but also to all cats that had lived before his time and to all cats that might live after him. "Cat" could even mean some imaginary beast that never existed and never would, outside his mind. By now "cat" no longer referred to something he actually saw around him; it referred to a category of things that existed only in his mind—in his map of the world. This is what we call abstract denotative meaning.

A symbol you use for its abstract meaning, then, refers to a category of things, and the category is one you've set up in your mental map. The category is not something that exists in the outside world; the objects you see around you every day don't come with labels like "cat" and "non-cat." That category is only in your head; it is something you do when you look at the world.

Categories in our maps of the world.   When you use symbols to refer to these categories, or abstractions, in communicating with someone else, that person must share your set of categories to understand what you mean. If someone knows what you're referring to when you say "cat," then that person also has the category "cat" in his or her mental map. Before the two of you can communicate effectively, your mental categories labeled "cat" must be roughly similar.

The categories don't have to be identical to permit reasonably effective communication; they just have to be fairly similar. You can easily carry on a perfectly reasonable conversation with someone who doesn't share exactly the same categories with you. For example, think about talking to a blind man about rain. Your image of rain is very likely predominantly visual. When you think of rain, you see rain falling. When the blind man thinks of rain, he hears its sound and feels it on his skin. But communication could proceed pretty well, considering that the two of you would be talking about such different categories.

The idea of abstraction, or categories in your mental map, may be easier to understand if you imagine your map of the world as a huge filing system that you use to attach meanings (or names) to the events around you. As you walk around noticing events, you mentally flip through the files looking for the file folder that best corresponds to each event you see. When you find a good match between a folder's contents and a specific new event you're looking at (say, a bluepoint Siamese kitten), you mentally file the event in that folder and use the name on that folder (the abstract symbol "cat") to refer to the object.

Language as a set of categories. The similarities between your mental categories and someone else's make language. A language is first of all an enormous set of categories for sorting and classifying the events we perceive, and of course it also includes a set of symbols for referring to these categories. If every speaker of English sorted the events he or she perceived into different categories, then the words of the English language would be nearly useless. Only because we all think in roughly the same categories do our symbols have meaning.

Levels of abstraction Not all abstract symbols and meanings are equally abstract. Symbols like "democracy" and "brotherhood" that refer to all-encompassing categories are more abstract than ones like "cat." "Cat" comes closer to actually pointing at something outside our heads than "democracy" does.

In fact, we can arrange groups of symbols by their level of abstraction. Look at this ordering of symbols, called an abstraction ladder:

Events

Objects

Living things

Animals

Mammals

Felines

Cats

Female cats

Gray female alley cats

This cat (a cat that can be pointed at)

This ladder begins at the bottom with the one symbol whose meaning is concrete and gets more and more abstract as it rises, until at the top is the symbol whose meaning is the most abstract meaning of all (as we're using the word): events. At each level, more and more of existence is included, until at the top everything is included. (Everything we could talk about is an event.) As we proceed up the ladder, the symbols become more general and less specific.

You, as a business communicator, can learn two important lessons about levels of abstraction. First, note that only the bottom symbol on the ladder is truly concrete. When you use that bottom symbol, your audience can look at the thing you've pointed at and see what you mean. Every symbol except the bottom one is abstract, and its meaning is in your head, where your audience can't look at it.

Second, note that the best messages nearly always use the lowest possible level of abstraction. Messages are more interesting and communicate better when they avoid high-level abstractions and use very specific symbols instead. Specific symbols create more vivid images in the audience's mind and are more likely to stimulate the audience to visualize your message. Sometimes beginners believe that using very specific symbols will make them appear condescending to the audience, but in fact it's almost impossible to be too specific. Of course, some subjects are naturally more abstract than others, and it would be silly to rule out all higher-level abstractions, but in most cases, try to use the most specific symbol you can. Specific is vivid.

Symbols and Their Emotional Meanings

Most symbols tell your audience not only the subject but also how you view the subject. They tell whether you see it as good or bad, pleasant or unpleasant, benevolent or threatening. What's the difference between a "discussion" and a "confrontation"? Between a "student" and a "scholar"? Between a "boss" and a "leader"? The difference is not that the person who uses these symbols is pointing at pairs of different events, rather, that the person is evaluating the events differently. This evaluative part of a symbol's meaning is called connotative meaning.[1]

Suppose a woman wants to comment about a 20-year-old man. What will she call him? She could call him a kid, guy, young man, dude, youth, male human being, or a number of other names. But she selects only one of these names, and she selects on the basis of her feelings about the man. Most events could be called a number of names. People must choose

---

1. This book's usage of *connotative* is the usage of social scientists who study language. *Connotative* is also sometimes used to mean a word's secondary meaning or any other meaning associated with the word's main meaning, whether emotional or not. That definition is less useful to business writers.

which name to call them, and they don't choose among these possible names at random. They select the name that carries the particular connotation they have in mind. In fact, you usually have difficulty referring to events without revealing, at least to some extent, how you feel about them.

Nearly all symbols have some connotative meaning. Even simple words like "cat" and "storm" have clear connotative meanings, and we use these meanings when we refer to a "catty person" or a "stormy relationship." When we refer to a "catty person," we're certainly not saying that the person physically resembles a short, furry, four-legged house pet; we're saying that our evaluation of the person's character resembles our evaluation of a cat's character.

The good-bad dimension is common to most connotative meanings of symbols. That is, most often a connotative meaning tells us whether the communicator thinks the subject is good or bad. And the connotative meaning is quite separate from the denotative meaning. In fact, if we list words having very similar connotative meanings, we find that they "point to" a wide variety of things:

Weakling	Tyrant
Rotten	Demagogue
Junk	Polluted

These words are related because they all say, "This is bad," even though their denotative meanings are very different.

Some words have such vivid connotative meanings that we use them where denotatively they make little sense. The denotative meaning of "stupid car" is nearly nil—cars can't be smart or stupid. Yet connotatively, the phrase is rich and vivid in meaning. The symbol "stupid" is used for its obvious connotative meaning. Most expressions involving the common four-letter obscenities work this way.

Associative connotative meanings A special kind of connotative meaning arises because people associate a symbol with certain feelings or memories in their mental maps. The word "no" evokes strong feelings in most people, largely because they've associated it with feelings of rejection since infancy. People often react very emotionally when you say no, even when what you're refusing them isn't very valuable at all; their mental association of your refusal with the pain of earlier refusals creates a response far out of proportion to the facts.

We often react to the associations evoked by a symbol as though we were reacting to the actual object the symbol denotes. Many people shudder at the thought of eating fried rattlesnake, snails, or grasshoppers. The meat is not that unpleasant, I'm told, but the associations are. A young man who has tried them reports that earthworms are tolerably edible, if you deep-fry them until crisp. Nutritionally they're fine—for someone else.

When a score of brewing companies produce practically identical products, an advertising agency has difficulty promoting any real merits of one over the others. As a result, we see one brand sold because of its associations with glacier-fed streams in the Rocky Mountains, another because of its associations with tough, masculine cowboys, and another because of its associations with sports heroes. Ads for soap, cars, cosmetics, processed food—in fact, for most mass-marketed consumer items— usually emphasize artificial associations much more than any functional merits of the items. Even when one product is functionally superior to its competitors, such as a toothpaste with decay-preventive agents, its advertising usually emphasizes associative meanings much more than functional superiority.

Managing connotative meanings   Skill in creating messages with the appropriate connotative meanings is very marketable in our society, though regarded as a bit shady by many people. Advertising agencies, corporations, and political organizations often pay extravagant salaries to their "image merchants."

A somewhat more modest skill in managing connotative and associative meanings is a valuable asset for business people at all levels. At the very least, a competent communicator recognizes that symbols do have connotative meanings and tries to compose messages that are free of discordant or inappropriate connotations. The person who goes through life ignoring the connotations his or her messages arouse in audiences' minds may be constantly puzzled by their unexpected reactions. The skillful communicator understands how the connotative meanings of words affect audiences, and he or she can draw on these meanings to improve communication. Symbols that have strong connotative meanings are very powerful tools; they can communicate very effectively when used consciously and intelligently.

Dictionary Definitions

Occasionally someone suggests that the dictionary definition of a symbol is its denotative meaning, but if you examine dictionary definitions you'll see that this isn't true. Especially when connotative meanings are important to a symbol's meaning, the dictionary suggests them quite clearly, although it doesn't separate them from denotative meanings.

Here are some excerpts from dictionary definitions:

demagogue 1: a person, especially an orator or political leader, who gains power and popularity by arousing the emotions, passions, and prejudices of the people

junk 1: any old or discarded material, as metal, paper, rags **2**: anything that is regarded as worthless, meaningless, contemptible, or mere trash

tyrant 1: a king or ruler who uses his power oppressively or unjustly **2**: any person in a position of authority who exercises power oppressively or despotically

As you can see, these definitions include both denotative and connotative meanings. Dictionaries would often be quite misleading if they didn't suggest connotative meanings.

Nonverbal Symbols

Words and phrases certainly aren't the only symbols. They're the ones we're most aware of, but other symbols are also essential to the business communicator.

Expressions and gestures as symbols   Facial expressions, gestures, tone of voice, and body language communicate important meanings. Though such symbols are less clearly coded than verbal symbols, they communicate almost as clearly—sometimes even more clearly, because the language of gestures and facial expressions transcends many verbal barriers. A smile means very nearly the same thing in most of the world.

We can easily illustrate how facial expression and tone of voice contribute to a sentence's meaning. Take the sentence, "I'm sure glad to see you." Say it with a big smile first, then say it with a heavy scowl. The sentence changes meaning almost from one pole to the other because you've changed the key symbol for interpreting it—your expression.

Consider another sentence: "Sarah was very good at typing today." Say the sentence over and over, each time emphasizing a different word. Notice that your tone of voice seems to change and the sentence's meaning clearly changes. "*Sarah* was very good at typing today" means that someone else probably wasn't. "Sarah was very good *at typing* today" means that Sarah must have performed poorly at something else. And so on.

Body language, as many current books and articles demonstrate, is also a communication symbol. Body-language symbols are especially important in personal relationships, liking and disliking, attraction and repulsion, aggression and submission, and so on. Such symbols are often especially honest messages simply because the communicator is unaware of sending them. It's hard to misrepresent your feelings if you're communicating them unconsciously. And even when you notice the messages your body is sending, they're relatively difficult to control. An excellent actor can do it; most people can't.

Actions and life-styles as symbols   What people—and organizations —do often communicates more loudly than words. All of us can think of childhood situations in which someone performed a symbolic action—of honesty, brotherhood, or love—so impressive that we remembered it vividly years later. Actions can sometimes be powerful symbols, rich in meaning.

The way people order their lives can communicate symbolically, too. Nothing illustrates a person's values quite so vividly as the way they're played out in his or her life-style. Often the way people live portrays their values more accurately than what they say about their values. Every life represents one person's decisions about which values are inviolate and which values can be compromised. Usually the compromises are evident only in the way people act. Often, in their thoughts and comments, they themselves haven't recognized how they've made these compromises.

People sometimes feel this conflict between a company's words and its deeds. For example, many companies portray themselves as service-oriented: "If we can help in any way, please let us know." If they behave correspondingly, fine. But if customers get no help when they request it, then all the writing in the world about service orientation won't be very persuasive. The word must be matched by the deed.

FURTHER EXPLORATION

1. Think of situations in which someone might say, "The store is crowded." How many different meanings might that sentence convey? You should be able to identify eight or ten at least.

2. For two or three hours when you're in a group of people, watch for statements that (1) contain no "I" or "me," so they appear to be statements about the outside world, but (2) are mostly statements about the speaker's own mental map. List some examples. Were such statements frequent or infrequent?

3. Make an abstraction ladder for the symbol "car." Review the discussion of levels of abstraction to see exactly how the ladder is constructed. See how many levels you can make in your "car" ladder. Is there any limit?

4. Can a meaningful sentence be constructed in which every symbol has a concrete meaning?

5. Select six symbols that have clear connotative meanings and describe each connotative meaning. Does everyone perceive the same connotative meanings in these symbols? To what degree do people share connotative meanings for most symbols?

6. Pick a national TV advertisement and describe the associative meanings it uses. What feelings does the advertiser try to associate with the product or service?

6
Language and Perception

Without knowing the force of words,
it is impossible to know men.
Confucius

"Then you should say what you mean," the March Hare went on.

"I do," Alice hastily replied; *"at least—at least I mean what I*
say—that's the same thing, you know."

"Not the same thing a bit!" said the Hatter. *"Why, you might just*
as well say that 'I see what I eat' is the same thing as 'I eat what I
see'!"

"You might just as well say," added the March Hare," *that 'I like*
what I get' is the same thing as 'I get what I like'!"

"You might as well say," added the Dormouse, which seemed to be
talking in its sleep, "that 'I breathe when I sleep' is the same thing
as 'I sleep when I breathe'!"
Lewis Carroll

ost of your knowledge of the world has come through communication. You've learned much through personal experience, of course,
but you've learned much more by hearing and reading messages. Your
knowledge has been heavily influenced by the communication process.
Language, particularly, affects your perceptions, but your mental map affects
them even more fundamentally. This chapter explores these effects and
discusses how to minimize their impact on communication.

HOW ENGLISH AFFECTS YOUR PERCEPTIONS

Your perceptions are shaped by the language you use to create a map
of the world. Because you and I speak English, we see the world in a certain
way; if our native language were Urdu, we'd surely look at the same world
quite differently.

That our language encourages us to notice some things and discour-
ages us from noticing others is hardly a new discovery. If a speaker of
English wants to talk about a running man, for instance, the language
almost forces him or her to notice four aspects:

1. When the running took place—in the past, present, or future

   The man ran.
   The man runs.
   The man will run.

2. Whether the running is completed or continues to be performed

   The man ran.   The man was running.
   The man had run.   The man had been running.
   The man will run.   The man will be running.

3. When the speaker's observation of the running occurs in time

   The man will have been running. (At some future time, the running
   will have been in progress.)

   The man had run. (At some past time, the running had already been
   completed.)

4. Whether the running is actual or hypothetical

   If the man were running . . .
   If the man had run . . .
   Were the man to run . . .

If you spoke a language that didn't require these distinctions, you'd probably still notice them when they were significant. But usually you'd ignore
them. In fact, in many other languages such distinctions are actually difficult to express. Be aware, then, of how English biases your perceptions.

64

HOW THE MAPPING SYSTEM AFFECTS YOUR PERCEPTIONS

Your mental map helps you identify events in the outside world by attaching meanings to patterns of nerve impulses and storing the vast knowledge you've collected. It serves as your memory. And most of the time, it serves you well. But occasionally, its working leads you to draw wrong conclusions about the outside world.

Writers on semantics, the study of the relationship between symbols and their meanings, have devoted careful attention to this kind of problem.[1] This section discusses some of their key findings.

Polarization: Two-Valued Thinking

Obviously not everything in this world is either black or white. In fact, most events fall into gray areas. But your mapping system makes it very easy to perceive the world in terms of absolutes, in blacks and whites. For example, you might say, "Everything in the world can be divided into two categories: things that are green and things that aren't green." This statement seems to make perfect sense. But the minute you begin to test a statement like this against the outside world, you find difficulties. Go outdoors and try to divide what you see into green and nongreen things. Where's the boundary between green and blue, or green and yellow? What about an oak tree? It's partly green (for part of the year) and also partly black. Consider another example. Try to describe the color of the palm of your hand. You'll use words like pink or orange or brown to describe something that's neither pink nor orange nor brown. It's all of these colors and at the same time none of these colors.

The real world is rich and complex. By reducing that complexity, your mapping system helps you deal with it. Your map tends to classify the world in either-or terms; it will, if you let it, eliminate the gray areas. In fact, it makes thinking and talking about the gray areas difficult even when you insist on considering them.

Problems of Abstraction

Suppose we need to describe, say, a person named Gerald Corlew. There are many ways we could do it, and all involve listing several of his attributes, selecting them according to our audience's needs. We might describe him by saying he's a:

Man	Student
23-year-old	Beer drinker
Husband	Private pilot
Father	Dodge owner
Roman Catholic	Taxpayer

---

1. See Alfred Korzybski, *Science and Sanity, an Introduction to Non-Aristotelian Systems and General Semantics* (Lancaster, Pa.: Science Press, 1933). For a more popularized treatment, see S. I. Hayakawa, *Language in Thought and Action*, 3rd ed., (New York: Harcourt Brace Jovanovich, 1972).

Now consider how we've made this description. We've taken little pieces of Gerald Corlew's life, given them labels, and listed them. We've abstracted. When we say, for example, that he's a 23-year-old, we're selecting one little piece of his life. His 23-year-old-ness certainly doesn't exist apart from the rest of his life, except in our minds, so when we abstract that fact we're performing an artificial mental exercise.

This kind of abstracting is certainly not limited to descriptions of people. Most mapping involves abstraction. For example, when you look at a great, tall, leafy thing and call it an "oak tree," you're abstracting and isolating only part of a whole thing. There's certainly more to that thing than oak-tree-ness. When you watch a football play and say, "Greene scored a touchdown," you're abstracting only one piece of a very complex event.

Your mapping system's ability to abstract is extremely useful, but it tends to lead into two semantic traps: judgment by category and allness.

Judgment by category   No two X's are alike (substitute any noun you like for the X). In the outside world, we seldom find two X's that are enough alike that there aren't any important differences between them. No two cops are alike; no two business people are alike; no two professors are alike; no two Italians are alike; no two oak trees are alike. In spite of what any teacher tries to tell you, not all students are alike.

Here's the trap. An important (and usually useful) property of your mapping system is its provision of familiar categories and convenient labels for them. Therefore, it's easy to place in a category two things that share a single quality and forget that they have many other dissimilar qualities. Though they share one quality, they're not identical. It's too easy to think, "This thing is an oak tree (or a cop, or a professor, or a welfare recipient, or a Ford), and that thing is an oak tree (or whatever), and so this thing and that thing are alike." After you've attached the same label to two things, you forget all the differences and remember only the similarity.

Remember that the real world wasn't created just for the convenience of people who use the English map to classify things. Common sense and our observations of the outside world should suggest that most things we classify as being alike probably all differ from one another in every way imaginable—except for the one common trait that our label abstracts.

Allness   Suppose we add one element to our description of Gerald Corlew: Gerald Corlew is in prison. Now our picture changes—drastically. In fact, for many people the other elements in our description nearly disappear. To them, this element tells all.

Allness is the trap of assuming that one label for a thing tells you all about that thing. Allness is like judgment by category applied in reverse. Instead of assuming that things with the same label are alike, now you assume that one label tells you all there is to know about that thing.

If you've ever spent much time with a two-year-old, you can easily understand how people make assumptions that lead to allness problems. For weeks at a time, the child will walk around pointing to everything in sight, asking, "What's that? What's that?" Of course, no one tries to explain to such a young child that when we say, "That's a truck," we're abstracting just one quality of the thing being pointed at and ignoring all its other qualities and that the label "truck" certainly shouldn't be construed as a complete description of the thing.

Of course, as the child grows older, he or she should develop more sophisticated notions about how a language works. But the child, like most of us, probably won't think very much about how a language works after he or she learns it. Therefore, the extremely simplistic mapping notions that we worked out at age two or three tend to stick with us. We call them "common sense."

Like the two-year-old, we like labels. Labels make it easy to carry mental images around to remember and discuss difficult concepts. The world is very complex; therefore, some simple categorizing and labeling make life easier. But when they get out of control, parts of our maps don't correspond to the outside world. Language is just a convenient fiction; events in the outside world are the facts.

Static Viewpoint

You've noticed that the outside world constantly changes. Yet your mental map tends to treat it as though it were static.

For example, many people who've visited Washington, D.C., would probably agree with the statement, "Washington is a hot, humid city." But most people visit Washington during the summer when the weather is often hot and humid. That's how they map it—"Washington: hot and humid." That's how they talk about it. The time element is very easy to forget; obviously Washington is not always hot and humid; it's very seldom hot and humid anywhere in the United States in February.

People change, often radically; institutions change; business conditions change; rocks and trees change; the whole universe changes constantly. But if you're not careful, parts of your map get frozen in place. Your map doesn't keep reminding you that what was true once may not be true now. In fact, it encourages you to think, subconsciously, that something true is true for all time; that it always was and always will be true.

Many people have had experiences similar to one of mine. I once considered a job teaching in the same academic department that I'd earned my undergraduate degree from. As I interviewed some of my former teachers—people who would be my colleagues—at times they talked to me as though I were still the same person who had studied under them nearly ten years earlier. I knew that, although I'd changed enormously during those ten years, they were looking at the me_{1970} and seeing (at times) the me_{1960} instead. Even though these teachers were especially skilled communicators and every single one of them had studied material like this intensively, they still found it almost impossible to avoid applying some of their (not always complimentary) evaluations of the me$_{1960}$ to the me$_{1970}$ they were talking to. One reason that "a prophet is without honor in his own country" is that the prophet's countrymen can't help looking at him or her and seeing the dirty, scrawny little kid who once stole apples from their orchards.

Most things that are true are true only under certain conditions. Washington is hot and humid on many summer days. To avoid the static viewpoint, form the habit of testing statements against the outside world. Ask yourself, "Under what conditions is this statement true?" Or "When was this evaluation true?" Or, best of all, "Under what conditions will this statement no longer be true?" If your map is wrong, checking it against the outside world may reveal the error.

Direct Observations Versus Personal Conclusions

Some statements I make result directly from my observation of the outside world, such as, "There are two light fixtures in my office ceiling." On the other hand, some statements I make result from my mental processing of information from the outside world. For example, I might observe those fixtures and come to the conclusion, "My office is very well lighted." Grammatically, linguistically, and structurally, nothing about the two sentences even hints that one results from direct observation and the other from a personal conclusion. Observation statements and personal-conclusion statements are grammatically and linguistically alike. Language gives you no warning of their great difference in meaning.

Banning all personal conclusions from conversation would be silly. They're important and necessary. Remember, however, that every personal conclusion is a matter of probability. When I say, "My office is very well lighted," on the basis of counting the light fixtures, I really mean something like, "I think it's probable that my office is very well lighted." By talking about probabilities, I remind myself and my audience that I don't know from observation that the statement is true—perhaps neither fixture works or both are poorly placed to light my desk.

A direct observation is fairly likely to be true; a personal conclusion may or may not be true. When you recognize a personal conclusion, you can at least estimate its probability of being true or false. But if you report your conclusion to someone without saying that it's personal, then that person is prevented from using it intelligently; you've given the person no reason to think in terms of probabilities.

A company report writer will lose the readers' confidence quickly if they discover that he or she doesn't clearly distinguish direct observations from personal conclusions or doesn't clearly label each one. Direct observations (facts) are the raw material of management decisions. A knowledgeable observer's personal conclusions may carry a great deal of weight, but only if readers know they can trust that observer to label facts as facts and personal conclusions as personal conclusions. The two look alike in writing; the writer has to indicate which is which.

Bypassing

Bypassing is a very simple semantic problem. It occurs when people use the same label to mean different things, or use different labels to mean the same thing. Some of the world's great misunderstandings have arisen through bypassing situations. American and Soviet politicians sneer at each other's claims of being truly democratic, when in fact each could make a good case that his or her country is very democratic indeed—according to his or her way of mapping "democratic." The same label refers to quite different categories in the politicians' maps. Also because of bypassing, steaming political arguments often cool off very quickly when the two adversaries discover that, underneath the overheated rhetoric, there are two minds in almost perfect agreement. They're using two labels to say the same thing.

Bypassing occurs because of two half-conscious assumptions people make about language and labels: (1) that words can be used in only one way (the way I use them, of course!) and (2) that words "have" meanings. As we've seen, neither assumption is correct. Even simple words are used in many ways; my very incomplete little desk dictionary lists 12 different usages for "cat," 28 usages for "do," 18 usages for "have," 29 usages for "fact," and none of these specifies subtle shifts of meaning or possible connotative meanings. And meanings aren't part of the words; the meanings exist entirely in the minds of people who use the words.

To avoid bypassing, simply focus on your audience's mental map rather than your own. For all practical purposes, your message really means what your audience thinks it means, no matter what you think it means. Your audience will react to it according to what the audience thinks it means. When you're trying to communicate effectively, the audience—to coin a phrase—is always right.

When the person you're addressing keeps attaching unintended meanings to your messages, try to attune your message to that person's map, even if you believe he or she is bullishly wrongheaded. If you insist that your message is correct and that the other person perceives it incorrectly, then you can't communicate. But if you're very flexible about accommodating your message to your audience's way of attaching meanings, you may communicate very effectively.

Although bypassing problems are simple to describe, they're extremely confusing and irritating. The incorrect "commonsense" notions about words and meaning that cause bypassing problems are so strongly entrenched in people's mental maps that rooting them out is extremely difficult. Even skilled and knowledgeable communicators occasionally get embroiled in bypassing because for a moment they stopped thinking about what they were doing and let "common sense" take over. You have to stay alert!

INTENSIONAL AND EXTENSIONAL ORIENTATIONS

All the above semantic problems arise because it's very easy to focus upon your mental map and forget about the territory in the outside world that it's supposed to represent. Your map is convenient and essential for storing knowledge about the outside world, but it's only as good as its degree of correspondence to that world. The map is a convenient fiction. The better it corresponds to the outside world, the more it helps you deal with the world successfully.

Few people are so stubborn that they'd drive off the side of a mountain because the autoclub's road map says there's supposed to be a road there. When the road map and the evidence from your own eyes disagree, you conclude that the road map is wrong. But each of the semantic problems we've discussed results from believing that your mental map is right, regardless of what happens in the outside world.

Usually the disagreement between your mental maps and the outside world isn't that obvious. The disagreements that cause most difficulties are subtle, partly hidden ones, in which external evidence doesn't force itself upon you. In these cases, not bothering to look carefully at the outside world is easy, and most people don't bother. This is the intensional orientation—a viewpoint so completely focused on the map itself that it ignores the territory the map supposedly represents.

An extensional orientation, on the other hand, focuses carefully and consistently on territories in the outside world and continually tests parts of the map against them. Most of all, the extensionally oriented person pays attention to the results of such map testing, and, upon getting hints that the map may be wrong, he or she is willing to consider changes in the map.

During the Middle Ages, scholars actually did argue about how many angels could dance on the head of a pin. Where did they get evidence for the argument? From the writings of earlier scholars, of course, the same place they got evidence on every other topic. Their common sense told them that the way to answer questions about the world was to consult the writings of Aristotle and other classical scholars. If Aristotle's map of the world didn't answer the question directly, then scholars could deduce an answer from things Aristotle did say. When Galileo and others began inspecting the outside world and mapping it from their observations, the scholars were outraged; such an obviously wrongheaded venture could (and did) destroy their intensional world.

Using evidence from their mental maps, people have proved beyond any doubt that heavier-than-air objects can't fly, that rockets can't travel in the vacuum of space (there's nothing to push against), that a car in a quarter-mile drag race can't exceed about 125 miles per hour, that Edsels would sell like hotcakes, and that traveling more than twelve miles per hour in a car would take your breath away and you'd suffocate. The intensional orientation is not dead!

The semantic problems we've discussed in this chapter are caused primarily by an intensional orientation. Each yields to the same treatment: be extensional! Keep your eye on the outside world.

FURTHER EXPLORATION

1. Over the next several days, collect examples of the semantic problems discussed in this chapter. Look for them in your direct experience and in what you read and hear. For each example, which of these problems was involved? How would an extensional orientation have helped to prevent or minimize the misunderstanding?

2. List points that could describe you. When you've listed 12 or 15 points, stop and consider each one. If that were the only point someone knew about you, what image of you would he or she have? Which point might create the most accurate image of you? The least accurate? (Remember your conclusions when you write a résumé one of these days.)

3. According to this chapter, "When the person you're addressing keeps attaching unintended meanings to your messages, try to attune your message to that person's map, even if you believe he or she is bullishly wrongheaded." Should you ever not do this? For example, can you imagine situations in which it would be morally wrong or poor communication strategy to do this?

4. To illustrate the concept, "Meaning is in the mind of the perceiver," think of a statement that various people would perceive differently. Describe how their perceptions of it differ. Can you think of a statement that two given persons would perceive exactly the same way?

II

Basic Principles and Techniques of Business Communication

Some people are born with a great deal of writing talent; almost intuitively, they can write messages that communicate extremely well. For the rest of us, however, good writing is anything but intuitive. It's hard work. Fortunately, we can learn by analyzing the methods and techniques that naturally talented writers use. And that's exactly what business communication experts have been doing over the last four or five decades. The five chapters in Part II distill the results of these years of analysis.

The techniques we'll discuss are entirely practical because they arise from real-life experience. Talented writers use these techniques naturally to produce outstanding writing; the rest of us can learn to use them consciously and deliberately. (Actually, very talented writers learn to write even better by studying these techniques, and they're often the most eager learners.)

CLARITY AND ADAPTATION

The basic requirements of an effective message are fairly simple: it must be clear and adapted to your audience's needs and viewpoint. If your audience understands your message and considers its view of the subject natural and sensible, then it has the best chance of being effective. To be clear, most messages (especially routine ones) should be simple, at least mildly friendly, and right to the point. These goals are often straightforward, and you can probably achieve them in many of your messages already.

Readability, Tone, and Organization

As your messages get complicated, clarity is harder to achieve. For that reason, a more detailed study of how excellent writers achieve clarity is worthwhile. We find that they often use techniques for (1) achieving high readability (simplicity), (2) achieving the desired tone (friendliness), and (3) organizing messages effectively (getting right to the point). In the next four chapters, we explore each of these techniques.

Planning, Writing, and Revising

To adapt your messages to your audience, you must analyze the audience's viewpoint. Although you can occasionally analyze and adapt very quickly as you begin writing, usually you'll need to spend some time at it. Such planning is the first of three stages in the writing process.

One of the clearest marks of beginning writers is their attempt to do the whole writing job in one step. They begin communicating by picking up a pen, and when they complete a draft of the message, they quit. Experienced writers know better. They know that writing is too complicated to be done well all at once—there are too many things to think about. Most good writers divide the job of writing into the planning stage, the writing stage, and the revising stage.

The planning stage   In the planning stage, you adapt your message to the audience. You analyze the audience's psychology, motivations, present knowledge of your topic, and feelings about it. You also think through your communication goals—how you intend to affect your audience.

Based on this audience analysis, you can consider possible ways to approach your subject and present your major points. You can decide how to organize your points so they best inform and motivate your audience. And you can find ways to communicate any sensitive parts of your message without causing offense or ill feelings. By the end of the planning stage, experienced writers often have some quick notes on their goals and their audience analysis and a brief outline of the message.

The writing stage   In the writing stage, you concentrate on getting your ideas down on paper as quickly as possible. Using your outline, write the message straight through the message. If you get stuck searching for the right word or phrase, leave a blank space and continue. Working quickly maximizes your natural ability to make your ideas flow smoothly from one point to the next. Since you'll revise later, you needn't worry now about grammar, spelling, optimum word choice, or any of the other mechanics that make writing such a chore. You'll take care of the mechanics in revision.

When you finish your rough draft, set it aside and do something else for a while. When you come back to revise it, you'll be able to see it very objectively, almost as though it were written by someone else. The most important purpose of the writing stage, everything considered, is to get your ideas out in front of you where you can revise them into a good message.

The revising stage   Your job in revising is to reevaluate all the tentative conclusions you drew in the planning stage. Is this message likely to be effective? Will your readers understand it? How will it make them feel? Would it be more effective if you organized it differently? Would it work better if you explained some of the points differently? Make all the necessary changes to improve it. Then look at the sentences one by one. How could the ideas be stated more clearly? How can you use transitional phrases or numbered points to help the reader understand how the ideas relate to one another? How can you rephrase sentences for variety and interest? Finally (and only then), check the grammar, spelling, and punctuation. This step is very important, but do it last, after you've phrased your message in the most effective way.

BEGIN WORK IMMEDIATELY

Dividing the writing process into three steps is logically sensible and practically useful. It's sensible because each step is small enough for most writers to manage, so you don't get confused by trying to think about too many things at once. And this division is practical because an enormous amount of real-life experience shows that it works, not only for naturally talented writers, but also for everyday managers who must learn to write well.

The three-stage writing process is explained more fully in Chapter 11, but the time to begin using it is right away. Practice problems for this part of the book are clustered together, beginning on page 152. As soon as you finish reading this introduction, do three or four of them. Plan your messages, write quickly, then revise. Work toward clarity by making your messages simple, friendly, and right to the point.

As you finish reading each chapter in Part II, once again do three or four practice problems and apply the techniques you've learned. The three-stage process will help you just as much now as when you write more complicated messages later. By starting now, you'll be shaping your writing habits into ones that will serve you well for a lifetime!

7

Readability

I am a Bear of Very Little Brain,
and Long words Bother me.
Winnie the Pooh

Let thy speech be short, comprehending much
in few words.
Ecclesiastes 32:8

Make things as simple as possible—
but no simpler.
Albert Einstein

Readability is the efficiency with which writing can be read and understood. Your writing is readable if your audience can understand it quickly and easily.

Several factors affect readability. One is that some ideas are harder to understand than others. Most of us find math books difficult to read for this reason. When a subject is inherently complicated, most writing about it will have relatively low readability. Good writers take extra pains to compensate for the natural difficulty of such topics.

Two other factors that affect readability are correctness in grammar and spelling. Good grammar is important because it presents familiar sentence patterns; when sentence patterns are unexpected, the writing is harder to decode. Similarly, spelling errors make writing harder to read.

HOW TO WRITE READABLY

This chapter describes other factors that affect readability and ways to increase the readability of your writing.

Use Simple Words and Short Sentences

If we analyze writing that's easy to read, we notice first that it uses everyday language. As Figure 1 illustrates, such writing favors simple words over difficult ones. And it uses short sentences rather than long, complicated ones—or at least the average sentence is fairly short. Most good writers find that an average sentence length of 15 to 18 words works well.

In fact, the style of good business writing shouldn't be impressive at all. And that's an advantage, because if people are impressed with your writing style, then they've been distracted from your message. You want people to think about your message rather than your writing style. Everything considered, the best way to impress people with the value of your ideas is to communicate them as efficiently as possible.

Incidentally, you should keep your paragraphs fairly short, too, normally not longer than about ten or twelve typewritten lines long. Short paragraphs make a page look more inviting to read. Very long paragraphs look so dreadfully complicated that many readers just skip them.

Write the Way You Talk Within Reason

The reason simple words and short sentences work so well is that people are used to them. They're the building blocks of everyday talk. Listen to a conversation, and you'll hear simple words and short sentences.

Listen to yourself talk, too. If you're like most people, you're very good at talking; you can express yourself clearly and smoothly in conversation. You've spent 19 years or more developing that skill, and for that reason, people may tell you to write the way you talk. To a certain extent, that's good advice—but only to a certain extent.

Precision Steel Corporation
P.O. Box 1980 • Pittsburgh, PA 15218 • 412/219-1144

November 18, 1983

Mr. Frank Madieros
Allied Engineering Associates
13128 Commercial Court
Framingham, MA   10703

Dear Mr. Madieros:

I'll be glad to arrange for you and Ms. Tawnies to tour our Data Processing Department on Tuesday, December 2, at 11:00 a.m. Gerard Washington, manager of our VAX 11/780 computer system, will be available at that time. He'll be glad to tell you about our experience with the VAX and to answer any questions you may have.

We've had very good results from the VAX. Digital Equipment Corporation, manufacturer of the system, met our installation schedule and has provided the level of support we needed on the equipment. We were able to convert from our old PDP-11/45 system very smoothly and quickly. Therefore, we can strongly recommend the VAX for the kinds of applications you mentioned in our phone conversation this morning.

When you arrive at the plant, please park in one of the visitor's spaces in Lot 23 at 129th and Center Streets. Then go to Gate 5 directly across 129th Street from the parking lot. I'll have visitor's passes waiting there. If you'll be bringing anyone else besides Ms. Tawnies, please phone ahead so I can get passes for them.

I'm looking forward to seeing you and Ms. Tawnies on the second at 11:00.

Cordially,

Hilbert Gardinier
Director of Data Processing

Figure 1 Simple words and short sentences

If you take that advice too literally, it can make your writing less clear. Conversational language is full of slang, half-stated ideas, sentence fragments, and other such structures, as Figure 2 illustrates. These structures work in conversation, largely because body language, facial expression, tone of voice, and a variety of situational clues fill in any gaps in meaning. In writing, you can't use all this extra information; you must communicate without it. Therefore, when you write, be careful to use full sentences and make sure your ideas are fully expressed.

If you bear that caution in mind, you can profit from the idea of writing the way you talk. Here's how. When you sit down to write, imagine that your readers are sitting across the desk from you, and just mentally tell them what you have to say. Then write it down the way you "said" it. (Of course you'll remember to use complete, grammatical sentences and express your ideas clearly.)

When you've finished your rough draft, test it by imagining again that your readers are across the desk from you. Read what you've written as though you were telling it to them. Does it sound right? Do you talk that way? Are there words or phrases in your message that you'd never say aloud? If you wouldn't say things a certain way, then maybe you shouldn't write them that way either.

If you use it sensibly, the technique of writing the way you talk can be very successful. It allows you to apply much of your oral skill in writing situations. Just as your oral skill makes your ideas easier to understand, this technique can make your writing more readable.

Be Direct and Concise

To be efficient, business writing should be direct and to the point. And it should make its points without extra words. Since the reader's time is valuable, the writer shouldn't take up any more of it than necessary. This rule doesn't mean you should leave out supporting ideas that the reader needs to understand your main points. Anything that's necessary should be said. But you should carefully stick to the necessary points and make them in reasonably few words.

Directness and conciseness are achieved in the planning and revising stages of the writing process. Here's how.

1. In the planning stage, be sure you organize your ideas before you begin to write. Much of the unnecessary verbiage in business writing occurs because writers pick up their pens before they realize exactly what they want to say.

2. In the revision stage, be sure you haven't drifted into the bureaucratic language that many people believe is proper business writing. Some business writers do indeed have very pompous and wordy styles, full of clichés and unnecessary phrases, as in Figure 3. But the most successful business communicators carefully avoid such gobbledygook—it interferes with their ability to communicate.

On the Telephone

Hello, John? Roger Whelan, down in shipping. . . . Yeah. Me too. . . Yeah, it was fun. . . . Say, John, about those forms from Helen, are we going to get delivery, uhh. . . . I know, next month. Look, John, that really makes a problem for, uhh. . . . Well, we're supposed to be going ahead with the conversion. . . . On those forms, yeah. . . . Look, is there a copy of that form someplace? We could use the copier and make ones for the time. . . . Well, can they at least get us one drawn up so we can go ahead? . . . Great, John. Listen, after you talk to 'em, will you give me a call? A couple of the people down here are really getting worried. . . . Yeah, well. But when we do get the forms, it's going to be a tough time to get all that stuff done all over again. . . . Yeah, I'll tell 'em. Thanks, John. Goodbye.

In a Memo

DATE: December 5, 1982

TO: John LeFevre, Administrative Services Section

FROM: Roger Whelan, Shipping and Receiving Department

SUBJECT: NEW SHIPMENT-COMPLETED FORMS NEEDED IMMEDIATELY

We need to get the new shipment-completed forms from your office as quickly as possible. Helen Lefteros indicates these forms aren't scheduled to be delivered until next month, but conversion to the new record system has already begun, and we need those forms to report shipments right now. Our concern is not only that processing of shipment reports will fall behind, but also that, when the new forms are delivered, we'll have a month's paperwork to catch up on.

If there's no way to speed up delivery, please get us at least one copy of the form right away. Then we could use the copier to make working copies for the interim.

Figure 2 Spoken and written messages

Gobbledygook Version

Dear Mr. Heraldsen:

In response to your inquiry of 24 September regarding your order #bG/bG4862184.6M, submitted to this company on 10 August, you will be glad to know that we are making every effort in order to expedite shipment of the merchandise which was ordered. By way of explanation to you of the delay which has occurred relative to this order, our supplier, which is D. E. Shippen Office Forms Company, Inc., has experienced delays of several months' duration in the receipt of raw paper product through normal delivery channels, and as a result thereof, that company's production processes are retarded due to the fact that raw material shortages result.

In recent communication from D. E. Shippen Office Forms Company, Inc., relative to this set of circumstances, it was indicated that their shipments of raw materials have been partially reinstated, and as a result it is expected that this company's production processes will be resumed at near-normal levels at an early date. Your order #bG/bG4862184.6M has been assigned an elevated priority in the processing of production scheduling upon resumption of our production operations. As a consequence, shipment of your goods per your order may be expected at the earliest practicable date upon resumption of our deliveries from D. E. Shippen Office Forms Company, Inc.

We are glad to be of assistance relative to this or any other matters, and if you should experience any further delays or have any questions regarding our operations, please bring these to our immediate attention.

Very truly yours,

Better

Dear Mr. Heraldsen:

We're doing everything we can to get your order #bG/bG4682184.6M shipped out. D. E. Shippen Office Forms, our supplier, is facing a severe paper shortage, but Shippen indicates that they expect to be back in full production soon. Your order is one of the first we'll ship when we can start production again. We hope to make delivery very soon.

Cordially,

Figure 3 Avoiding gobbledygook

3. Revise to cut out unnecessary words and phrases, as the writer in Figure 4 did. As you review your rough draft, you'll nearly always find some words and phrases you can remove without changing the meaning. Remove them.

4. In revising, try to condense ideas into fewer sentences. Often you'll find that the ideas in two or more sentences can be condensed into one sentence, with an improvement in readability (Figure 5). It may surprise you that material can be easier to read when you pack more ideas into sentences. But sentences that contain only one or two simple ideas are hard to read, since most people are more comfortable taking in information at a faster pace.

After you've spent some time revising for directness and conciseness, you'll find yourself revising less and less because you'll automatically write a more efficient first draft. At that point, your developing habit patterns will start taking over the job. You'll never completely outgrow the need to revise for conciseness, but you'll certainly make quicker work of it.

Vary Sentence Length and Structure

As you work toward a direct and concise writing style, watch out for one major hazard: choppiness. Writing is choppy when it contains a series of sentences with the same structure and roughly the same length. As Figure 6 shows, choppiness makes the writing very hard to read. A piece of choppy writing is hard to read aloud, and you can immediately see why. As you read, the pitch of your voice rises and falls in precisely the same pattern, sentence after sentence. This pattern gets boring very quickly; it gets almost painful after a while.

Once you can identify choppiness, correcting it is very easy. As you revise, carefully vary the length and structures of consecutive sentences. Use some short sentences and some long ones. Use some introductory clauses and phrases and some parenthetical phrases within sentences. Use a comma and a connecting word (such as *and*, *but*, or *so*) to join two logically related statements into a compound sentence. Use a transition to clarify the logical relationship between two sentences or break up a monotonous pattern. Figure 7 shows some ways to do these things.

The idea is to break up the sameness of a series of sentences by introducing the natural variety that you hear in conversation. The natural style of conversation tends to be simple and uncluttered. But if you listen carefully, you'll notice that people use varied sentence patterns as they talk. In writing, simplicity of style doesn't mean that each sentence is written in the simplest possible pattern. It means that you try to avoid the needlessly complicated and ponderous style that bothers people. There's plenty of room for varied sentence lengths and structures.

DATE: September 30, 1983

TO: Vincent Ghilberti, Director of Sales

FROM: Adrienne Lefler, Marketing

SUBJECT: Proceeding on Cincinnati Project

~~It's my sincere and considered conviction that~~ The ~~proper~~ time has arrived ~~and the agreed-upon preconditions are met, so that Sales and Marketing should plan~~ to go ahead with ~~the implementation stage of~~ the Cincinnati project. ~~At the present time,~~ We've ~~successfully~~ established a ~~significant~~ base of ~~customer~~ accounts in southwestern Ohio, ~~through the efforts of central and regional sales personnel,~~ and we're now ready, ~~in my considered opinion, to proceed~~ to set up a new~~ly created~~ sales district based in a ~~new~~ Cincinnati ~~area~~ office. ~~location, as per our earlier plan.~~

As soon as ~~you've had an opportunity to review the status of these developments and~~ we receive your OK, Marketing will ~~proceed, as planned, to~~ set up ~~and implement~~ an intensive ~~media~~ advertising campaign, ~~which, as you're aware, has already been~~ fully budgeted, and ~~set in motion the various tasks required to~~ implement ~~the rest of~~ the plan we've ~~jointly~~ agreed on.

Figure 4 Revising by deleting extra words

Unrevised

Dear Ms. Goldfarthing:

    We've refunded the purchase price of the sweater you returned recently. The sweater was a blue Orlon pullover. It cost $14.88 plus $.74 sales tax. Therefore, a total of $15.62 is refunded. This amount has been credited to your account.

    Perhaps you're still in the market for a sweater. We're having a closeout sale on all remaining Orlon sweaters at the end of this week. The selection in your size is still good. The prices will be quite attractive. Stop in and look them over.

Cordially,

Revised

Dear Ms. Goldfarthing:

    We've refunded the purchase price of the blue Orlon pullover you returned recently. Since the sweater cost $14.88 plus $.74 sales tax, we've credited a total of $15.62 to your account.

    If you're still in the market for a sweater, stop in at the end of the week and check the prices at our closeout sale on all remaining Orlon sweaters. The selection in your size is still good, and the prices will be quite attractive.

    Stop in and look them over.

Cordially,

Figure 5 Revising by combining sentences

DATE: November 26, 1982

TO: Purchasing Department

FROM: Catherine Verland, Industrial Engineering

SUBJECT: Special Marking Pens

Choppy

We're working on a special project. We need to order some marking pens to fit unusual requirements. We need the pens to highlight words in a set of documents we're working with. We then need to copy the documents on a standard office copier. The highlighting should show on the copies as gray shadow. The highlighted words should clearly show through. We've experimented with several yellow marking pens. They didn't work.

We'd like for you to find us a special product made for this purpose. Otherwise we'd like for you get us samples of a number of yellow marking pens for testing. We'll need several dozen of these pens in the next few months. We'll have a continuing need for more over the next few years.

Better

For a special project, we need to order some marking pens to fit unusual requirements. We need the pens to highlight key words in a set of documents we're working with, and then we need to copy the marked documents on a standard office copier. On the copies, the highlighting should show as gray shadow, and the highlighted words should clearly show through. We've experimented with several yellow marking pens without good results.

Can you either find us a product made for this purpose or get us samples of a number of yellow marking pens and highlighters for testing? In the next few months, we'll probably need several dozen of these pens, and we'll have a continuing need for more over the next few years.

Figure 6 Eliminating choppiness by varying sentence length and structure

Simple Sentences

The man finished the job. He checked his watch.

More Varied Structures

The man finished the job, and he checked his watch. (Compound)

The man finished the job and checked his watch. (Complex)

When he finished the job, the man checked his watch. (Complex)

The man checked his watch after he finished the job. (Complex)

Having finished the job, the man checked his watch. (Complex)

The man finished the job. Therefore, he checked his watch. (Transitional expression)

Simple Sentences

The report was finally completed just after 2:00 A.M. It was ready for the morning staff meeting.

More Varied Structures

The report was finally completed just after 2:00 A.M., so it was ready for the morning staff meeting. (Compound)

The report wasn't completed until just after 2:00 A.M., but it was ready for the morning staff meeting. (Compound)

The report, finally completed just after 2:00 A.M., was ready for the morning staff meeting. (Complex)

Even though the report wasn't completed until just after 2:00 A.M., it was ready for the morning staff meeting. (Complex)

The report was completed just after 2:00 A.M., in time for the morning staff meeting. (Simple)

The report was completed just after 2:00 A.M. As a result, it was ready for the morning staff meeting. (Transitional expression)

Figure 7 Adding variety to your sentence structure

Use the "People-Doing-Things" Sentence Structure

There are two basic English sentence structures:

The child hit the ball. (Active voice)

The ball was hit by the child. (Passive voice)

Notice that both sentences say exactly the same thing. The first sentence uses the standard subject-verb-object pattern. The second actually reverses that pattern, with actor being named after the action. The object-verb-subject pattern is called the passive voice. The reason the two patterns are important to remember is this: a series of sentences in the passive voice tends to sound stuffy and bureaucratic, the opposite of the simple, direct style the business writer wants to cultivate. As Figure 8 illustrates, a string of passive-voice sentences is boring to read.

For certain purposes, the passive voice is perfectly legitimate. For example, to emphasize the object of an action rather than the actor, a writer might put the object at the beginning of a sentence. (What was hit? The ball was hit.) Or a writer might want to discuss an action but not the actor's identity. The girl who reports, "Dad, the baseball was hit through the Smith's kitchen window," has completely avoided the question of who hit it.

Normally, however, a business writer should avoid the passive voice. An easy way to avoid it is to write sentences about people doing things. That is, the subjects of sentences should be people, and wherever possible the verbs should be action verbs—ones that describe actions that can be observed.

In the beginning, you should work on the people-doing-things structure in the revision stage. Check your message sentence by sentence to see whether the subject names one or more persons and whether or not the verb describes an action you could see. If they don't, then try to rephrase them so they do. Usually you'll quickly see how to make the needed changes, but if not, go on to the next sentence. In the average message, you can probably structure the majority of sentences in terms of people doing things. Then you'll seldom make the mistake of using a long, boring string of passive-voice sentences.

Distribute Emphasis Effectively

A typical message normally communicates two or three major ideas and a number of minor ones. One of the writer's problems is to make sure the reader can tell the difference between major and minor ideas. In speech, this distinction is not much of a problem because the speaker's tonal emphasis, facial expressions, and body movements emphasize the main ideas. In writing, however, this supplementary information is unusable, so the whole job has to be done by words on a piece of paper.

When people think of emphasizing an idea in writing, they often think of underlining, capitalizing, using red ink, and other such mechanical devices. Although occasionally useful, these devices are too strong

Passive Voice

DATE: July 11, 1983

TO: All Employees

FROM: Helen Segueri, President

SUBJECT: EMPLOYEES TO BE REIMBURSED ONLY FOR COACH AIR FARE

Employees are to be reimbursed by the company only for coach fare when travel is undertaken for company purposes. This policy is to be applied to all employees, including executives and salespeople, as part of the Executive Committee's current program for cutting of costs.

First-class fares purchased by employees will be reimbursed by the company at the coach rate for that flight. No employee will be reimbursed by the company for first-class air fare under any circumstances.

People Doing Things

DATE: July 11, 1983

TO: All Employees

FROM: Helen Segueri, President

SUBJECT: MAKE AIRLINE RESERVATIONS FOR COMPANY TRAVEL AT COACH RATE

The next time you call to make airline reservations for company travel, be sure to ask for the coach fare. The Executive Committee has voted to ask all employees, executives and salespeople alike, to fly coach as part of our current program to cut costs.

If you decide to travel first class, your reimbursement will be at the coach rate. We will not reimburse any employee for first-class air fare under any circumstances.

Figure 8 Passive-voice sentences versus sentences about people doing things

and distracting to use time after time in message after message. Overused, they impair clarity rather than enhance it.

For everyday purposes, writers use other techniques to emphasize main ideas: (1) position, (2) space, and (3) word choice.

Position   The audience is most likely to remember the points that come first and last. This is true whether the message is conveyed in a letter, report, paragraph, speech, or any other unit of information.

The audience is most likely to remember the first point, next most likely to remember the last point, and least likely to remember the middle points. Only when a middle point is inherently very interesting and appealing will it be as memorable as the points at the beginning and end. Most people take this fact into account in planning messages. They plan beginnings and endings much more carefully than middles.

Correctly positioning key points is not difficult. Devise your message plan to place the most important points at the beginning and end. Within your message, plan the beginnings and endings of paragraphs carefully, too. And when you want to deemphasize an idea you must mention, consider placing it in the middle, where it will naturally be less memorable.

Space   If you write three paragraphs about one idea and just a sentence or two about another, people will naturally assume the three-paragraph idea is the more important. The more space you give an idea, the more weight the reader will give it.

How, then, do you discuss an extremely important idea that requires little explanation and a less important idea that requires much explanation, both in the same message? In such cases, carefully offset the reader's natural tendency to assume that the longer explanation covers the more important point. Devote more space to the important point than you normally would or use position and word choice to emphasize it.

Word choice   A point phrased in vivid language is more likely to stand out than one phrased in flat, unemotional language, as Figure 9 illustrates. Advertisers take great care to create vivid and memorable images of their products, partly by phrasing ads in the liveliest language they can find. If you normally write in the relaxed, informal style we're discussing, you naturally tend to use interesting and lively words. To emphasize a particular idea, however, search very hard for the phrasing that brings it to life for the reader.

One way to use word choice for emphasis is to depict the idea in human terms, with people-doing-things sentences. Another way is to use real-life details that help the reader visualize the idea. Yet another way is to associate the idea with the reader's experiences—to show how it affects the reader personally. Bring the reader right into the picture by using "you" in your phrasing. These techniques can be used together.

Flat	Vivid
Our sales nearly doubled last quarter.	Our sales increased from $345,210 in the previous quarter to $662,992 last quarter, a 92% increase. On an annual basis, this is nearly a 370% growth rate.
The Wonderflex is a fine fishing rod.	Because of the carefully hand-wrapped and bonded stainless steel guides on the Wonderflex, you can be sure of completely free line action on every cast.
Fran has been doing very good work.	Fran coordinated the reorganization report last year and wrote nearly all of it herself. Implementation of its major recommendations led to a 13% increase in productivity in the department in the first half of this year. Moreover, she designed and ran two major training series, both rated outstanding by the supervisors' council. She completed these projects in addition to her normal work.
The Por-TV is light enough to carry anywhere.	The Por-TV weighs only 3 pounds, 13 ounces—less than a six-pack of your favorite canned beverage. You can easily carry it to the beach, the mountains, or the football stadium.
This report is too long.	This report takes 384 pages to support only two simple recommendations. It weighs a pound and a half more than my whole briefcase.
Anaheim is a city in southern California.	Anaheim, the home of Disneyland, is a city of 167,000 people located just southeast of Los Angeles, California.

Figure 9 Flat versus vivid phrasing

READABILITY TESTS

Once your message is written, a test of its readability can be useful. You should informally assess every message's readability as you revise it. When a message is extremely important, you may want to test its readability more formally.

Informal Tests

Checking the readability of your own writing is harder than it may seem, because you're so familiar with your message. To you, adding the correct voice inflection and emphasis as you read your writing is just second nature, but determining how someone else would interpret it can be difficult.

Yet you can detect many readability problems in your writing if you get some mental distance from it. One way is to write a rough draft and then let it lie for a day or so before you revise it. After that much elapsed time, the writing is almost as unfamiliar as though someone else had written it, and you can now see it afresh.

Another way is to read your writing aloud. When you hear it rather than see it, you can often perceive things you hadn't noticed before. Go off someplace by yourself (where you won't feel embarrassed) and read aloud in a steady, flat voice. Don't add much vocal emphasis; remember that the reader will "hear" your message only through the expressionless words on the page. As you read, notice where it's hard to make the words come out right. If you stumble, surely your reader, who knows less about your writing than you do, will stumble too. If you run out of breath in a sentence, your reader will likely find it long, too. If it doesn't sound like you, it won't represent you very well.

A Formal Readability Test

Occasionally, a piece of writing is so important that revising it deserves a great deal of care and time. In such cases, a formal readability test may be worthwhile. One such test is the Gunning Fog Index, named after its developer, business communication consultant Robert Gunning.[1] Among the several widely accepted tests, the Fog Index is especially easy to use.

To compute the Fog Index of a piece of writing, follow these four steps:

1. Select a writing sample at least 100 words long. For more reliable results on longer pieces, test several 100-word samples selected at random. When counting words, count anything having spaces around it as one word. Thus "seven hundred fifty" is three words, while 381,552,348 is one word.

---

1. Robert Gunning, *The Technique of Clear Writing*, rev. ed. (New York: McGraw-Hill Book Company, 1968), pp. 38–39.

2. Determine the average number of words per sentence. Count the independent clauses in the sample (each independent clause of a compound sentence is considered a sentence for this purpose) and divide the number of words by this figure.

3. Determine the percentage of "hard" words. Count the number of words of three syllables or more and divide by the total number of words. Among the hard words, do not count (a) capitalized words, except at the beginnings of sentences; (b) words that are combinations of short, easy words such as "barkeeper," "nevertheless," "grasshopper"; or (c) verbs that become three syllables by adding -ed or -es, such as "trespasses" and "pretended," but do count verbs of three syllables ending in -ing. Count hyphenated words only if one part is three syllables by itself. Do not count numerals as hard words.

4. Add the two figures computed above and multiply by 0.4 to obtain the Fog Index. Figure 10 illustrates the computation. The Fog Index indicates the number of years of education an average reader would need before finding the piece of writing readable. Normally writers aim for a Fog Index somewhat lower than the educational level of the intended readers. Thus most newspaper and magazine articles have a Fog Index of about 9 or 10; even *Scientific American* articles average about 11 or 12.

Since the Fog Index evaluates only two of the factors in readability, it cannot determine that a piece of writing is actually readable. It can, though, give you a danger signal if your writing tends to be difficult to read. If your writing often has a Fog Index higher than 11 or 12, concentrate on keeping sentences shorter and phrases simpler.

READABILITY IN NONROUTINE MESSAGES

Up to now we've been discussing normal readability goals and rules of thumb for achieving them. But in some situations the normal goals may not apply. Most of the messages you write assume that readers are middle-class American business people or consumers who have at least some college education. And most of your messages assume that the readers don't share the language of your specialized field. When these assumptions don't apply, you may need to analyze your readability goals more explicitly.

In technical reports for highly knowledgeable readers, for example, conversational phrasing may seem out of place, and you may have difficulty structuring sentences to show people doing things. In such cases, you may be entirely justified in phrasing your material somewhat more formally. Remember that writers of *Scientific American* articles for a Ph.D. audience can keep the readability down to an eleventh- or twelfth-grade reading level. Even when material is technical, it shouldn't sound stiff and stilted. In such technical reports, legitimate technical terms may help you express ideas efficiently. When computer specialists write to one another

The following passage is selected from the introduction to a report for a shoe manufacturer. For computation purposes, each sentence or independent clause is followed by // and each "hard" word is underlined.

```
        The Black Shoe Company produces and markets men's dress
shoes in the 35-75 dollar price range.//   Styles are
conservative.//   The shoes are very well made and are fully
repairable, making them unique in today's men's shoe market.//

        The Black Shoe Company owns its own retail outlets, an
unusual pattern in the shoe industry.//   Stores are run by local
managers,// but the company retains controlling interest in each
store.//   Most of the stores are located in the East and
Midwest,// and the company wants to expand further in the state
of California.//   Present California stores are located in Los
Angeles, San Francisco, San Diego, and Sacramento, the four
largest markets in the state.//

        The company would now like to locate a new California store
in one of the state's smaller markets.//   Such a store would not
only increase the sales of Black Shoes, but it would also serve
as a test case to help find out the feasibility of further moves
into smaller California markets.//   The cities of Fresno and
Bakersfield have been selected by the company as possible sites
for the new store.//
```

Number of words	183	
Number of sentences	12	
Average words per sentence		15.25
Number of "hard" words	13	
Percentage of "hard" words		+7.10%
Total		22.35
Multiplication constant		×0.40
Fog index		8.94

Figure 10 The Gunning fog index

about "inputs" and "interfaces," for example, these terms have specific technical meanings. In other settings, though, such terms are mere jargon and interfere with clear communication.

Most people have to guard against writing too formally. Thus they're constantly working toward a more relaxed, more readable style. When your goals call for formality, you have little trouble adjusting; in fact you must carefully avoid overcompensating and becoming too formal.

Your greatest difficulty arises when your audience analysis calls for an easier reading level than normal. At such times, you can safely exaggerate your use of the the guidelines in this chapter. Thus you can strive for extra variety in sentence length and structure with an average sentence length that's shorter than normal. You can take extra pains to structure sentences to show people doing things, perhaps demonstrating key points by real-life examples. You can spend extra time revising, and carefully examine each phrase for possible rewording in a less formal, livelier way.

Since you have a variety of techniques for increasing readability, be sure to use them all when the reading level must be especially easy. Avoid making all sentences short and all words simple, though. Not all people who read at a lower-than-average reading level are stupid, and certainly all readers resent being talked down to. If you remember to vary your sentence lengths and structures, your message is less likely to sound condescending.

FURTHER EXPLORATION

1. Find a piece of writing you think is hard to read and analyze it, using the terms from this chapter. Compute the Fog Index of a sample and check the writing for its application of the other principles discussed here. Identify why it's hard to read. Select about three or four sentences and try to restate them more clearly without omitting any details.

2. Write a choppy paragraph, then read it aloud. Is it hard to read? Ask two or three friends to read it and see whether or not they can figure out what's wrong with it.

3. Try to find a passage of very stuffy, bureaucratic writing. In it, identify each use of the passive voice and each gobbledygook phrase. Try to rewrite the passage so it's more readable.

4. Are there any occasions when business writing should not employ the readability principles discussed in this chapter? Why?

The writing problems for Part II begin on page 152. If your instructor has not already assigned specific problems, choose some that interest you and begin work on them now.

8
Tone

"*When you call me that, smile.*"
Owen Wister (The Virginian)

Apt words have powers to suage
The tremors of a troubled mind.
John Milton

Speech finely framed delighteth the ear.
2 Maccabees 15:39

The tone of a message is what the audience sees of the communicator's personality. It's the feeling the message conveys.

Business writers normally cultivate a tone that creates a pleasant image of themselves and their companies. Occasionally, messages must be stern warnings or demands, but usually the audience should perceive a pleasant, friendly communicator. The most important reason for a good tone is simply that it's courteous, making communicating more pleasant. But a good tone can also help induce the reader to respond favorably and cooperatively. Feeling cooperative toward a pleasant person or a helpful organization is easy.

The revision stage of the writing process is when good writers carefully attend to tone. As your good writing habits develop, you may find that the tone of your first draft is often very close to the tone you're striving for. When that happens, revising for tone can be just a matter of verifying that you've achieved your objectives and polishing your phrasings. Even when you begin to achieve a good tone regularly, however, keep consciously monitoring your tone as you revise.

Most of this chapter discusses ways to achieve a pleasant, friendly tone. At the end, we consider ways to achieve other kinds of tone when necessary.

ACHIEVING A PLEASANT, FRIENDLY TONE

One obvious way of appearing pleasant and friendly is to say and do things the audience likes. If you're giving good news, your message naturally sounds pleasant, so you should emphasize the favorable aspects of your messages and downplay the less favorable ones.

Much of the time, however, you can't count on good news to create a pleasant tone. Often messages must convey neutral information, sometimes even bad news; in those cases, you must depend on careful phrasing to convey the proper feeling. In fact, when the news is good, careful phrasing can enhance the good feeling.

An Informal and Relaxed Writing Style

A big step toward good tone is to develop an informal, relaxed, and readable writing style, as discussed in the previous chapter. Such a style automatically sounds open and pleasant, the way you probably sound when you're talking to your friends. Thus as your general writing skill grows, your ability to achieve the desired tone will improve, too.

Incidentally, contractions—such as *you're, isn't,* and so on—can help you achieve a relaxed and informal tone. Your English teachers may have warned you against using contractions in essays, but business messages aren't essays. And contractions are quite acceptable here.

Friendliness and Enthusiasm

If you observe business people talking to one another or to customers, you'll nearly always sense a feeling of basic friendliness in the interaction. People are nice to one another, not only because it's common courtesy and because it increases business, but also because it makes the workday more pleasant for everyone concerned. A feeling of friendliness keeps the gears of business well oiled.

Friendliness and enthusiasm go together; enthusiasm sounds friendly. When people are talking together (rather than writing), feelings of friendliness and enthusiasm are expressed largely in tone of voice, facial expressions, and gestures. As we've seen, however, these channels are not available to the writer. Listeners can see the big smile on your face, hear the enthusiasm in your voice, and see you lean forward as you speak about your topic; readers, however, can see only the words you write on paper. Therefore, those words must express not only your ideas, but also your feelings. The words alone must do the whole job.

Since you talk all day and write only occasionally, you tend to choose words for their appropriateness to talking rather than writing. For most purposes, this tendency works out well enough. But it does leave your written messages seeming rather flat and unenthusiastic much of the time. For that reason, you should exaggerate—just slightly—the enthusiasm of your phrasing when you write.

Make an extra effort to select words that communicate enthusiasm about your ideas. A business person sitting across the desk from her audience can say, "I'm willing to do what you ask," with a big smile and such vocal enthusiasm that her feelings are perfectly clear. When she puts those same words on paper, however, the big smile and vocal enthusiasm disappear, and the words sound like unwilling agreement. On paper, to get the same effect she might say, "I'll be delighted to do it. It'll be my pleasure." Figure 1 provides further examples.

As a general rule, try to put friendliness and enthusiasm into messages through slightly exaggerated enthusiasm (as compared with your normal spoken phrasing) rather than by adding whole sentences about friendship. Such sentences tend to sound insincere and clichéd unless they're extremely carefully phrased, and you can usually convey the needed level of friendliness by stating your key points pleasantly and enthusiastically.

Mature Self-Confidence

A good self-image for a business person to cultivate is this: "I'm a reasonable person who makes reasoned decisions." Someone with that kind of self-image who works at living up to it has a considerable advantage when writing to an audience. If the decisions are well-reasoned ones, then the writer can write about them with a feeling of confidence that they will be accepted.

Spoken with Enthusiasm

We had profits of 14.83 percent last year.

Written

Last year was an outstanding time for us, with profits rising to a near-record 14.83 percent.

Spoken with Enthusiasm

Because of your good safety record, we've agreed on a new reimbursement plan for use of your personal car on company business.

Written

Over the last two years, you and other employees have reduced accidents to less than half the national average per mile driven. Because of this tremendous record, we're able to announce an improved reimbursement plan for use of your personal car on company business.

Spoken with Enthusiasm

I think Joan Malmquist's plan could work.

Written

I think Joan Malmquist's plan may be just the idea we need to meet the present crisis.

Spoken with Enthusiasm

Mr. Rennart's credentials meet the requirements of the job.

Written

Because of his credentials, Mr. Rennart looks like a top-notch applicant for the job.

Figure 1 Slightly exaggerated enthusiasm

For example, people who consciously reason things out seldom need to apologize for their actions, because their decisions have been made in light of the facts available. If such people prove wrong, they may find that explaining the situation is more appropriate than apologizing. As Figure 2 shows, apologies only remind the audience of the unpleasantness of the

Apology

Please accept our sincere apology for the delay in shipping the 12 Model AF-19 Duct-Mounted Air Purifiers you ordered. I can certainly imagine how frustrating it must be to have customers for these high-margin products and no products to deliver.

Unfortunately, we must ask your forbearance for an additional period before we can deliver these units. Current shortages of electronic chips used in the controller panel of these units are expected to continue. The manufacturer predicts a delay of about 45 days until these items can be delivered.

Once we receive shipment of these chips, our production facilities for the controller panels will be heavily overloaded, and our best guess is that it will require approximately 15 further days to process the backlog before your order can be shipped.

We're deeply sorry that this additional 60-day delay will be necessary, and we do appreciate your patience with us.

Reasons

When I received your letter, I immediately checked the status of your order for 12 Model AF-19 Duct-Mounted Air Purifiers. Our production people tell me that these units should be in your store in approximately 60 days.

As you've probably read, heavy increases in the use of sophisticated electronic chips, including those in the controller panel of our AF-19 purifiers, have occurred in the last two or three years. The manufacturer of our chips has dramatically increased capacity for these devices, but they're only now catching up to demand. We're promised the chips we need within 45 days, and we confidently expect to ship your units within 15 days from then.

Once these high-margin units are in your store, we know your customers will appreciate the computerized control capabilities that the electronic chips make possible. Once this present situation is resolved, we anticipate shipping all further orders within three days of receiving your order.

Figure 2 Apology versus reasons

event the writer is apologizing for; the apology calls forth bad feelings rather than good ones. Explaining why the event happened and why you took the action you did is usually better than an apology.

Mature writers convey their confidence that readers will accept their message. Immature writers, on the other hand, may say, "I hope you understand," or "I hope you agree." Such comments are an open admission to the reader that the writer lacks confidence; no writer makes such comments unless he or she thinks the reader may not understand or agree. You don't say, "It's not raining outside," unless there's some question about whether or not it's raining. Similarly you don't say, "I hope you understand," unless there's some question about understanding.

People with mature self-confidence take time to determine what's reasonably expected of them in a situation and what information they need, they expend the energy necessary to gather that information, they apply their best judgment in light of the facts available, and then they can explain surely and confidently how they arrived at their conclusions. Their mature self-confidence earns the confidence of others.

Courtesy and Sincerity

When we discuss courtesy and sincerity, we're concerned not so much with what the writer says as with what the reader perceives. The important question is this: does the message seem courteous and sincere to the reader?

Certainly the writer's real motives often come through in his or her writing, and if the writer tries to be courteous and sincere, the reader may perceive it. But an intention to be courteous is not enough; the writer should also consider the audience the message is intended for. What kinds of comments would the audience consider tactless or tasteless? What kinds of sentiments would the audience accept as sincere? How will the audience perceive the message?

An important factor in assessing courtesy and sincerity is the relationship it suggests between writer and reader. Although companies differ somewhat on this point, business people generally view one another and their customers as social equals. Ordinarily business people are most comfortable with one another on an informal, first-name basis. In this context, the exaggerated expressions of courtesy that appear when one party is of much higher status than the other aren't appropriate. Business people don't talk down to one another, and they get uncomfortable when someone talks down to them.

You may find it helpful to think of courtesy and sincerity as opposing forces to be held in balance, as Figure 3 demonstrates. In your writing, try to be as courteous as possible, short of sounding insincere, and as sincere as possible, short of sounding discourteous. Overly courteous writing can sound so gushy and fawning that the reader won't believe you: it sounds insincere. And sincerity carried to the point of brutal honesty about every aspect of your reader's business can quickly become discourteous.

Too Courteous

I'm certain, Mr. Hovatter, that a brilliant and perceptive entrepreneur such as yourself can inspect the following simple weekly production report and deduce that. . . .

Too Sincere

With your lack of formal training, Mr. Hovatter, no doubt you'd have difficulty understanding a normal weekly production report, so let me summarize the following figures by pointing out that. . . .

Balanced

As you can see in the following weekly production report, . . .

Too Courteous

No doubt the esteemed members of the committee have considered all possible factors in this question; I would simply like to emphasize one small point.

Too Sincere

Here's a factor I doubt you've considered.

Balanced

I believe the following factor is very important in this question.

Figure 3 Courtesy versus sincerity

      Two expressions are especially useful in establishing a tone of courteous sincerity: "please" and "thank you." If you're careful to use them sincerely, they're two of the most useful phrases in business communication. In asking someone to do something, "please" helps make the request pleasant. This approach is especially valid when you're the boss and the request might otherwise appear as a command. If you're forcing the reader to do something, though, "please" would probably appear insincere, and it shouldn't be used.

      "Thank you" is similarly very useful when the reader will believe you mean it. When your reader has done something especially helpful, your "thank you" conveys pleasant, warm feelings. If you use it routinely, though, "thank you" loses most of its effect.

Viewing Ideas Positively

The difference between a positive idea and a negative one is all in your viewpoint. For example, if you must refuse a speaking engagement, you could view it negatively and talk about what a shame it is that you have a previous engagement on that date and how sorry you are that the coordinator must find another speaker. Or you could view it positively and talk about the how the other engagement represents an important opportunity for your company and how eager you are to set an alternative speaking date.

Or if your competitor's product is being compared with your company's, you could view the situation negatively and admit shamefacedly that your product lacks several of its competition's features. Or you could take the negative approach of directly attacking all the competition's shortcomings that you're aware of. (This is a questionable tactic, mainly because your audience knows you're biased and may not believe statements of this kind coming from you.) But if you take the positive approach, you could talk about your product's special features, being especially careful to stress features the competition lacks.

One of the most important qualities of a good communicator is the ability to see the positive side of a situation and discuss it from that side. At the beginning, you may have difficulty remaining positive. With practice, however, this outlook will become a matter of habit, and then it'll be easy.

Saying no positively is a special case. Very likely, the first word you ever understood in your life was *no*. You understood it, and you hated it! People don't like to be told no. The word triggers an unpleasant emotional reaction resulting from all the frustrations and irritations they've experienced since they were nine months old. But sometimes writers must say no. How can they do so without triggering this reaction? The fact is that anything that can be said negatively with words like *no*, *won't*, *never*, *cannot* can also be said positively. It's just a matter of learning to phrase the negative concept another way.

Saying no positively has two advantages. First, it tends to eliminate unpleasant emotional reactions either partly or completely. Often the word *no*, and not the refusal itself, triggers the emotional reaction. (Sometimes the thing being refused isn't something the reader values very highly anyway.) If you avoid the word *no*, you avoid the emotion.

Second, saying no positively helps you remember to provide reasons for your refusal. Once the reader understands why you're refusing, he or she can see that you're not refusing just to frustrate or irritate. Perhaps the reader will see that, in your shoes, he or she would have made the same decision.

A good formula to remember when saying something negative is this: don't say what you can't do; say what you *must* do instead. See how the formula is applied in Figure 4. Figuring out positive ways to say no may seem a bit awkward and unwieldy as you begin to practice. Very quickly,

Negative	Positive
We can't ship your order until August 10.	We'll be able to ship your order on August 10.
Therefore, we can't return your check.	Therefore, we've deposited your check and credited your account with this amount.
Under the circumstances, we can't grant credit.	Under the circumstances, we'll be glad to re-examine your credit application in six months; perhaps at that time, your present situation will have changed, and we'll be able to open an account for you.
No exceptions to this rule can be allowed.	This rule must apply equally in all situations.
Don't hesitate to let me know if you have any questions.	Feel free to let me know if you have any questions.
This dress is not available in pink.	This dress is available in blue, yellow, charcoal, and white.
When you travel on company business, you won't be reimbursed for first-class fare.	When you travel on company business, you'll be reimbursed only for the lowest available fare, which is normally coach fare.
Therefore, I can't raise your grade from B to A.	Therefore, your grade must remain B.

Figure 4 Saying no positively

however, you'll find that being positive is just as natural as being negative. Being positive is an easy and worthwhile habit to acquire.

WRITING TO CREATE VIVID IMAGES

Vivid writing makes your ideas come alive. Often it's not enough for the reader simply to understand an idea; sometimes the reader must be made to feel its impact. For that to happen, the idea must be driven home with much greater intensity; it must create a truly vivid image. Good writers use three techniques to achieve vivid images: (1) selecting specific details rather than general symbols, (2) explaining ideas in terms of people doing things, and (3) involving the reader as a participant in the explanation.

Using Specific Details

Remember the last time you went to a football game. Remember what it was really like: the green grass on the field, the sound of the cannon that was fired after every touchdown, the loud guy behind you who made rude comments to the coach after every play, the smell of the popcorn, the clean uniform of the substitute who came in during the third quarter. Then remember reading about the game in the newspaper the next morning. How much of that real event did the newspaper capture? True, it did tell you some things about conditions as the coaches saw them (which you probably didn't perceive at the game), and it did describe the key plays and the outcome. But how much it missed!

That's the way most writing is. Out of all the specific details of a real event, a writer picks just a few to report. And in a factual account, a good writer sticks to the key points. But the factual account of that football game certainly didn't engage your feelings the way the real event did, with all its activity and excitement and suspense. Even though the sportswriter tried to capture at least some of that excitement (and probably had the skill to do so), the newspaper account was very flat, even a bit boring, compared with the real game.

A key difference between the game and the newspaper account is the amount of detail available to your perception. In the 150 or so minutes you spent at the stadium, you perceived an enormous number of specific events that made up your experience of the game. In the newspaper story, the description had to be cut to a reasonable length. After all, an account of all the sportswriter's perceptions at the game would take more space than the whole newspaper. In cutting, however, a good writer is careful not to leave an account that is so general and abstract that the audience doesn't even get a taste of what it would have been like to experience the whole game.

This example illustrates why specific detail is so important in writing, especially when the writing must engage the reader's emotions. Very specific detail is what real-life experiences are made of; you certainly don't experience the kind of generalization found in most writing. A flavoring of specific detail in a written message gives the reader a taste of the real experience and helps focus the writer's attention on the real-life aspects of that experience.

Stop reading at the end of this paragraph and look around you. In a few seconds, mentally describe the place you're in. Then think about how to describe it more specifically. *Where* are you? If it's a large place, *how* large? *How many* feet by how many feet? If it's well lighted, *how many* fixtures are there? *How many* windows? *What* material is on the floor? *What* color? If the walls are plaster, is it smooth or pebbled? *What* color? *What kind* of chairs? *How many? Who* is in the room with you? *What* are their names? Note at least six specifics, then jot them down.

Asking specific questions Now set aside your list of specifics for a moment while we consider various ways of adding detail to a piece of writing. No doubt you noticed that certain words in the paragraph above were emphasized: who, what, where, how, and how many. Each asks for more detail. And the specifics these little words call for are the specifics of your real-life experience of the room. Very likely you aren't experiencing, for example, three boys, one girl, and one older woman; but George Madariaga, a guy named Jerry whose last name you don't know, another guy you don't know at all, Emily Farr, and Mrs. Chen.

One way of getting from the general to the specific, then, is to ask repeatedly who, what, when, where, how, and how many. For example, look around the room you're describing and ask yourself, "Who's there?" You may answer, "a girl." Then ask, "But who is she?" You may answer, "a girl I know." Then ask, "But who is she?" You may answer, "Emily Farr." Ask the question, then ask it again of your answer—and again and again, until you've gotten as specific as you can.

Notice that there are two ways to answer the question of how large the room is. One works and one doesn't. Suppose you ask yourself, "How large is the room?" You may answer, "Very large." Then ask, "But how large" You may answer, "quite large." Then ask, "But how large?" You may answer, "extremely large." This sequence can go on and on, but there's no progress. Your description isn't getting more specific. But suppose you answer, "It's about 25 by 30 feet." Then ask, "How large is that?" You may answer, "It's about the size of a regular college classroom." Notice how much more informative these answers are. They're really getting specific; you're beginning to create a lifelike image in the reader's mind.

Using specific nouns generally works better than using specific adjectives or adverbs. If you can replace an abstract noun with a more specific and concrete one, do it. If you find that you're trying to be more specific by adding lots of adjectives, stop and make sure you're really building a specific image for the reader.

Choosing specific verbs Often verbs can be made more specific for vivid imagery. Many writers tend to overuse "is" sentences (sentences with the verbs *is, was, were*, and so on). Such sentences are almost always rather general. For vividness, write sentences about people doing things, and use the most specific action verb you can think of. Wherever possible, the action should be observable. For example, if a young woman went out the door, did she storm, slink, march, stride, or just walk out? All these verbs create more specific images than "went out."

However, in your practice with specific verbs, carefully avoid describing things that didn't really happen. For example, perhaps the young woman did just walk out the door. In that case, "walked" is the most accurate verb to describe what she did. If you say she stormed out the door, you've misrepresented what happened. "Stormed" is a fine word, but use it only when someone really storms. A serious problem arises when you try to "improve on" reality. Your reader will sense that you're exaggerating and suspend belief. Be specific, but be realistic, too.

Using specifics selectively   Don't use specific details indiscriminately. Try to select, from all you could say about an event, the details that create a vivid picture of it. If, for example, the size of the room where the event occurred is irrelevant, then ignore it. Select other topics to talk about, using believable specifics that help create a supporting image for your message. Thus vivid writing is sprinkled with specific details, not overwhelmed by them; if you try to make everything specific, the message will simply get too long. Instead, carefully plan the specifics to obtain the maximum effect from relatively few additional words. Selecting what to be specific about is part of the challenge.

Now look over your list of specifics about the room. First, consider which six or eight details would give a reader the best glimpse of what the room is like. Which specifics should you select? Think for a moment and decide, right now.

Next consider each of these specific details. Can you be even more specific? Concentrate on this task for five minutes or so. It's the best practice you can get. Then be even more specific. Exactly who? Exactly what? Exactly where? Exactly how many? Make each phrase more specific. Keep working until you're pretty sure each one is as specific as you can make it. Then force yourself to make each one still a little bit more specific.

Now go through your list and look very suspiciously at every adjective and adverb. Could you achieve the same effect, or a better one, by making the noun or verb more specific and omitting the adjective or adverb? Try it.

Finally, compare this final description with your first one. It's almost certainly much better—much more vivid in its imagery. And in doing this little exercise, you've learned two things. First, you've learned how to write vividly by using specific details. Second, you've learned that, when it's important to create vivid images, there's no substitute for reviewing your first draft and revising again and again and again.

Explaining Ideas in Terms of People Doing Things

In the preceding chapter, we discussed the people-doing-things sentence structure as a way to make your writing more readable. Actually, this structuring technique is much more powerful than that. Fully applied, it can pay great dividends for a relatively small investment of effort. Here's how to make this technique pay off for you.

When a TV advertiser wants to drive an idea home to an audience, he or she dramatizes it; that is, the advertiser actually makes a little movie illustrating the idea. You can do the same thing in writing. You can invent some characters—or even better, use real-life characters—to dramatize the idea you're expressing. Then you can draw a little word cartoon, complete with action, for the reader. Carefully developed, such a cartoon can have strong impact.

Thinking of your message in terms of word cartoons, or 30-second TV ads, allows you to learn from your extensive exposure to TV advertising and profit from the experience of very talented and highly paid ad writers. After all, you should be able to get some return from the years you've spent sitting in front of the TV set! From all the thousands of commercials you've watched, you've developed a pretty good feeling for how advertisers present ideas simply and strongly. Now you do it.

A key part of TV advertising is that ideas are presented in dialogue— actual conversations. If you find you can do it realistically, then you can use dialogue too, and it can be a good way to make ideas seem real. To be effective, of course, word cartoons have to be reasonably realistic; otherwise, they can sound a bit corny. But word cartoons do generate very vivid images in the reader's mind and help the reader identify emotionally with your message. Figure 5 shows an example.

Even if you decide that the dialogue approach isn't appropriate in a given case, you can still talk about people doing things. Events in the outside world don't "just happen" in the abstract. Someone actually does something to make them happen. In your phrasing, depict real people taking action, so the reader will perceive clear images. Instead of "Our prices have increased," say, "Our suppliers have raised their prices." Instead of "Your order will be shipped within 24 hours," say, "When I receive your order, I'll make sure it's shipped within 24 hours." Instead of "Paychecks will be available in department offices on the first of each month," say, "Your department office will have your paycheck for you on the first of each month."

Involving the Audience in the Explanation

Of all the characters who appear in your writing, the reader is the most important. If the idea you're explaining affects the reader, phrase it so the reader is involved as an actor. If you're asking the reader to do something, say "Here's what to do," "Here's how you can do it," or even "Please do this." Be sure to use "you" (either implied or explicit) in that explanation. After all, if you were talking across the desk to that person, you'd use "you." Why not do that in writing?

This point is especially important when you're explaining an idea that will probably encounter some emotional resistance. It's easy to see

Excerpt from a Letter Justifying a Cost Increase

As I'm sure you're all too aware, the price of almost everything has gone up in the last few months. Our price for raw milk has increased a bit more than 40 percent. Labor costs are up 23 percent. Postage is up 30 percent. Even the cost of our cardboard mailing packages is up 27 percent.

In the face of these price increases, we could have compromised the outstanding quality of the products we sell. By doing this, we could have cut enough corners to continue our previous price list for another year. But we know that, when you send gift packages of Coos Bay Cheese Products to your friends at holiday time, you want only the highest-quality products to arrive in their homes. That's why we're sure you'll appreciate our decision to maintain the high standards we've been proud to hold over the last 50 years, even though it means we have to raise our prices.

Word-Cartoon Version

The other day Jim Miller, our chief accountant, walked into my office and sat down. "George," he said, "we've got a problem. Look at these figures: the price of raw milk is up more than 40 percent from a year ago. Labor is up 23 percent. Postage—up 30 percent. Even our cardboard mailing packages are up 27 percent. We've not breaking even, George. We're going to have to do something."

"What do you think we should do, Jim?" I asked.

"We only have two choices," he said. "We can cut some corners, or we can raise prices."

"But there's no place left to cut, except in quality—you know that! We've already cut everything else to the bone. Of course, we could save some money by cutting quality. But if I were a customer, I'd want to be able to count on the quality of the products when I sent gift packages to all my friends during the holidays."

"I guess you're right, George," he said. "The only thing we can do is raise prices. Let me go back to my office and see what I can do on a new price list."

When I picked up the phone later that afternoon and Jim told me the price increase would average only about 12 percent, I was delighted! And I think you'll be happy, too, to know that you can still count on the same high quality standards in Coos Bay Cheese Products that you've always received, even in these inflationary times.

Figure 5 A vivid word cartoon

that addressing your readers by a group label ("All employees should. . . ." or "We know our customers would want. . . .") will appear impersonal to them. But even more important, a group label makes it difficult for them to build a concrete image of the point you're explaining. It lets them off the hook. They can say, "Oh, did you mean me?"

Just as it's difficult, though not impossible, to be too specific in your writing, it's very difficult to overdo the "you" in your writing. It's probably possible to say "you" too often, but you're very unlikely to do it.

TONE IN NONROUTINE MESSAGES

Up to now we've been discussing techniques for achieving the kind of pleasant and mildly friendly tone that's appropriate for most business messages. Once in a while, though, your analysis of a situation may identify a need for another kind of tone. Usually such situations involve warnings or firm demands for action.

As you analyze such situations, remember that the readers' responses may depend much more on their estimate of what you'll actually do than upon the stiffness of the message's tone. If they think you'll take serious action, they may respond as you demand; if they doubt you'll act, then your tone may make little difference. In fact, if they consider your tone to be hostile, that may reduce your chance of getting the desired response. A hostile tone may suggest that any future relationship and possible future gain is out of the question. A hostile tone may also elicit anger and opposition instead of cooperation. In these situations, a neutral and very factual tone in a message that clearly states your case may often be the most effective approach.

All organizations, from time to time, must send letters documenting past unsatisfactory performance and demanding action. In such letters, a great deal of friendliness certainly isn't appropriate; that would make the writer appear weak and ineffective. Yet an extremely hostile and threatening tone can have exactly the same effect, by suggesting that the writer must substitute bluster and bullying for real authority.

In such situations, emphasizing only the present situation and what now needs to be done may be useful. Although reviewing the situation's history may be necessary (as in reporting unsatisfactory employee performance), your goal is usually to solve the present problem. So it makes sense to emphasize that point in your message. Also, most people naturally feel defensive and hostile when someone emphasizes their faults and past failures, and that hardly creates an atmosphere for planning future solutions.

Perhaps this defensiveness can be avoided somewhat by carefully concentrating upon the objective facts of the situation, with minimum personalization. In the words of the maxim, "Condemn the deed, not the doer." This is when passive-voice sentences and discussions in terms of happenings rather than people doing things may be useful.

If your analysis indicates that a stern tone is needed, remember that the written word is by nature flat and unemotional in tone and that a very factual, objective message will normally appear stiff and aggressive. In addition, if the facts are unpleasant to the reader, the tone will seem negative regardless of how you write the message. It's seldom useful to do more to create a stern tone.

FURTHER EXPLORATION

1. Is the pleasant, friendly tone discussed in this chapter suitable for messages that say something disagreeable? Try to think of some situations in which you believe it wouldn't be suitable. What tone would be better in those situations?

2. When you're talking with a close friend, jokingly exaggerate your enthusiasm about the subject for a few minutes. Later, consider how you were talking and especially your choice of words. How did your word choice differ from your normal word choice? How should you slightly exaggerate the enthusiasm in your writing through word choice?

3. Mentally experiment with the balance between courtesy and sincerity. Imagine a conversation with someone (perhaps a relative). How could you be overcourteous? Does that really seem insincere? How could you be oversincere? Does that really seem discourteous?

4. How do you change your messages when you communicate with someone of higher status than yourself? For example, how differently do you speak to a close friend than to an instructor? Or to the president of a large organization? Be as specific as possible about the differences.

5. Think of some situations in which messages could take a positive or negative viewpoint. In each, try to find the best way to view the subject positively. Select one situation that interests you and think about it from time to time over several days; discuss it with your friends, if possible. In that situation, how much difference will it make to the reader if you take a positive rather than a negative viewpoint?

6. To see how professionals communicate vivid images, pay careful attention to TV ads over the next few days. Separate the visual from the verbal techniques by first watching some ads with the sound turned off (so you can see the visuals without distraction), then listening to some ads without watching the screen. In each ad, what key image is the advertiser trying to establish? Identify techniques you could use to create vivid images in your writing.

Remember to continue working on the writing problems that begin on page 152.

9

Organization I: Organizing Paragraphs

*Let us always devote ourselves first
to the steps of preparatory work.*
Hu Shih

Writing isn't hard; it's no harder than ditch-digging.
Patrick Dennis

M ost beginning business writers already realize the value of organizing their ideas into paragraphs. The technique is simple, at least in principle: among the ideas a message must discuss, sets of similar or related points are clustered together. Each cluster is then organized as a paragraph, and the paragraphs are sequenced according to their logical relationships to one another. Thus all the message's points are organized for maximum logic and clarity.

WHY WELL-ORGANIZED PARAGRAPHS WORK

The reason why this kind of organizing is very important lies in the way the human mind takes in information. Think of the reader's mind as a filing system. To receive and store information efficiently, the system must sort the information and file it logically. Once information is stored, then, its systematic filing allows accurate and efficient retrieval (remembering) for later use.

The efficiency of such organization is easy to see if you imagine trying to remember a list of 25 random objects that might be found in your room at home. That would be a hard job! To do it, you might spend 30–60 minutes firmly committing the list to memory. But if you could organize that list somehow, the job would be much easier. You might list the objects in the order they appear in the room, starting at the door and moving around to the right until you're back to the door. Or you might sort the objects into groups: clothing, furniture, grooming aids, and so on. Any way you can organize those 25 objects will help you remember them more easily and accurately.

When you write a letter or memo, you're asking your reader to do a learning task very much like the one above. And even the shortest report presents the reader with a much more complicated learning task. The help you provide by carefully organizing your material can make that task much easier. As Figure 1 (pages 115–16) shows, organizing really works.

If you neglect this organizing, then you're asking the reader to do it, and the reader probably won't bother. Organizing takes some effort, as every experienced writer knows. And few readers expect to make such an effort to understand and remember messages. In fact, if you try to make your reader work at all, he or she may decide to ignore the message. Remember, the responsibility for successful communication lies with the writer, not the reader.

The traditional ways of organizing paragraphs represent the practical lore developed over 2500 years by writers faced with problems very similar to yours. During that time, writers learned by experience that certain kinds of learning aids are very helpful to readers. In this chapter, we explore these traditions.

The Information

The desk dictionary provides information about the derivation (roots) of words, which is often helpful in determining their precise meaning. It also shows the proper division of words into syllables, essential information when you need to hyphenate a word at the end of a typed line. A spelling dictionary, or word finder, is quicker to use, although the information it provides is more limited. The desk dictionary gives the accepted definitions of words, the way literate speakers and writers of English commonly use them. It indicates the spelling of unusual plurals and other irregular forms, which can be very helpful. The spelling dictionary also indicates how to divide a word if you must hyphenate it at the end of the line. Because it's shorter and you don't have to look through so much material to find the word you want, the spelling dictionary, or word finder, is a particularly useful reference tool during the final revision and typing of messages. The desk dictionary is a guide to the world of words and provides several kinds of information. The spelling dictionary provides less information, but the information it does contain is more accessible.

A Possible Outline

I. Desk dictionary--a guide to the world of words--contains
several kinds of information:

   A. Correct spelling

   B. Proper division into syllables

   C. Spelling of unusual plurals and other irregular forms

   D. Ways words are used by literate communicators

Figure 1 Organizing information into paragraphs

II. Spelling dictionary or word finder--convenient reference in
final revision and typing
A. Information limited to spelling and division into
syllables
B. Shorter, thus information is more accessible and quicker
to use

The Organized Version

A desk dictionary is a guide to the world of words. It
contains several kinds of information that are helpful to the
business communicator. First, it tells how to spell words
correctly. Second, it shows the proper division of words into
syllables, essential information when it's necessary to hyphenate
a word at the end of a typed line. Third, it indicates the
spellings of unusual plurals and other irregular forms, which can
be very helpful. Fourth, it provides information about the
derivation (roots) of words, which is often very helpful in
determining their precise meaning. And finally, it defines the
accepted uses of words, the ways literate speakers and writers of
English commonly use them.

A spelling dictionary, or word finder, is a more
specialized source of information that's particularly convenient
to use in the final revision and typing of messages. It tells
how to spell words and indicates proper division into syllables.
Because the information in a spelling dictionary is more limited,
it's also easier and quicker to use. Since definitions and other
information are omitted, you don't have to look through so much
material to find the correct spelling of the word you want.

Figure 1 (continued)

WRITING A PARAGRAPH

As we've seen, paragraphs are clusters of ideas that are more closely related to one another than to the other ideas in the message. Once you've thought through your message and grouped ideas into these clusters, you're ready to structure the paragraphs.

Paragraph planning, which consists of selecting main ideas and planning the sequence of supporting points, is part of the planning stage of the writing process. By the time you begin writing, these steps should be completed.

The Main Idea

To structure a paragraph, begin with the main idea. Look at the points in your first cluster and ask, "What's the main thing I'm trying to say in this cluster?" or "What's the main thing the reader wants to know here?" Once you determine the main idea of your paragraph, write it down. Much of the time, the main idea will make a fine opening sentence for your paragraph.

The Supporting Sentences

Very likely, once you've written a main-idea sentence for a cluster, you will see at least one way to order the remaining points into a written paragraph. If your original cluster of ideas is a good one, then the remaining points in it should clearly and obviously relate to the main idea. Ideally, you'll be able to arrange them so that adjacent points relate to each other as closely as possible. Several patterns often occur in the supporting sentences of a paragraph: (1) the supporting sentences may simply say more about the main idea, (2) they may provide details explaining the main idea or providing reasons for it, (3) they may be examples of the main idea, or (4) most likely, they may combine these patterns.

Once you've written the first draft of your message from your outline or notes, you've given your reader a set of learning aids that should significantly ease the task of remembering the information in the message, as Figure 2 illustrates. You've grouped the points to be remembered into related sets, and you've preceded each set with a main idea that the other points fit into.

Transitions: Signposts for the Reader

As you revise your first draft, maximize the value of these learning aids by providing clear signals, or signposts, that show how the various points relate to one another. These signposts are called transitions.

Paragraph transitions Once you've written a first draft, you've converted your clusters into a series of paragraphs. To help show the reader how these paragraphs relate to one another, near the beginning of each paragraph add phrasing that refers to the main idea of the preceding par-

You can probably make your writing go faster by doing all your writing in the same place. Since you're well aware that writing is hard work, you'll certainly find a place to write where distractions are at a minimum and other conditions are right. You'll soon collect all the materials you need there, so you won't have to stop and search for a dictionary or a sheet of paper. And you'll quickly find the best arrangement for your writing tools, so the things you need are right at hand.

But most important, by consistently writing in the same place, you will train your mind to concentrate whenever you go to that place. You'll find yourself ready to start writing, without the usual 10 or 15 minutes of mental gymnastics to get your mind working. The power of suggestion can be a powerful tool when used in this constructive way.

Figure 2 Main ideas (italic type) and supporting sentences (roman type)

agraph. These added words make it perfectly clear how each paragraph relates to the one before it.

Often this relationship can be stated clearly in one of the words or brief phrases that we think of as transitional phrases, such as "therefore," "thus," "for that reason," "in addition," and "also." Sometimes, you can demonstrate the relationship by repeating key phrasing from the main-idea sentence of the preceding paragraph. For example, the paragraph you're now reading uses the repeated-phrasing device ("this relationship") to transition from the preceding paragraph's main-idea sentence, which is the middle sentence. In other cases, a series of paragraphs may provide reasons for some main idea, and you can demonstrate the relationship simply by numbering them "first," "second," "third," and so on. Whatever method you use—and you may have to invent your own from time to time—you should begin each paragraph with a clearly worded reference to the main idea of the preceding paragraph.

Sentence transitions   The next step in the revision stage comes as a surprise, even to many fairly experienced writers: as you revise, clearly and explicitly relate each sentence to the one before it. Much of the time, the sentences in your draft will already be related. In revising, however, ensure that every single sentence contains words signaling how it relates to the one before.

As Figure 3 illustrates, many of the devices that guide the reader from sentence to sentence are simply normal elements of writing. You probably already use them most of the time. Occasionally, however, you

Good communicators plan telephone calls in the same way they plan written messages. Before <u>they</u> place <u>a call</u>, <u>they</u> visualize the person <u>they'll</u> be talking to and try to analyze how that person may react to <u>their</u> message. <u>And they</u> plan goals for <u>the conversation</u>, <u>too</u>, determining exactly what <u>they</u> want to accomplish. <u>These</u> form the basis for notes containing the points <u>they</u> want to cover during <u>the call</u>. <u>Such an outline</u> helps ensure that <u>they</u> won't have to <u>call back</u> right away to make <u>further points</u>.

Figure 3 Many sentences contain several sentence transitions

may have difficulty thinking up a transition. Sometimes this happens when you've made a big jump in logic that you haven't noticed, and the difficulty signals you to reconsider what those sentences say. With a little rewording, you may be able to relate the subject matter of those sentences more closely so that one sentence really does lead into the next.

Often, though, a transition problem arises simply because writers aren't aware of the wide variety of possible transitions. Figure 4 describes the major ways to make transitions from one sentence to another. As you practice your writing, review this list from time to time and broaden your transition capability.

In particular, as you revise, go through your paragraphs quickly, ensuring that every sentence relates to the previous sentence in one of the ways shown in Figure 4. Often, reading a paragraph aloud will help you identify breaks in the idea sequence that aren't identified by clear transitions. Soon you'll develop a feel for the kind of flow these transitions provide, and you'll recognize breaks in the flow even without checking for transitions. Once that happens, you'll maintain smooth transitions from point to point almost entirely by habit. That's the payoff from your early hard work!

PRACTICE: THE KEY TO GOOD PARAGRAPHS

As you've seen in this chapter, the basic techniques of good paragraphing aren't particularly difficult or complicated. In fact, you already use many of them. And improving your paragraphing skill is important. As your messages become longer and more complicated, good, clear paragraphs are an invaluable aid to the reader.

The way to improve your skill is by practice. In the planning stage of your practice work, consciously think about the development of each

1. Use a connecting word showing the logical relationship of the sentence to the preceding one.

   The usual connectors include *and, but, so, thus, therefore, however,* and *nevertheless.* It's almost impossible to overdo this transitional device, since it provides the clearest of signposts. In any doubtful case, use this device.

   Example: On the basis of our investigation, we believe the defects are caused by improper storage methods by the customer rather than by defects in design or manufacture. *Nevertheless,* we recommend that the company replace these defective units and all our other units in the customer's present stock.

2. Repeat a key word or phrase from the preceding sentence.

   The word or phrase you repeat should carry the meaning forward.

   Example: The fall season is an extremely busy time for us. No doubt it's a busy time for you too.

3. Use a synonym in the sentence for a key word or phrase in the preceding sentence.

   In this way, you carry the meaning forward, although not in exactly the same words.

   Example: The units you ordered were shipped to your store by truck earlier today. These fast-moving items sell very quickly as the summer holiday season approaches.

4. Use an antonym in the sentence for a key word or phrase in the preceding sentence.

   Just as synonyms carry the meaning forward, antonyms do too.

   Example: Clarity is the essence of good writing. Obscurity should be avoided at all cost.

5. Use a pronoun in this sentence that refers back to an antecedent in the sentence before.

   Pronouns include the usual *I, he, her, its, our, you,* and *them.* They also include *this, that, these, those, some, any, another, others, none,* and *all.*

   Example: I believe Ms. Shourdon is very well qualified for this position. She has the necessary education, and her work experience provides excellent background.

6. Use a word in the sentence that's immediately recognizable as forming a pair with a word in the preceding sentence.

   Such pairs include writer-reader, talking-listening, time-clock, pen-paper. For this device to work, the reader must see the connection between the two members of the pair quite clearly.

   Example: The upper part of the form is for identifying information about the customer. The lower part is for information about the specific transaction.

Figure 4 Devices for sentence transition

paragraph. Outline each one. In the revision stage, verify that each paragraph has a clearly stated main idea and that the paragraph's other points relate directly to that idea. Then verify that each paragraph explicitly refers to the subject of the preceding one. Finally, verify that each sentence clearly relates to the previous sentence through one of the transitional devices discussed here.

You can significantly improve your ability to write well-developed paragraphs as you use this book. To improve, you must think about paragraphing and work on it every time you write a practice message. By the time you finish this book, good paragraphing will be almost completely habitual with you, and people will understand your messages much more easily.

To be a good writer, you need to know more about the structure of a paragraph than a single chapter in a textbook can teach you. In his excellent little paperback, *Writing to the Point: Six Basic Steps*, William J. Kerrigan has provided the kind of material I think would be helpful.[1] Many of the ideas in this chapter follow his more extended discussion. His book is well adapted to self-study.

FURTHER EXPLORATION

1. Select a passage of informational writing (not fiction) that you find easy to read and analyze its paragraph structure. The passage should be several pages long so you can see how relationships between paragraphs are handled. First, go through the passage paragraph by paragraph, underlining the main idea of each one; the main idea may not always come first. Second, draw a box around each paragraph transition. Finally, circle each sentence transition. How often are paragraph and sentence transitions missing? Where they're missing, did you intuitively notice an unexpected break in the idea flow?

2. Using a first draft of your own writing, repeat the analysis described in Exploration 1. If you find a paragraph with no apparent main-idea statement, try adding one. Where paragraph transitions are missing, add them. In each paragraph, be sure that every sentence after the first includes a sentence transition. If you can't think of one to add, that's a signal to rewrite one or more sentences. Is the new version easier to read than the old one?

---

1. William J. Kerrigan, *Writing to the Point: Six Basic Steps* (New York: Harcourt Brace Jovanovich, Inc., 1974).

3.   Analyze your own or someone else's paragraph in the following way. Underline the main-idea statement. Then, for each remaining sentence, determine which other sentence it supports most directly. Some of the remaining sentences probably directly support the main idea sentence; others probably directly support other supporting sentences. Some may not directly support any other sentence in the paragraph; circle these. As a result of your analysis, should you reorganize the paragraph to clarify the sequence of ideas?

Remember to keep working on the writing problems that begin on page 152.

10

Organization II: Organizing Messages

I never come across one of Laplace's
"Thus it plainly appears" without feeling
sure that I have hours of hard work
before me.
N. Bowditch

Too many writers are premature; they
should organize their ideas better before
writing a piece. I do tremendous
organizational layouts on many pieces
before I actually write them; I take notes
on matchbook covers, napkins, anything.
Woody Allen

Just as well-structured paragraphs make a message easier to understand, so does a carefully planned sequence of points. The order in which ideas are presented can help the reader understand them clearly. This chapter discusses tactical planning decisions involved in organizing your messages.

PLANNED ORGANIZATION ENHANCES COMMUNICATION

Carefully sequencing the points helps you organize your thoughts clearly as you plan your message. Considering what you'll say first, second, and so on gives you an easy and natural way to think through your message. As you try to sequence your ideas, you'll quickly see gaps in your logic and places where your ideas need further explanation. You'll also notice whether or not your points actually support the conclusion you want to draw.

In addition, clear organization will help the reader follow the logic of your message. A well-organized message leads the reader step by step through its points, never forcing the reader to guess how you arrived at your conclusions. Moreover, clear organization demonstrates that you've carefully and logically developed your ideas before beginning to write, and that gives the reader increased confidence in them.

Finally, clear organization enhances your message's readability and tone. Even though we've been discussing readability, tone, and organization as though they were separate topics, the separation is artificial—just a convenience for understanding a large body of material. Actually, well-organized messages are much more readable than disorganized ones. And disorganized messages convey an image of sloppiness and carelessness that's almost as plain as a direct insult to your reader.

Thus organizing is vital to the writing process. It's a key step in the planning stage.

BEGINNINGS AND ENDINGS

For more than 2500 years, writers and speakers have understood that the beginnings and endings of messages are more important and require more careful planning than the middles. As we saw in our discussion of emphasis, a message's beginning and end are positions of natural emphasis. Thus the points made in those places are more likely to stick in the reader's mind than those made in the middle.

The beginning of a message sets the stage for the reader's perception of the whole message. The subject of the beginning is the subject the reader will expect to hear about throughout the remainder, and the tone and viewpoint of the beginning are the ones the reader will assume apply to the whole message. Thus a message's opening words establish a viewpoint that will affect the reader's understanding of the whole message. For these reasons, the beginning is typically the most important part of a message.

The end of a message, on the other hand, will be the most recent in the reader's mind after reading. It's the last chance to influence the reader. But even more important, it's the one place where an idea can be discussed in light of all the other points. Thus, for example, when a message is designed to get action, the strongest call for action usually comes at the end, when all the reasons for it can be fully appreciated.

In long messages, beginnings and endings normally are nearly equal in importance. Both should be used to full effect. The beginning establishes the message's subject, viewpoint, and tone. And the ending pulls all the points together, firmly cements them in the reader's mind, examines future implications, and calls for any needed action. Particularly in oral presentations, many public speakers consider endings even more important than beginnings.

In routine business letters and memos, however, the beginning is very important, and the ending is not. The reason is the way business people read their mail. The sad fact for you as a business writer is that, on the whole, people don't much want to read your messages. Your reader is an extremely busy person with more mail on his or her desk than can possibly be read fully. Reading the mail, after all, is a minor part of a manager's very demanding job.

In every morning's mail, the manager finds the usual stack of ads, catalogs, and periodicals, which can be discarded or quickly marked for later reading. There are also interoffice memos; some of these are actually written for this reader, but most arrive because he or she is on one of the many routing slips, or internal mailing lists, in the organization (such memos are addressed, for example, "To all employees," or "To all project managers"). Finally, there are letters of varying importance.

Thus your reader sits down at the desk to go through the mail, pulls the wastebasket near, and "reads" the mail into the wastebasket. Don't misunderstand; your reader doesn't just dump the mail into the trash. That would be too risky. Somewhere in that mail are five or six vital pieces of information, and they must be found. But the rest, for most managers, is a pretty dismal collection of irrelevant junk.

Your typical reader, then, quickly scans the first page of each piece checking for assurance that this piece, like most of the rest, is unimportant and can be discarded. And your job is to get your message through in spite of that. That's why the opening is so crucial: if you say something important in the opening sentence or two, even the skimming reader will see it. If you say it anyplace else, then only readers who read past the beginning will see it. What you say at the end isn't very likely to be seen.

BASIC ORGANIZATIONAL PLANS FOR ROUTINE MESSAGES

The two most commonly used plans for organizing business messages are the direct plan and the indirect plan. In unusual circumstances, the alternative-elimination and the chronological plan are also occasionally used when they fit the logic of your points.

Direct Plan

Remember the last time you sat at your desk with a writing job to do? If you're like most people, you spent a substantial amount of time sitting there, staring at that blank piece of paper (wishing you were somewhere else), and trying to figure out how to start. What should you say first? How should you say it? For most people, the hardest part of writing is getting started—getting the first usable sentence down on paper.

Here's a way to get past that painful first step: think of all the points you must make, and determine which one is the main point. Ask yourself, "What do I most want this reader to know?" or "What does this reader most want to know?" The answer to one of these questions is your main point—the first point of your outline and (possibly) the first sentence of your message.

Putting the main point first has important advantages to writers and readers alike. It helps writers avoid the wasted minutes (or hours) spent sitting and looking at a blank sheet of paper. Very often, once the initial sentence is down on the page, you'll quickly see how the rest of the material in a routine message can be organized.

Putting the main point first also employs a key principle of the psychology of reading and listening: people tend to remember the first point in a message better than other points. Finally, as we've seen, putting the main point first increases your chance of getting it across, even if busy readers only skim the message. If the main point is in the middle or at the end, skimming readers would miss it completely, as Figure 1 shows.

Your readers also benefit when the main point is first; they then know the key idea of the message while they read the other points. If they know what you're driving at, they can look at the other ideas in context. If your main point is a conclusion supported by the points that follow, then readers can easily understand the points as they read because they know what conclusion the points are supposed to support. If your subordinate points are details related to the main point, then your readers will understand the details more clearly because they can fit them into the whole picture.

Putting the main point first is one of those rare techniques that allows the writer to have his or her cake and eat it too. You benefit two ways—the message becomes easier to write, and it also becomes easier to read. That's a good combination.

Putting the main point first is called the direct plan of organization. After the main point, according to this plan, you present the subordinate points arranged for maximum clarity. You can arrange these points in decreasing order of importance, with the least important at the end, or use another sequence when the logic of the material suggests one. In most routine direct-plan messages, when you get to the end of your subordinate points, you quit, with no closing summary or wrap-up, as in Figure 2. The direct plan of organization is best for almost all short informational messages, and it's also well suited to most longer messages.

Unrevised

DATE: November 27, 1982

TO: A. B. Reaume, Shipping Supervisor

FROM: Alfred Minor, Routing

SUBJECT: Truck Routes

Several months ago, we discussed the delivery route situation. At that time, routes 5 and 13 were expanding to the point where drivers were hardly able to cover them without overtime each week. Consideration was given to dividing these two routes into three, setting up a new route that would include parts of routes 5 and 13 and would take in several new areas not now covered by our delivery system.

As you may remember, these two routes overlap in the north county area. And that's the area of maximum current growth, which is continuing, possibly even accelerating. Thus, in my considered opinion, we should implement the plan for splitting routes, effective immediately. Only when we do this will we reap the anticipated benefits.

I've drawn maps showing my proposals for the revised routes 5 and 13 and the new route 20. I'll be glad to discuss these with you whenever you wish.

Revised

DATE: November 27, 1982

TO: A. B. Reaume, Shipping Supervisor

FROM: Alfred Minor, Routing

SUBJECT: Additional Delivery Route Should Be Started Now

The time has come to add another delivery route to cover the north county and nearby areas. Routes 5 and 13 are continuing to expand, as we discussed several months ago, and those drivers can seldom cover them without overtime. The new route would relieve the pressure by taking over parts of routes 5 and 13, and we could fill it out by including several new areas not now covered by our delivery system.

The maps attached show my proposals for the revised routes 5 and 13 and the new route 20. We can make this change as soon as I receive your OK.

Figure 1 Revising a message to use the direct plan

THE ASLOW COMPANY

1448 QUIMBY LANE • KELLY, LOUISIANA 71441 • (318) 716-9200

February 26, 1985

Ms. Sylvia Horvath
255 Griesor Road
Charleston, SC 29935

Dear Ms. Horvath:

The Kyusan 4011B cassette tape deck you ordered was shipped
this morning from our Cleveland warehouse by the Railway Express
Agency. It should arrive in Charleston within ten days.

I'm confident that you'll be happy with your new tape deck.
The special low-noise circuitry in this unit produces recordings
so quiet that they meet the highest professional standards. When
you're ready to order extra-low-noise cassette tapes at a very
attractive price, check the enclosed price listing and drop us a
line.

Your local REA office will notify you when your package
arrives and will indicate the exact shipping charges, which
should be in the neighborhood of $5. You should look over the
shipping carton very carefully before you accept delivery and
report any damage to the REA agent; REA is responsible for any
damages sustained during shipment.

Cordially,

Kenneth Cedarlind

personal feeling [handwritten annotation]

Figure 2 A direct-plan letter

Indirect Plan

Once in a while, perhaps two or three times in a hundred, putting the main point first interferes with communication rather than aiding it. In such cases, you can use an alternative plan called the indirect plan of organization, which has many of the advantages of the direct plan.

Indirect-plan messages, in which the main point is at or near the end, are of two kinds: First are messages whose main goal is to impart information that's best revealed by delaying the main point. Second are messages whose main goal is to deal with readers' strong emotional reactions.

When goals are informational   Sometimes your readers won't be able to understand your main point until you've explained it. It may involve technical terminology they aren't familiar with or background information they don't have. Here we're referring not to situations in which readers won't understand all the implications of the main point, but rather situations in which they literally won't know what you're talking about.

At other times, readers' preconceived ideas would lead them to reject your main point if you simply state it bluntly at the beginning. Figure 3 illustrates such a situation; department heads will naturally reject the idea that they should give up control of an activity unless they see good reasons for the change. In such cases, your readers will be more likely to accept your main point once they've examined the reasoning behind it.

There's little benefit in saying something your readers won't understand or accept. Therefore, in these cases, putting the main point at the end of the message has some advantages. One advantage is that the second most emphasized position in a message is the end. Since you can't use the position of strongest emphasis for your main point, why not use the second strongest? Even the reader who scans lightly through the message is fairly likely to notice what's said at the very end—that's certainly more likely than their noticing something said at any particular place in the middle.

From the writer's viewpoint, a message whose main point is at the end is somewhat more difficult to write than one whose main point is in the first sentence. But knowing how the message will end does help focus the organizing task and make things far easier than if there were no plan at all. In any case, remember that the indirect plan is not at all the same as the old tactic of "beating around the bush," a favorite approach of people who can't figure out how to say what they want. When its main goal is to inform, a message should be direct and concise whether it uses the indirect or direct plan.

When goals involve emotional reactions   On some occasions, your analysis may indicate that the reader is likely to react strongly and emotionally to the main point. Sometimes this reaction occurs when you must communicate unpleasant or unwanted news; other times you want to

```
DATE: March 8, 1983

TO: All Department and Division Heads

FROM: Francesca Fentini, Comptroller

SUBJECT: Newspaper and Magazine Subscriptions


     Many departments and divisions subscribe to newspapers,
magazines, and technical journals.  These periodicals provide
useful, sometimes essential, information to the people who make
important decisions in the company.  Therefore, the company has
underwritten the cost of these subscriptions, totaling more than
$35,000 per year.

     In many cases, sharing could eliminate the need for
duplicate copies of periodicals.  For example, the company
receives a total of 27 copies of the Wall Street Journal every
day, 34 copies of Time and 31 copies of Newsweek every week, and
10 or more copies of over a dozen technical journals every month.
Some of these periodicals are widely circulated and very heavily
used, and in those cases multiple copies are needed.  In other
cases, however, departments have ordered separate subscriptions
for one or two readers.  In at least one case, 10 copies of a
journal have been ordered for only 13 readers.

     It obviously benefits the company when employees have
access to important business and technical information, and any
steps that would reduce such access would clearly be against the
company's interests.  It does appear likely, though, that
increased sharing of periodicals would allow full access while
saving a substantial amount of money.

     Therefore, beginning with the July 1 budgeting period, all
periodical subscriptions will be channeled through the company
library.  Department heads should compile a list of periodical
subscriptions needed in each department and send the list to the
company librarian, who will investigate the possibility of
various departments' sharing copies when that's feasible.
```

Figure 3 An indirect-plan memo

arouse strong feelings in your reader, as in persuasion. In such cases, prepare the reader emotionally for the main point before you reveal it.

When your main goal is to deal with the reader's feelings about the message, the beginning and end usually focus on those feelings. The main information appears neither at the beginning nor the end; often it comes near the end. When the emphasis is on emotions, conciseness and directness become less important, and very clear, vivid writing is at a premium.

This principle doesn't mean that your writing should be aimlessly long-winded; on the contrary, each word should focus clearly on helping to shape the reader's response. But you should use more space to spell out your ideas in ways that will have emotional, as well as intellectual, impact.

Details of the techniques and organizational plans you can use in highly emotional situations will be discussed in Part III of this book.

Alternative-Elimination Plan

If a message's goal is to evaluate several possible courses of action and recommend one, the alternative-elimination plan may be best.

Using this plan, you first explain the situation and introduce the alternative courses of action. Then you eliminate the least suitable one by presenting evidence of its unsuitability. Then you eliminate the next-to-least suitable one, and the next, until only one course of action remains, which you then recommend. Figure 4 is an example.

Partial, rather than full, use of the alternative-elimination plan is best for some messages. Often, of several possible courses of action, all but two can be eliminated. For those two, however, a variety of factors, both positive and negative, must be considered. Then you can present the remaining discussion through the more familiar direct plan.

Chronological Plan

If you're tracing the history of a subject, it's often easiest to understand in a time sequence, or chronological order. Thus the chronological plan may be suitable.

Note two cautions about the chronological plan, however. First, when you use chronology, remember that not every sequence needs to be traced from prehistoric times all the way into the distant future. It's easy to get carried away with recounting history and go too far with it. Often two or three chronological steps tell as much of the story as any reader wants to know.

Second, chronology isn't the only way to explain a subject's development over time. Often, a subject's history can best be explained by dividing it into parts and discussing each part separately, regardless of the exact time sequence. Sometimes the parts can be presented chronologically; sometimes they're clearer if presented from some other viewpoint. Thus you should keep an open mind about possible organizational plans for material that involves sequences of events. Consider carefully what order will make the major points easiest to understand.

Combinations of Plans

Although brief messages normally stick to one of the plans discussed above, as messages get longer, organizational plans can become more complicated.

In a four- or five-page report, sometimes the overall pattern and most of the subdivisions are presented through the direct plan, but one subdi-

Dear Professor Hugill:

The Site Committee for the 1986 North-Midwest Regional Conference of the International Political History Association has concluded that the conference should be held in one of the Oshtemo-area motels that have conference facilities and overnight accommodations for the approximately 50 people expected to attend. Several area motels have the necessary space.

Three plans were suggested:

1. Meetings could be held in the SMU Student Center, and attendees could stay in vacant dormitory rooms.
2. Meetings could be held in the Student Center, and attendees could stay in local motels of their choosing.
3. Meetings could be held in a local motel, with attendees staying in that same motel.

Checking with the Residence Office at SMU, we found that arrangements cannot be made for attendees to stay in residence halls. Although students will be on Thanksgiving vacation at the time of the conference, nearly all rooms will contain the belongings of returning students, and it isn't practical to ask students to remove their belongings from the rooms for this brief period.

In the past, when attendees have stayed overnight some distance from the meeting site, many have complained about the difficulty of obtaining transportation to and from the site. Therefore, we've concluded that holding meetings in the Student Center, at least five miles from the nearest motel, isn't advisable. The cost of meetings room and meals at the Student Center and at local motels is nearly the same.

Thus it appeared most practical to select a local motel for meeting rooms as well as overnight accommodations. Managers of the several motels with the capacity for this group should be contacted immediately, since their schedules are often drawn up as much as a year in advance.

Cordially,

Dr. Georgia Crain, Chair
Site Committee

Figure 4 The alternative-elimination plan

vision (perhaps involving very technical information) is presented through the indirect plan. Similarly, one part of a message could be presented through the chronological plan, while the rest could be presented through the direct plan. Even in fairly short messages, hybrid or combination plans sometimes fit your needs best, so it's worthwhile to consider combining plans for the clearest possible explanation.

ORGANIZATIONAL PLANS FOR NONROUTINE MESSAGES

The organizational plans we've discussed in this chapter apply equally to routine and nonroutine messages. For routine messages, planning your organization may involve only a few seconds of thought before you begin writing. For nonroutine messages, such planning is part of an extensive planning stage, probably resulting in a written outline of your message.

When messages are short, about five pages or fewer, the first step in planning your organization is to think about the beginning and end. As messages get longer and content is more complicated, though, the logical sequencing of the body of the message becomes more important. In such cases, you should probably plan the sequence of your main points first and then consider the beginning and end. In fact, when experienced writers compose complex formal reports, they often write the body of the report before planning the beginning and end. Only when they have the body in front of them, they feel, can they effectively devise beginnings and endings. We'll discuss this approach further in Part IV of this book when we consider report writing.

FURTHER EXPLORATION

1. Think of situations in which you'd use the indirect plan for a message. Imagine ones in which the reader wouldn't understand the main point at all and ones in which the reader wouldn't accept the main point at first. Are such situations common or uncommon?

2. If you needed to ask a parent or close friend to loan you a substantial amount of money, how would you organize the message? Imagine the details of that situation and outline the message.

3. Minutes of meetings are traditionally organized chronologically. News reports of the same meetings are usually organized through the direct plan. Why are the two kinds of reports organized so differently?

Remember to keep working on the writing problems that begin on page 152.

11

The Job of Writing

What is written without effort is in general read without pleasure.
Samuel Johnson

The main rule of a writer is never to pity your manuscript. . . . I say that the wastepaper basket is the writer's best friend.
Isaac Bashevis Singer

God does not much mind bad grammar, but He does not take any particular pleasure in it.
Erasmus

E arlier we saw that good writers divide the job of writing into three steps: planning, writing, and revising. In this chapter, we investigate that three-step process in detail.

HOW EXPERIENCED WRITERS WRITE

Do experienced writers really plan, write, and revise? You bet they do! Novelists do. Textbook writers do, if they want students to learn something from their books. More to the point, experienced business writers do, when they're writing nonroutine messages.

As you remember from our discussion at the beginning of this book, business writers do two kinds of writing: routine messages and nonroutine messages. They write routine messages when they're very confident they can handle the writing problems and when they have to write quickly. In this situation, they rely on good writing habits to produce effective messages from first drafts. Nonroutine messages are the ones they don't feel completely confident about, the ones they expect to spend some time on, and the ones that are too important or too difficult to knock out in five minutes.

At this point in your study, you should probably treat all business messages as nonroutine. If your work will be graded, then it's nonroutine writing by definition. But beyond that, when you treat your practice work as nonroutine, you gain the maximum opportunity to learn from it. Careful attention to every point now will help you develop habits that will serve you well in the future.

No one, including you, expects to write nonroutine messages quickly. The question is how to spend extra time on a message most effectively. One possibility (which beginners tend to try first) is to put pen to paper immediately, but work very slowly and painstakingly, carefully considering every nuance of every word as they go along, to produce an outstanding message in one draft. That's the hardest possible way, and it's usually not very effective either. If you use that approach, you'll be sitting there with pen in hand trying to write down sentences and thinking about organizational tactics, spelling, transitions for smooth flow, your audience's viewpoint, word choice, grammar, and a hundred other details, and no one can think about that many things at once. Not only are the results depressing, since they don't represent the quality of work you can do, but the job itself is depressing, since it's terribly confusing to try to consider so much at once. That approach has nothing to recommend it, except that you've probably promised yourself that, as soon as you get through the cycle once, you'll quit, whether the result is any good or not. That's not a very mature approach.

Experienced writers have found that, if they use the plan-write-revise approach, they can complete nonroutine writing jobs in the same amount of time as usual, but with much less anxiety and frustration. And the results are nearly always better. Dividing the job into three separate steps allows you to take on a series of manageable decisions one at a time. When you're planning, you don't have to worry about writing-stage decisions, such as word choice. You'll take care of those decisions in the writing stage. And when you're writing a first draft, you can completely ignore decisions about spelling and grammar for the moment. You can do that because you'll go over that first draft later for spelling and grammar and other revision-stage matters.

The amount of time you spend on each of these stages may vary considerably with the circumstances. In short messages, you might typically spend about a third of the total time on each stage. In long messages, the planning stage might take only about a quarter of the total time, the writing stage only about a tenth of the time, and the revising stage about two-thirds of the time. Certainly, as messages get longer, you spend proportionally much more time on thorough revision.

Experienced business writers really do plan, write, and revise. They know it works. Isn't it worth a try?

THE PLANNING STAGE

The planning stage includes the steps you take before drafting the message. It's a thinking stage, for the most part, rather than a doing stage.

In the planning stage, you think through all the key elements of the communication situation: the audience, your communication goals, the information you want to communicate, possible message structures, and the specific content of the message. If the message is difficult or lengthy, you may make extensive notes during the planning stage and write a detailed outline. If the message is extremely straightforward and simple, you may be able to hold all your key planning conclusions in your head. Most messages fall midway between these two extremes, calling for some sketchy notes about the audience and goals and a brief content outline.

Audience Analysis

It's essential, before you begin writing, to picture the reader clearly in your own mind. Unless the communication seems personal to you, it's hardly likely to seem personal to the reader either. Try to visualize the reader personally as you write. This practice helps you see your writing as communication between you and your reader rather than just an exercise in putting words on paper. If your audience consists of many readers, picture a typical audience member in your mind.

In your audience analysis, besides mentally picturing your reader, you seek answers to some specific questions, as was done in Figure 1. First, what do your readers know about your subject? Are they familiar with its background, or is this the first they've heard of it? Will they immediately recognize why you're writing about this subject, or must you fill them in? Do they already understand the technical terminology of this subject?

```
Audience: all company employees who drive rental cars on company
business

        About 80% of rental car expenses arise from use of rental
cars in the Sales Department.  Salespeople have a very different
work style from in-plant executives, and they recognize that
procedures useful to other employees are often awkward or
impossible for them to implement.  They tend to be suspicious of
company directives and carefully maintain practices that allow
them to do their type of work successfully and conveniently, even
when the company frowns on such practices. They sometimes
perceive company policies as hostile to them and their work
goals.

        Nonsales users of rental cars are nearly all executives of
middle to high rank.  Compliance from such people cannot be
commanded, though in-plant executives tend to cooperate if they
remember the policy at the time it applies and if they understand
the reasons for it.
```

Figure 1 Notes on audience analysis

Second, how do your readers feel about this subject and about you as a communicator? Will your news be welcome or unwelcome, interesting or dull, expected or surprising? Will they probably believe you? What preconceptions do they hold about you and your organization?

Third, how do your readers view this subject? How does their perspective differ from yours? How must you compensate for their viewpoint?

Finally, now that you've drawn some conclusions about your readers, how can you maximize communication with them?

Goal Setting

One of the most important planning steps is to be specific and explicit about your goals. Remember that a message hardly ever has just one goal; even the simplest message usually has several interrelated goals. The clearer your goals are in your own mind, the clearer you should be able to make your message.

For example, if you want your readers to take action, you must determine exactly what that action is, as in Figure 2. Often the desired action has two components: the complete action they should take ultimately, and the initial step they should take immediately. If these actions aren't completely clear in your own mind (and it's surprising how often they aren't), then how can you possibly make them clear in the audience's

```
       Major goal: to induce users of rental cars to stop buying
    the supplemental insurance at company expense

       Secondary goals: (1) to assure readers that this is a
    rational policy based on careful analysis of costs vs. benefits,
    (2) to assure readers that their own liability won't be increased
    by this policy, and (3) to build confidence in the competence of
    the management of this department and the company
```

Figure 2 Notes on goals

mind? In addition, be clear about why the readers should take that action. How will they benefit? How will their organizations benefit? What must they know to understand these benefits and believe they'll obtain them?

Or if you want your audience to understand some idea, you must know exactly what the idea is. Writing the main idea down is a good way to verify that you've identified it correctly and completely. Writing objectifies it, gets it out in front of you where you can inspect it. If you can't write the main idea down in a quick note to yourself, then how do you expect to get it written down in a message to your audience? In support of the key idea, what other pieces of information will be needed? What evidence must be presented? What details will make the main idea clear and understandable?

Besides your knowledge goals, consider goals related to the readers' feelings. In nearly all messages, your goals include having them feel that you and your organization are competent and pleasant to deal with. Also, do your goals for this message include cultivating any particular feelings toward the subject? Do you want your readers to feel that your message says something good? Something bad? Must you overcome any preexisting feelings, as revealed by your audience analysis, to accomplish these goals?

Often your communication goals arise from someone's inquiry or request, which you're answering in your message. When this occurs, your goals are partly defined by the request you're responding to, but you should also ask yourself what motivated the request and what your reader will probably do with the information you provide. By doing so, you'll often find additional goals that your message should meet, namely, providing further help your reader probably needs or precluding a further request later on.

Information Gathering

At this stage in planning, consider what information you'll need to accomplish your goals. What evidence will you need to back up your points? What details will you need to clarify your points?

The planning stage is the time to gather the needed information. If the information is short and simple, maybe you can make usable notes on a single page. But if it won't fit on half a page or so, then you should seriously consider a simple note-card system. Note cards are standard 4" × 6" or 5" × 8" cards on which you jot the information you intend to use in your message. Put only one piece of information on each card. Cite exactly where each piece of information came from; many people put the source note in the upper right corner of each card, as in Figure 3. As you begin organizing your message, you can sort the cards into various orders. Since each card has only one piece of information on it, sorting is easy and straightforward.

Note cards have several advantages for planning your message. They're easy to keep track of, since they're distinctive in shape and stiffness. They're considerably easier to work with than a bunch of odd-sized scraps of paper, and they're easy to sort into a given order. For many long letters and memos and nearly all reports, they're essential.

In gathering information, your major sources are normally (1) your own knowledge; (2) your company's files; (3) various kinds of reports, including computerized reports; and (4) other people. To become an effective manager, you must be familiar with these sources of information.

If you know what kinds of information are in the files and how to get them, you'll often find historical information there. Most present-day situations have already been faced by someone in the past, and the files usually record that person's response. Old reports also contain a tremendous wealth of information. It's surprising how often today's assigned

Source: Karen S. Baecht
Acctg. Dept., phone
conversation 10/13/83

Total spent in mid-south sales district in fiscal '82 on $5.50/day rental car supplemental insurance: $3503.50. She had to search individual records to get figures; it would be too expensive to search out figures for other units.

Figure 3 Sample note card

report virtually duplicates one done several years ago, and that old report often contains extremely valuable historical information that can be used as background in the present report. In addition, the old report records someone's approach to the problem and sources of information, and these can be valuable supplements to your own thinking.

In your company, cultivate the acquaintance of experts in areas you may have to write about. A quick phone call to someone you know may save days of digging for a piece of information you need.

Planning the Organization

Once the information is available, you can begin thinking about how to organize it. Usually, using the direct plan, you'll think through the information and select the main point to go at the beginning, and then you'll put the remaining information into some logical order that's easy to understand.

If you've made note cards, organizing is very easy. You can sort them in various orders until you find the order that's simplest and easiest to understand. Once you've sorted your cards into the final order, number them consecutively so you can quickly resequence them if they're dropped on the floor.

If you think you may use some organizing plan other than the direct plan, now is the time to experiment with the other possibilities. Material oriented to the reader's emotions should be planned at this stage. For instance, in your outline don't just say "buffer paragraph," but plan the content of the buffer paragraph. That way, when you sit down to write, everything is laid out in front of you and you can concentrate completely on getting words on paper.

Outlining

If your message will be at all complicated, outlining can be one of the most time-saving steps in the planning process. Yet many people are very negative about outlining. Often, they're negative because they think of outlining as a formal process that depends on remembering when to use Roman numerals, capital letters, and lowercase letters as indices. But the outlining we're talking about is for your eyes only, so it can be as informal as you like.

At the minimum, an outline consists of sketchy notes that help you remember the sequence of points in your message. Often, however, you can get more value out of your outline through some indenting or other marking to indicate the message's major divisions, as in Figure 4. The original purpose of the numerals and letters in formal outlining was to help the writer see the pattern of the message. If you think they're useful, use them; otherwise, develop your own system to show the structure.

If you've used note cards in gathering information, you can outline simply by sorting your note cards into a given order. When you outline this way, you'll probably have to make some additional cards to include

```
Don't pay extra $5.50 for insurance on rental cars

    Standard insurance on rental car contract is $600

      deductible collision

    $5.50/day extra buys full coverage

Supplemental insurance is poor value for company

    $3503.50 spent in one sales district alone in '82

    Only 7 rental car accidents in whole company

Policy won't affect employees' personal liability

    Company will assume responsibility for first

    $600.00 loss in rental car accidents on

    company business

Expense account vouchers showing the supplemental

 insurance charge on rental cars won't be paid
```

Figure 4 Rough outline

points not already recorded. When you finish sorting, you'll have a small stack of cards for each major division of the message, and you can devise some method of indicating to yourself the order of the stacks. Many writers who outline this way label one corner of each card in pencil. In this system, the first division of the message is section A, and the cards in that small stack will be A1, A2, A3, and so on. Labels are similarly derived for sections B, C, and so on.

If a message is very short and simple, you could probably outline it adequately in your head, with nothing on paper. This is a very risky procedure, however, and it isn't recommended even for short messages. Here's why: the outline's major value is its objectivity; it's out in front of you where you can criticize it and check it for completeness and logical flow. When you make changes, they're down on paper where you can see them. An outline in your head is hard to envision clearly, and it's even harder to criticize and revise. When you make changes, you'll probably forget some of them. Even worse, you may forget the whole outline under the pressure of writing. Practically every experienced writer has had that happen, which is why such writers outline on paper. Then they know they have an outline.

THE WRITING STAGE

The whole purpose of the writing stage is to get a version of the message on paper so you can work it over and turn it into a good message. That's all. No one will ever see that first draft but you—not the typist, not the reader, not your teacher, not your boss. As you write the draft, you'll know with absolute certainty that it can't possibly be used as the final draft of the message. It's a first draft.

The first time you write a real first draft, you may find the task depressing. After all, you're not used to doing work that you know ahead of time won't be good enough to use. But after only one or two first drafts, you'll begin to sense the freedom and creativity that this step allows you, and soon you'll come to see it as relatively enjoyable. Every good writer first writes a first draft, then revises it into a good message.

Since the first draft is for your eyes only and will surely need extensive revision, feel free to make it rough and dirty. Use the paper that's most comfortable for you, even if it's not particularly pretty, and triple-space or even quadruple-space the lines so there's plenty of space for revising. Write the first draft as quickly as you can, straight through from beginning to end. Don't allow your old writing habits to slow you down. If you get stuck on a word or sentence, leave space for it and quickly go on. Filling in that space will be a job for the revising stage.

The reason for writing quickly is very simple: it lets you make the most of the substantial communication skills you have—speaking skills. The faster you write, the more your writing resembles speaking, and you're probably very good at explaining yourself clearly and smoothly aloud. If you slow down, then your thinking will very likely get way ahead of your writing, and you'll lose this natural clarity and smoothness.

If you can type, try typing your first drafts. Here the emphasis is on speed, and mistakes are no problem (as long as you can see what you meant). See Figure 5, for example. Your first-draft typing speed will quickly soar with a little practice. If you can't type, you may want to try dictating your first draft into a cassette tape recorder or any recording device you have available. You'll spend much of your career dictating messages, and you might as well start learning how to do it right now.

In short messages, it's a good idea to write from beginning to end, because that maximizes the natural smoothness and flow of your writing. But in longer messages, experienced writers usually draft one section at a time in just about any order. When they've assembled all the information for a given section, they write that section. Then when they've assembled all the information for another section, they write that one. If assembling the information is no problem, they often write the easiest section first as a way of getting started. In longer messages, they draft the beginning and the end last, so they can draft those sections with clear knowledge of what the sections in between actually say.

Since writing requires such a high degree of concentration, it's worthwhile to take actions or use aids that will help you concentrate.

DATE: February 3, 1983

TO: All employees

FROM: Andrea Claire, Executive Vice-President

SUBJECT: Car Rental Insurance

When you rent a car on company business, please don't pay the extra $5.50 a day for supplemental insurance. The standard insurance included in the fee for a rental car provides $600.00 deductible collision insurance; the $5.50 supplement raises this to full coverage.

The supplemental insurance is a poor value to the company. In one sales district alone last year, $3503.50 was spent on this coverage, and there were only seven accidents in the whole company involving rental cars, so the company will simply pay any amount up to $600 called for under the usual insurance.

This change will not change your personal liability in case of accident on company business in a rental car in any way. Expense account vouchers showing the $5.50 charge for supplemental insurance will not be honored.

Figure 5 Rough draft

One of the most useful is to select a place where you'll do all your writing. Do all your writing there and never use that place for other activities, certainly never for relaxing; whenever you go to that place, your mind will thus be cued to start concentrating. If you use a certain place for studying and never for relaxing, that may do for writing too.

When you revise your first draft, you'd prefer to approach it as though you'd never seen it before. A major purpose of revision is to find things you didn't notice when you wrote the draft, so you want to see it anew.

For that reason, it's a good idea to let the first draft cool for as long as possible before you go back to it. A day or two may be plenty. If possible, allow time in your work schedule for this. If you can't let the draft cool for very long, then at least take steps to put it completely out of your mind for a time. Do something else that's completely different. If you can only spare a few minutes between drafting and revising, be sure you spend those few minutes completely away from the writing process, doing something that's fun. Try to clear your mind of the draft as completely as you can.

THE REVISING STAGE

At this point, you have a completed first draft of your message ready to revise. You also have a set of notes you made in the planning stage on your audience analysis, goals, needed information, and outline, including your organizational plan. These are the basic tools for revision. You'll also need a pencil, a good eraser, a pair of scissors, and a stapler.

To revise effectively, be as objective about the first draft as possible. Most people get ego-involved with their writing and defensive in the face of criticism, even from themselves. Many experienced writers actually pretend they're revising someone else's writing; they then feel free to be brutally critical, as they suspect the reader will probably be. They believe that this approach helps them revise more effectively.

A basic principle of revising is to avoid completely recopying any substantial part of the message unless you are forced to. Don't make changes by recopying. If changes are small, pencil them in the margins or between the lines (did you remember to triple-space or quadruple-space?). If you have too much material to insert or you're shifting sentences and paragraphs from one place to another, cut the pages apart with scissors, put the pieces in the correct order, and staple the pieces to backing sheets. Make the process as easy as possible mechanically.

To be most effective in the shortest time, revise by reviewing the message for one specific factor, then reviewing it again for another factor, and so on until all factors have been checked. If you try to review the message once for all possible factors, you're again trying to think about too many things at once, and revision becomes frustrating and needlessly complicated.

It makes sense to revise for some aspects before others, because changes in certain aspects of the message may dictate major changes in others. Make all the big changes (such as general organization) first, so you're fairly confident in later steps (such as checking the spelling) that you're working with copy that's final. Here's a suggested order of revision steps.

1. Check for effective organization. First, review your preliminary notes on organization or your outline and make sure your plan worked out effectively. That is, should you now reconsider that plan? If another plan would be more effective, use your scissors to reassemble the draft in that new order.

Then check the draft for complete conformance to your plan. Are all the pieces in the right places, or are some points out of order? If you see problems, snip the draft apart and staple the pieces into the proper order.

Finally, verify that the major organizational signposts are in place. Does the beginning, for example, actually fit the message as it turned out, or does it suggest you'll provide more or less than the message really provides? If the end is significant, does it fit the actual message content? If the message has subdivisions, is the beginning of each subdivision clearly signaled for the reader, and does each beginning fit the subdivision's content? Add, or snip and staple, as necessary.

2. Check for clarity. Review your audience analysis notes so they're fresh in your mind; then put yourself in the reader's place and see whether or not the message is as clear as possible.

A great many business messages depend on the logically developed reasoning: a proposal and supporting evidence, a request and the reasons for it, an explanation why and how something happened. If the message, or part of it, fits this pattern, then does it describe all the necessary steps in the logic, and does the logic make sense? Is each of these steps fully explained in its proper place, or are the pieces of the argument scrambled? If any step in the logic has been omitted, is the step so obvious that it can remain unsaid (or have you described steps so obvious that they should be omitted)?

In addition, is the terminology familiar to your reader? If you have any doubt, use nontechnical terminology that you know the reader can understand. Finally, is the message's viewpoint likely to seem sensible? Does the message reflect your own viewpoint, or does it successfully reflect the reader's natural viewpoint toward the subject? If the message is cast in the reader's habitual reasoning patterns and assumptions, it will be easier to understand.

3. Check for tone. Carefully review your goals, concentrating on those relating to tone. Then review your audience analysis notes and put yourself in the reader's place. Thinking as the reader would, review the message to be sure it accomplishes its tone and image goals. Make any changes that will help it achieve these goals.

Then, still thinking as the reader, review the message again, looking for parts that may unintentionally jar the reader. Will the reader draw inferences you didn't intend? Could something possibly be seen as offensive or belittling? Is the implied relationship between writer and reader appropriate to the situation?

4. Check for readability and continuity. By this time, most of the basic phrasing of the final message is probably in place. Probably your scissoring and stapling is finished. Now you can polish the phrasing.

First, review the message, maybe several times, looking for ways to clarify and smooth the phrasing. Can a simpler or clearer word be substituted for a hard one? Can rephrasing a sentence emphasize the key phrase more clearly? Can rephrasing clarify the logical relationship between two sentences? When you find passages that somehow don't seem smooth or easy to read, try various ways of rephrasing them.

Second, go through the message paragraph by paragraph. In each one, identify the main-idea sentence and verify that each other sentence logically relates to it. Then be sure that each sentence contains an explicit reference to the sentence before. Review "Sentence Transitions" in Chapter 9, if necessary.

Finally, verify that each paragraph begins with a clear reference to the preceding one. Review "Paragraph Transitions" in Chapter 9 for details.

5. Check for correct grammar, spelling, and punctuation. At this point and not before, you're ready to consult your dictionary and grammar manual. Until now you've been making changes that could still introduce additional problems in mechanics. Now all those changes are finished, and you're ready to do the final polishing.

When you find a passage that may contain a mechanical error, the best procedure is to look up the possible error in your dictionary or manual and correct it. Not only will you ensure the correctness of the passage, but you'll also be learning how to write such a passage correctly the next time. An alternative, of course, is to rephrase the passage to avoid the word or structure that's creating the problem.

Your draft may look something like Figure 6 after the revision stage.

```
DATE: February 3, 1983

TO: All Employees

FROM:  Andrea Claire, Executive Vice-President

SUBJECT: Refuse Supplemental $5.50 Insurance on Rental Cars


     Next time you step up to the car rental counter on company
business, please refuse the $5.50 per day supplemental insurance.
If amounts must be paid under the car rental agencies' standard
$600.00 deductible insurance, the company will simply pay them.
This change will not affect your personal liability in any way.

     The supplemental insurance, which raises the collision
coverage to full coverage, is a poor value to the company.  One
sales district alone spent $3503.50 on this coverage last year,
and there were only seven accidents involving rental cars in the
whole company during that period.
```

Figure 6 Final version

THE PRODUCTION PROCESS

Knowledgeable and effective use of modern methods of producing messages on paper will save you a tremendous amount of communication time during your career. Therefore, even though you may not have access to the most modern devices now, you should anticipate using them and prepare to use them quickly. In this section we look at the new technology of word processing and how you can save time by dictating your messages.

Using Word Processing Systems

Although many offices still use standard typewriting methods to produce written messages, most will soon be using computerized word processing equipment to speed up the task.

Computerized word processing differs from standard typing methods in two principal ways. First, when the message is typed at the keyboard, it's recorded electronically rather than just being typed onto paper. Although some word processors do produce a paper copy of the message as it's typed, more often the typed characters are displayed on a video screen. Once the message is recorded, it can be played back to print a copy on paper at any time.

Second, the message as recorded can be changed very easily, usually with just a few coded keystrokes. Letters, words, even whole paragraphs can be added, deleted, changed, or moved from one place to another very quickly and easily. Margins can be reset to be wider or narrower, spacing can be varied, other changes can be made in the typing format, and the processor almost instantly readjusts the recorded text for the next printing. Because changes and corrections can be made so quickly, computerized word processing often allows much quicker turnaround of your message at each production step. Perhaps even more importantly, since each round of revision involves no retyping, it can't introduce new typing errors into the message.

As a communicator, you'll write or dictate your first draft, and a word processing operator will enter it into the computer's memory and give you a rough typed copy, triple-spaced, with very wide margins for revision. You'll mark revisions on the rough copy, and the operator will enter your changes and quickly produce a new rough copy for your approval. Since changes can be quick and easy, you may find it useful to go through two or three rounds of revision and reprinting rather than trying to do the whole job in one round. No matter how many changes you make, no one will ever have to retype your message from beginning to end and thus introduce new errors. When you feel your message is ready for final typing, you'll instruct the operator to print it, giving any special instructions about format that are needed.

Complete retyping of a message is costly, time consuming, and error-prone. Computerized word processing eliminates retyping and makes the production process much more flexible and much better adapted to the writer's needs. In an organization that uses it wisely, its direct saving through reduced typing costs is far overshadowed by its value in making written communication easier and more effective for executives.

Using Dictating Machines

Probably no one has felt comfortable using a dictating machine for the first time. You didn't expect to type expertly the first time you tried, and you should similarly expect to spend some time learning to use a dictating machine well. Once you learn, dictating will save you a tremendous amount of time, so the learning is well worthwhile.

Learning to use a dictating machine is a two-step process. First, you must learn the mechanics of operating the machine, and, through it, giving information to your typist. Second, you must learn to integrate dictation into your process of written communication.

The mechanics of dictating The first step in learning to dictate is to become completely familiar with the controls and functions of your particular machine. Most machines include at least a start-stop button, a volume control, and some method of coding the locations on the recording of beginnings and endings of messages and any correction notes. Before you use your machine seriously, these controls should be so familiar that using them is almost automatic to you. If your organization provides training in your machine's use, take advantage of the first opportunity. Such training can quickly familiarize you with the machine and speed up the process of learning to use it effectively.

A dictating machine is intended to help you transmit information to a typist conveniently. Therefore your dictation is a dual communication: you're communicating the message itself to its audience, and you're also communicating instructions to your typist. If you remember your typist's communication needs as you dictate, you can considerably improve the quality of the final message.

First and foremost, the typist must be able to hear what you're saying clearly and distinctly. Hold the microphone at the prescribed distance from your mouth and adjust the volume control for maximum clarity. Speak naturally, but distinctly, especially at the ends of sentences, where most people's voices tend to drop. Use the on-off switch to avoid long pauses while you're thinking or looking at your notes. Most beginners' recordings consist of long passages of heavy breathing, punctuated occasionally by ear-splitting throat clearings, "uh's," and a word or two of the message itself here and there. Try to get past this stage through practice sessions before you try to use the machine seriously. And spot-check your recordings from time to time to be sure you haven't fallen into bad habits.

Before the message begins, your typist must know how you want it transcribed. Is it a letter, memo, or report? Do you want a rough copy for correction, or do you want final copy? Does it go on the organization's standard letterhead stationery with the usual single carbon copy, or do you want something special? Put these specifications at the beginning of your message.

Finally, your typist must be informed very clearly about the spelling of any unfamiliar names or terms, capitalization, punctuation, and beginnings of sentences and paragraphs. You'll soon learn how much of this information to provide, but at first provide too much rather than too little. Your typist must also know as soon as possible when you've changed your mind about any phrasing; use the machine's correction marking to signal such changes.

You and your typist will be working as a team to produce your message, and in many organizations you'll be working with this same typist time after time. Therefore, take time to give your typist a quick course in the working methods you find effective. Most typists feel, as you probably did when you started this book, that having to revise indicates a weak writer rather than an experienced one. If you explain what you're doing, however, your typist should be happy to provide quick rough-draft-quality transcription of your dictation for you to revise. Once your typist understands how valuable the planning-writing-revising process is, you should be able to get the kind of typing you need at each stage.

Dictation and the writing process

Dictation and the writing process   Dictation is part of the writing stage in the writing process. If you intend to dictate your message, then you must execute the planning stage completely and (at least in the beginning) somewhat more carefully than usual. Before you pick up the microphone to start dictating, have a written outline of your message in front of you.

An outline is more important to a dictator than a writer, because when you're dictating, it's very cumbersome to check what you've just said. To get the most benefit, keep dictating quickly and smoothly throughout your message. Because an outline helps you keep track of what's been said and what comes next, some sort of outline is essential.

Dictating is advantageous in the writing stage, because it lets you take maximum advantage of your present oral communication skills. It lets you draft the message at your normal speaking rate and get the resulting smoothness and flow into your message. It does not, however, make any other magical improvements in your writing. All the voice inflections, for example, that made the message so much clearer and more enthusiastic on the recording will be completely flattened when the message is reduced to typed characters on paper.

Therefore, plan to revise dictated material just as you'd revise material drafted on paper. In fact, as you're learning to dictate, treat all your messages as nonroutine and plan to revise them. At the beginning of each message, tell the typist you want triple-spaced rough copy for revision. Later, when you're more confident, you can treat many short dictated messages as routine. Even then you'll probably continue making at least short notes of your message before dictating. At that point, you'll get the full benefit of dictation, and it will really speed up your writing.

FURTHER EXPLORATION

1. How applicable do you think the techniques and working methods of novelists and other professional writers are to your own business writing? Or is your writing too different from theirs to benefit from their methods?

2. Analyze your instructor as an audience for your messages. In your analysis, what questions would lead to helpful information? Make notes of your conclusions. Will this analysis be helpful in your future writing?

3. The next time you write a business message, write notes on your goals first. Did these notes specifically help in your writing and revising?

4. Experiment to find the very quickest way to write a first draft. Everyone's approach to writing is different, so keep experimenting until you find your own fastest drafting method. How much time can you save in the writing stage?

5. What are some good ways to let a first draft cool when you can't wait very long before revising?

6. Revise a finished piece of your own writing as though it were a first draft. Work quickly, checking one aspect of it at a time. Can you improve it significantly?

7. How much of the process described in this chapter do you think applies to preparing a speech or other oral presentation? Outline the steps you'd use.

8. What steps, like those described in this chapter, would help you prepare for an important telephone call or face-to-face conversation? Outline a working plan.

The writing problems for Part II begin on the following page.

WRITING PROBLEMS

1.   Assume that you must obtain the instructor's permission to enroll in a business-communication course. Write your prospective instructor a short, persuasive letter outlining your educational background, business and writing experience, major or projected studies, and career plans. Select facts that will enable your instructor to evaluate your achievements and decide favorably about your potential abilities. Show your instructor that you have the background and skills needed to profit from the course.

2.   Begin keeping a file of all nonpersonal mail you receive during the next month. Include all direct-mail advertising, business letters, letters and notices from your school and employer, and every other written message you get, except for mail from your parents or friends and personal mail that you don't want the instructor to review. At the end of the month, select five of these messages that you think are particularly interesting—because they illustrate either good or bad communication principles—and write a memo to your instructor about these five, indicating what's good or bad about them. Be specific; say why they're good or bad and how they could be improved. Submit the memo and the five messages to your instructor.

3.   Select five ads for products you're interested in and write to each of the advertisers for further information about the products. To increase your chances of getting a reply, select ads for special-interest products rather than ads in general-circulation magazines for consumer goods that are sold through mass distribution channels. Check ads in hobby magazines or special-interest publications.

To help get a custom reply that will be interesting to analyze later in the term, ask at least three specific questions about the product. Try to ask questions that you think might not be answered on the standard printed fact sheet or brochure that the advertiser may send you. Prepare and mail the five letters, then turn in copies to your instructor for evaluation. If you want to keep salespeople away from your door, avoid ads for insurance, encyclopedias, and investment opportunities. (See also problem 12, Chapter 18, and problem 1, Chapter 20.)

4.   At the end of the term, you and your roommates moved out of the house you rented at 3207 Mason Street. As informal treasurer of the group, you paid the bills, and this morning you received the forwarded bill for an additional month's trash hauling. Apparently, whoever was supposed to cancel the trash hauling forgot to do it. Down in the fine print on the bill you found the statement, "Accounts may be terminated only in person or in writing; no telephone terminations will be accepted." Since you don't have time to drive to the office of Gregory and Sons Hauling, Inc. (843 Tenth Street, your city), write a letter that will do the job. Enclose your check for the current month's service.

5. On a trip to Colorado last summer, you bought a ski jacket at Boulder Mountain Supply (2440 Johnson Street, Boulder, CO 80917) for your friend Barbara back home. When she tried it on, you found that you had guessed her size wrong—the jacket was just too big. In addition, she says she'd prefer a style of jacket that's available locally at a much lower price. You don't doubt that Boulder Mountain's jacket is a good value, but it isn't the type of jacket Barbara wants. Boulder Mountain said it would accept the return of the jacket for a full refund of $67.95 plus $2.41 tax. Attach your letter to the outside of the package, enclosing the sales slip (which you saved). They should credit your bank card account.

6. Your school mails reports of students' grades directly to home addresses. You've found that grades usually arrive about three weeks after the end of exams. Exams have now been over for seven weeks, and you're still awaiting the results. Perhaps processing has been delayed or the school has your address wrong. In any case, you'd like to see your grades as soon as possible. Write a letter to the campus Records Office.

7. The six-month history of your new business, College Copy and Typing Service (1532 College Avenue, your city), has been one of growth beyond your highest expectations. By applying the latest word processing techniques and equipment (allowing you to underbid the competition for the large-volume jobs), you've grown from a small office doing walk-in trade to a business with eight full-time word processing operators and five other employees.

Recently, you noticed that some of the operators bring their own dictionaries and other reference books, but others have to borrow such reference books when needed. To maintain a businesslike setting, you've decided to supply operators with spelling dictionaries at company expense. The one you've always preferred is *Quick Speller*, published by Eastern Press (233 Beacon Street, Boston, MA 02115). It's in a convenient 8½" × 11" format, which makes finding a word very easy, and it's uncluttered by pronunciation guides and other information that word processing operators don't need. Draft a letter ordering 12 copies to be shipped immediately, billed to your office.

8. The Richard E. Herttua Real Estate Agency (443 West Spring Street, Davenport, IA 52809) buys its normally small quantities of office supplies locally, but for special projects and large purchases it takes advantage of the volume savings offered by Foti and Paul Office Supplies (P.O. Box 2876, Chicago, IL 61818). Next month the agency plans a mass mailing to all residents of the district, including a form letter with individually typed inside addresses. Allowing for moderate spoilage, they'll need 18 reams of 20-pound rag bond stationery, 16 boxes of number 10 envelopes of equivalent quality, and 24 carbon ribbon cartridges for Electric Model 72 typewriters. The agency has established credit with Foti and Paul and requests billing with the normal quantity and early payment discounts. Write the order.

9. As program chairperson of your state's Future Business Leaders Club, you're in charge of the state convention that's scheduled for a week from Friday in your city. This morning you received a call from the manager of the hotel where the convention is scheduled saying that a fire occurred last night, and extensive smoke damage will require about a month to repair. Frantic calls to the three other establishments with facilities and meeting rooms for the 143 registered delegates (and 25 or so others who usually show up) found them fully reserved for that weekend. You'll have to call off the convention.

Your group doesn't have the budget for 143 telephone calls all over the state, and your college couldn't help you on this. But the college has offered to let you use its word processing facilities to type a form letter to all 143 registrants. You have a list of names and addresses. Write the form letter to notify registrants that the conference is cancelled.

When the hotel manager called about the fire, she offered your group the first priority on a Friday and Saturday of your choice after repairs are completed. Unfortunately there's no assurance that repairs will be completed before the end of the school term, so you can't set a new date now. You'll notify registrants of the new date as soon as possible. In the meantime, you'll hold each registrant's $20 registration fee. Anyone who wants this fee refunded should write to you, and you'll send it.

10. Revise the following memo.

```
DATE: September 19, 1983
TO: All business faculty
FROM: Business Students Association
SUBJECT: Meeting Announcement
```

Please read the following message to your classes:

The Business Students Association is an organization of interested business students dedicated to the development of further knowledge about business careers, enhancement of necessary business career skills, and further contacts for the beginning careerist. The club is now accepting applications for new members. See any member for forms.

The next meeting will be on October 23, at which Mr. Jordan A. Orosz of Orosz Associates will speak. Interested students are invited to attend.

Consider the following questions: Is there a more effective way to reach business students at your school than by asking instructors to read announcements? (Do instructors really read such announcements?) What information will motivate students to apply for membership? (Imagine reasonable details that may be necessary.) What information will students need to attend the meeting next month? (Provide reasonable details.) What's the best way to organize this kind of message? What's the best format to use? After deciding how to communicate this information most effectively, produce the message.

11. Since your high school days, you've been a fan of the TV news magazine program *60 Minutes*. You like the in-depth coverage of controversial issues, and you've often wished that other networks would screen similar programs. That's why you were delighted last night to see a new national program, *10 PM*, with reporter Jane Byther as host. Topics included a confrontation between representatives of independent truckers and other trucking groups and an investigative report on pollution caused by common practices of municipal sanitary districts. The style was hard-hitting and interesting, and the material was the kind that's seldom explored on the normal news programs. You especially enjoyed the show's production gimmick: at the beginning, the end, and the commercial breaks, you got to see and hear the action in the control booth as the director cued changes in the picture and sound. Although you've never written a fan letter before, this time you want to do what you can to encourage the network to continue the show, and you also want to encourage the local station to continue carrying it. Supplying reasonable details from your imagination, write a fan letter for this show, addressed to your local network TV station.

12. In a small business management course last semester, you wrote a term paper on management problems in small machine shops. Mr. Ryan Menchinger, co-owner of Hermel Die Casting, Inc. (23 First Street, Eau Claire, MI 49111), spent two afternoons showing you how his company works and answering questions in detail. In addition, he lent you copies of three issues of *American Metal Market*, whose articles you found very helpful. The information he provided became the core of your paper. He asked you to return the magazines, and he wanted to see a copy of your paper.

Now that you've submitted the paper, write a thank-you letter to send to Mr. Menchinger along with the three magazine issues. You've forgotten to stop by the professor's office to pick up the graded term paper (you got a B+), and you don't have a backup copy of it. When you get it back, you'll make a copy for Mr. Menchinger.

13. Large companies that advertise on national television have a problem when people write in and suggest advertising ideas. Ads are planned months, sometimes even years, in advance, and they're planned in integrated, systematic ad campaigns that support companies' current goals. Ad ideas from consumers seldom fit into campaigns that are in the planning stage, so they're seldom helpful. But even worse, the fact that an idea has been submitted exposes the company to the risk that the consumer's idea will be similar to one that's already in the works.

To grasp this problem, put yourself in the position of a consumer who's become interested enough in a product to write down an advertising idea and send it to the company. The company rejects your idea, but six weeks later you see that company using almost exactly the same idea in a national ad. You've heard about the monumental costs of these ads, and you find it irritating that the company seemed to steal your idea—maybe even more irritating that their rejection of the idea may have been a ploy to avoid paying you for it.

You can easily understand, then, that a company doing a lot of TV advertising finds itself in this situation fairly often, and it wouldn't be unusual for submitters of ideas to sue for payment. Worse, if the company gets into this position, it would be vulnerable to purposely dishonest lawsuits. Suppose a friend of yours works at an advertising agency and you could find out what ads a company is going to run three or four months hence. All you would have to do is to send in a nearly identical idea (as though you were an innocent consumer), wait for the ad to run, and sue for payment.

To see how companies handle this problem, write to two or three large national consumer-goods companies that advertise heavily on TV and ask them to send you a copy of the form letter, if any, that they use to reply to submitters of ad ideas. Identify yourself as a student of business communication preparing a report for your class.

Alternatively, think of a plausible advertising idea that a large company could use and submit it. Then see how the company responds.

When you receive the replies, report as your instructor directs.

14. As a buyer for Applied Microsystems Company (20735 Old Salem Road, Woodburn, OR 97072), you're responsible for soliciting bids from potential vendors (sellers) on supplies and materials. When a department submits a requisition for items, you compile a list of potential vendors and send each vendor a Request for Bid (RFB) on those items. The RFB is a set of forms listing the items sought (with space to enter the price bids) and requesting information on the terms and conditions of sale. Since much of your work is on federal government contracts, RFBs for orders totaling more than $5000 include forms on which vendors must document compliance with federally required equal opportunity and affirmative action employment programs.

Recently, several small orders (under $5000) have been won by S & L Electronics (45 Low Way, Daleville, IN 47334), a regional supplier. Consequently, you've included S & L on the list of potential vendors for a much larger order. Apparently, your assistant has received their bid, because this letter was on your desk for signature this morning. Certainly you can word the message better.

Dear Mr. Lemessurier:

You made several errors in your response to our recent RFB #5530-91. You specified your bid on nearly all the items on the RFB, but you left certain items blank. If you're to become a successful bidder on orders of this size, you will have to understand that you must bid on all the items; our company cannot be expected to pick and choose item by item within a single order. Successful bidders on orders of this size would certainly realize that they often have to provide some items in an order at a small loss, making up the difference on other items that can be supplied more profitably. Unless you bid on all items, your response cannot be considered seriously.

In addition, you did not return the federally required compliance forms. If you have determined on principle not to provide this information, then please let us know so we can drop your company from further consideration as a vendor for orders totalling over $5000. If not, then you should know that governmental regulations force us to document compliance by all vendors of orders for more than $5000. I know it's a lot of trouble to produce those figures, but if you don't show compliance, we cannot order from you. Don't blame us; blame Uncle Sam.

I must reiterate that before we can consider your response to any RFB, you must be completely responsive to the request. When you do not respond fully, our hands are tied.

Cordially,

15. Mr. Garrett G. Hartsuyker, of Garrett Stationers (Providence Square, Lebanon, IN 46052), has sent you (Century Distributors, Inc., 28 Market Avenue, Lafayette, IN 47902) a very prickly letter. He says your bill is nearly $500 higher than it should have been for the paper and office supplies he buys from you at wholesale, and he says he won't pay until you get it straightened out. Indeed, he hasn't paid his monthly balance due during the last two months. Your normal quick credit check showed Garrett Stationers with a top credit rating, so other than stopping shipment on further orders and continuing normal past-due billing notices, you took no action. Now you must reply to Mr. Hartsuyker's letter.

Your investigation shows that Garrett Stationers purchased $1655.15 worth of supplies from you in December and January. Further examination of the hand records of that period turns up a return shipment from Garrett of $488.18 that was never credited. It's impossible at this point to tell why; perhaps a clerk mislaid it, or maybe two sheets of paper stuck together when someone was posting returns. In any case, you've lectured the staff members (again) at this week's staff meeting, so they'll be even more careful than usual for a while.

Since the mistake in billing was your fault, you won't charge Mr. Hartsuyker the usual late-payment penalty if he'll remit $1166.97 by return mail. You'll release shipment on his current orders as soon as you receive payment.

Write Mr. Hartsuyker. Besides explaining the above information, tell him that, if mistakes ever occur in his account again, you should receive payment at least for the amount he knows to be due. When he refuses to pay anything at all on a partially disputed bill, then you have to put a hold on his current orders, and his nonpayment fouls up your accounting process. At the worst, his nonpayment could lead to a stain on his fine credit rating. After all, you're not trying to cheat him; if you make mistakes, they're honest errors.

16. As Customer Relations Manager for Kronco Recreation Equipment Company (4265 Dayton Drive, Lorain OH 44055), you've received a letter from D. V. Hetue (355 Waylon Drive, Huntington, WV 25724), saying she purchased one of your company's large backyard swing sets through a local discount house. After assembling the unit and setting the four vertical posts in concrete in her backyard, Ms. Hetue discovered that the trapeze bar (one of four swinging attachments) was missing from the box. Obviously it was too late to return the set to the store, so she wrote you a very irritated letter. The swing set was a present for her seven-year-old daughter, and the birthday was marred by the missing part.

Your company's view is that, in any system involving human beings, errors are bound to occur sooner or later. (You can't blame Ms. Hetue for being upset that the error happened to her.) You've found that very few packing errors occur with your line of swing sets. Even so, your company takes care to hire mature, conscientious (higher-paid) packers to ensure correct packing. Perhaps the missing trapeze bar was removed at the store before the sale; had the box been opened? This is the usual cause of shortages. All packed sets are inspected for completeness before shipment. An inspection slip should have been included in the package; request that she return the inspection slip in a return-addressed envelope you'll include, so that the responsibility for the shortage can be assigned. Write Ms. Hetue that you've processed a shipping order marked "Expedite" (immediate shipment) for the trapeze bar. She didn't mention whether the mounting hardware (hooks and chains) was missing also; just in case, you've added that to the shipping order.

17. Since a purchasing department is constantly in communication not only with every other department of the company but also with outside suppliers whose goodwill is vital, effective written messages are important. Thus, one of your jobs as Assistant to the Director of Purchasing is to spot-check the memos and letters from your department's seven buyers. In this way, your boss hopes to identify trouble areas before they develop.

In this afternoon's review session, you found the following memo from one of your buyers. When you show it to your boss tomorrow morning, also show her how you would have written it.

DATE: December 16, 1983
TO: Bernard L. Laux, Vice-President, Finance
FROM: Carrol Findahl, Buyer
SUBJECT: Requisition for Worksheet Forms

We regret to inform you that procurement under your recent requisition number 99304 for eight-column worksheet forms has been delayed. In this requisition, your department requested that the worksheets be purchased from a specific designated vendor, V&Z Printing Company. As requisition instruction 17.D.6.a indicates, items can be ordered from designated vendors only when such a procedure can be justified in the interests of the company. Normally, items can be purchased at the most favorable price though our standard sources of supply. Only when items are of special design or are not available through standard sources is a designated vendor permitted. There was no indication in the appropriate space on the requisition that this was the case. If it is the case, then perhaps your subordinate who filled out the form neglected to provide that information. It should be indicated how this eight-column worksheet form is different from standard forms of that type and why V&Z Printing is the only supplier who can provide a satisfactory item to our company. There must be a clear showing before a buyer has authority to accept a designated vendor.
These procedures can be abrogated only under emergency procurement conditions as certified by a vice-president of the company.
Purchasing can provide quick, efficient, and economical procurement only when departments provide us with full information and follow company procedures. Delay and increased costs inevitably follow attempts to undercut established company purchasing policy.

18. As Credit Manager of Haroldsen's Department Store (Main and Washington Streets, your city), you're faced with a tough one. According to a letter on your desk yesterday morning, Mr. Norman F. Rancour, Jr. (2893 Old Charleston Pike, Huntington, WV 25704) ordered a $349.50 modern oak coffee table from your catalog last May 12. The table was a housewarming gift for Mr. and Mrs. Roman J. Virchis (1626 Lake Robin Avenue, your city), two extremely important clients of his. In his May letter, he asked you to deliver the table immediately and charge the price, plus tax and special gift handling and delivery fees, to his United Bank Card. Since he intended to list the cost as a business expense, he's been waiting ever since for the charge to appear on his bank card statement, and it hasn't appeared. He's worried that perhaps the order was never delivered to Mr. and Mrs. Virchis.

The results of yesterday's investigation are in, and the worst has happened. The order was delivered all right, but the reason Mr. Rancour hasn't received an accounting is that the charge was made to the Virchis's account instead of his. His gift card was enclosed as requested. It seems the Virchises have an account directly with your store, and whoever wrote up the shipment ticket was in too big a hurry to read Mr. Rancour's letter carefully. It happens that the clerk who initialed the shipment ticket has since left the job, so there's no way to inquire further.

In your position, you can readily understand that this situation is embarrassing to all. Mr. and Mrs. Virchis received a gift with a bill attached, and apparently they were motivated by politeness not to raise questions. Mr. Rancour's attempt to cultivate two important clients certainly has not been helped. And of course Haroldsen's has suffered a black eye. Haroldsen's ability to provide special services is precisely what attracts its top customers.

At this point there's nothing you can do to turn back the clock and undo the damage, but at least you can help rescue Mr. Rancour. After crediting the Virchis account for the total of $362.90 and charging that amount to Mr. Rancour's United Bank Card account, write Mr. and Mrs. Virchis a letter that will satisfy them about Mr. Rancour's good intentions. You will, of course, do this while preserving Haroldsen's fine reputation. (See also the following problem.)

19.   Now that you've written the Virchises (see the preceding problem), you must explain the situation to Mr. Rancour. It won't be easy, but it must be done. It's against store policy to give Mr. Rancour anything more than your best explanation—no gifts, discounts, or other gimmicks. Your goal is to explain the situation clearly (so Mr. Rancour can take steps to rehabilitate his standing with the Virchises) and to retain any further business Mr. Rancour may have in your city.

20.   For the manager of the Surf Harbor Inn (14391 Harbor Boulevard, San Diego, CA 92112), write Ms. Thelma Dauz, Facilities Coordinator, AGVA National Convention, sending 2600 copies of your motel brochure and special AGVA reservation return cards you've had printed for enclosure in the convention announcement package she'll send to each AGVA member. Ms. Dauz will be writing additional promotional material for the convention, so you'll want to suggest points she could use, selected from the brochure. Be sure to point out that AGVA members should use the reservation cards to get the special rates (printed on the cards) of $32 for a single room and $20.50 for a double room per person per night. Write Ms. Dauz at her business address (Administrative Services Department, Jabar Services, Inc., P.O. Box 419, Orange, CA 92666). These main themes are presented in detail in the brochure:

- Extra-large rooms, all beds king-size
- An ocean or harbor view from every room
- Olympic-size pool and both ocean and harbor beachfront
- Recreational facilities, including tennis courts, 18-hole pitch-and-put golf course, and sailboat rentals for guests
- Romero's Harbor Restaurant for seafood, which has been named in lists of America's best restaurants
- La Casita Restaurant, gourmet Mexican food
- The Surf Room, with nightly entertainment
- Seven convention meeting rooms, with thoroughly up-to-date facilities for groups the size of AGVA
- Only 10 minutes from San Diego Airport and 15 minutes from San Diego Zoo and Sea World; free guest van service for airport and major tourist attractions

21. Revise the following form letter; a typist will fill in the blanks before mailing each copy.

```
This is to inform you that your membership in Valley Racquet
Club will expire on the last day of _____. Unless
you pay the annual dues of $_____ by the first day of
_____, you will forfeit all privileges of
membership. Reinstatement of membership at that time will
require repayment of the $_____ initiation fee.
    Plans for the coming year call for a much needed
refurbishing of the locker room area, with new paint and
refurbished lockers. In addition, the budget includes funds
for completing the club room and entertainment area with wet
bar that was begun three years ago and installing the nine
new handball courts. The new pool and sauna should be in use
before the end of the year.
    As a reminder, note that, for the above amount, you're
entitled to full use of all VRC facilities seven days a week
as you wish on a first-come, first-served basis. No further
court fees or other fees are charged.
```

22. To provide writing exercise for a fellow student, write a "bad-example" first draft of a letter or memo. To be a good exercise, your version should illustrate poor writing clearly enough so others can see what's wrong with it, but it should be challenging enough so the problems it presents in the revision stage are more than just trivial. Make the project understandable either by adding an explanatory paragraph or by including situational details in the draft so that the student can understand the situation. To constitute a good exercise, your bad-example draft must be completely self-explanatory. (See also the following two problems.)

23. Exchange bad examples (the kind written in the preceding problem) with another student and revise that student's bad-example draft. Be sure you identify all the problems it poses (there may be more than one) and write a draft that communicates the message well. If necessary, supply reasonable details from your imagination to solve the problem. (See also the following problem.)

24. Exchange papers with a different student after completing the preceding two problems. You'll receive both that student's bad example and a partner's revision of it. Write a critique of both papers in a memo to your instructor. Explain what problems the bad example poses and what techniques you'd use to improve it. Also evaluate how well the revision solves the problems. Detail any suggestions for further revision that would make the message as effective as possible. Be complete and to the point.

Extended
Case Studies

INTRODUCTION

The three extended case studies presented here are an alternative way to practice the writing skills you've learned in this book. Each case consists of a number of writing opportunities that all relate to the same situation. As you continue to work on a case during your study, you become familiar with the communication situation and more comfortable dealing with the problems it involves.

The ABMC case and the Education and Training case provide most of the writing practice for a semester's study. Problems are included that provide practice with the full range of writing situations discussed in the remainder of this book. Each case may be supplemented by selected writing problems from individual chapters as needed.

The Forms Design minicase is a set of seven writing problems suitable for beginning or intermediate practice as you study Chapters 7–13.

THE ABMC CASE

Assume the identity of Pat Dixon, Administrative Assistant to Peter Santos, North Central District Sales Manager for the American Business Machines Company. ABMC manufactures and markets a complete line of typewriters, dictation equipment, duplicators, copying machines, and other office word processing equipment.

You've just completed your eight-week orientation session at the company headquarters, and this is your first morning on the job in the North Central district. Mr. Santos spends about an hour describing the kinds of work you'll be doing over the next few months. In the beginning, he says, he'll simply assign you specific tasks to perform, but as time goes on he'll assign you a number of other tasks to perform on your own initiative. He introduces you to the office staff of 6 people and indicates that you'll be meeting the 19 salespeople over the next week or two as they come into the office.

You spend the rest of the morning looking over the office policy manual and a copy of the sales catalog.

Notes: In the problems that follow are materials that realistically simulate information that Pat Dixon might find in the in-basket. If you're asked to repond to a letter or memo received in the office, you'll have a copy of that document, sometimes with instructions from Mr. Santos added. When oral instructions are given, you'll have a printed summary of them.

The materials you're given are designed as realistically as possible. Respond as realistically as you can. In some instances you won't be told specifically what to do; you should then decide what response, if any, is appropriate. You're expected to take some initiative in handling such matters.

In some problems, you'll be given notes on the standard business or office procedures you'll need to know about to respond.

Summary of the Facts

Your name:	Pat Dixon
Your title:	Administrative Assistant to Sales Manager, North Central district
Boss:	Peter Santos, Sales Manager, North Central district
Company:	American Business Machines Company
Staff size:	6 in the office (besides you and Mr. Santos), 19 in sales

ABMC Problem 1
Suggested reading: Chapter 2

On your desk you find two books and a note from Mr. Santos that says, "Jerry Halvas has loaned me these two books. Let's get copies for the office library."

The books are *The Sales Desk Manual*, by Lynne Peters, and *The Customer Isn't Always Right*, by Theodore Cleaver. Both are published by The Sales Book Association (420 Beacon Street, Boston, Massachusetts 02191). A couple of quick telephone calls reveal that local bookstores don't stock these books. Since no price information is listed in the books, write to ask the publisher to send the books, bill your office, and ship right away.

ABMC Problem 2
Suggested reading: Part II and Chapter 12

Summary of instructions from Mr. Santos: Each salesperson uses a small folding cart to carry demonstration equipment into customers' offices. These carts are getting old, and we'll soon have to replace them. I've seen other salespeople using small, collapsible roller tables that would be a big improvement. Will you please check with three or four of our equipment suppliers and get prices?

The tables are made of fiberglass with metal frames. They have two shelves about 18 inches wide by 24 inches long, with the lower shelf about 6 inches above the floor and the upper about 2 feet off the floor. The casters are about 4 or 5 inches in diameter—casters smaller than that would make a table tippy when crossing bumpy sidewalks and parking lots. The tables must fold very compactly for packing in car trunks.

Note: Draft the body of a letter to an equipment supplier. A typist can address each final copy of the letter to one of ABMC's regular suppliers. These letters will be for Mr. Santos' signature.

ABMC Problem 3
Suggested reading: Part II and Chapter 12

```
Pat:
I have to be away for a couple of days. While I'm gone, will
you please get a memo to the office staff and salespeople
telling them we'll have a special staff meeting on the
twenty-third of next month, beginning at noon. They should
reserve the whole afternoon for this. This is an important
meeting—sometimes the sales personnel treat these special
meetings lightly and don't go to much trouble to attend.
We're giving them a full month's notice of this meeting, so
there should be no excuse for missing it.
                                              Peter Santos
```

ABMC Problem 4
Suggested reading: Part II and Chapter 12

Summary of oral instructions: For some insane reason, Pat, I've agreed to talk to the Huntington Exchange Club next month on the topic of "Humor in Business." Thinking about what on earth I could say, I remembered an amusing little publication called *The Wolf Magazine of Letters*, put out by a business forms company in Ohio. I'd like to be able to hand out copies of the current issue and talk about it. It's a little leaflet-sized collection of humorous and interesting letters published every second month, as I remember it. They publish it and send it to business customers and potential customers, I assume. I'd like 25 free copies of one issue. Will you see if you can get the company to send them to me? Some of the club members are business people, but I'm not sure that all of them are. Any payoff to the forms company in terms of increased business will be minimal, but I'll be sure to give full credit in my talk, and the forms company's name will be on the little magazine. Write the Wolf Envelope Company (1750 East 23rd Street, Cleveland, OH 44101).

ABMC Problem 5
Suggested reading: Part II and Chapter 12

```
3341 Flogland Hall
Blossomland Community College
Clearwater, MI 49101
January 20, 1983

Mr. Peter Santos
ABMC Sales Office
28 Business Park
Chappington, IL 60192

Dear Mr. Santos:

     As program chairperson of our Future Secretaries
Association here at Blossomland Community College, I'd like
to invite you to come tell our group about the equipment
marketed by American Business Machines Company. A topic we'd
be interested in is future developments in office machines,
although you may have prepared material in a related area
that you'd rather present to us.
     Our group meets on campus in Room 2294, Flogland Hall on
the first Thursday of each month. If your schedule permits,
we'd like you to speak to us on March 4 or April 1 at 7:30
p.m.
     We're looking forward to hearing your talk. Will you
please let me know which date would be best for you?

Cordially,

Constance Ravelli
```

Summary of oral instructions: Talks like these are great advertising for ABMC, and besides, I like to do it. I accept every invitation I can. Let Constance know I'll be there March 4 with our slide-tape presentation, "The Office: 2001." I'll need a screen and a place to plug in my tape recorder and projector. The talk and show will take about 40 minutes, and I'll be glad to answer questions for as long as they wish.

ABMC Problem 6
Suggested reading: Part II and Chapter 12

Summary of oral instructions from Mr. Santos: There's been some talk, Pat, of locating a warehouse and distribution center for ABMC products in this district, and the Planning and Facilities Division is making a feasibility and location study right now. Since our salespeople cover this district pretty intensively, they may have some useful ideas about where such a facility could be located. This kind of center would be very helpful to us, because it would shorten delivery times significantly within our area. It should be very near the major truck, rail, and air terminals, and since it'll include a small display area for our products, it should be accessible to the heaviest possible concentration of our customers. No doubt every salesperson will want it located in his or her area, but some may be able to make very strong cases for their areas, and we ought to hear from them. Please get a memo to each salesperson on this. Of course, all this discussion is still tentative; in fact, we aren't even sure that we'll add a new distribution center at all. So salespeople shouldn't jump the gun and begin talking to customers about this yet.

ABMC Problem 7
Suggested reading: Part II and Chapter 12

```
Pleasantville High School
1400 High Street
Pleasantville, Minnesota 56297
January 9, 1983

Mr. Peter Santos, Sales Manager
American Business Machines Company
28 Business Park
Chappington, Illinois 60192

Dear Mr. Santos:

     I have been wondering whether I will ever be able to
tell my students that they can have confidence in products
made by American Business Machines Company. I certainly can't
have much confidence in the promises you make!
     I wrote three months ago to ask you to invite a speaker
to talk to my secretarial practice class about the new ABMC
Wordmaster word processing system. You promised to send a Mr.
Henry McQueen to address us on January 8 at 2:00. Mr. McQueen
never appeared.
     A simple telephone call, Mr. Santos, would have let me
know that Mr. McQueen wasn't coming, and I could have made
other plans. Was that too much to ask?

Sincerely,

(Mrs.) Silvia Sprat
Business Education Instructor
```

Handwritten note on bottom of letter: McQueen—What about this? Peter Santos

Memo attached

```
DATE: January 12, 1983
TO: Peter Santos
FROM: Henry McQueen
SUBJECT: Talk to Business Class
```

     I was never scheduled to go to a business class on January 8 as far as I know, Mr. Santos. Back in September, I gave your secretary my schedule for that week because I was scheduled to attend a school administrators conference in Duluth. So I would have known I'd be tied up January 8 if anyone had asked me about making a speaking date with Mrs. Sprat. I've rechecked my files, and I'm sure I never got any notification of this speaking commitment; if I had, I would have told you so you could arrange to shift the date.

Handwritten note on bottom of memo: Pat—Let's get a letter off to Mrs. Sprat and see if we can pacify her. McQueen is very conscientious, and I'm sure our wires got crossed somehow. See if you can get Mrs. Sprat to set another date, and this time we'll be sure Henry knows about it. I'll sign the letter.

Peter Santos

ABMC Problem 8
Suggested reading: Part II and Chapter 12

Summary of oral instructions: Pat, I'm asking you to take charge of the physical arrangements for our spring district sales meeting on May 20 and 21. You'll be responsible for reserving the necessary space for us and making sure the physical arrangements are taken care of.

     To get the best facilities and lowest costs, I'd suggest you start by contacting six or eight local motels that have meeting rooms. Check with the managers to see what they can do for us.

     We'll need a meeting room for about 25 people on both days, all day and evening on May 20 and all day through late afternoon on May 21. Check the costs on the room itself, since these vary somewhat. Included in our cost estimates should be noon meals for both days and an evening meal for May 20. Be sure they can provide a cash bar before the evening meal and ask whether there's any charge for this.

     In addition, we'll need single rooms (one person to a room) for about 14 people for the nights of May 19 and 20. Sometimes these places offer a group rate for blocks of rooms like this.

     The only other thing I can think of that we'll need is a projection screen. Oh, we'd better get coffee in the middle of the morning and afternoon. And maybe rolls with the coffee in the morning.

Note: One way of approaching this assignment is to send a note to each manager indicating the full facts and asking him or her to contact you when the answers are completely assembled. This step can save you from making several calls back and forth to get all the information straight. If you simply write the text of the letter, a secretary can type copies and address them to the motel managers on your list.

ABMC Problem 9
Suggested reading: Part II and Chapter 12

Denise Fuson, Sales Manager of the large Downtown Plaza Motor Hotel, is the first to reply to your request for cost estimates for the May district sales meeting (see the previous problem). Her letter provides cost figures for a block of 14 single rooms, the three group meals, and rolls for the morning breaks, and she indicates that the cash bar is no problem. She doesn't mention costs for the meeting room, morning and afternoon coffee, cash bar, or projection screen. Perhaps these are included in the meal and room costs, but she hasn't said so. You'll want these matters settled in writing before you make a final decision. Reply to her letter.

ABMC Problem 10
Suggested reading: Part II and Chapters 17 and 18

Your search among local motels for a site for the May district sales meeting is complete (see the previous two problems). You checked with Merrit House, Traveler's Inn, Mayfield Inn, Wingate Motor Inn, Vacation Villa, Motor Hotel 54, Downtown Plaza Motor Hotel, and Harold Hanson's Motor Lodge. Both Wingate Motor Inn and Motor Hotel 54 were fully booked for May 20 and 21. The facts are in for the other motels. Summarize the following facts in a report to Mr. Santos so he can quickly make an informed decision.

Merrit House charges charges $20.00 per day for a meeting room, and Vacation Villa charges $25.00 per day. Traveler's Inn, Harold Hanson's Motor Lodge, Downtown Plaza Motor Hotel, and Mayfield Inn include the price of meeting rooms in the meal charge.

Downtown Plaza Motor Hotel gives block rates on 12 or more rooms at a rate of $47.00 per night for a single room. At Traveler's Inn, the lowest rate is the normal commercial rate of $35.00 per night for a single room. Mayfield Inn gives block rates on 10 or more rooms at $31.80 per night for a single room. Merrit House normally gives block rates only on 15 or more rooms, but will offer a block rate on 14 rooms at $43.90 per night for a single room; for fewer than 14 rooms, the normal commercial rate of $58.00 per room applies. Vacation Villa charges $33.75 per night for a single room, which is apparently the standard room rate at that motel. Harold Hanson's Motor Lodge offers a special rate of $39.00 per night for a single room to organizations using its meeting rooms. All these prices include applicable taxes.

Your inspection reveals that accommodations at all these motels are pleasant and acceptable in every way. Accommodations at Merrit House are especially luxurious.

Meals at Vacation Villa are catered by Levinson's Food Service. Meals at Traveler's Inn are catered by the Gatepost Restaurant. Both are served only in buffet style. The four others provide in-house meal service and can provide either buffet service or full service.

It's assumed that a light luncheon such as salad and cold cuts would be wanted for Thursday noon, a full dinner such as steak or prime rib would be wanted for Thursday evening, and a plate luncheon such as baked chicken or ham would be wanted for Friday noon. The following approximate prices are based on such menus, with all service, tips, and applicable taxes included.

Merrit House charges $5.60 and $6.80 for the lunches and $14.30 for the dinner.

Vacation Villa charges $7.35 and $8.25 for the buffet lunches. The dinner consists of a smorgasbord featuring roast beef, fried chicken, and shrimp cocktail for $11.80.

Traveler's Inn charges $8.50 for the buffet lunches (only a single menu is available) and $16.00 for a smorgasbord dinner featuring a large variety of Oriental foods in addition to roast beef and chicken.

Harold Hanson's Motor Lodge charges $5.90 and $7.20 for the lunches and $17.40 for the dinner.

Downtown Plaza Motor Hotel charges $4.70 and $5.50 for the lunches and $11.00 for the dinner.

Mayfield Inn charges $6.70 and $7.90 for lunches and $15.80 for the dinner.

Based on your inquiries among salespeople and local friends who eat out frequently, the clear choice for quality of food is Mayfield Inn, regionally known for its fine food. Harold Hanson's Motor Lodge has an outstanding reputation for prime beef. The Gatepost Restaurant, which caters meals at Traveler's Inn, is well regarded for Oriental food. Food ratings for Merrit House and Downtown Plaza Motor Hotel ranged from so-so to negative. No one you talked to knew anything about Levinson's Food Service, which caters meals at Vacation Villa.

Neither Vacation Villa nor Traveler's Inn can provide a cash bar, since neither has a liquor license. All the others provide the cash bar without a fee. Mayfield Inn and Harold Hanson's Motor Lodge provide peanuts, chips, and other snacks with the cash bar.

Downtown Plaza Motor Hotel and Harold Hanson's Motor Lodge provide morning and afternoon coffee to users of meeting rooms. Downtown Plaza Motor Hotel provides rolls at a cost of $.80 per roll, suggesting an average allowance of two rolls per person. Harold Hanson's Motor Lodge provides rolls at $1.75 per person. Vacation Villa includes morning and afternoon coffee in the room charge; it can't provide rolls, but a nearby shop has excellent rolls available in quantity. Merrit House and Traveler's Inn each charge $.70 per person for coffee at each coffee break. Merrit House provides rolls at $1.30 per person. Traveler's Inn has no provision for rolls and made no suggestions. Mayfield Inn charges $1.95 per person, but includes a variety of soft drinks, orange juice, and milk; rolls in the morning and a selection of snacks in the afternoon are also included in the flat charge.

Vacation Villa charges $25.00 to provide a projection screen, suggesting that it would be less expensive to provide your own. Traveler's Inn can't provide a screen. The rest provide projection screens at no charge.

All six motels urged immediate reservations, since facilities are limited.

ABMC Problem 11
Suggested reading: Part II and Chapter 12

After receiving the facts cited in the previous problem, Mr. Santos has selected Mayfield Inn as the site for the May district sales meeting. Write Roger Adcock, Manager, to make the final reservation.

Note: Confirm all the prices and requirements explicitly in your letter.

ABMC Problem 12
Suggested reading: Part II and Chapter 12

Write the managers of the five motels that were rejected as the site of the May district sales meeting (see the previous four problems). Thank them for quoting prices for your meeting and politely indicate that you won't be using their services.

Note: Compose a form letter. A secretary can address each copy. Telling these people you've made a decision spares them having to contact you further about your plans.

ABMC Problem 13
Suggested reading: Part II and Chapters 12 and 15

Summary of oral instructions: As you've probably noticed by now, Pat, ABMC puts a high premium on keeping the communication lines open between salespeople and customers; we think it's crucial. As a result, it's our policy that all nonroutine correspondence—that is, everything except routine billings—must go through the salespeople to the customers. Except in unusual cases, nonsales personnel don't communicate directly with customers.

Last Friday, this policy paid off. Here's a copy of a letter from the accounting office to one of Jim Montoya's customers. The letter will have to be rewritten, but Jim didn't have time to dictate a new version when he was in the office last Friday. This letter needs to get out right away.

Will you please draft a new version for Jim's signature? Here's the original version:

```
Dear Mr. Olson:
```

In regard to your refusal to pay on statements #4465–GL–901–8 and #4465–GL–901–9, this office has carefully audited your October and November billing. It is our determination that you did purchase $3461.92 worth of goods during that period, as you claimed in your complaint of October 19.

We have further determined that on July 22 we did pick up return merchandise from order GJ34829B3TH.12 in the amount of $1174.37. The driver issued you a hand credit memo; however, he did not report that nor did he complete an official credit form (as he is required to do) for our credit department.

Consequently a record of credit was not entered in our computer, and this department cannot be held accountable for the discrepancy in your billing.

Because you have withheld payment as a result of our disagreement, Mr. Olson, your account balance is now determined to be $2287.55, and it is now more than 60 days past due. If we receive full payment for that amount, we will reopen your account and release shipment on the orders we have been holding pending clearance of your credit. We will not assess the normal late–payment penalty this time, Mr. Olson.

In the future in the event that you should ever again wish to raise complaints against our computerized statement, our accounting procedures and our shipments to you would be expedited if you would mail a check to clear your account along with your letter of complaint. You may rest assured that we will treat you honestly if you treat us honestly.

```
Cordially,
```

Note: In writing to Mr. Olson, you must explain the company policy stated in the final paragraph. Along with his letter of complaint, Mr. Olson should have mailed his check for the amount he calculated that he owed. In this respect, he certainly was wrong.

ABMC Problem 14
Suggested reading: Part II and Chapter 12

Handwritten note from Mr. Santos: Pat—I'm not sure what all this means, and I don't have time to figure it out. Please study it and get out a memo on it to everyone on the sales staff. We've had some questions about this. I have some copies of the form needed. We'll have to consider released time on a case-by-case basis, if the question comes up.

DATE: January 4, 1983
TO: ABMC District Sales Manager
FROM: Jim Jenkins, Director of Sales
SUBJECT: Reimbursement for Enrollment in College Courses

Several times in the past few months salespeople have asked whether the company will pay the costs of tuition and books for employees who enroll in college courses related to their jobs and whether released time will be given to take college courses that are offered during working hours. Neither the Sales Division budget nor any of the District Sales Office budgets contain any funds that could be used for this purpose. I'm sorry to inform you, therefore, that the Sales Division can't reimburse its personnel for costs incurred in taking college courses. A copy of the Training Division policy on this point is attached. Please inform all sales personnel about this matter.

Training Division Policy #4503.11

This policy applies to all employees except Production Division employees below the rank of supervisor, Administrative Services and Physical Plant employees below the rank of supervisor, and clerical employees below the rank of secretary. In order to encourage personnel to develop greater professional competence in their respective fields and to prepare for professional advancement, personnel registering in credit courses at the college or graduate level in institutions of higher education accredited by the regional accrediting associations will be reimbursed for the direct costs of tuition, registration fees, and required course textbooks and other materials upon successful completion of such instruction. Certification that the college course will contribute to the employee's professional growth will be provided by the employee's direct supervisor and countersigned by the supervisor's direct superior unless the supervisor is at the rank of vice-president or higher. Successful completion is defined as completion with the grade of C (or equivalent) or higher. Costs of travel and nonrequired materials such as paper and clerical help will not be reimbursed. Submission to the Training Division of receipts for all expenses, approval of the direct supervisor that the course fulfills the requirements of this policy, and documentation of successful completion are required before reimbursement from the Training Division budget can be made. Supervisors are encouraged to allow released time for personnel to enroll in credit college courses for professional development when departmental or divisional schedules permit. Released time is encouraged only when scheduled meetings of credit college courses occur during

regular working hours. If possible and necessary, personnel
may be required to make up working time outside the normal
working hours. If the credit college course can be taken
outside the individual's normal working hours, no released
time should be given. To receive reimbursement, personnel
should submit Training Division form 4503B to the Training
Division in accordance with the instructions on that form.

ABMC Problem 15
Suggested reading: Part II and Chapter 12

Summary of oral instructions from Mr. Santos: As you may know, besides
marketing through retail office equipment dealers, ABMC sells directly to
the corporations on the Fortune 500 list (a list of the 500 largest American
corporations published annually by *Fortune* magazine). These companies
purchase office equipment in such large volume that we find it efficient
to serve them directly rather than through retail dealers.

   This year's Fortune 500 list will be published soon, and I'd like you
to draft a form letter of congratulations to be sent to the chief executive
officers of companies that are listed for the first time. Making the Fortune
500 list is an important milestone in a company's life, marking its admission into one of the most exclusive groups in the world. ABMC is proud
to have been a Fortune 500 company for many years.

   One benefit of a company's being on the Fortune 500 list, of course,
is the efficiency and economy it gains by dealing directly with ABMC and
other large suppliers. Our salespeople will be calling on such companies'
administrative managers, and your letter should mention this. This point
should be subordinated, however, and your letter should emphasize the
congratulations.

   When you and I arrive at a final draft of this letter, I intend to propose
that it be sent over ABMC President Williamson's signature to all newly
listed Fortune 500 companies.

ABMC Problem 16
Suggested reading: Part II and Chapter 13

Dear Mr. Santos:

   John Green, your salesperson here in Toledo, has
suggested that you may be able to help us. For a term paper
in my office management class, I'm trying to find out the
relative distribution of various brands of common office
equipment. I'm particularly interested in comparing the six
or eight best-selling brands of word processing systems and
copiers to see which brand is in greatest use in the Midwest.
I feel that this information will help me in my office
management career and that it'll also help others in the
class who will someday be purchasers of office equipment.

For this paper, I'll need to know the annual sales in numbers of units for the North Central district for each model of your word processing systems and copiers. Since such figures for the recent year may not be complete, perhaps it'd be best if you could send me the figures covering the last two or three years. I'm certain you must have such figures readily available, and I'd appreciate it if your secretary could copy them for me.

I'll very much appreciate whatever help you can give me on this project. If you'd like to see the resulting term paper, I'll be glad to send you a copy.

Cordially,

Paul Tanaka

Pat:

As you might imagine, sales figures, especially by product line, are very closely guarded information in most industries, because such information could considerably help our competitors in planning their sales strategies. Our company policy has always been to maintain the strictest confidence about sales figures. We wouldn't release them in any case, but especially not when Mr. Tanaka is offering copies of his report to us and presumably also to our competitors. Even if he had the figures, they wouldn't be comparable to those of our competitors, since our North Central district is very different from the composition of their sales districts that also cover northwestern Ohio. Please refuse his request very tactfully; he'll be a purchaser of office equipment in a few years as an office manager, and we don't want to offend him more than necessary. Write him over my signature.

Peter Santos

ABMC Problem 17
Suggested reading: Part II and Chapter 13

Pat:

I've got a problem. For the last five or six years, I've gone down to Southern Michigan University and spoken to the chapter of Pi Omega Pi at one of their winter meetings. Pi Omega Pi is the national honorary fraternity for future high school teachers of business; I was a member of the Southern Michigan University chapter when I was in college. This year they waited so long to invite me that I already have unbreakable commitments for the three dates they have open.

I know how this happens; students who are trying to run an honorary fraternity on the side are very busy and just

don't get around to things as quickly as they ought to. But
this time they've missed the boat completely.

I'm very sorry to miss this opportunity, because it's
not only a chance to go back and help the school, but it's
also a chance to remind a group of people—people who'll be
recommending office equipment to high schools in a few years
—that we're in business. High schools buy a lot of office
equipment for classroom use.

Please write to Ms. Marcy Bromstein for me and let her
know that on March 18 I'll be right in the middle of my
vacation, and I expect to be skiing down the slopes in Idaho.
On April 15, I'll be involved with our first-quarter sales
managers' conference in Seattle, a meeting I can't possibly
afford to miss. On May 20, as you know, we'll be here at the
spring district sales meeting, which I'll be leading. These
are the three dates she said she had open. I'm a little
irritated that they waited so long to invite me, and I know
they're going to be disappointed that I can't come; it's
almost an annual tradition.

Peter Santos

Note: This letter is for Mr. Santos' signature.

ABMC Problem 18
Suggested reading: Part II and Chapter 13

Dear Mr. Santos:

How would you like the chance to familiarize nearly 80
prospective secretaries with the unique advantages of ABMC's
new Wordmaster word processing system? We'd like to help you
do just that.

Here in Onsalagin High School, we graduate about 80
secretaries each year. We feel that these young people should
have an opportunity to learn the basic functions of a modern
word processing system, since many of them will be entering
jobs in which such equipment could be put to good use. We
seem to have a chance to help you promote this piece of
equipment, and you have a chance to help us train competent
young secretaries.

We see two possibilities for you. You may find it useful
to place a sample Wordmaster system in our model-office
classroom for a period of about seven to eight weeks during
the year to give each student an opportunity to learn to
operate the unit. Or you may find it more useful to place a
sample unit in your sales outlet here in Onsalagin, which is
just a block from the school, and let each student spend some
time with the unit there. Of course, it may be some
imposition on Modern Office Supplies Company to have 80
students each spending several hours practicing on the unit
in the store.

Because we must spend a substantial sum of money on regularly replacing the many typewriters and other office machines used in this program, we see no possibility of purchasing a Wordmaster system for these students' use.

Can you give us the opportunity to help these young secretaries prepare for office careers?

Cordially,

Hermann L. Schippers, Business Manager
Onsalagin Public Schools

Pat:

Please reply. We have more than 40 typewriters and some other equipment in Onsalagin High School, so we don't want to offend them unnecessarily. We have only 11 Wordmaster demonstrators in the whole district, and we can't possibly tie one up for two months on this. Our 19 salespeople would shoot me! Anyway, school administrators talk to each other a lot, and if we give one to a school, the other schools will expect one, too. Maybe they can justify buying this unit if they'd put it in the administration offices of the school system and let students use it there. Their educational discount would reduce the price under $4000 (they get 22 percent off). See if you can sell them on that.

Peter Santos

ABMC Problem 19
Suggested reading: Part II and Chapter 14

Summary of oral instructions: I'd like you to spend some time drafting a memo to our salespeople when you get a chance. Here's the situation: Most of our salespeople, except for the two who live here in town, get into the office only once a week. That's when they turn in all routine orders and do other paperwork. (As you know, they call in once a day with rush orders and other nonroutine messages.) During the seven hours or so each person spends in the office, we find that he or she spends something like three to four hours just getting the paperwork in order—getting orders drafted for clerical processing and so forth. Several years ago, we equipped each salesperson with a small, battery-powered cassette tape recorder to use as a dictating unit. The unit is very convenient to use, and it's especially suited for use in the car between calls. The problem is that the salespeople aren't turning in orders and other paperwork via cassettes.

Dictating this material would save time and money for both the salespeople and the office. If they'd dictate their orders right after receiving them (and while driving to their next appointment), then they wouldn't have to draft notes for typing while they're in the office. Doing this would save time and enable the secretary to type the orders for each salesperson's approval before he or she leaves the office that day. We often find now that orders turned in while the salesperson is in the office have to be read over the phone for his or her final approval, because the secretary doesn't have time to type all the orders before the end of the day. Orders handled this way are often both delayed and fouled up; reading the order over the phone doesn't allow truly accurate correction. If our salespeople would just turn in their half-dozen dictated cassettes when they enter the office, then all the orders could be typed for their approval by the time they're ready to leave in the afternoon. This procedure would also give each salesperson more free time to talk with me and do other important work here in the office.

The cassette recorder would also help reduce order errors. I know that many errors creep in simply because our salespeople don't look at the notes they made when they talked to the customer until they're ready to write up the order in the office several days later. During that time, the notes have gotten cold and the salesperson can't remember exactly what was said. If our salespeople would dictate their orders and other material right after leaving the customer, many of these potentially embarrassing and costly errors could be eliminated.

I've talked to the salespeople about this several times over the last three or four years. Will you try a memo on it please?

ABMC Problem 20
Suggested reading: Part II and Chapter 14

You've decided to hold your May district sales meeting at the Mayfield Inn. While inspecting the facilities there, you noticed that they have an indoor pool. You're certain that the salespeople would enjoy using the pool, but they'll be in meetings almost continuously both days of the event. It has occurred to you, and Mr. Santos agrees, that the salespeople would really enjoy a late-night swim after the Thursday evening meeting. Unfortunately, according to the sign on the door, the pool closes at 10:00 P.M.

Write a letter to the manager of the Mayfield Inn requesting that the pool be left open on Thursday evening, May 20, until midnight. The company will be willing to pay a small fee, say $10 or $20, for the use of the pool, although this fee probably won't cover the cost of keeping the pool open. Perhaps the best inducement you can offer is that the motel will be building goodwill among the salespeople, many of whom spend several nights a month in local motels when they visit the local ABMC office.

ABMC Problem 21
Suggested reading: Part II and Chapter 14

Pat:

The attached policy statement arrived this morning. Please draft a message on it to our salespeople. Salespeople have established routes and overnight stops, so this may be an unpopular change. Be as persuasive as you can; let's see if we can avoid friction with the home office on this issue.

                                               Peter Santos

DATE: January 7, 1983
TO: All District Sales Managers
FROM: George Spock, Comptroller
SUBJECT: Motels

The company has negotiated an agreement with U.S. Travel Inns, Inc. (USTI) that provides a 5 percent rebate on all overnight lodging by ABMC personnel at the motels in the USTI chain. USTI will give this rebate in addition to the normal commercial discount it gives to our employees and others.

Based on employee travel records, we've determined that more than 75 percent of employee overnight lodging could be supplied by the more than 220 USTI motels located throughout the nation, thus giving our company a substantial saving. You've received enough copies of the USTI directory to distribute to all employees who travel on company business. Employees are directed to obtain overnight lodging in a USTI motel whenever possible.

To obtain reimbursement for overnight lodging in communities where a USTI motel is located, an employee must stay in that motel. Exceptions will be permitted only when no USTI motel is located within 25 miles of the place where lodging must be obtained, when space is not available at a USTI motel within 25 miles of that place, or when meetings or conferences are scheduled beyond the employee's control in other facilites and the employee must obtain lodging at the meeting site to participate fully. All employee expense vouchers listing overnight lodging in hotels or motels other than those in the USTI chain must be accompanied by a statement explaining the reason for the exception. Exceptions will be considered on a case-by-case basis, and reimbursement for overnight lodging may be denied when an exception claim is determined to be invalid.

When staying at a USTI motel, employees should request the normal commercial rate. Each quarter, ABMC will submit employee reimbursement records to USTI for the 5 percent rebate. In communicating this policy to your employees, please emphasize that this rebate is not to be claimed at the time the employee pays for lodging.

ABMC Problem 22
Suggested reading: Part II and Chapter 15

Summary of oral instructions from Mr. Santos: Under a new Indiana public school funding regulation, school districts are encouraged to instruct high school business majors in the use of word processing equipment. The state will provide special funding (called Title 14 funds) for the purchase of instructional word processing equipment according to a formula based on the number of students registered in advanced secretarial courses. The ABMC Wordmaster word processing system is one of seven brands approved for purchase under Title 14 funds.

Sales to school districts are handled through 16 of our largest retail dealers throughout Indiana who can provide the standard ABMC educational discount of 22 percent (which means a unit price of less than $4000), full installation and on-site testing at delivery, and comprehensive after-sale service by ABMC-trained technicians.

Purchases of equipment under Title 14 funds are handled in most school districts by the district business manager, who is normally an assistant superintendent of schools. We have a list of names and addresses. Please draft a form letter to be mailed to these people along with our 26-page Wordmaster specification brochure and our educational price list. These business managers should be well informed about the Title 14 program, so the letter's purpose is to refer them to their nearest appropriate dealer (determined by region) and to encourage them to consider the Wordmaster as a possible system. Dealers will soon be contacting them to arrange demonstrations of the Wordmaster for them and for their high school's business teachers.

The Wordmaster system has two features that make it especially attractive for educational use. First, ABMC is widely known in the industry for the quality of its keyboards (as many business managers and most business teachers will realize). The keyboard in the Wordmaster is not only state-of-the-art in design, providing optimum "touch" for fast typing, but it's also designed for maximum durability under the hard use it'll receive in the classroom. Second, the Wordmaster includes a "document privacy" feature not found in competitive units, which allows an operator to specify a secret password for each document stored on file. To read or change that document, the password must be given. Thus one student's work can be protected from access by other students, and any material entered by instructors can be similarly protected. (The brochure provides further information about keyboard quality on pages 4 and 5, and the document privacy feature is explained on page 17.)

ABMC is happy about the Title 14 program not only as an opportunity to sell equipment to school districts, but also because it'll increase the number of trained word processing operators available to other purchasers of Wordmaster systems. According to a recent federal government estimate, word processor operation is one of the fastest-growing jobs in the country, with an estimated growth rate of over 130 percent for the coming decade.

Note: Your form letter should include spaces for insertion of the names and addresses of school business managers and the names and addresses of regional dealers. Mr. Santos will sign it.

ABMC Problem 23
Suggested reading: Part II and Chapters 12, 13, and 14

Pat:

Here's a form letter our Claims Office is asking us to send to a list of dealers who've been having claims problems with the company. Since we serve as a channel for all such correspondence, the letter has come through us. This letter seems designed to lose friends and alienate dealers. Will you please rewrite it?

Peter Santos

We respectfully advise you that you are wasting time and money returning parts.

You are following the wrong procedure. At present, you are returning parts without a request from the factory. Under many existing circumstances, such parts are not needed to serve as a basis for the required claims decision. Where a recurring problem has been identified and the probability of a given part failure is known to be high, Product Engineering does not require an inspection of each individual failed part. Consequently, you are wasting the time and money spent on crating, preparing papers, and shipping charges.

You should discontinue returning all parts and concentrate on returning as quickly as possible only those parts for which you receive requests upon our examination of your initial statement of claim. At present, the time between the date of failure and the date of the credit memo issued to your account is too long. Also you have too many dollars tied up in delayed claims decisions. It should be possible to have failed parts in Rochester two weeks from the date on the Parts Return Request form.

What you must do is wait for a Parts Return Request form and then make arrangements for them to arrive in Rochester as soon as possible. If a Parts Return Request is not issued within thirty (30) days of submission of your claim, then you may dispose of those parts. If a recent claim of yours has been disallowed, we are sorry. Any comments you have will be welcomed. Thank you for your cooperation.

Note: Consider whether this situation should be treated as good news, bad news, or persuasion.

THE EDUCATION AND TRAINING CASE

Assume the identity of Chris Novak, Assistant to the Director of Education and Training, Thompson Manufacturing Corporation. Your new boss, Andrea Walsh, hired you as her assistant after your six-month orientation period with the company. In your first conversation with Ms. Walsh, she told you about some of the duties and responsibilities you'll be assuming over the next few months, saying that at first she'll simply assign specific tasks for you to perform, but as time goes on you'll be on your own more often. She also introduced you to the office staff of 11 people—secretaries and training specialists.

Ms. Walsh indicated that, since she normally dictates her paperwork late at night, she'll often assign work to you in dictated notes or memos rather than by talking to you during the day, when she has a heavy schedule of meetings and conferences. This doesn't mean that you're not to interrupt her during the day; if you have a problem she needs to know about, you should certainly arrange to see her. This is just a timesaving way for her to give you instructions.

The case materials you're given here are designed as realistically as possible. Respond to them as realistically as you can. In some instances, you won't be told specifically what to do; you should then decide what response, if any, is appropriate. You're expected to take some initiative in handling such matters. In some problems, you'll be given notes on the standard business or office procedures you'll need to know about to respond.

Summary of the Facts

Your name:	Chris Novak
Your title:	Administrative Assistant to Director of Education and Training
Your boss:	Andrea Walsh, Director of the Education and Training Department
Company:	Thompson Manufacturing Company
Staff size:	11 secretaries and training specialists

E and T Problem 1

Suggested reading: Part II and Chapter 12

When you returned from lunch today, you found this note on your desk:

Chris:

    To help you get an understanding of our operation, I'll be asking you to write memos and letters over the next few weeks about several of our training programs. This afternoon, will you get a memo to Harold Stolte, Director of Personnel? Harold asked us to investigate the feasibility of developing a training program to teach interviewing skills to his hiring officers. Please report these findings:

- If the following arrangements are suitable, Education and Training will develop the program.
- Written authorization will be needed from the Personnel Department by the end of next week.
- To get a reasonable return on cost, at least 12 employees must participate, all of whom have the qualifications and appropriate job responsibilities to benefit from the program.
- Total cost is around $4000. Education and Training could pay a maximum of $1200; Personnel pays the rest.
- Dr. Catherine Wong (Ph.D. in psychology from Harvard) of Indiana University would be available for a two-day session next month. She's done similar sessions before; good reports from clients.
- Arrangements would have to be made for people to fill in at participants' desks for the two days. Participants can't be running in and out of the sessions.

Please draft this memo and have my secretary type it under my name this afternoon.

Andrea Walsh

Note: Your memo should state, concisely but clearly, all *the information Ms. Walsh has asked you to state.*

E and T Problem 2
Suggested reading: Part II and Chapter 12

This note from Ms. Walsh was on your desk this morning:

Chris:

Harold Stolte has orally authorized the training program in interviewing skills for his personnel people [see the previous problem]. He'll be giving us written authorization in the next day or two. We need to line up Dr. Wong right away. Please write a letter to Dr. Wong this morning for my signature offering her $1400 plus direct expenses (including travel) of up to $750 to run the program. Her fee is to include all payment for her time and the time of any assistants she employs. The expense allowance will cover the costs of any materials she prepares and of course the travel costs. (She should submit an itemized accounting after the program.) We expect 12 to 14 participants for a two-day program, with the total session time—including morning and afternoon breaks—running approximately 14 hours long. We've already discussed with her the dates of February 17–18, which fall on a Thursday and Friday, and these appear to be the best for us.

When she confirms this agreement—right away, we hope—she should list the equipment she wants us to provide (overhead projector, flip chart, etc.). When we talked on the phone earlier, she mentioned a short textbook on interviewing that our participants should read before the program begins. If she'll provide ordering information, we'll buy copies for each participant beforehand at our expense.

Andrea Walsh

Note: Since this letter and her reply of acceptance will consitute your company's only contract with Dr. Wong, you should be completely clear about the terms of the agreement, especially the financial arrangements.

E and T Problem 3
Suggested reading: Part II and Chapter 12

Chris:

Vice-President Mallinson has asked each department head to submit a two-year projection of equipment needs. Please get a memo to all members of the department, including secretaries, asking them to suggest equipment that must be replaced during this period and new equipment that we should consider buying. I'll want you to follow up on this, so be sure you get specific information about what's needed: suggested brands, models, prices, possible vendors, and so forth. To ensure time to gather the information before the deadline two weeks from now, give staff members only four to five days to respond to your request. Encourage them to think carefully about equipment needs two full years away, because we'll no doubt have a devil of a time getting any major purchases approved that aren't on this list. We may be able to substitute brands or models as new units are introduced, but we probably won't be able to add completely new items. Staff members should give this matter top priority in their thinking.

Andrea Walsh

E and T Problem 4
Suggested reading: Part II and Chapter 12

Several staff members have made the same inquiry in connection with the two-year projection of equipment needs that you asked them to prepare (see the previous problem). They use audiovisual equipment extensively—cameras, projectors, and audio recorders—and much of it must be replaced periodically. In reviewing replacement and new equipment needs, they'd like information about the various pieces of audiovisual equipment that are currently on the market. Often they know the features they'd like, but they don't know the model numbers or prices of units that offer such features. Perhaps, as one person suggested, the Purchasing Department uses a standard reference manual or catalog in processing requisitions for such items. In an interdepartmental memo, relay this inquiry to Jason Breitweiser, Director of Purchasing.

E and T Problem 5
Suggested reading: Part II and Chapter 12

Jason Breitweiser just phoned to tell you that the Purchasing Department uses the Stone and Barton catalog of audiovisual products as its main reference in processing requisitions for camera, projection, and audio recording equipment (see the previous problem). He's sent you a spare copy through interoffice mail. Prices listed in the catalog are discount prices, he said, which are usually within a few percentage points of the lowest prices available on such equipment. He said that the Purchasing Department normally uses Stone and Barton prices in preparing preliminary audiovisual-equipment price estimates, such as the two-year projection your department is now working on. He suggests that you do the same. You can easily see that this approach would simplify each staff member's task in specifying equipment models and prices. At the same time, you'd like to establish that Breitweiser is the one who suggested using Stone and Barton prices. If the prices quoted in your projection are ever questioned, you'd like to base your pricing on his authority. Write him a memo for the record that puts his suggestion into writing for your files. Perhaps you could frame it as a thank-you note for his help.

E and T Problem 6
Suggested reading: Part II and Chapter 12

Chris:

By now you've no doubt seen the form that our departments use to request a feasibility study on developing some specific training program for them. Apparently, Jerry Polinger has sent us one of those forms and hasn't been very specific about what he wants—maybe he doesn't know exactly what he wants. Jerry is the Director of Production Engineering, the department that designs our production processes, and the one thing that's clear is that he wants us to set up a short training course to help his engineers convert to using the metric system. Our whole plant will be converting to the metric system over the next ten years, and Jerry's engineers must get to work on this conversion immediately.

Bill George, in our office, wrote a memo to Jerry asking for clarification of Jerry's request for a feasibility study on this program; the memo is for my signature. Bill left on vacation this morning, and I think he must have been in a hurry to get this off his desk, because this memo isn't something I want to sign and send. Will you rewrite it and give it to my secretary to type under my name? If you treat the matter positively, just telling him what we need to know, then I'm sure the memo will be more tactful.

Andrea Walsh

DATE: January 14, 1983
TO: Jerry Polinger
FROM: Andrea Walsh
SUBJECT: Errors in Request for Feasibility Study

You've made several errors on the form you submitted
requesting a feasibility study on our designing a training
program in the metric system for your engineers. You
indicated that you expect approximately 15 participants in
the program, but according to the company roster, you have
only 9 people in your department, including yourself. If the
program is to include personnel from other departments, we
must know what departments will send participants and design
the program appropriately.

You also neglected to state the desired length of the
program and the amount of money your department can invest in
it.

In order to process a request and conduct a feasibility
study, we must have correct and complete answers to all the
questions asked. Incomplete information only delays the
completion of our study. Since we face a heavy demand on our
services in Education and Training during the late summer
months when you want to schedule your program, we must have
specific information on the above-mentioned points. If this
information isn't supplied, we can't conduct your program.

E and T Problem 7
Suggested reading: Part II and Chapter 12

Chris:

As you've probably figured out, the sales training
programs we run are our bread-and-butter operation; without
them we'd be out of business in Education and Training.
Because we're able to employ a good-sized staff mainly to run
the sales training programs, we can use our people to set up
a small number of other programs of various kinds for other
departments.

I wanted you to understand this because we have a touchy
point to make to the company's 11 regional sales managers.
Every four months, we run a training program for the
salespeople in each of these regions. Two of the three yearly
programs are put on in some central city in the region. The
third, a three-day program, is run here in the headquarters
offices. This three-day program is very important because, in
most cases, it's the one time that the salespeople spend some
time in the plant. It keeps them in touch with the thinking
of the people here, and it gives them a chance to talk
informally with people they'd never see otherwise.

The problem is this: top management has decided to transfer the travel budget for these training sessions from our department to the regional sales offices. This means that we'll no longer be able to pay travel costs for salespeople who come to these meetings. We no longer have the budget for it. Last year the total cost of travel to these 33 training programs exceeded $171,000, an expense that must now be met by the regional sales offices themselves. Money has been added to each of their budgets for this purpose, but in the complexity of a long and detailed budget, they probably haven't even noticed the addition.

Please draft a memo to the regional sales managers telling them about this budget transfer. Be sure to emphasize that the reason we can no longer pay this travel cost is that the money isn't in our budget anymore. Be as positive and tactful as you can—we don't want to get them so irritated that they'll begin questioning the value of these training programs.

                                                    Andrea Walsh

E and T Problem 8
Suggested reading: Part II and Chapter 12

Chris:

Carlos Aguilar, one of our Education and Training specialists, has been getting concerned about some problems we're having with the way departments initiate the development of training projects. Sometimes the department heads are afraid that, if they let us study the project and prepare a proposal, we may not be willing to run the training program the way they want it run. Perhaps at certain times in the past, there were problems of this kind. So instead of submitting a formal request for a feasibility study, they go ahead and develop the program themselves and let us know about it only when it's an accomplished fact. Often we not only could have helped with the administrative details of setting up the program, but we also could have suggested alternatives that might have saved some money. If the department doesn't feel that our alternatives are workable, of course they have the final say.

After Carlos complained bitterly about a situation that arose last week, I suggested he draft a memo to all department heads that reviews the procedure for requesting the study of a proposed training program. His memo (below) certainly isn't very tactful, and it has some other problems, too, as you can see. Will you please draft a memo on this?

                                                    Andrea Walsh

DATE: January 17, 1983
TO: All Department and Division Heads
FROM: Education and Training
SUBJECT: Incorrect Training Procedures

At the present time, a number of departments are following the wrong procedure for initiating training program requests. Fully organizing a training program in a department, when Education and Training offers the assistance of trained professionals who work full-time in this area, is a waste of a department's time and resources.

The correct procedure for a department to follow when contemplating a new training program is to initiate discussion with a member of the Education and Training staff. After some preliminary discussion, the department should submit a request for a feasibility study, answering completely and factually all the questions asked on the form. Then Education and Training will study alternative approaches to the training program and report fully on available alternatives. The department that requested the study always makes the final decisions about the program.

Departments that seek to subvert this procedure by secretly developing programs and presenting them to Education and Training only for budget approval are not only misappropriating company resources but are also implying doubt about the professional competence of Education and Training staff members. Education and Training is sorry that some proposed programs could not be adequately funded during the last year, but that is not the fault of this procedure. It is a result, partly, of the actions of those who have refused to follow this procedure and thus denied themselves consideration in Education and Training's advanced budget planning.

E and T Problem 9

Suggested reading: Part II and Chapter 13

DATE: January 19, 1983
TO: Chris Novak
FROM: Andrea Walsh
SUBJECT: Letter to Professor Jennings

Dr. Luther C. Jennings, of the College of Education at Southern Illinois University, has invited me to spend a couple of days on campus lecturing to his classes in educational methodology. He's indicated that the two dates on which he could schedule such sessions are October 23–24 and November 6–7, saying that we'll have to hit one or the other of those dates to fit into the school schedule.

Unfortunately, I'll be in Omaha on October 23 running
our Mid-Plains district sales training session, and I
wouldn't be able to get to Carbondale until very late in the
day on the 24th at best. And I'll be spending both November 6
and 7 in San Diego setting up the Pacific district sales
training session and running it on the 7th. It looks as
though my schedule rules out a trip to the campus during the
fall term.

I'd like to have a chance to visit the campus, for two
reasons. First, I can compare notes with the educational
theorists, and I've always come back from sessions like these
with terrific ideas for improvements in our programs. Second,
I can do some quiet recruiting for Thompson Manufacturing
among the best of the school's graduates. When our recruiters
appear on campus through the placement office, they have to
interview any student who signs up. But when I can sit down
for an evening with the professors, I can get the names of
the very best graduates for us to contact personally later.
This kind of recruiting is worth a lot of money to the
company.

Please tell Dr. Jennings what the situation is. Make it
clear that this is not a brush-off, that I do want to talk to
his classes when our schedules can fit together. Tell him to
keep me on his list.

E and T Problem 10
Suggested reading: Part II and Chapter 13

Earlier, Ms. Walsh asked if you'd be willing to represent the company by
working on the city's United Fund campaign. She said that, although you
wouldn't be paid directly for your work on the campaign, you'd be given
some released time for daytime meetings, and your participation would
be a favorable factor in future promotion decisions. Since you've enjoyed
your participation in Junior Chamber of Commerce service projects and
other civic activities, you readily agreed. Here's a letter you received
yesterday:

Dear Chris:

The Executive Board of the United Fund is very pleased
that you've agreed to join us in this year's campaign.
Representatives of Thompson Manufacturing have been among our
most skillful and energetic workers in the past, and I'm sure
this year will prove to be no exception.

We were quite pleased to note that your work is in the
area of training, because one of our greatest needs is for
people who are knowledgeable in this field. We'd like to
invite you to use your professional expertise in the
campaign. The job of Training Director involves organizing

and leading about 12 training sessions for United Fund
canvassers. Since this is the kind of activity your
department conducts, we think you'd be the obvious choice for
the campaign's Training Director.
      Will you please let me know in the next few days if
you'll accept this post in the campaign?
Cordially,

Todd Thatcher, Chairperson
United Fund Executive Board

This morning you showed the letter to Ms. Walsh. She suggested you beg
off, for two reasons. First, the job is incredibly time-consuming. You'd be
organizing and running about 30–40 hours of training, and you'd be doing
everything yourself—even worrying about details like scheduling rooms
and providing pencils and paper for participants. Second, since you've
only been working in the training field for about six weeks now and you
haven't actually seen a training session in operation yet, perhaps (she said
tactfully) you should get your feet wet gradually rather than taking on a
large training job like this one as your first experience.

E and T Problem 11
Suggested reading: Part II and Chapter 13

This morning Ms. Walsh asked you to come into her office. She spent
some 20 minutes explaining the outcome of Jerry Polinger's request for
a feasibility study on a training program in the metric system for design
and production engineering personnel (see earlier problem). Here are your
notes of the conversation:

- Polinger and other department heads agreed on a maximum of
  $30 per participant for a one-day program; 15 participants expected;
  total bill $450.
- Minimum possible cost for administration is $125.
- Remainder ($325) must cover instructional costs: instructor's fee
  or salary, instructional materials, other costs.
- Outside instructor who has expertise in the field will demand
  about $500 plus expenses; any instructional materials would be
  additional.
- We tried to find a young, relatively inexperienced but qualified
  faculty member at a nearby community college or high school to
  run the program at a low fee—couldn't find such a person.
- We tried to find programmed materials that are available for self-
  study—nothing was suitable.
- Possibility: resubmit proposal early in the next budget, when more
  money may be available; a good program will cost $50–$60 per
  participant.

- Possibility: Jerry could run the program on his own as a seminar (each participant takes part of the material and teaches to others); seminars often work when all participants have the technical background to understand the material, as these people do. A strong leader is needed to keep things on track and on schedule.

In a memo to Jerry Polinger, report the results of the feasibility study.

Note: Be sure to give Jerry enough information about the feasibility study's outcome to enable him to make an intelligent and informed decision on what to do about this program.

E and T Problem 12
Suggested reading: Part II and Chapter 14

Chris:

    I'd like you to try your hand at a little sales job. Here's the situation: Education and Training has always had a slack period during the company's September-through-December rush. In September and October, salespeople are ordinarily much too busy to attend training sessions, and of course in December we don't ask them to be away from home any more than necessary. During that same period, the home office people are usually pushed to get out the fall and end-of-year shipments, so home office departments aren't asking us to schedule training programs for their people between September 1 and December 31. As a result, except for the 11 regional sales training programs around the country in late October and early November, we run almost no programs during these four months.

    Of course, our staff spends some of this time making long-range plans and preparing for future programs, but frankly we don't need four whole months to do that work. It's really too long a slack period.

    If we could get some departments here in the home office to schedule their training operations between September 1 and October 15 or during December, we could even out our work load quite a bit. Of course, areas like Sales, Production, and Shipping are busy right then. But Accounting, for example, could probably move some of its annual training sessions to this period, and I'd think Information Systems and some of the engineering areas could, too.

    They'd get two important advantages, as I see it. First, because our instructors aren't so busy at this time, more time would be available to develop outstanding programs and prepare good presentations. (Don't suggest, though, that our work during rush periods isn't well done.) Second, because our facilities are underused during this time, departments could expect some cost reductions. For example, we'd seldom,

if ever, have to use (and pay for) meeting rooms other than
our own conference rooms, which are free. And unless a
session is on some special topic that our instructors aren't
prepared to present, we'd seldom have to pay the high fees
that outside instructors charge. (Don't let them
misunderstand this: we're not offering any across-the-board
price cuts or bargain-basement prices during this period; we
only want to say that departments ordinarily can expect some
savings by scheduling sessions during this period.) Will you
please draft a memo to all home office department and
division heads to tell them about this?

Andrea Walsh

E and T Problem 13
Suggested reading: Part II and Chapter 14

Chris:

Because it's increasingly difficult to recruit qualified
computer programmers, the Information Systems Department is
funding a program to train selected employees to become
programmers. Any employee may apply for the training program.
Applicants will be selected primarily on the basis of their
scores on a programming aptitude test; a record of reliable
and conscientious work in their present job will also weigh
positively. Previous computer programming experience isn't
required or expected.

Our goal is to select six trainees, who'll be paid $1380
per month during the eight-month program. At the end of this
period, successful trainees will be eligible for the position
of Programmer IV at a starting pay of $1530 per month.
Although the company can't guarantee that positions will be
available to every graduate of the program, Information
Systems has consistently had openings for more than double
this number of Programmer IVs annually in the last several
years.

This program is an attractive opportunity for the
employees who qualify. It offers office and assembly-line
employees an opportunity to enter a respected profession
whose members are in high demand. To get similar training in
community colleges or private technical institutes, they'd
not only receive no salary for their work, but they'd also
probably be paying substantial tuitions. The Programmer IV
salary is higher than typical clerical and assembly-line
salaries, although the training-period salary may constitute
a salary reduction for some applicants. Trainees now in
positions covered by union contracts will lose seniority
rights in their present positions upon entering the program.

It's inappropriate to try to sell people on a major
career change the way you'd sell a new brand of toothpaste or
a magazine subscription, but we need to describe this program

as positively and persuasively as possible. Please draft a
letter for distribution to all employees that announces the
program and encourages them to request further information
from our office.

Andrea Walsh

E and T Problem 14
Suggested reading: Part II and Chapter 14

Chris:

Ever since we had to turn down Jerry Polinger's request
for a training program in the metric system for his
production engineers and design people [see earlier
problems], I've been keeping my eyes open for some way of
getting that project done within the budget. In my
conversations around the district, I asked about possible
opportunities. Yesterday I found a possibility that Jerry may
want to consider--it could be a really good deal.

Dr. Wilbur Skaggs of the University of Nebraska has run
about 20 training programs over the last couple of years in
exactly the field Jerry is considering: training engineers to
convert to the metric system. Professor Skaggs is already
scheduled to run a training session, I found out, at
Consolidated Paper Products here in town on the eleventh of
next month. I asked whether 15 of our people could sit in on
Consolidated's training session, sharing costs, but
Consolidated didn't want to get involved in all the problems
that might raise. So I then asked Professor Skaggs whether
he'd consider running a second session in the same trip,
either before or after the Consolidated program. After some
discussion of our financial situation, he agreed to run a
program for us like the one he's doing for Consolidated for a
total fee of $450, including all expenses. This session could
be either on the tenth or twelfth of next month.

This could be a real bargain for us. Ordinarily Dr.
Skaggs charges $600 for running the all-day program plus
something like $500-700 for travel expenses and materials.
Only because he'll be in town anyway and because all
materials will already be prepared for the Consolidated
program is he willing to lower his fee to meet our budget
restrictions.

If Jerry can come up with the money to pay $37 per
participant (a total of $555) instead of the $30 maximum we
discussed earlier, we can manage to cut our administrative
costs to $105, rather than the $125 we had allocated. This
cut would allow us to meet the program's cost.

I'd like to see Jerry take advantage of this bargain and
have Dr. Skaggs run the program. Will you write a memo
that'll persuade him to do it?

Andrea Walsh

E and T Problem 15
Suggested reading: Part II and Chapters 17 and 18

You've received a number of staff suggestions about equipment purchases over the next two years (see earlier problem), and the deadline for formulating a final list is fast approaching. You've followed up on each suggestion as necessary by calling possible vendors and getting brand names, model numbers, price information, and so forth. You haven't taken time to shop for the best prices on items, but you've assembled standard list prices from readily accessible sources. Now your report to Ms. Walsh should efficiently summarize this information to allow her to make intelligent and informed decisions about the items to be included on her final list.

Ms. Walsh gave you a list of items. She proposes replacing her desk chair with the Slater Hi-Boy Tilt model, which Thompson Manufacturing central supply office provides at $297.00. She also proposes replacing two older overhead transparency projectors and three older slide projectors. Replacement of the current overhead projectors by the equivalent current model, the Brown L900, will cost $362.50 each. Replacement of the current slide projectors by the equivalent current model, the Weston Cartridge 328, will cost $269.80 each. Finally, she proposes buying an overhead projector table similar to the two current Jefferson J14-220 tables; the proposed model is currently available at $173.90. All the above audiovisual prices are taken from the Stone and Barton office and audiovisual products catalog.

Elvira Wedley, secretary, proposes replacing two office typewriters. She strongly favors the ABMC Adjust-Type model. Midtown Office Equipment Company quotes prices from $1048.55 to $1372.45 for this model depending on the options selected. Ms. Wedley also proposes buying an additional five-drawer file cabinet to match those now in the office. The Thompson Manufacturing central supply office quotes a price of $168.14 for this item. Finally, she proposes buying an electric collator for assembling the department's many reports and instructional materials. Midtown Office Equipment Company quotes a price of $653.00 on the Thornton Deluxe Electric Collator.

Donna Ferlow, secretary, proposes buying a word processing system. She says she can show how it'll save a substantial amount of typing time and allow more efficient preparation of training materials. She favors the ABMC Wordmaster system, quoted by Midtown Office Equipment Company at $5340.00, including installation and a one-year service contract, which is normally included in the purchase price. (You quickly checked two other vendors and found alternative systems at comparable prices.)

Bob Verdugo suggests that, if any slide projectors can be replaced, the new units should definitely be compatible with the current dissolve control unit. The Stone and Barton catalog shows that the Weston Cartridge 428, at $317.90, would be required. Bob also proposes buying another dissolve control unit, the Weston model 302-19 at $97.20.

Bob Verdugo, Dave Ziegler, Dawn Denton, and Paul Lotze all propose replacing their portable cassette tape recorders with more modern units. Dave Ziegler says he's looked over current models and favors the Suhatsu 300. The Stone and Barton catalog quotes a price of $104.95 for this item. (According to departmental records, all the present cassette recorders were purchased at the same time; should all nine of them be replaced now?)

Paul Lotze proposes buying an automated storyboard software package for the company's ZBL 430 computer. He says he can show substantial benefits in preparing slide sequences, and users' reviews of the package are enthusiastic. The package is available from Digisoft Automation for $5400, including first-year service. He says Jeanne Patacsil in Marketing and Neil Silverthorne in the president's office are making similar proposals. Some coordinated budgeting may be possible. Use of the package would require the installation of a computer terminal in the office. He recommends the Trimloc 2700 terminal with Trimloc VUE printer; the best price based on his research is $917 for the terminal and $720 for the printer, plus shipping charges from New England Electronic Center in Springfield, Massachusetts.

Bill George proposes buying a computer terminal for office use in preparing several programs for Information Systems. He says he spends an excessive amount of time arranging to use the Information Systems terminals to prepare courses. The Trimloc terminal would meet his needs; it may be worth considering regardless of whether the storyboard software package is recommended for purchase.

Dawn Denton proposes buying another seven-shelf bookcase for her office. The Thompson Manufacturing central supply office quotes a price of $239.40 for this item.

Dave Moen proposes buying a 45-inch circular conference table and three armchairs for his office, a request he says he's repeating. He lists Thompson Manufacturing central supply office inventory number R559-25 for the table at $147.30 and inventory number H3-556 for the chairs at $93.90 each.

Carlos Aguilar proposes buying a second camera and copy stand for creating 35mm slides. He says the present camera and stand are often in use when he needs them, and it's wasteful of film for two people to alternate their use of this unit during the same period. He recommends the Bolens Radex camera and stand, which are listed in the Stone and Barton catalog at $429.95.

The remaining staff members had no suggestions.

THE FORMS DESIGN MINICASE

The Hobson Equipment Corporation began after World War II when founder Gerald McInis bought some war surplus vehicles and hired local mechanics to rebuild them as farm machines. The venture was quite successful, and over the last few decades the company has evolved into a major supplier of earthmoving equipment, with offices and production facilities in Hobson, Iowa. The company now employs over 900 workers, including management and office staff totaling more than 250. This is the setting for the following writing problems. In each problem, you'll be asked to assume the identity of some participant in the developing forms design project at Hobson Equipment.

Forms Design Problem 1

Suggested reading: Part II and Chapter 12

Your identity: staff assistant to Edgar F. Cataulin, Administrative Manager

In his office today, Mr. Cataulin asked you to write a memo for his signature requesting that the Training Department study the feasibility of an in-plant short course in forms design. Your notes of the conversation:

- The present situation is lamentable.
- A recent count of the forms used in the company identified over 650 different forms.
- Many forms could be combined.
- Most forms could use updating.
- A few forms are so poorly designed that they're nearly unusable, even by people who know what they're supposed to be used for.
- The cost in work-hours because of the company's poor forms is incalculable.
- A systematic study of forms is necessary—essential!
- Participants should be representatives of all staff departments; all departments use many forms—especially Accounting, Personnel.
- The Data Processing Department needs ideas to improve printout design.
- Get an expert (professor? consultant?) in for 2–3 days, all-day sessions.
- Important goal: increase the awareness of the importance of good forms design (most people aren't even aware of the problem).
- Better forms are an absolute must; top priority.

Capture Mr. Cataulin's enthusiasm tactfully in your memo to Azon E. Grenfell, Training Director.

Forms Design Problem 2
Suggested reading: Part II and Chapter 12 (also, review Chapter 14)

Your identity: Azon E. Grenfell, Training Director

Ed Cataulin is a man of many enthusiasms—some of them eccentric, some sensible. This time you can see real merit in his idea of doing something about forms design in the company. You too were shocked to discover how many forms the company uses, although you've long been aware that many of them are terribly designed—anyone who has to fill them out knows that. But your expert opinion (for which you are highly paid and occasionally respected) is that training a large number of people to design forms is the wrong way to solve the problem. There's no doubt that such a training course could be set up, and it would certainly do some good. But forms design is not a simple field in which everyone can become an instant expert, and many of the problems will require a more professional approach than 10 or 12 hours of study can provide. We need more than a "quick fix."

You believe that the company should hire a professional forms designer to consult with department personnel. Such a staff member could work closely with these personnel to build skills among those who often create new forms (such as the Accounting and Personnel people) and could also help the Data Processing people become sensitive to design considerations in their printouts.

If the company isn't ready to hire a full-time forms designer, then why not retain a professor at one of the nearby universities as a part-time regular consultant? Several local professors have the necessary expertise; you can supply names and credentials. Ed's department would be the appropriate one to do the hiring (and pay the cost), since a project of this kind would normally be handled by Administrative services.

Reply to his memo. He thinks that your department should fund this project, so you must make a convincing case that solving the problem is really his department's responsibility.

Forms Design Problem 3
Suggested reading: Part II and Chapter 12

Your identity: staff assistant to Edgar F. Cataulin, Administrative Manager

In a meeting you attended this morning in Grenfell's office, Ed Cataulin and Training Director Azon Grenfell finally agreed on what to do about forms design. Since the company depends so heavily on forms for collecting and transmitting basic information, they felt that the long-term solution would be to hire a full-time forms design specialist. To begin with, however, they agreed to make sure that such a specialist could produce benefits that would justify the cost. Toward this end, they telephoned Dr. Charles T. Guntrup, Professor of Administrative Services at the state university. They described the problems and the desired solutions, and they also discussed arrangements for retaining Dr. Guntrup as a consultant. These arrangements include five days per month, selected by mutual agreement, to be spent at the company office in Hobson and a fee of $175 per day plus travel reimbursement at actual cost. Dr. Guntrup is to bill the company each month for the fee and bill separately for the expenses. All work is to be done by Dr. Guntrup personally at the company site.

After talking with Dr. Guntrup, Cataulin and Grenfell agreed on the following project objectives:

- To study the design criteria of certain forms selected by Cataulin and Grenfell.
- To propose and justify the redesign of forms, if necessary.
- To supervise the implementation of redesigned forms, including the retraining of personnel.
- To report impressions of the company's forms situation and suggestions in a monthly meeting with Cataulin and Grenfell.
- To present a report at the end of six months that evaluates the need for a full-time forms design specialist, documents the benefits from employing such a person, and details a job description.

Finally, Cataulin and Grenfell agreed (after some heavy negotiating on both sides) to split Dr. Guntrup's fee and expenses evenly between the two department budgets.

After the meeting, Cataulin suggested that you write a memo for the record, based on your notes of the conversation, documenting the points of agreement between the Administrative Services Department and the Training Department. Write that memo.

Forms Design Problem 4
Suggested reading: Part II and Chapter 12

Your identity: staff assistant to Edgar F. Cataulin, Administrative Manager

Mr. Cataulin also asked you to draft a letter (for his signature) to Dr. Guntrup that discusses the company's forms design problems, presents Hobson Equipment's proposed project objectives, and formally offers him the proposed consulting position. Dr. Guntrup's favorable reply will complete the arrangement, so be specific about the work to be done, the schedule of reports to be made, and the terms of payment. Ask Dr. Guntrup to begin work as soon as possible; in his reply, he should propose a project schedule that includes suggested dates for his work at the company.

Forms Design Problem 5
Suggested reading: Part II and Chapter 12

Your identity: Dr. Charles T. Guntrup, Professor of Administrative Services at the state university

In a letter to Ed Cataulin at Hobson Equipment Corporation, accept the terms of the consulting arrangement they've offered. In the next two weeks, you must complete the present university semester, preparing and grading final examinations and grading term papers. The following week (check the calendar for dates) you propose to spend Monday and Friday at Hobson. After that, you propose to spend every Friday there and one additional day per month selected by mutual agreement among Cataulin, Grenfell, and you. You agree tentatively to the objectives proposed by Cataulin, although as a professional consultant you must reserve the right to propose revisions in these objectives as your investigation progresses. Since you'll be performing your work at some distance from your home office, you assume that Hobson Equipment will provide you with a desk and file, along with the minimal clerical assistance necessary for any correspondence or other written materials you may need to prepare.

Forms Design Problem 6
Suggested reading: Part II and Chapter 12 (also, review Chapter 14)

Your identity: Dr. Charles T. Guntrup, Professor of Administrative Services at the state university

After spending three months working with Ed Cataulin and Azon Grenfell on their company's forms design problems, you feel the time has come for them to obtain certain specialized technical assistance. You've identified a number of problems that could be readily solved by a good graphics designer. You've noted repeatedly in discussions with Cataulin and Grenfell that their problems with computer printout design are actually symptomatic of more pervasive documentation problems in the Information Systems area.

At the state university, you're fortunate to have unusually well qualified colleagues in both these fields. Professor Timothy R. Kloos, Art Department, has a strong background and credentials in precisely the areas where graphics design help is needed. He's served as consultant to companies throughout your region and is highly recommended by past clients. Dr. David A. Peairs, Information Systems Department, is an internationally known authority on technical documentation with strong recommendations from clients nationwide.

You propose that Professor Kloos be engaged to spend approximately three days at company headquarters consulting with staff members and reporting results and that he be commissioned to spend approximately three additional days on actual design work to be done at the university. You suggest a consulting fee of $175 per day, plus expenses, and an allowance of $300 for assistance and materials.

Your proposal for Dr. Peairs is more extensive. You propose that the company engage him in a continuing relationship similar to your own. That is, he should be directed to work with the Information Systems staff over a period of months to help them evaluate the benefits of hiring a professional technical documentation specialist and to prepare a job description for such a specialist. Because of his national reputation, Dr. Peairs normally accepts consulting assignments at $300 per day, plus expenses.

You've discussed these points with Cataulin and Grenfell in some detail. They appear reasonably optimistic and have asked you to put your suggestions in writing. Your written statement will serve as the basis for their own proposals for supplementary budget support for these projects. Write the letter.

Forms Design Problem 7
Suggested reading: Part II and Chapter 13

Your identity: staff assistant to Edgar F. Cataulin, Administrative Manager

You're to draft a reply to Dr. Guntrup, who has proposed that the company engage two additional consultants, one in graphics design and one in technical documentation. Neither recommendation has been accepted.

The proposal to engage a graphics design consultant was rejected on the theory that it would be better to delay action until the new forms design specialist has been hired. This specialist may already have the necessary skills or may prefer alternative means of achieving the goal. Even if the specialist does decide to engage Professor Kloos (the recommendation will be kept on file for the specialist's reference), it would be better for him or her to make the contact with Professor Kloos as a basis for a possible long-term relationship. It's felt that the benefits of immediate action are outweighed by the potential benefits of allowing the new person to make the decision and establish the contacts.

The proposal to engage a technical documentation consultant was the subject of a meeting with Information Systems staff. They didn't feel that technical documentation was a high priority, and their own staffing proposals for the next budget won't include any new people in this area. They didn't reject the importance of technical documentation; they simply felt that other needs were much more pressing. It's now clear that Information Systems staff doesn't recognize the problems created for the rest of the company by poor printout design and other documentation shortcomings, and a long-term program of educating the Information Systems staff will be essential to the solution. Such education may be part of the forms design specialist's job. It'd be folly to bring in a consultant against the wishes of the department involved; except in a life-or-death situation, no one would seriously consider such an action.

Write Dr. Guntrup, describing the outcome of the proposals; this letter is for your boss' signature. Remind Dr. Guntrup tactfully that, according to the original plan, he was to submit at the end of six months a report evaluating the need for a full-time forms design specialist and presenting a job description for that position. In that report, he may want to discuss again his proposals to retain Professor Kloos and Dr. Peairs. If he's prepared to submit that report now, he should do so. At the same time, he should indicate what further professional consultation on his part, if any, he believes Hobson Equipment should consider. Make it clear that you aren't in any sense firing him, but only inviting him to reevaluate the original goals and schedule and to confirm them or suggest revisions to them.

III

Writing Letters and Memos

U p to this point, you've been studying background material that's useful in all kinds of business writing. In this part of the book, you'll put your knowledge to use as you practice writing some common types of short business messages. Each chapter in this part analyzes sample messages to help you develop your power of analysis, and includes practice problems at the end.

LETTERS AND MEMOS: FORMAT

Most short business messages are typed in letter or memo format. The letter format is used for more formal messages, including nearly all messages sent outside the organization. It's also used occasionally for official messages from the organization to an employee, such as an announcement of a promotion or raise. Typing formats for letters are described in Appendix A beginning on page 483.

Memo format is used for less formal messages, including nearly all messages addressed to someone inside the organization. It's also used occasionally for very informal messages to readers outside the organization. Standard memo formats are described in Appendix B beginning on page 495.

Most short reports are typed in letter format (if addressed to someone outside the organization) or memo format (if addressed to someone inside the organization). Extremely formal short reports may be typed in formal report format with a title page and other formal-report parts, as described in Chapter 19.

LETTERS AND MEMOS: CONTENTS

The variety of situations in which people write letters and memos is nearly endless. Scholars in this field have listed several hundred types of letters and memos, and their lists aren't even intended to be exhaustive.

In the coming chapters, we consider three basic organizational plans for short messages: a plan for communicating good or neutral news, a plan for communicating bad news, and a plan for persuading. The applications of these plans are quite varied, as the following examples show.

DIRECT-PLAN MESSAGES: GOOD NEWS OR NEUTRAL INFORMATION

Acknowledgment	Invitation reply
Adjustment approval	Job instruction
Adjustment request	Notice
Announcement	Notification
Appointment	Offering of a favor
Appointment reply	Offering of information
Appreciation	Order
Claim	Personnel evaluation report

Collection notification
Collection reminder
Complaint
Condolence
Congratulations
Credit application
Credit approval
Credit request
Favorable reply
Favorable reply to claim
Favorable reply to credit request
Favorable reply to order
Favorable reply to request
Inquiry
Inquiry about a person
Inquiry reply
Introduction
Invitation
Invitation for credit

Policy
Praise
Procedure
Recommendation
Remittance
Remittance request
Reply to congratulations
Reply to invitation
Reply with sales possibilities
Request
Request for adjustment
Request for credit information
Request for recommendation
Reservation
Seasonal greeting
Sympathy
Thanks
Unsolicited favorable message
Welcome

INDIRECT-PLAN MESSAGES: BAD NEWS

Acknowledgment, back order
Acknowledgment, declined order
Acknowledgment, delayed order
Acknowledgment, incomplete order
Acknowledgment, indefinite order
Adjustment compromise
Adjustment refusal

Back order response
Credit refusal
Employment refusal
Favor refusal
Order refusal
Refused request
Unfavorable reply
Unfavorable unsolicited message

INDIRECT-PLAN MESSAGES: PERSUASIVE MESSAGES

Campaign series sales letter
Collection appeal
Collection inquiry
Collection ultimatum
Continuous series sales letter
Interview follow-up letter
Job application letter
Persuasive claim

Persuasive policy complaint
Persuasive request
Persuasive request for credit
Prospecting sales letter
Résumé
Special request
Unsolicited sales letter
Wear-out series sales letter

Obviously, the number of types of short business messages makes it fruitless to describe specific approaches to each one. Doing that would make this book far too long. Besides, you don't really have to learn different approaches to 50 or 100 types of messages, because each type is a largely commonsense application of the basic principles of one of the three basic organizational plans.

Therefore, over the next few chapters we'll concentrate on the three basic plans. In some cases, we'll consider how a basic plan is applied to a specific situation. Studying such cases will help you see how to adapt that particular plan to most situations. After studying these chapters, you should understand the three basic plans very clearly and know how to adapt them to nearly any situation you might encounter in your career.

12

Direct-Plan Messages

*Read over your compositions, and where
ever you meet with a passage which you
think is particularly fine, strike it out.*
Samuel Johnson

*I knew one that when he wrote a letter
he would put that which was most material
in the postscript, as if it had been a bymatter.*
Francis Bacon

The direct plan is the commonest way to organize business messages. As we've seen, it allows the reader to receive information most efficiently, and it's a simple, easy way for the writer to organize ideas.

The direct plan is used when the message's main goal is to convey information. It's usually the best organizing plan when the information will come as good or neutral news to the reader. (See Figure 1.) This plan isn't so well suited to situations in which (1) the reader won't understand the main point (perhaps because of technical terminology) if you state it at the beginning, (2) the reader's preconceived ideas will lead him or her to reject the main point immediately unless you begin by showing the reasons for it, or (3) your main goal involves dealing with the reader's emotional reactions to the information. In such situations, you should consider the indirect plan.

In the direct plan, the message's focal point is at the beginning. The main point is located there, and all the other points support what's said there. In a direct-plan message, the ending is much less emphasized than the beginning. In fact, in messages of only a page or so, there's no explicit ending at all; the message simply stops after the last point is made.

ORGANIZING DIRECT-PLAN MESSAGES

The steps in organizing a direct-plan message are (1) identifying and stating the main point, (2) planning the order of supporting points, evidence, or arguments, and (3) devising a suitable ending.

The Main Point

The first statement in a direct-plan message should normally be the main point. In unusual cases, it could be preceded by some friendly comment (such as congratulations, if appropriate), but nearly always the main point comes right at the beginning.

In the planning stage, begin your organizing by identifying the main point. Depending on the circumstances, the main point may be what you most want the reader to know, or it may be what the reader most wants to know. If the reader isn't expecting the message, then certainly the main point will be the central item you want to convey. If the reader expects the message, then you may want to state a main point that will satisfy the reader's expectations by telling what he or she wants to know.

In your planning, formulate the main-idea sentence exactly as it will appear in the message. Since it'll be the first sentence in the message, it should not only state the main point but also attract interest, often by demonstrating how the point affects the reader personally. Using your audience analysis notes to consider how the reader views this point, experiment to find the formulation that best attracts interest and most clearly conveys the main point.

August 2, 1983

Mrs. Roberta Morganstern
596 Second Street
Port Clyde, Maine   04855

Dear Mrs. Morganstern:

    Here's your lease for apartment #2056 in the College Towers
complex beginning October 2, 1983. Please sign the top copy of
the lease and return it as soon as possible.

    I've applied your $820 check to your account as follows:

First month's rent	$310.00
Last month's rent	310.00
Security deposit	200.00
Total	$820.00

    I'll make arrangements to be sure your apartment is fully
cleaned and ready for occupancy when you arrive here in Lexington
on October 2.

Cordially,

James MacPherson
Manager

Figure 1 A direct-plan letter

The Supporting Points

Now that you know what the first sentence says, you may immediately see some reasonable ways to organize the supporting points. If they develop evidence or argue for the main point, then they should be organized in the most logical order. If they're details that further explain the main point, then they should be organized in the clearest way. Often the clearest way is to arrange them in descending order of importance, from most important to least important. While you're thinking about the supporting points, look for ways to personalize them and orient them to the reader's interests. The more interesting your message appears, the more likely the reader will continue reading.

The Ending

If your direct-plan message is shorter than a page or so, it almost certainly needs no ending material. After it discusses the last supporting point, it should just stop, as the message in Figure 2 does. Longer messages, such as direct-plan reports, may need ending summaries simply to help the reader remember the large quantity of information that was presented. In addition, the endings of longer messages may repeat any request for action that was made in the beginning.

```
DATE: August 29, 1983

TO: All Employees

FROM: Roland U. Landweer, President

SUBJECT: Screening for High Blood Pressure


    The company will provide free blood pressure tests for all
employees who wish to participate during work hours on September
13 and 14 in the outdoor lunch area behind the Administration
Building.

    Hypertension, or high blood pressure, is a serious
condition that increases the risk of heart disease and other
illnesses, but it's readily controlled under the care of your own
physician.  The test is quick and entirely painless.

    This screening is voluntary, and you're under no obligation
to be tested.  Results will be communicated to you immediately.
No record of your test results will be kept by the company.

    Supervisors and department heads will be scheduling release
time for employees who wish to participate.
```

Figure 2 A direct-plan memo

Remember, however, that the focus of a direct-plan message, even a longer one, is on the beginning. If you let your message build to a climax at the end, then you'll be departing from the direct plan and reducing the efficiency with which it can be read. So even if the message ends with a call for action and the reasons for acting, the main presentation of the material should be at the beginning. The end is simply a reminder.

SOME ROUTINE DIRECT-PLAN MESSAGES

Widely varied types of messages use the direct plan—far too many for us to consider individually. Several types of routine direct-plan messages, however, can illustrate the way messages use this plan.

The Direct-Plan Request

A request is a message asking the reader to do something. You should organize a request in the direct plan when you think the reader may already be willing to do as you ask without having to be persuaded.

In planning a direct-plan request, note that the call for action is the main idea, so it should come in the opening sentence. To soften your request so it doesn't sound like a demand, you'll often use the word *please*. If opening with the request seems inappropriate, then perhaps an organizational pattern better suited to persuasion is needed. In a direct-plan request, your reader should see your call for action simply as information.

Figure 3 shows a common type of direct-plan request in which the requested action is one the readers are expected to perform as part of their jobs. The request's purposes are to ask them to complete the report by a specific date and give them additional information they'll need to write it. Thus the opening request for action is followed by details and by information that readers will need to perform the action.

A direct-plan request usually ends simply by stopping at the end of the supporting points. In some cases, though, it's possible to make a subordinated reference to the requested action in the final sentence or two. In Figure 4, the end reminds the reader that action is needed, yet the reminder is worked into a sentence that by no means repeats the main point. The closing request for quick action or action within a certain period is often used as a reminder in this way. Here, as a mild incentive, the action is linked to an outcome the reader would like. Notice also that the beginning states the request in rather general terms, and the supporting points clarify precisely what is asked for and why. When the request is so complicated that it can't be smoothly stated in a single main-idea sentence, the main point should be a summary, or general statement, of the request.

The Direct-Plan Inquiry

An inquiry is a request for information. In many ways, it resembles the direct-plan request, since it asks the reader to do something—namely,

DATE: May 24, 1983

TO: All Department Heads

FROM: Suzanne Lefebvre, Vice-President, Administration

SUBJECT: PERSONNEL PROJECTIONS DUE MAY 31

   Please get your department's quarterly personnel projection to me by May 31. Beginning on June 11, the Executive Committee will be holding sessions to determine personnel allocations, and I want to meet with you to discuss your projected changes in time to prepare our general plan.

   Although the recent PH-55 contract will involve selective personnel expansion in certain areas, please remember that our current long-range projection assumes a mild contraction in personnel in the coming two or three quarters. Therefore, if you plan to request additional positions, your justification will need to be clear and strong. I would view any justifiable savings in personnel very positively.

Figure 3 A direct-plan request

Dear Ms. Sulieman:

   We'd like to conduct tests, as you suggested, of the two tape recorder models you showed us in your interesting demonstration last Monday. We believe one of the two may be the recorder we need for each of our sales representatives. They appear to be sturdy, knockabout machines that can stand up to daily use on the road yet provide the high-quality dictation capabilities we need.

   Please provide us one unit each of Model YR-1780 and Model SR-1901 for approximately one week's testing here in the home office. That will allow selected salespeople to try using them briefly and allow several experienced stenographers to transcribe tapes made on them.

   We'd like to finish testing on these units and write the complete order for 70 to 80 machines in the next two or three weeks, so I'm hoping to have the units for testing very soon.

Cordially,

Figure 4 A direct-plan request

send us information. Most requests, however, ask for a fairly simple action, whereas an inquiry normally asks for answers to a whole series of questions. Thus the structures of the messages aren't quite the same. In inquiries, the reader is typically expected to answer the questions as a matter of course. Thus the direct plan is normally appropriate. If persuasion is needed, see Chapter 14 for guidelines.

The opening sentence of a direct-plan inquiry should indicate that you're asking for information and state at least the general topic of the information you want. For example, the inquiry in Figure 5 begins by asking for "more information," which by itself is a fairly general request. Quickly, though, the message provides the context in which the information will be applied (a study of the 1300 present forms), and it begins refining the topic on which further information is requested. If the reader may benefit from providing you the requested information (for example, by eventually selling you the goods you're inquiring about), then you may want to mention this in the opening.

Often, an inquiry's supporting "points" are a series of specific questions you'd like answers to. In that case, you might enumerate these questions, as in Figure 6. Enumeration can be used for a list of points of roughly

---

Dear Professor Flores:

    I'd like more information about the model program for forms design that you discussed in your recent article in <u>Management and Administration Magazine</u>. Since I was recently given responsibility for studying the more than 1300 standard forms my company uses, ranging from order forms and job applications to standard computer printout formats, I'm very interested in your conclusions. It's of course very expensive to print and store this many forms, and any justifiable reduction in this number would be welcome.

    In your article, you stated that a typical company should be able to reduce the number of forms it uses by about 15 to 20 percent by elimination and consolidation. However, if two forms designed for slightly different purposes are consolidated into one, then probably the resulting form will be at least slightly less suitable for either of its uses than the original two were. How do you evaluate the tradeoffs in such situations to decide whether to retain the two forms or consolidate them?

    I've already ordered copies of each information source you mentioned at the end of your article. If you can suggest references to more extensive information specifically about form consolidation, I'd like to have your recommendations.

Cordially,

Figure 5 A direct-plan inquiry

DATE: October 23, 1982

TO: Samuel Reichel, Director of Marketing

FROM: Oscar Quinones, Director of Personnel

SUBJECT: Administrative Associate Position

     I have several questions about your October 16 proposal to the Executive Committee to eliminate the Executive Secretary position and to establish an Administrative Associate position in its place.

    1. Will each administrative unit that now includes one or more Executive Secretary positions automatically be entitled to corresponding Administrative Associate positions, or will each unit have to request and defend the allocation of such positions?

    2. Will all personnel now ranked as Executive Secretaries automatically be ranked as Administrative Associates after the change? Since stenographic skills were weighed heavily in the qualifications for Executive Secretary and would hardly be considered in the qualifications for Administrative Associate according to your proposal, some of our present Executive Secretaries may not formally qualify as Administrative Associates.

    3. Once Administrative Associates with little or no stenographic skill begin filling positions, who will perform clerical tasks of the highly confidential or sensitive nature that are now performed by Executive Secretaries?

    4. What's the relationship between the Administrative Associate position and the present Administrative Assistant position, now generally held by early-career male employees?

    I'd like to see these points clarified before the Executive Committee considers the matter further.

Figure 6 A direct-plan inquiry

equal weight, all focusing directly on the main point rather than building on one another. In Figure 6, each enumerated point is one of the questions Mr. Quinones mentioned in his opening sentence.

The Direct-Plan Reply

The routine reply is one of the most common types of business messages. If you're using the direct plan, then the main point of a reply should be the thing the reader wants to know, as the openings in Figure 7 illustrate. After the opening, the direct-plan reply provides details or other supporting points, as are usual in direct-plan messages. If the reply answers a series of questions, then enumerating your answers may be clear and convenient.

The Direct-Plan Acknowledgment

An acknowledgment says, "I received what you sent." Not only is it courteous to acknowledge receipt of many types of messages and goods, but in certain cases the acknowledgment is necessary to serve as a written receipt for goods or an acceptance of an order. If, in reply to a request, you take action that isn't visible to the reader, then sending an acknowledgment eases the reader's mind and lets you reemphasize the goodwill you've built up by doing what he or she asked. And when someone sends you

```
DATE: May 24, 1983

TO: Tara Wolfe, Comptroller

FROM: V. X. Landino, Director of Personnel

SUBJECT: CURRENT HIRING SUCCESS RATES


     Here are the figures you requested on our hiring success
rates by job category and department, in the first three quarters
of this fiscal year.  As the attached table indicates, . . .




Dear Mrs. Halyk:

     I'd be happy to spend Thursday morning, March 5th, with
your fifth graders to talk about careers in veterinary medicine.
I'm glad to hear that several of your pupils have suggested this
topic. . . .
```

Figure 7 Openings for a direct-plan reply

something valuable that doesn't prompt any other response, your acknowledgment says thank you.

Although the acknowledgment's purpose is to indicate receipt, it seldom makes much sense to open simply by saying you received the item. That's usually pretty obvious, since you are replying at all. If your whole purpose is just to say you received the item, as Figure 8 does, then a better opening would be to thank the reader for it. If you intend to take some action, then a good opening would be to say what action you intend to take, as the opening in Figure 9 does. In Figure 9 the credit line is necessary because the writer is shipping goods first and billing the store after shipment. Terms of 2/10, n/30 mean the writer will give a 2 percent discount if the store pays within 10 days of invoice; the full net amount is due in 30 days.

Anytime your message involves your company's product or service, consider including brief resale material. In Figure 9, for example, the middle paragraph is intended to resell Ms. Harkhani on the wisdom of her decision to stock Gardenyear carts. Even though she's already placed an order, resale material of this kind helps to confirm for her the merits of the product. Resale material is usually used in correspondence that will arrive between the time of the order and the time of delivery, thus helping to maintain the buyer's enthusiasm until the product or service itself arrives. Your company probably budgets a substantial sum to communicate promotional messages to potential buyers, and your routine messages are a very inexpensive opportunity to assist these promotional goals in a direct, personalized way.

```
DATE: August 19, 1983

TO: Morris Cohn, Lab Manager

FROM: Sharon Melton, Industrial Engineering

SUBJECT: Preliminary Test Results


    Thank you for your prompt delivery of preliminary test
results on the plastic valve samples.  Some of the raw data
you're getting looks very good, and I think there's every reason
for optimism at this point, as you've suggested.

    We're looking forward to your complete October 15 report,
after which we'll make a final design decision.
```

Figure 8 A direct-plan acknowledgment

```
Dear Ms. Harkhani:

     On Thursday we'll be shipping by motor express the three
Model H5 Gardenyear Lawn Carts you ordered.  We've established
the $500 credit line you requested, and shipments will be made on
our normal 2/10, n/30 terms.

     We appreciate your order, and we know your customers will
like the unique Gardenyear design because of the cart's easy
loading and unloading.  Other garden shop owners tell us that,
once several units move out of their shops, word of mouth quickly
leads to additional sales at an attractive 43 percent markup.
And the quality engineering that goes into these products makes
for satisfied customers in the long run.

     I'm enclosing 50 copies of the Gardenyear promotional
brochure for distribution to your customers and several copies of
our order form for your use.

Cordially,
```

Figure 9 A direct-plan acknowledgment

If you do include resale material, simply claiming that your products or services are the best in the world or making other such general claims is not very effective. After years of exposure to mass advertising, people are pretty much deaf to such claims. Instead, select one or two particular selling points of special interest to the reader and concentrate on them. Keep it brief; two or three sentences are about all most readers will pay attention to. Consider the examples in Figure 10.

PLANNING NONROUTINE DIRECT-PLAN MESSAGES

When you're writing an unfamiliar or complicated message, use the full three-stage approach to writing, as described in Chapter 11. Each nonroutine message has its own peculiarities, so each needs the full analysis and careful revision of that approach. The following examples of nonroutine direct-plan messages illustrate the problems you may encounter.

The Directive

A directive is a formal statement of procedure. It prescribes the way a certain task must be performed, and as such it becomes part of official policy. Figure 11 shows an example. Because a directive is formal, most writers treat it as a nonroutine message.

```
     Both you and your clients will appreciate the protection
provided by the 416-pound tear strength of the My-Fiber mailing
envelopes you ordered.  Despite the roughest handling in transit,
the report your client takes from the envelope will look perfect,
just like the copy on your own desk.


     The triple-stitched construction and expertly hand-sewn
fittings will keep your customers happy with their Wilder-Tote
bags for season after season, and their friends will be
impressed, too.


     You'll begin using your Writer's Desk Manual the day it
arrives.  The 24 steps to a clear report in Chapter 4 give you 24
easy, understandable ways to improve your very first project.


     Weighing only 28 pounds, your fiberglass RollaTabl is
guaranteed to hold a 400-pound load without strain--if two strong
men can lift the load, the RollaTabl can carry it handily.
```

Figure 10 Resale material

The first step in planning a directive is to determine precisely what the procedure is. This step may seem obvious, but often a procedure is completely formulated only when it's written into a directive. Until then, the procedure has probably been discussed only among executives whose viewpoints are so similar that they don't need to describe it precisely.

Even when a procedure is fully spelled out, however, it still needs careful inspection by the writer. What situations will the procedure be used in, and who will use it? Does the procedure, as stated, really fit those situations? What exceptions will arise, and how does the procedure apply to them? What further assumptions must someone make to apply the procedure correctly? If all this sounds a bit petty and legalistic, that's because a directive is, in a small way, a legal document. And few people look so foolish in public as the directive writer who must immediately issue daily bulletins clarifying what the directive really meant.

Once you feel comfortable with the procedure you'll describe, begin a thorough audience analysis. The problem with most directives is that they must be understood by everyone who will play a part in the cited procedures, and often that means everyone in the organization, from top to bottom. Top executives are accustomed to getting information from written documents, but many others in the organization aren't. Often, the

```
DATE: May 17, 1983

TO: All Employees

FROM: Helen G. Bromwell, Vice-President, Administration

SUBJECT: Summer Hours for Administrative Offices June 6
         to September 2 Will Be 7:30 a.m. to 3:30 p.m.


        This summer, on a trial basis, we'll shift our
administrative offices to an earlier schedule.  From Monday, June
6, to Friday, September 2, offices in the Administration Building
will be open from 7:30 a.m. to 3:30 p.m.  Production divisions
will continue on the normal three shifts.
        A skeleton crew will staff the Personnel Department and the
Sales Office on the regular 9:00 a.m. to 5:00 p.m. schedule
through the summer for the convenience of employees and customers
who need the services of these offices between 3:30 and 5:00 p.m.
        At the end of the trial period, administrative employees
will be asked to comment on the possibility of (1) continuing
these early hours throughout the rest of the year or (2)
returning to normal hours during the winter months and then
shifting to early hours again the following summer.
```

Figure 11 A directive

employees aren't at all stupid, as their creativity in finding ways to circumvent the procedure will demonstrate, but they aren't used to reading complicated, legalistic documents. Every possible technique to achieve high readability must be used.

Therefore, directives often go through quite a number of revisions after they're drafted. In fact, after the writer has revised extensively, directives are often circulated to others for comment and further revision. Important directives are sometimes even tested by asking a small cross section of employees to read them and explain what they mean. Such testing indicates weak spots in the directive and often in the procedure itself.

The Special Goodwill Message

A wide variety of messages is sent to build goodwill among readers. Such messages include handwritten congratulatory notes to promoted colleagues, holiday greetings to customers and suppliers, and welcoming letters to new employees, customers, or community members.

To get the most benefit from such messages, make them part of a planned goodwill program. If they're written only sporadically, they'll no doubt do some good, but the results will be spotty. Worse, having to write

Dear Mr. Speegle:

We appreciate the confidence you expressed in American Business Machines Corporation by your recent stock purchase. We share your optimism about the future of ABMC.

To help you be fully informed about ABMC, we've enclosed a brochure describing the company and its products and a copy of our most recent annual report. We'll be sending further reports at least every three months to keep you abreast of our progress and our plans.

If you ever feel you'd like additional information, please let us know. We want our owners to be able to take pride in their association with ABMC.

Cordially,

Figure 12 A special goodwill message

an individual message for each occasion is a time-consuming task, which you may soon start putting off. With a planned program, you'll soon develop skeleton outlines for each basic type of message, so you can write individual goodwill messages quickly and painlessly.

In planning goodwill messages, you should usually avoid blatant commercialism, since that can interfere with building goodwill. Yet, since goodwill messages are often addressed to people who wouldn't otherwise be acquainted with your products or services, such messages are especially valuable opportunities to inform them. As Figure 12 illustrates, the balance between useful information and blatant commercialism is often delicate, and maintaining it is a challenge in every stage of the writing process.

The Memo for the Record

Many vital working agreements within organizations are made in face-to-face or telephone conversations. Often such agreements involve significant exchanges: my department will do this now, and in return your department will do thus and so in the future. Unless such agreements are recorded for future reference, participants are relying very heavily on one another's memories for the details. If success in your job depends upon someone's fulfilling such an agreement, you may want something in writing that makes the agreement clear. That's the role of a memo for the record, as illustrated in Figure 13. Sometimes the participants in such an agreement recognize that someone should write it as a memo and send copies to everyone involved. Often, however, no one thinks of that at the time, and only later do you realize that you should create a memo for the record.

```
DATE: June 23, 1983

TO: David R. Holdaway

FROM: Linda Lowary, Chair, VisCom Program Design Committee

SUBJECT: Preparations for Final Presentation


        After our meeting this morning, I checked with Colette
Johnson in Marketing and Wayne Windus in Transportation, and
we'll be able to go ahead with plans for our final presentation
on July 9, as we'd hoped.  All who should attend have put the
date on their schedules.

        I appreciate your offer to verify the historical data and
to rework the projections in line with our discussion.  As soon
as I receive that material from you, I'll begin preparing the
visuals we'll need for the presentation.  I hope to begin on
these by the week of June 9 at the latest.
```

Figure 13 A memo for the record

In that case, consider in your analysis that, by writing such a memo, you're questioning at least the accuracy of the other participants' memories, and some may feel you're questioning their integrity, too. Therefore, try to avoid blunt, tactless openings like "For the record, here's a summary of the agreement we made this afternoon. . . ." If you're just a bit inventive, you can probably avoid being that obvious and thereby let the other participants save face. For example, if there's a step in the agreement you can take immediately, you can orient the memo to it by saying, in effect, "Here's the information I agreed to provide. I'm looking forward to receiving thus and so from you, as we agreed this afternoon. . . ." Each situation is different, of course, but if you're sensitive to the inherent implication of dishonesty in a memo for the record, you should be able to devise an inoffensive approach when needed.

FURTHER EXPLORATION

1. For 10 or 12 practice problems at the end of this chapter, quickly identify the main point in the message you'd write. Do you sometimes find more than one idea that could be considered the main point? If so, determine which one would best introduce the message as a whole to the reader.

2. Can you imagine a situation in which a message should have two main points of approximately equal importance? How could you organize such a message to get the benefits of the direct plan?

3. Imagine that you're writing a letter for a club or other student organization to welcome new members and invite them to attend their first meeting. Draft two or three sentences of resale material you could use in that letter. Then draft three or four versions of the resale material, stressing different benefits in each version. Which version do you think would work best? Why?

4. For the same organization, draw up a plan for special goodwill messages. What occasions provide opportunities for such messages to members? To others? How could such a plan be used?

5. Plan a memo for the record that could be submitted to your instructor with your next assignment. The memo should note that you're submitting the assignment, and it should detail the steps you expect the instructor to take in response. How should you plan such a memo to make it tactful? Is there ever a classroom situation in which actually sending such a memo would be a good idea?

WRITING PROBLEMS

1. Write to a college or university, asking for its catalog. Since many catalogs are published in parts, specify the field of study and the type of degree (such as undergraduate, graduate, MBA) you're considering. Send a check for $5.00. Say you'll pay the rest right away if the price is higher; if the price is lower, the institution should refund the difference. (The institution may just return your check along with a catalog order blank that lists prices.)

2. In a wide variety of business fields, small journals are published to keep practitioners abreast of the latest developments in special-purpose products and services. These journals are often free to qualified subscribers, with publication and editorial costs paid from sales of advertising space. Distributing the issues free to qualified subscribers increases circulation and concentrates it among those whom advertisers want to reach, thus making the journals more attractive and cost effective to advertisers.

One such (fictitious) journal is *The Automated Administrator*, which carries articles and advertisements about current applications of automation to office systems: automated word processing systems, electronic office message systems, electronic mail, and other related fields. Since you'll soon be making the final selection among several models of word processing systems for a small-scale trial project in the office you administer, you feel you qualify as the kind of person *The Automated Administrator* accepts as a qualified free subscriber. Write to the circulation manager (14391 Page Mill Road, Palo Alto, CA 94300), indicating why you feel you qualify. The circulation manager will view yours as a routine request, so simply provide the facts.

3. As Manager of Industrial Relations in your company, you supervise the maintenance of the official company policy manual, a collection of key company policy statements and directives assembled in loose-leaf binders in your office, with copies in other major offices in the company. The manual consists of official statements on employment and compensation of salaried and hourly workers, employee benefits and discipline, materials purchasing and handling, security of classified documents, health and safety regulations, and many other topics. Over the last few months, you've found that the manual needs attention. Continual revision has led to careless misprints. Later statements supplant earlier versions, which are still in the manual. Extraneous material appears (such as the dates of 1971 holidays and special staff assignments for a major project that's now completed). The manual is organized according to the publication dates of the policy statements, so new statements are simply added at the end.

The major problem is that there is no table of contents or index, so particular topics are difficult to locate. Only a few people are familiar with the contents; all others are at a disadvantage. An index should be created.

You've recently hired an assistant, and one of his first jobs unquestionably should be to become familiar with the policy manual's contents. It occurs to you that he could kill two birds with one stone while studying the manual by creating an index and locating out-of-date sections. The indexing job simply means identifying key words in each policy by which company personnel would probably search for information (such as salary review, annual; parking regulations; discipline, procedures; safety rules). The resulting index will be an alphabetical listing of key words, with page references. Suggested changes and deletions (with an explanation of each) should be incorporated into a memo.

Write the memo that will assign the job.

4. Mrs. Linda Wilgus (665 North Branch Street, Roswell, NM 88202), would like to buy small, individual-sized boxes of breakfast cereal for her children. Her problem is that the packages of eight or ten small boxes available in supermarkets include cereal brands that her children dislike, and to get the five or six packages of brands her children will eat, she must buy several additional packages that they won't eat. Her grocer's order list doesn't include these small boxes in packages of single brands. She checked with a restaurant supply house and some other local sources and found that, even in case lots used by restaurants and institutions, one has to buy assorted brands. She'd be willing to buy in case lots if necessary. Her children attend a day care center while she works, and they take the small boxes of cereal with them in the morning for breakfast at the center.

Mrs. Wilgus now intends to write a letter directly to the manufacturer of the cereals that her kids like best, American Cereal Company (Battle Creek, MI 49017). Draft a letter for her that will get the desired result.

5. As a new owner of a Recordex Model 55 cassette recorder for your stereo system, you're irritated to discover that the balance control is calibrated incorrectly. The balance control sets the relative volume between the two recording channels, making one softer or louder relative to the other when you record. The control works, except that it must nearly always be set at about "2 o'clock" on the dial for accurate balance rather than at about "12 o'clock," which should be normal. That inaccuracy would be OK in a cheap unit, but for $465 you expected more. Write the mail-order discount company that you bought the unit from (Disco Audio Discounter, P.O. Box 477, Mission, TX 78572) and ask to have the unit repaired or replaced. (See also the following problem.)

6. For Disco Audio Discounter (see the preceding problem), reply to the letter about the Recordex Model 55 cassette recorder. You offer no repair service. On returns and exchanges, the customer pays the shipping both ways (the approximate cost is $8.45 each way); you'll make an exchange if the unit is returned complete and operable (except for the present complaint) in all the original packing within 14 days from the date of your letter. Complete repair should be effected by loosening the set screw on the balance knob with a small screwdriver and resetting the knob in the correct position; the customer may be able to do this in five minutes. The Recordex Company offers warranty service. West of the Mississippi, send to Audio Service (92445 Sepulveda Road, Phoenix, AZ 85030); east of the Mississippi, send to Grother and Company (45 Old Summit Parkway, Lawrence, MA 01845). Repair should be covered under the warranty if the conditions are as described; the customer pays the shipping one way.

7. As Head of Payroll for your company, you receive a printout after each payroll computer run that lists the "check this person" (CTP) cases identified in that run. Payroll entries are put in the CTP file under one or more of the following circumstances:

- An employee's time card shows more than 12 hours of work on one day.
- An employee's recorded earnings total more than $99.99 for one day.
- An employee's time card shows more than 56 hours of work in one week's pay period.
- An employee's recorded earnings total more than $467.99 for one week's pay period.

Entries in the CTP printout are checked by hand to ensure that neither errors nor misrepresentations have occurred.

You've now found that under the new union wage agreements that took effect last month, certain employees may be legitimately paid more than $99.99 in one 24-hour period. Indeed, the size of the CTP printout has nearly doubled in the last few weeks (a time of seasonal high overtime) simply because of legitimate cases of this sort. It's a waste of time for your people to have to check out all these cases by hand, and it's a waste of good paper to print the list. Write a memo for your signature to Rudolph J. Cihak, Jr., Head of Information Systems, asking that the payroll programs be revised to set $110.99 as the upper daily limit on earnings and $519.99 as the upper weekly limit for CTP purposes. Sometimes such computer changes seem to take forever, so press for immediate action on this. (See also the following problem.)

8. Assume the position of Rudolph J. Cihak, Jr., Head of Information Systems, and respond to Pauline Jolliffe, Head of Payroll, about the request to change the criteria for CTP entries (see the preceding problem). Her request poses a problem she didn't anticipate: changing the daily earning limit from a four-digit number to a five-digit number. This doubtless can be done, but the programming required may not be trivial. Simple-looking changes like this, if done hastily, can foul up the interrelationships of a complex set of programs like the payroll package.

As Jolliffe will probably remember, Information Systems made an ironclad agreement earlier this year to implement changes in major systems (like payroll) on a semiannual release basis. (This means that all changes requested are collected over each six-month period and then programmed and rigorously tested together as a system package before they're released for general use. This procedure promotes more rigorous testing than is likely to occur with a series of very small changes.) Jolliffe not only agreed to this procedure, but adamantly argued for it (in uncomplimentary terms, as a matter of fact) as a way of cutting down on the number of computer-based errors. She should be the first to understand your position. Remind her.

9. Sit in for George G. Bergant, Director of the VS748 Project to develop a new product line for your company. Each month the directors of each development project meet with the company's top-level Operating Committee to coordinate activities and consult on problem areas. You just received notice that the next meeting is Monday at 2:00. That's the day you already agreed to spend at Georgetown Engineering working on a critical phase of your project. Luis Pacheco is your chief engineer on the project; he knows all phases of it very well. Ask him to attend the meeting as your representative. You'll give him your minutes of past meetings and your notes to review before the meeting. He'll have to make an oral progress report on your project, but it should be straightforward—no special problems to report. He can take some notes on the meeting and brief you when you get back. You especially want to know what's happening with the procurement of equipment for testing metal samples that you'll need for the next phase of your project. If that issue isn't discussed by others, he should raise the question. If Pacheco cannot make this meeting, he should tell you immediately so you can get someone else. (See also the following two problems.)

10.   Since you didn't hear from Luis Pacheco (see the preceding problem), you assumed that the monthly project directors' meeting with the Operating Committee was competently covered, so you spent a very productive day yesterday at Georgetown Engineering. In your in-basket this morning was the following note from your boss, Product Development Vice-President Helen J. Exarhos.

```
DATE: July 25, 1983
TO: George Bergant
FROM: Helen Exarhos
SUBJECT: Representation at Operating Committee Meeting

    Several important questions relating to your project
came up this morning at the Operating Committee meeting. I
called your office and found you were out of town, so I had
to provide answers as best I could. I sure hate to shoot from
the hip on such important matters, and I hope I don't have to
do it again.
    Operating Committee decisions are, of course, critical
to the continuation of any project, and the monthly meetings
will have to be treated as top priority. I trust that that
will be the case in the future.
    Please stop by my office after lunch so I can fill you
in on developments at the meeting.
```

Knowing Helen's normally calm disposition, you realize that this is a serious reprimand. When you arrive in her office this afternoon, you'd better be ready to explain what happened. Obviously Luis wasn't at the meeting. Write him a note to find out why. (See also the following problem.)

11.   Luis Pacheco (see the preceding two problems) wasted no time in replying. Within an hour you received his return note.

```
DATE: July 25, 1983
TO: George Bergant
FROM: Luis Pacheco
SUBJECT: Meeting I Was Supposed To Attend

    I don't know anything at all about this, George. This is
the first I heard of it. I don't remember getting any memo on
this, and my secretary says she would have noted it on my
calendar automatically if it had arrived.
```

      I'm really sorry about this, George. Of course I would
have attended if I'd known. I fully realize how important
these meetings are.

Just to be sure, while you were waiting for Luis' reply, your secretary dug out the file copy of your memo. It was right where it should have been. "Why me?" you sigh. You sent the memo; Luis never got it. You shouldn't have just assumed he'd get it. Later you may have some comments for the manager of the interoffice messenger system (after you cool off); right now, draft an explanation for Helen Exarhos. Since her memo will remain in the files, you'd better put your answer in memo form for filing, too.

12. In the Contracts Department of your company, which you direct, you've installed a new ALM Model 9 word processor, a newly designed system with state-of-the-art features. In a conversation with Calvin Fondren recently, you described some of the unit's features and functions, and he asked if he could bring his group of 11 technical writers from the Product Service Department to see it in operation. After some checking with your staff, it looks as though 1:30 on Thursday of next week would be a good time. Your lead word processing operator would be on duty at that time to demonstrate all the features. Calvin and his people could stay as long as they want, since this should be a light workday, and they can even try out the machine themselves if they'd like to. If Calvin thinks it would be useful, you could check with Ellen Montooth, the local ALM representative, to see whether she could stop by that afternoon. Write Calvin a memo on this.

13. Mr. Walter Shumata (19 Telegraph Road, Chattanooga, TN 37405) has written you (Kent Lock Company, 14772 University Heights Blvd., St. Louis, MO 63130) asking for a new installation template for his deadbolt door lock, which he described well enough so that you know it's a Model 447. His friend had bought it and never installed it, and Mr. Shumata had received it secondhand—minus the printed paper template showing the exact locations of clearance and mounting holes. The Model 447 is an old item now out of stock, but it is a very strong unit, reinforced to resist jimmying. For maximum security, key blanks for this model are not publicly available; additional keys are only available directly from the company. Mr. Shumata has probably noticed the unorthodox key style. Copies of the template sheet are still available. He should send $.50 to cover handling and postage. With your reply, include the standard order blank for additional keys.

14. As the proud owner of a newly-built ranch house, you're now planning a quick-growing, low-maintenance yard. To reduce the need for mowing, you propose to use mostly ground cover rather than lawn. Lucero Nursery (Rte. 5, Macon, GA 31211) advertises a special patented strain of creeping juniper that they claim grows much faster than normal strains, hugs the ground (no more than eight inches high), and fills in more densely than normal to shade out weeds. These are just the qualities you're looking for.

Write for more information. What evidence can they provide to back up their claim? Will these plants thrive in your climate (zone 5 on the map in their catalog)? Are there special soil requirements? (Yours is heavy clay and inclined to be alkaline.) Why are these plants priced nearly twice as high as local creeping juniper? Will Lucero guarantee live delivery of robust plants that will take hold and thrive? Ask about special watering and fertilization requirements. You want all the information they can provide. Your order will be for about $300 worth of plants, if you buy.

15. As owner-manager of Cannell Flowers, Inc., you're the largest grower of holiday poinsettia plants in your region, with nearly two acres of greenhouses in production. One of the most important factors in growing poinsettias is to shorten the day length artificially in the fall to force the plants into early bloom. Thus, plants are fully developed and blooming approximately a month earlier than their normal late December period. There's nothing more useless to a flower dealer than a poinsettia just coming into bloom on December 26, so the forced blooming is necessary to your business.

You shorten the day length by movable screening, which can be pulled into place over the plants to provide simulated darkness or pulled back to admit daylight. The screening is expensive, short-lived, awkward to move, and only moderately effective. In short, you'd like an improvement. According to an ad in the magazine *Modern Flower Growing*, the new VVC Night Screen provides denser shading than is possible with movable screening, it's about half as bulky as other screens, and it's impervious to the normal greenhouse environment. Therefore, the initial installation is expected to last, by company test, for five to seven years.

Write Georgia W. Harnetty, Marketing Vice-President, Consaul Agricultural Products Company (P.O. Box 19, Eastport, ME 04631), for detailed information. Your present screening will need replacement after the current season, so you want all the information necessary to make a purchase decision. What testing has been done, and with what results? What present users can attest to Consaul's claims under actual growing conditions? Can Consaul ship in the quantity you'll need in the first quarter of next year?

16. Assume you've graduated from college, moved across the country, and taken a good job. Now three years have passed, and your pride in your alma mater leads you to want a jacket with the school insignia on it. After some inquiry, you find that the most likely source is the bookstore back at the campus. Write for price and ordering information on the jacket you're thinking of.

You've seen other people wearing just what you want: a ski-type jacket in blue, with a fairly heavy lining for cold weather, snaps down the front, elastic at the wrists, and a light hood stored in the neckband. You'll need the large size.

17.   Three years after graduation, you're seriously considering a move to a new job with a company in Cheyenne, Wyoming. One consideration is the availability and cost of housing. Your present family home is a 3-bedroom single-story frame house of about 1300 square feet. For the children's sake, you'd like to have a similar home in a good school district. Write to Larry Liptak Realty (445 Rodeo Drive, Cheyenne, WY 82001) for all the information the firm can send.

18.   On your trip to Big Sur last summer, browsing in an art shop in Monterey, you found two delightful ceramic pieces by local artist Frank Czajkowski. Since you put the pieces on display in your home, your friends have been so impressed that you want more Czajkowski pieces for holiday gifts. Write Lyla P. Cronin, Cronin Gallery (397 Seaside Way, Monterey, CA 93940), for information about availability of items, descriptions (and pictures?), prices, shipping information, and anything else you'll need to know. (See also the following problem.)

19.   Reply for Cronin Gallery to the inquiry about Czajkowski ceramic pieces (see the preceding problem). You have a limited selection of pieces in stock right now. Frank Czajkowski does ceramics mainly in the summer, so you don't expect to get more until many months after these are sold. Several are in the same style as those you carried last summer; others are smaller pieces in a much more delicate style that most people prefer. Prices depend on the item. The larger pieces run from $27 to $40; the more detailed, smaller ones run from $34 to $55. Since you do little mail-order business, you aren't equipped to provide photographs of pieces. You'll provide crating and shipping service at cost (figure about $10 for the first ceramic item and $6 for each additional item). You'll insure the shipment, but of course broken pieces can be replaced only if additional items are in stock.

You recognize that it's difficult to make selections under these circumstances, so you're willing to ship pieces and accept their return at full price, with the customer to pay the shipping both ways. You'll crate and insure your shipment, but any breakage not covered by insurance will be at the customer's expense.

You accept payment by major credit card. You'll be glad to make your best selection of the number of Czajkowski pieces desired, crate and ship them, and charge them to a credit card. The customer may return any of them (insured) for a full refund.

20.   As Administrative Services Manager for your company, you're responsible for the Telex service, which is part of the mailroom operation. The Product Design Department manager has requested that your department also provide facsimile service. Facsimile service, or fax, consists of making copies of a document, as a copier does, except that the master document is scanned by a machine at one site and the copy is made by a machine at a remote site by telephone connection. Drawings, signatures, and even photographs can be transmitted. (News services transmit newspaper photographs by fax.) A page can normally be transmitted in a minute or two.

A number of manufacturers make fax equipment, but you don't know very much about it. You'll want to know the equipment and operating costs. You don't know whether images sent by one manufacturer's fax machine will be receivable by another manufacturer's fax machine. What if the company you want to send a document to uses another manufacturer's machine? Is there anything special required in the way of telephone lines? One obvious use of fax is to transmit contracts and other documents bearing legal signatures. But are signatures sent by fax fully legal and binding or not? The Product Design Department is interested in using fax to transmit design drawings, but do the machines have sufficient resolution to provide the fine detail needed? What other answers do you need to decide whether to acquire fax capability and which manufacturer's unit to acquire?

Your assistant has found a list of names and addresses of fax manufacturers in an article (not otherwise very informative) in an office management journal. Write a form letter that you can send to each manufacturer to get the information you need.

21.   Invironments, Inc. (464 East Way, Minot, ND 58702) manufactures an innovative line of modular cabinets and bookcases suited to small apartment dwellers and others who need to disassemble such furniture for occasional moves. All units in the line measure 24 inches high, 36 inches wide, and 14 inches deep. Units may be attached so that one rests on top of another, side by side, or at corners in checkerboard fashion. When the owner changes apartments, units may be rearranged to fit the new room sizes. Invironments guarantees that it will stock all present items for ten years, so that additional modules will be available if needed.

Using the information in the firm's brochure, you've figured that you could fill a wall that's 9 feet 3 inches wide to a height of 6 feet if you bought four of their upright frame pieces, one stereo cabinet, two sliding-glass-front cabinets, and four bookcase modules. The total price should be $1172.80. Order these units in birch finish to be charged to your bank card and shipped by United Parcel (you pay shipping charges on delivery). Refer to your enclosed (imaginary) sketch of the arrangement you want and ask them to check to be sure that the units you're ordering will create it. Include your telephone number.

22.   One of the most popular products of Simpliflex Lamp Company (38 Palm Drive, Grand Rapids, MI 49506) is a spring-loaded desk lamp that stays in any position it's placed in. This unit has had higher sales to the general public in discount stores and general stationery stores than in specialized office furniture stores. As secretary to the customer relations manager, one of your tasks is to respond to inquiries from customers about the three mounting brackets described in the lamp's instruction sheet. One bracket is for mounting on a horizontal edge such as the edge of a desk, another is for mounting on a vertical edge such as the headboard of a bed (a surprising top seller), and the third is for mounting on a wall or other vertical plane. Each lamp comes with one of the brackets, but customers often discover after purchase that they really need a different one, and many outlets stock only one type.

Recently, you've been answering about 20 inquiries per week on the prices of these brackets. You simply note the desired bracket's price (each is $2.60 plus $.85 shipping in the United States) and ordering information (a check or money order should be s ent to the above address) directly on the letter of inquiry, but even such a simple procedure is getting pretty time-consuming. Therefore, you've decided to design a single form letter that covers all three brackets. Some resale on the sturdy, durable lamp would be appropriate; most people find the functional design with exposed frame and springs quite attractive. If your message works well, perhaps it could be included with each lamp sold.

23. Universal Electric, Inc. (9100 Bervor Street, St. Paul, MN 58118) is a major manufacturer of lighting equipment, including industrial and household fixtures and fluorescent tubes. The company's state-of-the-art line of plant-growing lights is a profitable but relatively low-volume line. These special fluorescent tubes are used by greenhouse operators to provide supplementary lighting, and they're also used by people who grow plants under lights at home. The spectrum of light they provide is scientifically adapted to the requirements of growing plants.

Distribution channels to serve greenhouse equipment suppliers were readily established, but sales to nonprofessional people presented more difficult problems. The average home installation might involve the sale of only 12 or so tubes, too small an order to be handled by direct mail (especially since shipping fluorescent tubes requires extremely careful handling). At the same time, few local electrical suppliers sell enough volume in this line to maintain substantial inventories.

Universal's solution has been to direct these low-volume purchasers to local suppliers and provide special rush shipment to suppliers on such orders. Although the normal processing cycle for other merchandise is 30 days or more to shipment, orders for the plant-growing tubes are taken out of normal sequence and placed in the very next shipment to that supplier, usually within 5 working days.

As Director of Customer Relations, your problem is that individual consumers often send orders directly to Universal. Your response to such orders and to requests for your plant-growing equipment price list is a mailing packet containing a form letter advising consumers of the proper purchase procedure, a price list, a specification sheet describing the various fluorescent tubes in the line, and a list of local distributors by city. Right now, you're not completely satisfied with the form letter you're using. Write a new one. It should be positive in stating the advantages of dealing with local distributors, yet firm in refusing to accept direct orders.

24. Since you completed your education two years ago, you've successfully begun a career in your chosen field. This morning you received a letter from Ms. Sandra Kersulis, program chairperson of the student club you belonged to on campus, asking you to appear on a panel of recent graduates to discuss the best ways of getting a job in your field. You're asked to make a presentation of about ten minutes (along with two other panel members) and then answer questions as a panel member. The meeting is scheduled for the second Thursday of next month at 7:30 P.M. in the same room where you used to take your business communication class on campus. You'd enjoy talking to students about job hunting, and you have some good ideas, so you'll agree to participate. Write Ms. Kersulis on campus and accept her invitation. (The student organization can be one you belong to, or it can be the student chapter of American Management Association on your campus. Your instructor may be able to supply an appropriate campus address.)

25. Take the place of John Kabaci, Purchasing Agent, Condor Industries (P. O. Box 5545, Butte, MT 59701, (406) 555-3200) and respond to the job application of Christine A. Audette (342 Birch Street, North Platte, NE 69101). Ms. Audette is an assistant buyer with a large North Platte company, and she's applied to fill your opening for a buyer. Her résumé outlines a background that well exceeds other applicants' qualifications. You want her to visit Butte, meet the Condor purchasing staff and officials, and get a chance to evaluate her potential future with the company. Ask her to plan a stay of about two days, arriving one morning by plane and leaving the next evening, or something like that. You will, of course, pay all expenses; she should submit an expense list after the trip. The job will be a step up for her, and her application was very enthusiastic, so you expect agreement. Ask her to consider dates and call you collect to tell you when she can come. Your secretary will make a motel reservation when you hear from her.

26. As a new customer service representative at Cliff House (P. O. Box 499, Goleta, CA 93017), a mail-order firm, revise the following reply to John R. Bestick (Rte. 5, Valentine, NE 69201), written by your predecessor just before her departure:

Dear Mr. Bestick:

This is to inform you that our company doesn't ship the Model
#48 Crockery Birdbath any longer. After many bad
experiences, we have found that private shipment of single
units of this item is too unreliable to be worth the trouble.
Few arrived unbroken. We do ship in truckload lots directly
to local dealers, where we can control packing and handling.
This way the breakage rate has been acceptable. You may be
able to locate a unit through your local garden store,
although we have no record of recent shipments to Valentine,
Nebraska.
      Otherwise, I'm afraid your best bet is to plan a visit
to Cliff House in Goleta on your next vacation. Our packers
will be glad to help you secure the birdbath you wanted in
your car or trailer for the trip home.

Very truly yours,

27. Each year *Disc Month* (P.O. Box 4919, Groton, CT 06340), a recording industry journal, publishes a statistical summary of the record business. In one part of this extensive summary, the journal includes statistics on the sales of records and tapes in retail outlets in the United States. As sales manager of Duke Records (main office: 3277 Old Salem Road, Corvallis, OR 97330), a major retailer with more than 20 large discount record outlets in four Northwest states, you've received a request from *Disc Month* editors for information about your average weekly sales per store of discs, eight-track tapes, cassette tapes, and reel-to-reel tapes in five categories (country, rock, and so on). It's a satisfying sign of your company's growth in the field that you're being asked, for the first time, to supply such information.

   Reply to *Disc Month* for Duke Records. Regretfully, you can't provide any information of the kind requested without full clarification of how the journal will use it. No identification of your firm whatsoever, allusion to any statistics as being yours, or use of your name in their printed results is permissible. In fact, any use of your firm's name in connection with the summary would be considered a violation of a trust. Since you're in a very competitive industry, keeping your sales (and sales problems) secret is an important and hard-sought goal. You feel that such sensitive information (which normally would be restricted to a small core of your top management people) should be viewed by only one highly trusted writer, who will lump together your statistics with those of other outlets and then immediately destroy the source material you provided. You must insist on these restrictions, and you want a full, clear statement of *Disc Month's* position in this matter before you proceed.

28. As head of the Production Engineering Department, you recently contracted with Bellsen Associates, a consulting firm, for time and motion studies to aid in designing a production plant for your company. This morning you received Bellsen's final report. Although the 84-page report will receive weeks of evaluation and study by your eight-person staff, a quick look suggests that it's excellently done. It certainly is beautifully produced, and the recommendations appear to cover all the areas you hoped would be included. You've authorized payment by the Accounting Department; payment normally takes 2 to 3 weeks. In the meantime, acknowledge receipt of the report. Bear in mind that, if you later discover deficiencies in the report, you'll be asking Bellsen to provide further information, so don't go overboard in your compliments.

29. One of your pet peeves at the mail-order discount audio supply store where you work (Universe of Audio, 1992 East Eighth Street, Seattle, WA 98102) is the incomplete order. When someone sends an order for "the Kramson receiver you carry, and bill my Visa account," it could be any of the six Kramson models you carry—and each of those might be priced slightly differently, depending on the circumstances.

Ms. Emily V. Myres (19 Bear Tooth Pass, Red Lodge, MT 59068) has made a number of mistakes in her order. She ordered two ALZ speakers that she said cost $171.40 for a pair, including shipping. Actually, the Universe of Audio discount price list (which you'll enclose) quotes one line of ALZ speakers in the $140 range per pair (exact prices depend on style and finish), and the next higher line is in the $210 range per pair. Ms. Myres must specify whether she wants the speakers in walnut, mahogany, or unfinished wood and whether she wants the floor-standing or wall-mounted models. You can ship any of these from stock. Shipping is always an additional cost for speakers; she'll pay the shipping charges on delivery. She must specify the shipping method, and she should be sure that the shipper she specifies has a terminal near Red Lodge or will deliver there. When you write your acknowledgment, do your best to keep the order.

30. Here's a letter of acknowledgment from a distributor, Druco Sports Equipment (14991 Trade Center Ct., Atlanta, GA 30317), to a retailer. See if you can improve it.

```
Roberts and Sons Hardware
554 Northern Blvd.
Leesburg, FL 32748

RE: Order #G-4418-RTL-55

Dear Mr. Steen:

     Thank you for your recent order. We would like to be
able to ship these items out to you immediately, as per our
standard policy.

     Unfortunately, the fourth item in this order is
erroneously designated. You list stock number 4483 as a
```

screwdriver kit in a plastic case. Please note in your
catalog that 4483 is polyurethane skateboard wheels.
Screwdrivers and screwdriver sets are listed on pages 23 and
42 of our catalog in addition to listings of special—purpose
tools in connection with various product lines. Your clerk
probably just neglected to copy the stock number correctly.

   Please note that this discrepancy reduced your order
below the $200 minimum on regular orders; therefore, we are
holding your full order pending correction of this item. When
your response is received, immediate shipment is anticipated.
We will wait to process billing on this merchandise until
that time.

   Repeat orders from regular customers such as yourself
form the mainstay of our business. We know you value the
accuracy of our order processing procedures as much as we
appreciate accuracy in the orders we receive. It is our
satisfaction to provide exactly the merchandise desired by
each customer. We look forward to your continued patronage.

Sincerely,

31. As Director of Administrative Services for Sturmer and Company,
you supervise a central copying service and oversee the installation and
use of the 17 office copiers in strategic locations throughout the company.
Until now, access to these copiers has been completely unrestricted, and
(as expected) there's been some employee abuse of this open access. The
company has been willing to tolerate a certain amount of private use of
company copiers by employees, but recently the use of copiers has risen
dramatically, and you can find no evidence of an unusual increase in
legitimate office copying.

   Therefore, you've ordered the installation of Copy-Cop, a small control box, on each office copier. Copy-Cop stops all use of the copier until
a plastic card (like a credit card) is inserted in its slot. Cards are coded
by office, and Copy-Cop maintains records of how many copies are made
under each card number. The goal is to allow official access to copiers
without restriction but to put some limits on employees' private use of
copiers. There's no intention of reducing the amount of legitimate copying.

   Explain the new system to all office employees. Each office has
requested the number of Copy-Cop cards it needs, and each office supervisor is expected to maintain control of the cards assigned. The Copy-
Cops will be turned on tomorrow.

32. Play the role of Margaret M. Sampey. On your desk this morning
you found the following memo, prepared by an assistant, for your approval.
If you decide that this isn't a very good way to communicate the message,
revise it. The facts are correct.

DATE: October 5, 1983
TO: All Employees
FROM: Margaret M. Sampey, Director of Personnel
SUBJECT: Discontinuance of Clerk-Typist V Rank

The Baulsen Company has determined that it would be in the company's best interests to discontinue the rank of Clerk-Typist V. This is the lowest rank of employment in the clerk-typist range. As of the first day of November, all positions carrying the Clerk-Typist V rank will be abolished. Employees at the rank of Clerk-Typist V and supervisors overseeing positions at this rank should take note.

The primary rationale for this discontinuance is the determination that recruitment of new employees at this grade level is no longer feasible, while at the same time maintaining a high-quality clerical staff at the present higher clerk-typist ranks is quite possible. That is to say, we are not able to hire qualified people at the pay level of Clerk-Typist V, yet we do not feel it is necessary to raise the pay levels of the higher clerk-typist ranks in order to attract qualified employees at those levels.

Supervisors overseeing positions at the Clerk-Typist V rank will be contacted in the next few days to determine whether the tasks assigned to that position justify an upgrade to Clerk-Typist IV. If they do not, then the position will be abolished. It is the assumption of Personnel that most or all present Clerk-Typist V positions will be upgraded.

Present employees at the Clerk-Typist V rank should contact Personnel as quickly as possible to schedule evaluation interviews and apply for an upgrade to the Clerk-Typist IV rank. All employees temporarily laid off in the course of this shift, either because of failure to meet the specifications of the Clerk-Typist IV rank or because of position abolishment, will be placed on a preferential rehiring list. Personnel on that list will be preferentially listed in candidacy for all future position openings for which they qualify. It is the assumption of Personnel that employees in positions upgraded from Clerk-Typist V to Clerk-Typist IV will correspondingly be upgraded unless evaluation raises serious questions about an employee's continued employment with the company at any rank.

Departmental budget officers should please note that the pay differential of approximately $107 per month between the ranks of Clerk-Typist V and Clerk-Typist IV will be automatically compensated through Personnel funds allocated for this purpose for the remainder of this budget year. Budgets for next year should be adjusted to reflect this increase.

33. As Director of Purchasing, Union Shipbuilding Company, clarify the handling of purchases from small businesses, minority-owned businesses, and businesses located in areas of high unemployment. Since your company builds ships for the navy and ships subsidized by the federal Maritime Administration (MARAD), your purchasing procedures are subject to federal regulations designed to ensure that certain types of businesses receive fair consideration as vendors of the materials you purchase. The facts in outline are as follows:

- Small businesses defined: for the manufacturing industry, the number of employees of a firm and its affiliates doesn't exceed 750; for the construction industry, the average annual receipts of a firm and its affiliates don't exceed $12 million for the last three fiscal years.

- Minority business enterprise (MBE) defined: at least 50 percent interest is owned by minority group members; if publicly owned, at least 51 percent of stock is owned by minority group members. Minority group members are federally defined to include Negroes, Spanish-speaking Americans, American-Orientals, American-Indians, American-Eskimos, American-Aleuts. Industry-wide source lists of MBE vendors are available.

- Labor surplus area (LSA) defined: a geographic area of unemployment as specified in the Department of Labor's publication, *Area Trends in Employment and Unemployment.* LSA firm defined: the firm is located in an LSA or holds a Certificate of Eligibility to participate in the benefits of the LSA program.

- Final determination of status of businesses as small, MBE, or LSA: depends on self-certification—statements provided by the firms themselves in annual written representations that document their status. Every firm added to computerized list of vendors' names and addresses is invited to complete certification forms to document its status as a small, MBE, or LSA firm. Buyers are to mail forms to all new vendors and repeat the mailing annually thereafter.

- Policy defined: the maximum practicable opportunity will be accorded to small, MBE, and LSA firms to participate in the performance of contracts of all kinds. Standard purchase order terms and conditions shall include a clause encouraging similar policies on the part of vendors and subcontractors. Price differentials are not paid in support of these programs.

- Procedure defined: upon receipt of departmental requisition or materials list, the buyer creates a prospective vendor list. Small, MBE, and LSA firms will be represented on vendor lists when possible. A computerized vendor name and address printout indicates which vendors qualify under each program. If the order will exceed $10,000 and the item is capable of being supplied by small business but no small business source can be identified, the buyer is required to notify the Purchasing Agent. Compliance under small business, MBE, and LSA programs is documented by the buyer on the procurement summary form (on which all details of each purchase are recorded).

Write a directive suitable for inclusion in the *Purchasing Department Policy Manual (Buyer's Guide)* in the form of a memo to all purchasing employees.

34. As Director of Personnel of Digi-Sta-Tronics, Inc., a fast-growing electronics company, you believe that the company has now grown beyond the point where top management can know every employee personally. No longer, for example, does the president meet with each newly hired employee during orientation day. Therefore, you feel, formal communications should be developed to replace the personal relationships of the past and help retain the valued small-company atmosphere as much as possible. As an example, draft a welcome letter that could be mailed by the president to each new employee's home.

Here are some of the things you should keep in mind as you write:
Most new employees are technical specialists whose careers depend on continued training to keep them abreast of current developments in their fields. The company fulfills this requirement with the highest training budget, in proportion to company income, of any organization in your area. All employees are eligible for tuition reimbursement for all outside course work and other training that contributes to their professional skills.

The rapid growth of the company continually broadens opportunities for employees to take on additional challenges and responsibilities. The company has successfully resisted being taken over by outside financial interests and is scheduled for listing on the New York Stock Exchange soon, a sign of long-term stability.

35. For a school club or other organization, write a goodwill letter of welcome to be distributed to all new students (or, if more appropriate, to all students newly eligible for membership). Explain your organization's goals, activities, and benefits to a potential member, remembering that the letter's primary purpose is to congratulate new students on entering college or meeting eligibility requirements. In your planning, consider at least five or six themes you could use. Select the best one as the theme of your letter, perhaps using some of the others as supporting ideas. Be sure to indicate how students can find out more about the organization.

36. As Assistant to the Vice-President for Administration, Oremen Research Laboratories, Inc. (48871 V Street, Wilmington, DE 19801, (302) 555-4001), write Professor Aaron J. Hsueh (Administrative Services Department, State University of Maryland, Salisbury, MD 21801) to confirm an earlier telephone discussion. Ask Dr. Hsueh to:

- Conduct a task-time study of the clerical staff. (How many hours per week are spent on various clerical tasks?)
- Develop a recommendation (based on the study results) on the feasibility of a word processing system in the company.
- Specify parameters and criteria (if relevant) for selecting specific word processing equipment.
- Serve personally as the project's supervisor/coordinator.
- Select and recruit other experts to assist as necessary.
- Allow the company the right to approve all persons working on the project.
- Perform all work at the company site. (Normal office hours are 7:30–4:15; his hours are completely flexible.)
- Bill the company monthly at $30 per hour for work done.
- Assist in progress reviews at the completion of each project stage to allow revised estimates of the project completion date.
- Begin work as soon as possible; the target completion date is September 1.

You estimate that the task will take approximately 160 work hours, as you've outlined it to him on the phone. The agreement may be terminated by either party at any time.

Invite Dr. Hsueh to call you if he's interested in proceeding on this basis.

37. Maintaining high quality control in producing your company's complex electronic assemblies is extremely complicated, and the only way to do it is through computerized statistical analysis of production output. That's why you, as Information Systems Manager (in charge of computer operations), and Nick Baclagan, Quality Control Manager, have been discussing hiring an employee to serve as liaison between your two departments, with the departments splitting the cost. Finally, at a meeting this morning, you agreed that the new position will be in your department (you'll do the hiring after consultation with the Quality Control Department), and Quality Control agrees to shift half the cost of this position from its budget to yours. As soon as this arrangement is ratified by the Operating Committee, you'll draft a job description for Nick's approval and start interviewing applicants. You're satisfied, and apparently so is Nick.

On such an important agreement, you'd rather not trust your memory and Nick's for the details. Write a memo to Nick confirming the arrangement.

13

Indirect-Plan Messages: Bad News

In things that are tender and unpleasing,
it is good to break the ice by some whose words
are of less weight, and to reserve the more weighty voice
to come in as by chance.
Francis Bacon

The words of his mouth were smoother
than butter, but war was in his heart:
his words were softer than oil,
yet they were drawn swords.
Psalms 55:22

In your practice so far, you've been concentrating on conveying information clearly and effectively. At times you've had to take the reader's emotions into account, but your main goal has been to make the reader understand facts. That's the first of the two basic types of communication situations. In the second type, which we'll consider now, dealing with the reader's emotions is the main goal.

In the second type of message, conciseness and efficiency become less important, and vividness much more important. In a neutral emotional setting, a fact can simply be stated and understood; needless elaboration is likely to interfere with communication. But to present that same fact in the face of emotional resistance may very well require a more vivid explanation. Points that would seem obvious in a neutral setting may need to be stated explicitly when emotions are strong, to make sure the reader will take them into account. In your study, review the techniques of vivid writing discussed in Chapter 8.

In addition, the tone of the message and the connotations of the words must be regulated much more carefully than in an informational message. In the presence of charged emotions, one small failure of tact or error in tone can be so magnified that it kills the intended effect of the message. On the other hand, very skillful and consistent selection of symbols to create the desired emotional reaction in the audience can enhance the effectiveness of the message enormously.

COMMUNICATING BAD NEWS

When you must communicate bad news, you can expect to arouse strong feelings of disappointment. And more often than not, bad news must be communicated to a reader whose goodwill and future business you want to keep. At such times, you try to communicate the bad news without creating any more ill will than absolutely necessary. The goal of the bad-news strategy is to avoid adding anger and ill will to the disappointment your reader will feel.

The bad-news strategy we discuss in this chapter can be used when both of the following conditions occur.

1. When the message is expected to upset the reader significantly. Very often, refusals belong to this category. When someone has asked you for something and you must refuse, he or she often reacts to your refusal with strong feelings of frustration, irritation, and sometimes rejection. However, not all refusals are likely to upset the reader. Sometimes requests reflect only casual interest; other times people ask for something simply to see whether or not it's available. The bad-news strategy is reserved for the times you expect strong feelings.

Just as not all refusals are really bad news, not all bad-news messages are refusals. For instance, if you must fire an employee or write a negative employee performance evaluation, then the bad-news strategy may be appropriate. If you must inform a customer that his or her payment record forces you to discontinue credit, you might use the bad-news strategy, even though that isn't normally considered a refusal. But since the bad-news strategy is so often used in refusals, this chapter uses refusals to exemplify bad-news messages (Figure 1). This focus makes the strategy easier to discuss, and affords us a consistent and relatively simple terminology.

2. When minimizing bad feelings is worth the extra time and cost. Quite frankly, using the bad-news strategy isn't always worth the effort, even when you know the message will arouse feelings of disappointment. Your time is money to you and your organization, and sometimes that money could be spent more productively than by writing messages in the more complicated bad-news format. Some organizations place a very high value on maintaining the goodwill of everyone they communicate with, and in these organizations the extra cost of writing somewhat longer and more difficult messages may be considered quite worthwhile. In other organizations, though, the circumstances of each bad-news situation are evaluated, even if only briefly, before a decision is made to write a bad-news message.

In some cases, it could be argued that no response at all is better than a bad-news message. The theory here is that even the most tactful reply confirms the disappointing refusal, and readers are sure to be upset when they read it. But if they never hear from the organization, they're never forced to realize that they've been refused, and sooner or later they'll forget the whole episode without ever being particularly upset. This approach is obviously inappropriate for most situations, but it does illustrate the kinds of options open to the writer.

You should understand very clearly before studying the bad-news strategy that it isn't the only way to handle bad news. In your career, you'll often find that some other approach seems more natural or appropriate. That's fine. If another approach seems better, use it. But when you can't think of a really creative way to communicate bad news, or when time is short, the bad-news strategy will work, and it's easy to learn to use.

THE PSYCHOLOGY OF THE BAD-NEWS STRATEGY

When you must communicate bad news, your readers will be disappointed. That's inevitable. But it's very natural for them also to be angry with you for disappointing them, and that's the reaction the bad-news strategy aims to minimize. However, you don't try somehow to sugar-coat the bad news so it doesn't seem bad any more, because that doesn't work very often.

If someone asks you for something, then that person probably feels that he is making a reasonable request and expects you to feel the same. The basic premise of the bad-news strategy is that such a request should

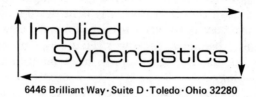

6446 Brilliant Way · Suite D · Toledo · Ohio 32280

January 19, 1983

Professor Jane C. Harrington
114f Hood Hall
Mt. Tabor State University
Portland, OR 97219

Dear Professor Harrington:

The data processing workshop you're planning for the
business people of Portland during the week of May 7 sounds like
a fine opportunity for them to learn about our field easily and
quickly. I can sympathize with the magnitude of the task you've
taken on, since I planned several of the programs that our
Customer Training Team uses to introduce new users to our system.

The system that Implied Synergistics is marketing is
specifically aimed at solving large-scale inventory problems in
petroleum distribution, which is a rather specialized
application. Therefore, our Customer Training Team's programs
are specifically designed to meet the needs of the wholesale
petroleum products field. Such programs would be of very limited
interest to the retail business people in your workshop.

We very much appreciate your compliment in inviting our
team to participate in your workshop. I have asked our
northwestern sales representative to contact you to see what kind
of contribution she can make. Sara Okel, who'll be calling you
later this week, is very knowledgeable about Implied
Synergistics' programs and about the whole field of electronic
data processing. I know she'll make a valuable contribution.

Cordially,

George Garabedian
Vice-President

Figure 1 An indirect refusal

receive a reasoned reply. The person who made the request should realize that you've seriously considered it and should clearly understand that your refusal is reasonable. It should be obvious that you aren't refusing capriciously, but because of carefully considered reasons. Ideally, at the end of your refusal message, the reader should be able to say, "I don't like being refused, but I can understand why. If I were you, I'd have to do the same thing." Such a response may not always be possible, but that's what you're striving for.

To achieve this effect, you must make the reader understand the reasoning behind your refusal before he or she realizes that you intend to refuse. The reason is simple. Once the reader sees that you're refusing, all the bad feelings that your message is designed to minimize will surface. And when the reader is angry, reasoning with him or her will not be easy. However, if you can show the reasoning behind your refusal before you reveal the refusal, you may neutralize a lot of the irritation that would otherwise arise. If you're refusing something that's really important to your reader, then you can't eliminate the disappointment, and you can't even eliminate the reader's irritation and anger toward you, but you can keep these reactions to a minimum.

The basic design of the bad-news strategy, then, is reasoning first, refusal second. In a memo or other informal message, the reasoning and refusal may constitute the entire message, as in Figure 2. Such a message uses the indirect plan discussed earlier.

The Reasoning

Let's look more closely at your viewpoint and your reader's. The reader, believing that a certain request is reasonable, has communicated it to you. You, believing that compliance with the request isn't reasonable, are refusing. Obviously, your viewpoint and your reader's must differ.

Once in a while, that difference lies in what each of you considers reasonable. Usually, however, the difference is in the facts available to each of you. To put it simply, you know something your reader didn't know when he or she made the request.

Facts The essence of the reasoning in a bad-news message, then, is to let the reader see the facts of the situation as you see them. You want the reader to come around to your side of the desk for a minute and look at the situation as it appears to you. Thus your reasoning emphasizes facts that the reader apparently hasn't considered. Often, the reader hasn't considered these facts because he or she couldn't possibly have known them. For instance, if someone asks you to be somewhere at a certain date and you have a prior commitment for that date, then that commitment will be the factual basis of your reasoning.

Priorities The emphasis in your reasoning is on facts. But you may also ask the reader to give those facts the same relative weight that you

DATE: September 15, 1982

TO: Dennis Ericksen, Supervisor

FROM: Jean Borkowski, Director of Physical Plant

SUBJECT: Use of South Parking Lot by Kite Club

Because we occasionally receive requests like yours to use the south parking lot for club and church activities, last year we checked with our insurance company to determine our liability coverage in such situations. According to our agent, our liability insurance covers only official company use of that property--that is, use directly related to official company activities.

Since our company values community service such as your present leadership in the Sunnyvale Kite Club, we checked to see how much it would cost to extend our insurance to cover community activities on our property. We found the cost prohibitively high. In addition, we considered the possibility of allowing organizations to use the parking lot after signing a waiver of any future claim against our company, but our lawyer indicated that such an arrangement would not adequately protect the company. As a result, we must limit the use of company property only to official company activities.

Figure 2 A refusal memo

give them. A fact the reader initially recognized but considered unimportant may be critically important from your side of the desk, and you want the reader to see why you're setting priorities as you are. For example, if you're asked to be somewhere and you have a prior commitment, then whether you fulfill that commitment or break it to meet with the reader is of course a matter of priorities. So besides communicating the fact of your prior commitment, you'll probably need to show the reader why that commitment is important to you, as Figure 3 illustrates. Sometimes all you need to say is what the prior commitment is. Other times you may need two or three carefully developed paragraphs to show why that commitment is so important to you.

To sum up, your goal in the reasoning is not to get the reader to agree with you, thinking, "Ah, now I can see that my request was indeed unreasonable." On the contrary, your goal is to get the reader to see that from your viewpoint the refusal is reasonable, thinking, "If I were in your shoes, I might come to the same conclusion."

Dear Mr. Johnson:

The work you're doing to help your fellow students learn more about the field of finance is very commendable. As Program Chair of the Finance Club, you're solving exactly the same kinds of scheduling problems you'll face throughout your career.

On your March 23 meeting date, I'll be presenting a proposal to our company's Executive Committee. This meeting, which will run from noon until late evening, is the conclusion of a project that five of us have spent nearly three months on. On April 18, your next meeting date, I'll be vacationing in Spain. My husband and I have arranged to spend three weeks camping and bicycling through southern Spain, and we're very excited about the trip.

I'm eager to meet your friends in the Finance Club and talk to them about our field. If other dates are open, please let me know. Otherwise, feel free to pass my address along to next year's Program Chair. I'd like to hear from you again.

Cordially,

Figure 3 An appointment refusal

The Beginning

As a practical matter, beginning a bad-news message by talking about the reasoning is very difficult. At the very beginning of the message, the reader is extremely alert to every nuance, and if he or she immediately realizes that you're leading up to a refusal, then you haven't succeeded in reasoning before the emotions start to rise.

Therefore, most bad-news messages begin with some comments designed to put the reader in a neutral, reasonable frame of mind for the reasoning that follows. Probably the most important reason for this material is simply to get away from the beginning of the message, where the reader is so attentive to each detail, and get the reader moving forward smoothly in the message. In fact, this section of the message is often called the "buffer," since it provides a buffer zone between the onset of the message and the beginning of the reasoning section.

The fact is that you start bad-news messages by "beating around the bush," but you do it skillfully. Beating around the bush has a bad reputation because most people do it so clumsily that it's quite obvious. It works only when the reader doesn't notice what you're up to. By the end of this chapter, you'll be an expert at it.

The Ending

In the body of the bad-news message, you've presented your reasoning and then revealed the bad news. When the ending comes, the reader's emotions are at their peak: certainly some disappointment, probably mixed with irritation and anger. Now what can you do in the ending?

Think back to a time when your spouse or valued friend was angry at you. What do you do at such times? Your first impulse is often to leave quickly and avoid the unpleasantness of the anger. But if you do, the other person is left to seethe and rage alone. By the time you return, perhaps he or she will have cooled off, so you've avoided the immediate unpleasantness, but by leaving you haven't done what you could to help the person calm down quickly. If you'd stayed, there might have been some unpleasant moments, but probably you could have hastened the cooling off and helped the person avoid much of the anger.

When you're writing you don't have to feel the reader's anger directly, so the choice is easy: you stay with the reader and communicate a bit longer. And you try to help the reader think optimistically about his or her future relationship with you instead of dwelling on the present irritation. The ending is successful if the reader finishes your message thinking, "I wish they hadn't refused me, but they're a good company, and it'll be rewarding to do business with them in the future." You've led the reader to focus on a future benefit rather than a present irritation.

PLANNING AND WRITING BAD-NEWS LETTERS

In this section, we consider how to plan and write each part of a bad-news letter effectively. First, though, we should consider the easiest way to write a first draft.

Few experienced writers draft the parts of a bad-news letter in the order they'll appear in the final version. They draft the reasoning section first, then the beginning. This approach is easier because the reasoning is the key section of the letter, and it's the part they've been thinking about very carefully in the planning stage. Once that section is drafted, it's relatively easy to fill in the rest of the letter around it.

More importantly, the reasoning is the part that must be just right for the letter to be effective. The beginning should lead smoothly into the reasoning, but if you write the beginning first, you'll be tempted to force the reasoning to follow the line of discussion you've established there. That would reverse the proper priorities. Instead, write the entire reasoning section first, and then force the beginning to flow into it smoothly. Then when the reasoning and the beginning are drafted, continue with the refusal and the ending. This approach can save you quite a bit of time in the revision stage, when you're polishing the transitions from one section to the next.

Although you'll draft the parts of a bad-news letter in a different order, we'll now examine them in the order in which they'll appear in the final version.

The Buffer Paragraph

In the opening, often called the buffer paragraph, you try to put the reader in a rational frame of mind for the reasoning that follows. To do this, try to create an emotional climate that's either neutral or slightly positive. To many beginners, this appears difficult. What on earth can you say that'll put the reader in a neutral frame of mind and won't be perceived as beating around the bush (which always seems offensive when noticeable)?

Agree with or compliment the reader Like experienced writers, you can usually come up with a suitable subject for the buffer paragraph in one of these ways:

1. Agree with something the reader has said or with an attitude you're certain he or she has. If your letter is a refusal, then obviously the reader has made a request. You don't want to begin by saying, "I agree that it would be a good idea to carry out your request," because in just a few lines you intend to refuse the request. But the reader has most likely said other things that you could agree with. If not, the reader has surely implied certain attitudes that you could agree with.

2. Pay the reader a compliment that you think will be perceived as sincere. If you can pay an honest compliment, then it may be a good subject for your buffer paragraph. But remember that the reader's judgment of your sincerity is the only judgment that counts. If the reader considers your compliment insincere, then your buffer paragraph will fail, even though the compliment honestly represents your feelings. In this case, the reader will probably feel that he or she is being buttered up and may become irritated and suspicious—exactly the feelings you're trying to avoid.

As we've seen, the subject of your agreement or compliment in the buffer paragraph shouldn't be the request you intend to refuse, yet it should be somewhat related to that request. If you stray too far from the main subject of the request, then the reader can see that you're delaying, and any experienced reader knows that people delay when they have bad news to tell. So the subject of the buffer paragraph should be related to, but not focused on, the topic of the refusal. It should be close enough to appear relevant, but not so close that it arouses false hopes.

Make a smooth transition into the reasoning The transition from the buffer paragraph to the reasoning paragraph must be graceful, or the reader will realize that you're shifting gears, that you've finished making pleasantries and are now getting down to business. And when that happens, you might as well be starting the letter right at that point, because the reader's careful attention will be rekindled.

The transition from buffer to reasoning should also be especially clear. Therefore, using a word or phrase at the very end of the buffer and repeating it at the very beginning of the reasoning is the strongest device. If you use a different device, be sure that it shifts the reader's attention very smoothly. Review the section on transitions earlier in this book for other possible devices.

One final note on buffers: one sentence can seldom accomplish everything a buffer should do. Most experienced writers assume that their buffer paragraphs will be about two sentences long. In the first sentence, they state the point of agreement or the compliment. In the second, they elaborate on that idea by saying more about it and try to employ the word or phrase they've chosen as the transitional device. By using two sentences, they give the buffer enough room to work, and they give themselves plenty of flexibility for inserting the transition. Figure 4 shows what good buffer paragraphs look like.

The Reasoning

No doubt you're refusing the reader's request for a good reason; if you didn't have one, you'd be writing a good-news letter instead. Since there *is* a reason, your first step in thinking about the reasoning section is to clarify that reason in your own mind. Why must you refuse?

Avoid disagreeable lines of reasoning   Try to avoid even thinking about that old standby, "company policy," as your reason. If granting the request violates company policy, then surely there's a good reason for that policy, and that reason will be much more informative to the reader than just the words "company policy." In fact, try to avoid using the word "policy" completely. Most people react negatively to that word because of previous bad experiences with it, and there's almost always a better way to describe the company's decisions. It's best to explain *why* the company does things a certain way.

Also avoid this kind of explanation: "If we do it for you, then we'll have to do it for everyone." Hogwash! People are different, situations are different, and there's plenty of room in any intelligently applied policy for legitimate exceptions. Very likely your reader sees his or her case as a legitimate exception and will be especially irritated by the weakness of your "explanation."

Sometimes the real reason for your refusal is basically selfish: complying with the request would simply cost too much money or time. You shouldn't necessarily discard such an explanation just because it might sound selfish. Most people accept the idea that businesses are organized to make profits, and explaining how the request would result in excessive costs is often very persuasive. Such a line of reasoning must be phrased

```
Dear Ms. Menchinger:

     The prospective program you've put together for the annual
meeting of the Associated Die Casters of Kentucky looks very
impressive.  Having put programs of this kind together myself, I
know what a busy time you've had during the past few weeks
contacting prospective speakers and getting commitments.

     I feel very sympathetic, because my own schedule is pretty
hectic at this time of the year, too.  For the weekend of your
conference, I've already made firm commitments to. . . .




Dear Professor Jamiesen:

     I agree that, when you're trying to help someone build
writing skills, there's just no substitute for examples of good
writing.  Having worked in Allied Industries' writing development
programs myself, I've seen the improvement that can come from
reading and analyzing examples of effective writing.

     In developing our programs, we commissioned a team of three
business-communication instructors from Ohio University to spend
three months assembling an extensive series of outstanding
examples of good business writing.  [The letter goes on to
indicate that the manual of examples cost the company more than
$7500 to develop, and the company cannot release it for use by
Professor Jamiesen's business communication students, as he has
asked.]
```

Figure 4 Buffer paragraphs and transitions

very carefully so the selfishness is not heavily emphasized. You can often achieve the proper emphasis by showing that prices to all customers would have to be raised, or services reduced, if the company granted such requests.

Explain the reasoning Once you've identified a line of reasoning in your own mind, turn it around and look at it from the reader's viewpoint. How can you make your explanation vivid and persuasive? There are three possibilities.

1. You may be able to show that, in the long run, the bad news benefits the reader. Figure 5 shows such a line of reasoning. In refusing credit to customers, for example, perhaps you can explain that any additional payments beyond their present ones would put a terrible strain on their budgets, with the likely result of bad credit ratings in the future. Or in refusing an employee's application for a job transfer, perhaps you can show that he

PFIRST FEDERAL
SAVINGS & LOAN ASSOCIATION
OF PERSHING

86 Chester Street   Pershing, Wisconsin 54330

February 3, 1983

Mr. Alfred J. Luna
355 Sandy Way
Richmond, WI 47374

Dear Mr. Luna:

    Congratulations on the beautiful landscaping job you've done on your property. Last summer I drove by your home on my way to work and was very impressed with your garden--particularly the roses. I know you must have worked almost every weekend to get such quick results.

    When you purchased your property four years ago, we agreed that your mortgage payment would be $182.00 per month. That figure included a yearly assessment of $465 for county property taxes and $143 for homeowner's insurance.

    Last year's countywide reassessment has resulted in an increase in your county tax to approximately $592 annually, and the cost of your homeowner's insurance has increased to $190 per year. These increases reduce your payment of the principal balance in your account by nearly $11.60 per month, a reduction that could ultimately result in a considerable extension of the contract period of the loan.

    To accommodate these increases totaling $174 per year, your monthly loan payment will be adjusted from $182.00 to $194.00 beginning with your March 1983 payment. Your mortgage loan will, of course, remain at its present very attractive interest rate of 8.5%, substantially lower than the rate on loans written today.

    Next time you're in the office, please let me take a few minutes to explain our new treasury bill savings plan, which pays as high as 14% compound interest. With your growing family, such a plan may be very attractive to you. The First Federal Savings and Loan Association of Pershing has been happy to serve you for these last four years, and we hope to serve you for many years to come.

Cordially,

Katherine Divjak
Vice-President

Figure 5 A bad-news letter stressing benefit to reader

or she would lose valuable seniority rights or other benefits. When such an explanation is valid, it's usually the most persuasive line of reasoning.

A problem with such reasoning can arise when your argument is difficult to understand or the long-term benefit might not be believable. In this case, trying to tell readers that you're refusing for their own good may backfire by creating needless irritation. Of course, you'll carefully avoid insensitive phrasing such as "It's for your own good"; people believe they know their own interests better than you do. But even if the phrasing is tactful, you may find it hard to convince the reader of some long-term benefit unless your case is quite clear and credible. When you can make such a case, this kind of reasoning may be the most persuasive of all.

2. You may be able to show that your refusal benefits a group of people that the reader can identify with. For example, in refusing a request for special service or an unjustified refund, you could explain that your prices to all customers (a group the reader can identify with) would have to increase to cover such special benefits to only a few. Although the reader might like you to make an exception in this case, as a customer he or she can surely understand that it wouldn't be fair to make all customers pay to satisfy one request. Often, as in Figure 6, the reader belongs to some group that would be penalized if your organization complied with his or her request. That group may consist of all customers, all employees, all students, or all family members.

3. You may be able to state the real reason in easily understood terms. You can do this by relating your reasoning to activities the reader is familiar with, such as personal shopping and budget problems. Often the reader's own letter gives you some information for making this kind of connection.

The key to this approach is creating a very clear and vivid image. Such an image tends to persuade all by itself; it draws the reader into the explanation so he or she identifies with the feelings you face in having to refuse. At the end of the reasoning section, the reader should be able to say, "I'm disappointed at being refused, but I can see that, if I were in your place, I'd probably have to refuse, too. This decision makes sense." If the reader can say that, how can he or she be angry with you?

Organize the reasoning If you're treating the message as routine, then once you've identified your line of reasoning and determined how to present it, then you're ready to begin writing. Routine message or not, if you started writing before this point, you've jumped the gun. You've tried to think and write at the same time, which hardly anyone can do well. Even in routine messages, try to separate the two activities so your approach can be well thought out before you start writing.

The most difficult problem in writing this section is to explain your reasoning without tipping your hand too early. Remember that the bad-news strategy depends on explaining your reasons before the reader real-

Dear Professor Vasquez:

The report assignment that your business-communication students are working on here in the Government Documents section of the library looks very interesting. And, of course, we're delighted that your 75 to 100 students are learning more about the census as a source of market information.

When 75 to 100 students all come in and use the same two or three government publications, you can imagine the result. At first the pages get a bit dog-eared and dirty, which is OK; that's what the material is here for. But then bindings start to loosen and the pages begin falling out. And finally whole books begin to disappear, section by section. That's what has happened to our copy of the 1978 Census of Business for Texas. Users of census materials expect to find a complete collection of census publications in our library, and it will be very expensive to replace that book.

Of course, we don't blame you for a student's stealing part of a census publication, but we'd like to make some suggestions in case you wish to ask your students to use census materials again. It may be possible to photocopy the useful sections of census publications and place them in the bookstore as required text materials for your course. Or you may be able to modify the assignment so that not all your students are using the same census materials.

To keep these materials available to all students and faculty, though, we must avoid the situation in which we have 75 to 100 students all working with the same few pages of the same publications; the documents simply aren't strong enough to withstand such rough treatment.

We're eager to have your students continue learning about government publications, and we hope to have them use our materials again in future semesters. Once we get this problem solved, I'm confident that this kind of research can remain a valuable part of your course.

Sincerely,

L. Gene Roberts
Government Documents Librarian

Figure 6 A refusal stressing benefit to group

izes that you're going to refuse. For the reasoning to work, it must be communicated to a reader who's calm and rational, not one who's just found out that he or she has been refused something. Therefore, try to avoid certain phrases ("I wish we could" and "I'm sorry") and words ("but" and "however") that nearly always signal a change in tone. "But" and "however" indicate that you're going to say something unfavorable ("I understand your problem, Ms. Ruis, but . . ."). A "however" in the second or third sentence of your reasoning will signal most readers that a refusal is coming.

One way to organize the reasoning is to begin with specifics and work toward generalizations or conclusions at the end of the section, as Figure 7 demonstrates. Begin by simply stating the key facts your refusal is based on. Then show how they lead to the conclusion that you must refuse the request. You're probably not accustomed to presenting an argument this way, so you'll have to work hard at it the first time or two. Once you master this technique, though, you'll find it's a very easy way to organize your reasoning, and it automatically helps you avoid revealing your conclusion.

The Refusal

Once you've planned or written your reasoning and buffer sections in detail, review them with this question in mind: "Have I already implied the refusal so clearly that it needn't be said explicitly, or must I add a sentence that states it unmistakably?" Often the buffer and reasoning sections indicate your refusal so clearly that it makes little sense to underscore it by stating it explicitly.

In considering this question, remember that the reader probably has some emotional resistance to being refused. And when someone doesn't want to recognize something, he or she may honestly miss implications that would be entirely apparent otherwise. Consider this possibility, and if you doubt that the reader will perceive the implied refusal, then state the refusal clearly.

In the revision stage, recheck your conclusion. Now that you can see the full phrasing of the whole letter, must the refusal be stated explicitly or not? In revising you can still add or remove a refusal sentence easily, so you can readily change your mind if necessary.

If you decide to state the refusal, then deemphasize it and state it positively. To deemphasize it, simply reverse the techniques of emphasis discussed in Chapter 7. That is, position the refusal in the middle of the letter, rather than the beginning or end. Perhaps you can put the refusal in the middle of a paragraph, with further explanatory material after it. At the very least, don't focus attention on the refusal sentence by putting it in a separate paragraph by itself; attach it to the end of the last paragraph of the reasoning section. Besides positioning the refusal for minimal emphasis, reduce its space by stating it briefly and avoid using vivid phrases in it.

 **Cyber-Security Systems, Inc.**

32222 Virginia Avenue ● Santa Clara, CA 95050

August 26, 1984

Ms. Hazel Sarif
Dobson Senior High School
922 Seventh Street
Dobson, ND   58081

Dear Ms. Sarif:

    We're highly complimented by your interest in more
information about Cyber-Security Systems, Inc., and our work in
computer security systems. Recent developments in this field
have indeed been fascinating, and our company is proud to be in
the forefront.

    After developing a series of software systems to protect
the security of computerized information, we prepared the booklet
you requested, "Protecting Computer Systems from Information
Theft," primarily to provide information to potential clients.
For that purpose, our printing of 4000 copies seemed ample.
After the recent reference to our booklet in the <u>Data Processing
Instruction Journal</u>, our supply has dwindled dangerously, and we
must hold the remaining copies for the use ~~use~~ of our sales
department.

    As soon as we're able to prepare new materials on computer
security problems for public distribu, you can be sure we'll
inform the <u>Data Processing Instruction Journal</u> and other
publications in the field, and we invite you to request copies at
that time.

Sincerely,

Joseph Guilbuelt
Assistant to the President

Figure 7 A bad-news letter

Stating the refusal positively isn't any harder than stating it negatively. Simply remember to take the proper viewpoint in your choice of words. A little formula sentence that may help you remember how to refuse positively is this: don't say what you won't do, say what you must do instead. Instead of "That's why we can't ship your order until the 20th," say "that's why the earliest we can ship your order is the 20th." Instead of "We must refuse," say "Here is what we will do instead."

The Neutral Close

Now that you've disappointed the reader, you must find something to say that may help him or her calm down and focus on the possibility of more pleasant dealings with you in the future. Think about your relationship with the reader and visualize the next contact you hope to have with him or her. How will that next contact be rewarding to the reader? How will he or she benefit from continued association with you and your organization? That's what the neutral closing should be about.

Avoid apologizing Once you've decided what to discuss, the most important thing is to avoid any further reference to the refusal or the unpleasant feelings it may have aroused. That's why an apology has no place in the neutral closing. In the first place, you're not sorry you made the decision; as your reasoning indicates, you made the best decision possible under the circumstances. You may indeed feel sorry that this particular reader happened to be adversely affected by the refusal, or you may be sorry you had to make the decision at all, but be careful not to tear down the effect of your reasoning by suggesting that you wish you had decided otherwise. Besides undermining your reasoning, an apology must necessarily remind the reader of the refusal's unpleasantness—which is exactly what you're trying to avoid at this point.

Consider including promotional material When your refusal is to a customer, one appropriate subject for the neutral closing may be promotional material about your products or services. In many cases, suggesting at this point that the customer buy from you may seem a bit crass and self-serving, but often your goal in writing the letter is precisely to obtain future sales. And if you phrase the promotional material to emphasize your desire to be of future service and deemphasize your desire to make money, this direct approach may be effective. You want the customer's business, so ask for it. But be sure to state how he or she will benefit from the transaction.

REFUSING AND OFFERING AN ALTERNATIVE

In some refusals, you're not quite refusing the reader flatly. You do have an alternative available, which, although it isn't exactly what was requested, is better than nothing. (If you believe the reader will find the

Dear Ms. Jonas:

    I'm delighted to hear that you're recovering from your illness and that you'll be back in school next week. I'm frankly amazed--and very happy for you--that you were able to recover from such a serious illness in only eight weeks.

    During the eight weeks you were away, our business writing class has been hard at work. Students have completed seven short-message assignments since the last one you turned in, and next Wednesday they'll be turning in final versions of a 12- to 15-page analytical report. I estimate that the average student has spent a total of 8 or 10 hours on the short assignments and perhaps 30 or 35 hours on the report.

    More important than the actual time involved, however, is that the students have spread this work over a period of several weeks, so they've had time to digest the material they're learning. It would be difficult, even for a student of your capabilities, to cover the same material in the three weeks remaining in the term and to complete the four short-message assignments coming up.

    I would suggest that you allow me to submit a grade of Incomplete for your work at the end of the term. This would give you more time to complete the work in the course, and it would also give you a chance to sit in during the next term on the lectures and discussions you missed while you were away. I'd be happy to have you join next term's class informally without registering or paying further fees, and I'm confident you can complete your work very successfully in that way.

    As soon as you're back on campus, please stop by my office. We can make arrangements then for you to complete the work.

Cordially,

Doyle Newton, Professor

Figure 8 A refusal letter with an alternative

alternative just as acceptable as the original item or action requested, then simply write an informational letter explaining the reasons for the alternative.)

In this case, since you can't do what the reader wants, you must still begin the letter just as though it were a standard bad-news letter, with the buffer paragraph and reasoning. But instead of explicitly refusing, switch at that point to explaining the alternative you propose. Then close by fully explaining the alternative, any procedures the reader must follow, and any other needed information. Since you're ending the letter on a positive note, the neutral close isn't needed, and the letter can end when you finish discussing the alternative, as Figure 8 illustrates.

Once you see how much easier the refusal-with-an-alternative is, you'll want to use it as often as you can. That's fine—as long as you remember that the alternative must be one that readers will perceive as genuine. They must consider it different from, and better than, nothing at all. Inventing an alternative when none really exists is tempting sometimes. But if your readers notice this dishonesty, they may be considerably more upset than they would have been even by a blunt, tactless refusal.

ROUTINE AND NONROUTINE BAD-NEWS LETTERS

Even to the experienced business writer, no bad-news letter is completely routine. That is, a bad-news letter, by its nature, requires a certain amount of analysis and planning before the writing stage, and few writers would willingly mail a first draft of one without at least some revision.

Once you gain some experience, though, some kinds of bad-news letters will come to be nearly routine messages. These are the borderline bad-news messages that convey only mildly upsetting news. In such cases, the planning stage might be abbreviated to a quick consideration of how to present the reasoning and what topic to use in the buffer paragraph. Then the message is quickly drafted. Finally, revision may involve only two or three quick readings of the draft to be sure each section accomplishes its aims and check for smoothness and mechanics. Thus, the whole process takes only a few minutes longer than drafting the message does.

These routine cases, however, are certainly the exceptions rather than the general rule. Normally, nothing less than a full-scale planning stage and revision stage will be enough to ensure good results.

FURTHER EXPLORATION

1. For six of the practice problems at the end of this chapter, determine what line of reasoning you'd use and what you'd say in the buffer paragraph. Just to prove you can do it, find four or five possible topics for each buffer paragraph.

2. Analyze how you felt the last time you were refused something important. What proportion of your feelings consisted of disappointment and what proportion consisted of irritation at the person who delivered the news? What did that person do, if anything, to help you get over the bad feelings? What could that person have done to communicate more effectively?

3. Experiment to see whether or not a buffer paragraph is really necessary in a bad-news letter by attempting to write such a letter with no buffer. Does the letter work without the buffer? If it works, was it harder or easier to write than a comparable letter with a buffer?

4. Over the next few days, think of possible buffer topics other than agreeing with or complimenting the reader. Would thanking the reader for his or her request work? Would some topics work only under special circumstances?

WRITING PROBLEMS

1. Twenty years ago, the Mannford slide rule was one of your manufacturing company's best-selling items. This top-quality precision rule was made in a variety of sizes and compositions ranging from a student model selling for about $10 to a laboratory-quality precision instrument at $438. Since that time, the market for slide rules has been almost completely eliminated by the inexpensive multifunction programmable pocket calculator. Two years ago, your company discontinued production of the last remaining item in this line and sold the design, the stock, and all rights to the product to Timms Engineering, Inc. (499 Brestford Ct., Coldwater, NY 13749). To your knowledge, Timms has disposed of the entire stock and doesn't intend to produce more slide rules. Three or four times a year, you receive inquiries or orders for Mannford slide rules. This morning's mail includes an order for a Series 37 rule that last retailed for $34.95. Professor Stanley Algamani enclosed a check for that amount. Explain the situation when you return his check.

2. As Director of Customer Service at Cleveland Glass Company (3910 East Shore Drive, Sandusky, OH 44870), you're responsible for mailing your company's various advertising and public service publications. A recent favorite is *Decorating with Glass*, a 68-page booklet containing decorating ideas based on your products and others. The booklet was widely publicized, both in your company's advertising and in articles in home and garden magazines, and a great many have been mailed. In fact, you recently mailed the last of the fifth printing of this publication.

Now your Marketing Services people have decided to revise the booklet with new designs and ideas before the next printing. They schedule completion in about two months; figure another two months for printing and binding. At this point, you're recording all incoming requests for *Decorating with Glass,* and you'll send out the new edition to this backlist first. Write a form letter to the people submitting requests and indicate why you can't send the booklet. Many will probably be completing their decorating before the new edition is ready, so the delay may reduce the booklet's value to them.

3. The campus activity that influenced you the most before your college graduation three years ago was your participation in the student chapter of the National Association of Accountants. You found the meetings informative and the activities fun.

This morning in your mail was an invitation from NAA back on campus to speak to the current group about your experiences since graduation. You'd be one of two speakers invited from among recent graduates. You eagerly checked your calendar for the meeting date, the first Tuesday of next month at 7:00 P.M., and you were sorry to discover that it was the day of your accounting firm's regional conference. The conference runs from early morning through the evening hours, and although it'll be interesting and useful in your work, you'd rather spend that evening on campus. Attendance at the conference is mandatory for all staff.

Write Ms. Shari Stucklik, Program Chairperson of the campus NAA, and tell her you must decline. It would probably be useful to her if you can be specific about future openings on your calendar on first Tuesdays of the month during the school year.

4. "What a relief," you sigh as you check your calendar and find you have an unbreakable appointment on the evening of the twelfth of next month. That's the evening the Pocatello Chamber of Commerce has asked you to make a speech on the future of the wilderness in Idaho. As Deputy Chief of the region for the Forest Service, your job includes many such speeches, and you recognize the vital importance of informing the public about future developments. On the other hand, this would have been your fourteenth talk to such a group in just two months, and you're just about talked out. After answering the same questions over and over and listening to the same complaints and arguments, it's very difficult to appear fresh and interested. You know you're getting stale.

In any case, the twelfth is the day of your regional inspection, and the brass from Washington will be in town to review your regional operations. There would be no possibility of getting away.

Reply to Lawrence W. McGuirk, McGuirk Realty (488 North Baird Street, Pocatello, ID 83201). Although your heart really isn't in it, you probably should offer to check other dates when the group has future meetings, if Mr. McGuirk will let you know when these dates are.

5. As Director of Marketing, Simplex-Bohr Marine, Inc. (3001 Main Street, your city), you've often been asked to talk to college student groups about opportunities in marketing and sales. You like to speak to students because you can not only make a pitch for job opportunities at your company, but you can also talk to some of the top students in an informal atmosphere before and after the meeting. In a field where there is a great deal of competition to hire top-flight graduates, this is a key part of your recruiting strategy. Perhaps most important, it's just plain fun to talk to people who are as attentive as students. Unfortunately, the three dates suggested by Mr. Alberto Guerra, the program chairperson of the student chapter of American Marketing Association who wrote to invite you, are impossible. On the second Tuesday of next month you'll be flying to Toronto to the annual trade convention in your field, which you couldn't possibly miss. The fourth Wednesday of next month falls in the middle of your company's annual sales training conference, and that's one of your most important yearly responsibilities; it's your busiest week. And the second Tuesday of the following month is the second day of your vacation, which you fully intend to spend lying on the beach in Honolulu with your family. Write Mr. Guerra; tell him that maybe you can speak another time. (Your instructor can supply an appropriate fictional campus address for Mr. Guerra.)

6. Fremont Die Casting Company (4 Meridian St., Waseco, SD 57791) is a small company producing aluminum and zinc castings used in manufacturing automobiles, power tools, and other metal assemblies. Although you have only about 50 employees, you're one of the larger employers in your small town. The high school industrial arts teacher in nearby Jordan has written to ask whether he can bring a group of about ten students on a field trip to your plant. After reviewing your insurance coverage, you conclude that you can't risk such a visit. Your operation is quite safe, as your near-zero employee accident rate shows, but the prospect of ten young people walking near open smelting pots of molten metal and high-pressure injection-molding presses isn't pleasant, especially when your liability insurance wouldn't apply. The cost of supplemental coverage, according to your agent, is beyond your small company's means. As part owner, reply to the request.

7. James Chan, a senior in management at Southern Michigan University, has written asking for sales figures, by model, for the minicomputers your company manufactures. As sales manager, you're responsible for replying. It's against company policy to reveal sales figures. Like most other computer manufacturers, you never release such figures for any purpose. Your refusal must be final.

Mr. Chan may already be aware that certain knowledgeable observers, including several prominent computer consulting firms, do formulate estimates of computer sales volumes by manufacturer. You neither confirm nor deny the accuracy of such estimates as they apply to your company, although you can point out that such estimates do not agree in detail. One readily available set of estimates is published by *Datamation*, a privately published computer industry journal, in each July issue. Others are published (generally at substantial cost) by leading consulting firms; some of these publications may be available in large university libraries or from academic experts in information systems.

8. Carl Luguena is the systems analyst in your Information Systems Department who specializes in designing and updating the various data processing systems for the production engineering department. Based on his conversations with members of that department, he recently submitted facts and figures to support a recommendation that the "Production Engineering Job Cost per Project Report" be discontinued. As information systems manager, you're responsible for taking action on such recommendations.

A quick check with Nancy Loquart, Production Engineering Manager, revealed that Luguena's facts are correct. Loquart has no idea why the report is produced. Although it's prepared weekly and distributed to her and five other staff members, it isn't currently used by anyone—it's just received and filed each week. All the figures available in that report are also available, in much more convenient form, in other data processing reports. She did mention that one recipient of the report is Comptroller E. Donald Frank.

A call to Don Frank provided one additional fact that Luguena apparently didn't know: the report is specifically required when the company enters into military contracts. Not only is it required when a contract is being fulfilled, but also before the company can even submit bids on military contracts; before bidding, the company must demonstrate that it follows "accepted business practice" by preparing such a report in the normal course of its business. The company has no military contracts now, and it has no immediate plans to bid on such contracts. However, current policy is to keep the possibility of future military contracts open. Thus, the report must be continued.

Write an official reply rejecting Luguena's recommendation.

9. As personnel director of a rapidly growing microelectronics company, you're responsible for administering an outstanding employee relations program that's highly regarded by employees and other companies in your region. The company strongly encourages and sponsors company sports teams, hobby clubs, and special-interest groups of all kinds. A substantial budget is provided to support such activities.

One rule of the program is that employee groups may use the company cafeteria annex for meetings during free periods, but they may not use any other on-site facilities. Meetings not suited to the annex must be held off the company's property. Wesley Purdy, president of the employees' computer club, has submitted a request that the club be allowed to hold meetings in the electronics repair lab. His arguments are as follows:

- The computer club fosters development of expertise directly related to the company's line of business that is then available to the company.
- The repair lab contains equipment that's needed in club activities, but no sensitive or specialized equipment that's likely to be damaged.
- No secret work or new product development is done in the repair lab.
- Several leading club members work in the repair lab, and they agree to be responsible for the use of equipment. (Wes says they're extremely strict about the correct use of equipment.)
- The lab manager has authorized the use of lab equipment at club meetings, and the equipment is currently used at meetings.
- It's riskier to move equipment to the annex than to move the meetings to the lab.

The meeting location policy was established by the Executive Committee, which consists of top company managers. Since Purdy's request appeared to be a legitimate exception, you made all the points listed above at an Executive Committee meeting and argued in favor of approving this exception without in any way changing the policy as it applies to other organizations. The committee refused, fearing that this exception would encourage many other requests for similar exceptions that they'd be reluctant to grant.

Communicate the refusal to Wesley Purdy. The purpose of the employee relations program is to encourage loyalty toward the company; try to refuse without making computer club members angry at members of the Executive Committee.

10. Phyllis Kelso of nearby Pleasantville has written to you, the manager of the Kerrigan Appliance Store, that the Morton Model 559 microwave oven she bought from you 13 months ago has stopped working. She said she took the unit to a local appliance repair shop, where they told her the main power transformer had shorted and must be replaced at a cost of $156, including parts and labor. Mrs. Kelso questions the reliability of a unit that has such expensive failures, and wants you to honor the guarantee by fixing the unit in your service department, even though the one-year guarantee expired last month.

Your salespeople are instructed to offer customers a service contract on all microwaves purchased; in effect, this contract extends the guarantee for two more years, and your records indicate that Mrs. Kelso signed your standard form refusing the service contract. In your experience, the Morton microwave is one of the most reliable of all small appliances—that's why its service contract is among the least expensive for appliances of any type. In any case, you can't extend the guarantee to cover this repair. The manufacturer, who offers the guarantee, wouldn't reimburse you for parts and labor, and you can't afford to absorb such costs yourself. The best solution you can suggest is that she bring the unit to your service department and let your technician check it out. Perhaps repairs can be made for less than $156, although you can make no promises.

11. You're the Customer Relations Director at Louisiana Scientific Instrumentation, Inc. (19 Main Street, Thibodaux, LA 70301), a rapidly growing manufacturer of small computers for hobby and small business use. Although LSI has been a success for over 15 years, the tremendous sales of the new line of microcomputers (about 175,000 units in the first year, making LSI the third largest in this market) raises entirely new management problems.

One of these is the sheer volume of customer inquiries. Small computers are complex and demanding, and even though your 445-page user's manual provides an enormous amount of information, a great many users have specialized applications requiring individualized explanation. You currently receive an average of about 350 inquiries from purchasers (besides inquiries from prospective purchasers) every week. Even with your current success, you're a small company, and your staff is spending every minute of spare time trying to keep up with the mountainous (and growing) backlog of inquiries.

Although the sheer volume of correspondence is overwhelming, even more frustrating is that few inquiries provide sufficient information to make a direct, complete reply possible; users don't know what facts you'll need. Most often, a knowledgeable (and expensive) electronics engineer or technician has to write the inquirer back for further information or provide a whole series of alternative answers for the user to weigh depending on the circumstances.

That's why the LSI top management has agreed to put a stop to this inflow; there will be no more written answers to customer inquiries. Instead, you'll establish a toll-free telephone inquiry line. It'll be installed by the end of this week, and in response to every customer inquiry you intend to send a form letter informing the inquirer of the toll-free number (800) 555-1101, and explaining why you can't reply in writing to his or her inquiry. You'll immediately send this form letter to inquirers in your present five-week backlog.

Two technicians supplied with a full library of reference materials will answer calls from 8 A.M. Eastern time to 9 P.M. Pacific time, five days a week. Because they can request further information from inquirers, the technicians should be able to provide complete answers to most inquiries in one call. But if any inquirer wishes to call back, further questions are welcome. You expect the lines to be very busy, but with persistence serious callers should manage to get through.

Write the form letter for reproduction over your signature. To save money and speed replies, no inside address will be used. (See also the following problem.)

12. As you collect your thoughts to write the form letter (see the preceding problem), you remember some statistics put together by staff members who've been answering inquiries. They're asked to categorize inquiries by subject, and summaries show that more than two-thirds of the inquiries are raising the same few questions (about 12). Most inquiries raise several questions, but they often include at least one of the "big 12." Your brainstorm: ask top technicians to prepare clear one-page answers to these 12 questions (add more questions later if the volume warrants this) and include these answers with your form letter when inquirers raise any of the "big 12" questions.

Further, since you're now keeping computerized records of inquirers' names and addresses (for later advertising mailings), why not computerize the reply process? Your data entry clerk will scan each letter very quickly to determine whether the inquirer has raised any of the "big 12" questions. If so, the clerk will note (by code number) which questions were raised, along with the name and address. If none of the "big 12" questions is raised, the clerk will enter a different code with the name and address. Then your computerized high-speed printer can print out your form letter to each inquirer, personalized with an inside address.

This procedure requires just one modification of your form letter. Now you need a basic form letter (as noted in the preceding problem), but you must structure it so an additional paragraph can be inserted by the computer if necessary, depending on the code number. For inquirers who asked one or more of the "big 12" questions, the paragraph noting the enclosed answer sheet(s) is automatically included; for inquirers who didn't, the paragraph is omitted. Both versions of your letter should be smooth and clear.

Note that many of these inquiries are very much like complaint letters. Customers are saying (in effect), "Why didn't you tell me before I bought the computer that such-and-such would cause problems?" Of course, since you didn't know they intended to use the computer for such-and-such, you feel justified in ignoring their irritation and simply providing information. Your telephone-inquiry technicians have been trained to take this approach; be sure your form letter does, too. Don't let the letter be interpreted as quarrelsome or overly defensive.

In the version you write, label the "big 12" paragraph clearly. The simple addition of this one paragraph (wherever it appears) is the only difference between the "big 12" version and the plain version; nothing else should need changing.

13. To help earn money for your education, you replied to a newspaper ad offering a part-time job. Your letter must have impressed the personnel manager of Capitol Construction Company, because you were one of three people invited for a job interview. Driving to the interview, you discovered that the company is more than 30 minutes from your apartment by car.

Yesterday Mr. Ronald Ferguson at Capitol phoned, offering you 20 hours of work per week with hours to be arranged to fit your class schedule; the job begins the week after next at a very attractive pay rate. You told Mr. Ferguson that you prefer to work only 10 hours per week, and he replied that they need someone for the full 20 hours. You spent the evening reevaluating your budget and your schedule, and you concluded that you can't keep up with your classes if you work 20 hours per week (especially if you count the travel time each day), even though the job looks interesting and the pay is tempting. Write Mr. Ferguson.

14. Valley Street Presbyterian Church (1902 Valley Street) is conveniently located near your college's campus. Accounting Education Service (433 Market Street in your state capital), a profit-making enterprise, has written to inquire whether it may rent a room in the church plant to house a three-night-a-week cram course for people who'll be taking the CPA exam on campus three months from now. AES represents itself as a company with well-established credentials of high quality (the church is invited to investigate) and a very high success rate in helping its students pass the CPA exam. It cites a number of local accountants as references.

The church's policy, long established, is to encourage local nonprofit groups to use its facilities at low cost or no cost, but to refuse facilities to profit-making organizations. However, since an educational organization, even if profit-making, might be considered acceptable by church officers, you (as church secretary) called several of the references and heard high praise of AES' quality and integrity. Then you called the church officers who must authorize such use of the facilities, and they unanimously reaffirmed the standing policy. They felt that any use of church facilities for profit-making activities is an inappropriate use of the property, especially since the church, as a nonprofit religious organization, is exempt from paying normal real estate taxes. Other profit-making educational groups have been refused the use of the facilities in the past. Write a reply to AES.

15. Take the place of Sandy Ritnauer, sales manager of The Forkner Dulcimer Company of Milo, Tennessee. This morning's mail brought an order for a Model 35 hammer dulcimer, in walnut finish, from Walter Jenune (8375 Brockton Turnpike, High Bridge, VT 05656). This top-of-the-line, two-bridge, four-octave instrument is one of the finest hammer dulcimers available anywhere in the world, fully justifying its $2,349 price tag. The hand-inlaid wood cabinet, made in the great tradition of fine crafstmanship handed down from father to son in your company for nearly 80 years, is truly beautiful. Mr. Jenune must be an excellent musician to appreciate the quality of this instrument and to play a hammer dulcimer of this size. Unfortunately, The Forkner Dulcimer Company markets its products only through selected retail dealers located throughout the United States. Your agreement with your dealers requires that all sales be made through them; because of the complexity and fragility of your instruments, processing direct sales to customers and providing the after-market service that's usually necessary isn't cost effective. Return Mr. Jenune's order and check. Refer him to Brannigan's Music Store (917 Mountain Peak Parkway, Lenox, MA 01240), his nearest retail dealer. Persuade him to make the 80-mile trip to Lenox for his instrument. Although your records show no deliveries of the Model 35 to Brannigan's, they do stock other, less expensive Forkner dulcimers, and they'll process his order for delivery of a Model 35 in less than 60 days.

16.   When Jonathan Salontov applied for a credit card at your department store, you (as credit manager) ran a routine credit check on him. The result: Mr. Salontov is classified as "slow pay" (frequent missed or past-due payments) by several present creditors. Under these circumstances, your policy is to refuse credit. Encourage Mr. Salontov to patronize your store on a cash basis until his present creditors can report full, regular payment. Remind him of your store's well-deserved reputation for top-quality merchandise, including many unique and original product lines not found elsewhere in your region.

17.   As a fast-rising young manager, you're strongly encouraged by your company to establish a record of participation in civic organizations. You've concentrated your participation in your city's Junior Chamber of Commerce, a group you particularly like. Apparently the feeling is mutual, because yesterday a fellow member phoned, saying he represented several current officers, and asked you to run for president of the organization. You were surprised and impressed, and you agreed to consider it. In the cold light of day, you've realized that the presidency would have both pros and cons. It would certainly impress your company's management, and it would be extremely satisfying to your ego. However, running for president and being president would be extremely time-consuming, and this time would be subtracted from the time available to perform your regular work successfully. You spoke with your boss about the question this afternoon, and he was obviously quite impressed that you'd been invited to run. Clearly, a term as president of the Junior Chamber of Commerce would be a strong plus in future promotion considerations. On the other hand, he made it equally clear that your value to the company lies principally in continuing to perform your job at your present high level. He said that he could be flexible in scheduling your vacation time to match periodic peaks in your presidential schedule, but he firmly ruled out any reduction in your managerial duties if you're elected president. Your spouse vigorously opposes your spending evenings and weekends on additional away-from-home activities.

You've decided not to run. To be completely sure of saying exactly what you want to say, put your refusal in writing.

18. As sales manager for a musical instrument manufacturer, you were delighted to receive a sizable order recently from a new customer, Roberts Music Store (4924 Beal Street, Oxford, ND 58231). Today the bad news arrived from your credit department: information submitted by Roberts Music Store, corroborated by the normal credit check, indicates that Roberts is a new business, undercapitalized, and shaky, as many new businesses are. With hard work and careful planning, some such ventures survive, but the odds are against it. Credit is denied.

It's your job to write Mr. Ernest Roberts, refusing credit and inviting him to pay cash in advance for the $21,852.18 worth of merchandise he ordered. When you receive payment for this order, or for a reduced order if he prefers, you'll ship immediately.

19. The University Curriculum Committee at one typical university is the major approval body for the curriculum as it appears in the university catalog. The committee considers departmental requests for changes in curriculum and also initiates its own inquiries.

After a recent inquiry, the committee has voted to restrict the maximum number of course credits earned in one department that can be applied toward graduation. The new limit will mean that a student can't take more than half of all the credits needed for graduation within the same department. This change will make it more likely that students will get a broad exposure to many bodies of knowledge and viewpoints, which is the ideal of liberal education.

Checking the catalog to see how many credits students must earn for the various majors (including prerequisites to required courses), the committee has found that majors in the Art Department, Biology Department, Communication Arts Department, and German Department exceed the new maximum.

As the chairperson of the University Curriculum Committee, write a memo that could be adapted and sent to the chairperson of each of these departments. (For example, write the memo to the Art Department so that it could be adapted for typing and mailing to the other departments.) Although the University Curriculum Committee unquestionably has the authority to demand changes in departments' curricula, remember that the change you're asking for will require a great many hours of work by the faculty and the chairpersons of these departments. You're asking for a major expenditure of effort from people who may not sympathize with the committee's aims in this case.

20. Partly because of your committee work over the last two years, your company has approved the establishment of a centralized word processing center. Your administrative assistant, Emily Guilio, has spent more than half her work time for two years assisting you on this project. She gathered facts, studied other companies' installations, talked to equipment vendors, and generally became a word processing expert. In addition, you're convinced that she has the skills to be an excellent manager. Therefore, you advised her to apply for the new position of word processing manager, head of the center. When your committee reviewed the applicants for the position, Emily's credentials placed her among the top three candidates, and she was invited to interview for the position. In the interviews, she impressed committee members with her administrative and communication skills, which are vital in this position, and with her knowledge of the word processing field. Although you argued strongly on her behalf, the committee selected a man from outside the company who's had actual office management experience. The committee has asked you to inform Emily of their decision. Although you'll certainly meet with her to tell her the bad news, write the official letter of refusal from the committee that you'll give her at that time.

21.   In your recent effort to hire an administrative services manager for the growing communications equipment division of a large electronics conglomerate, Dwight Yoder was one of the two strongest candidates. The person hired in this new position was to organize your reprographics (copying and duplicating) and records management (long-term document storage) operations and improve the management of your telephone and mail system. Mr. Yoder's credentials, including 15 years as a military officer working in all these fields, are impressive. If you could, you'd probably hire him. But since the time you advertised the position and interviewed Mr. Yoder, corporate headquarters has ordered a shake-up of your division's top management. Your division president and three vice-presidents have been replaced by new people from corporate headquarters, and a freeze has been placed on filling new positions for the next three months. Your request to complete the hiring process for the previously approved administrative services manager position was denied. Since the long-standing problems in reprographics and records management will only worsen over the next few months, you're confident of receiving permission to hire someone when the freeze is lifted, but no doubt Mr. Yoder doesn't want to wait. Write him. You'll keep his materials on file and contact him again when the freeze is lifted, though you're confident he'll find a suitable position before that time.

22.   As Information Systems Director, every three months you must write an official performance evaluation letter to each of the managers working directly under you. Your problem today is the performance evaluation for senior systems analyst Ivan Petoskey. A little over two months ago, Ivan's wife abruptly left him and his seven-year-old son, and he hasn't heard from her since. Understandably, Ivan was unprepared to provide care for his son during work hours, and you were supportive during the first few weeks as he devoted most of his attention to the necessary adjustments. Other staff members were glad to fill in at meetings that Ivan was scheduled to attend, and his staff generously covered his essential work. Everyone assumed that after a few weeks he would be back up to his former high performance level.

But that hasn't happened. Although things are much better than they were during the first week or two of his crisis, Ivan is still frequently missing important deadlines and meetings—often without prior notice. In the last week, for example, he failed to complete the final report on a new production scheduling system. That report should have been presented to the top management executive committee, and his staff indicates that all the development work had been completed on schedule. In addition, he was called out of a meeting with the MIS steering committee, which includes the heads of several departments, and left the building (presumably for a family emergency) before consideration of the agenda item he was to present. These are typical of the continuing problems. Your notes list eight such problems in the last five weeks.

You wish to be as understanding as possible; such a crisis could happen to anyone. You like Ivan personally, respect his professional competence very much, and sympathize with his heartbreaking difficulties. But at the same time, the work must be done—meetings attended, reports and other work completed on schedule, and so on. The work of your entire department is being adversely affected over a long period, and the situation can't continue.

Write the performance evaluation. Convey your feelings about the situation as honestly as you can. Be specific about the problems you perceive. Communicate optimism that the situation will improve, but be firm in indicating that it must improve. Remember that this evaluation must establish a basis for dismissing Ivan, should that prove necessary later.

14

Indirect-Plan Messages: Persuasion

*Here comes the trout that must be caught
with tickling.*
Shakespeare (Twelfth Night)

*When the lion fawns upon the lamb,
The lamb will never cease to follow him.*
Shakespeare (Henry VI, Part III)

The art of persuasion is nothing more than a systematic approach to a communication activity that everyone performs continually. We all have to persuade others to do things for us. To persuade, we needn't peer into the dark crevices of the subconscious mind; we can simply look at ways to carry out a commonplace communication as well as we can.

WHEN TO USE PERSUASION

A persuasive approach to communication is appropriate when you must get someone to do something that he or she wouldn't do if you merely requested it. This definition involves two elements. First, you want your audience to do something. Second, the action you want isn't something the audience would perform if you simply stated, "Please do this." To achieve your goal, then, you must go beyond simply providing information and even go beyond convincing your audience that you're right. Your message must also get your audience to act.

Persuasion involves dealing with emotions. To persuade, you must arouse emotions that will motivate the audience to do what you ask. Whereas in the bad-news strategy the goal is to reduce negative emotions, in persuasion the goal is to arouse the kind of positive emotions that will motivate the audience to do what you want.

THE PSYCHOLOGY OF MOTIVATION

People are motivated to act when they feel that the action is in their own best interest. And that's where the process of persuasion begins for the persuader. How will the readers benefit? What's in it for them? Before you can go any further, you must answer these questions.

Motivation in Theory

A number of philosophers and psychologists have developed theories of human motivation. One that's widely accepted and relatively easy to apply is the hierarchy of needs developed by Abraham Maslow.[1] Maslow suggests that a person's basic needs in life can be grouped into five categories that form a natural hierarchy:

Self-actualization needs

Esteem needs

Belongingness and love needs

Safety needs

Physiological needs

---

1. Abraham H. Maslow, *Motivation and Personality*, 2nd ed. (New York: Harper and Row, 1970). See especially pp. 35–58.

We as biological organisms have physiological needs for air, water, food, clothing, and shelter. We need these things to maintain life; deprived of them, we would die.

Safety needs refer to our desire to continue satisfying our physiological needs in the future. Clearly, the physiological needs of today aren't the only ones we're concerned about; we're also concerned about providing for tomorrow and the next day—for the future. Our safety needs are satisfied when we feel no anxiety about fulfilling our future physiological needs.

Belongingness and love needs refer to our desire for friendship, acceptance, and love from other people. These needs involve feelings of belonging and trust.

Esteem needs refer to our desire for prestige and status. Much human motivation toward leadership and power may be ascribed to this level of need.

Self-actualization needs refer to our desire for the kind of self-satisfaction that doesn't depend on anyone else's activities or attitudes. Self-actualization leads us to engage in activities that we know we can do well, whether anyone else recognizes our prowess or not.

The operation of this hierarchy is the interesting thing. First, each level of need must be reasonably satisfied before the next level above it becomes a motivator. That is, a person will have no great interest in safety needs until all immediate physiological needs are met. And the need for self-actualization won't motivate a person until all the needs below it are met. Second, once a given level of need is met, it no longer motivates strongly. That is, if your physiological needs are met and you're reasonably sure they'll continue to be met, then neither physiological nor safety needs will be important motivators for you.

To illustrate how these principles work, let's consider an experience most swimmers have had at least once. In youthful horseplay, a friend holds your head underwater as a joke; you can't breathe. In Maslow's hierarchy, the need for air is a physiological need, the very bottom level. When you're cut off from air, your need for it becomes a total and absolute motivator for you; you do anything necessary to get it. But when you have plenty of air to breathe, the need for air is no motivator for you at all. No one could get you to do something by promising to give you air to breathe. The needs that will motivate you are now higher-level ones.

Since most people you'll do business with have satisfied their physiological and safety needs, they'll be motivated largely by the remaining higher-level needs: belongingness and love, esteem, and self-actualization. And it's significant that these needs all relate to people's feelings, their emotional lives. In contrast, the physiological and safety needs relate closely to money. People use money to satisfy their physiological needs, and they provide for a continued supply of it—through education, personal savings, and investments—to satisfy their safety needs.

Motivation in Practice

Experienced persuaders tend to agree that most American business people and their customers respond to a hierarchy of motivators something like this:

Good feelings, such as prestige, esteem, and self-satisfaction

Objective nonmonetary benefits, such as saving time or effort

Monetary benefits, such as making or saving money

This hierarchy is certainly similar to Maslow's. Here's how experienced persuaders apply it.

Given the place of money in our society, money is the most obvious kind of benefit and an easy one to explain. If you can show your readers how they can make or save money by acting as you wish, then you can base your persuasion on this benefit. Money's influence as a motivator isn't simple, though. Since most people have satisfied their physiological and safety needs, monetary benefits must appeal to higher-level needs. Thus, persuasion typically emphasizes that the ability to make and save money confers prestige and esteem; people are admired for this ability. In addition, money is quantifiable and easy to think about. If you can show someone how to save $87.13, then your proposal may look more attractive than another that promises only $61.20. It is much more difficult to quantify and compare benefits like esteem, acceptance, and self-satisfaction.

When experienced persuaders can't use money as the benefit, they often consider other objective benefits next, such as savings in time or effort, convenience, conflict avoidance, and better job performance. The range of possible objective, nonmonetary benefits is large. Like monetary benefits, these too can be explained fairly easily, especially when you can connect them to higher-level needs.

Emotional benefits can also motivate people, once you show them that doing what you ask will make them feel good. You may now think that feelings are pretty weak and insubstantial as motivators, but Maslow and other theorists suggest just the opposite. And the experience of national advertisers does, too. Almost all national consumer advertising—the kind you see on TV and in magazines—is aimed at viewers' feelings. That's partly because the competing products in many fields are pretty much alike, with few real differences to talk about. But even when an advertiser can show an objective benefit of a product, as with decay-preventive toothpaste, the message concentrates on the good feelings the consumer will have from fewer cavities rather than on the monetary and health benefits. "Look Mom, no cavities," and "Daddy, Daddy! I only had two cavities," are hardly appeals to the audience's rationality. They're designed to reach the audience's feelings.

No doubt you've done a favor for someone and enjoyed a warm feeling of satisfaction from it. You aren't alone. In our society, most of the work in some very important fields is volunteer work done by people whose only reward is good feelings. Good feelings are real, and they're important enough to motivate people. Don't neglect this kind of motivator just because it may appear less substantial than others.

If you have some information about someone, especially if you know him or her, you may be able to make reasonably accurate guesses about what kinds of needs motivate that person most strongly. Your first step in planning is to make that analysis.

EXPLAINING THE BENEFIT

Once you've decided how you'll motivate your reader, you need to consider how to create very clear images—images that will enable your reader to imagine getting and enjoying the benefit, understand how easy it'll be to do what you ask, and visualize taking action. This is a place where the techniques of vivid writing, discussed in Chapter 8, come into play.

Part of the problem is that a persuasive message will meet some resistance from the reader. (If no one could resist your proposed action, then there would be no need for persuasion.) Because they resist, readers won't share your images unless you can communicate them clearly and vividly. At the same time, these images must be believable. If you exaggerate too much, the images may be very vivid indeed, but readers may react to them negatively. Many people are bothered by TV commercials that exaggerate feelings all out of proportion and make consumers look pretty dumb. The wife who sinks into deep depression over a ring of dirt on her spouse's collar, for instance, is hardly behaving realistically; in real life such a person would need psychiatric help. And to the extent that people are irritated by such exaggeration, the commercial fails to persuade. The images you create in your message should be believable.

DEALING WITH OBJECTIONS

In most persuasion, the reader's resistance is based at least partly on specific objections—that is, perceived negative factors. Therefore, your message must overcome these objections.

Often the very thing you want readers to do is what they will object to; they may feel it's too costly in money, time, or effort. Experienced persuaders have found that the objection can usually be dealt with in one of the following ways.

1. Ignore it. If the objection might not occur to the reader unless you bring it up, then don't bring it up. Or even if the reader may think of it, don't emphasize it by talking about it; you may be able to keep the reader's attention focused on positive factors, ones that are favorable to your case. Ignoring an objection works best when the objection isn't very important to the reader.

2. Acknowledge it calmly and stress other, more important positive factors. This technique tends to take the steam out of the objection. It tells the reader that you did consider the factor but concluded that the reasons favoring your proposal were more important. Phrase the message to deemphasize the objection and to create vivid images of other positive factors. In Figure 1, this approach is used to ask employees to spend more time addressing interdepartmental mail.

3. Turn it into an advantage. It's amazing how often a negative factor can become an advantage when examined from another viewpoint. And an objection often proves to be no objection at all when the facts of the situation are explained more clearly. Turning apparent objections into support for your position isn't a rare occurrence at all; in fact, it's common.

What's not so common is the kind of writer who will inspect apparently negative factors to see whether or not they can be turned into advantages. Most people simply assume that an objection must be just what it looks like, and they're defeated right from the start. Finding such advantages, therefore, requires some positive thinking, as Figure 2 shows. The way to turn an objection around is to look very carefully at it simply as a fact, stripped of all its emotional weight, and not as a problem filled with negative overtones. Then search for another way to view the situation in which that fact is no longer a disadvantage. Can that same fact be used to support your position, rather than detracting from it?

If you try to turn an objection around and can only come up with what really amounts to doubletalk rather than a real argument, you may want to think twice before using it. It's true that sometimes fancy phrasing can distract the reader from an objection, and sometimes that distraction is needed. But if the reader feels strongly about the objection and realizes that you're substituting fancy talk for serious thought, then your effort may backfire. The reader may begin to question other things you say if you show that you treat his or her objections this lightly.

CLOSING THE DEAL

As any salesperson will tell you, more sales are lost because the seller didn't close at the right psychological moment than for any other reason. A good salesperson knows when to close.

Fortunately, when you write a persuasive message, knowing when to close is easy. You close—you try to get some definite commitment from your readers that they'll do what you ask—right at the end of the message. By that point you've laid out the best reasons why they should comply, you've dealt with any objections they may have, and you've explained exactly what action you want. If they're ever going to be persuaded to act, it's right then. So press firmly for action. And whenever possible, ask your readers to take action immediately. With every passing minute, the intensity of their motivation fades. On this point the advertisers are exactly right: get them to act now!

TO: All Employees

FROM: F. Alan DeTomasi, Director, Administrative Services

SUBJECT: Speeding Delivery of Interoffice Mail

Here's a way you can cut the delivery time of your interoffice mail. If you'll spend one minute adding a mail substation number to each interoffice message, we'll guarantee its arrival anywhere in the company within four working hours of the time we pick it up.

In the past 18 months our company has tripled its size, and our old interoffice mail system no longer works efficiently. Therefore, we've established mail substations on each floor of each building.

If your outgoing mail includes a substation address, it'll be carried directly to that substation on the next hourly delivery truck. The substation addresses of each employee are listed in the attached company directory. Mail with no substation address will be taken to the central mailroom and sorted as always--we'll do our best to provide timely delivery.

We recognize that looking up each recipient's substation address takes a little time--about a minute on the average--but we think the benefits and cost savings of guaranteed four-hour delivery are worth that small step. If you know the recipient's location (building and floor), you can simply check the Quick List on the back cover of the directory.

Since all substations will be in operation by the end of this week, start adding substation addresses to your interoffice mail now. The improvement will be well worthwhile.

P.S. Please inform mailers outside the company of your new substation address. We guarantee four-hour delivery of substation-addressed outside mail, too, from the time the Postal Service truck delivers it to the mailroom.

Figure 1 A persuasive memo

DATE: September 11, 1983

TO: Executive Committee

FROM: Duwayne Kunstler, Administrative Manager

SUBJECT: SAVINGS IN CLERICAL COSTS

    In view of the recently announced budget cutbacks and the hiring freeze, it may seem like folly to suggest that we now implement the proposed pilot project in word processing. Actually, though, this is the ideal time to make the proposed $74,000 investment in word processing equipment. Here's why.

1. After a very short time (less than 18 months), the project will pay for itself by a substantial saving in clerical costs. My June 18 report provides figures based on other local companies' experience.

2. All three departments chosen to participate in the pilot project anticipate the loss of at least one clerical employee. Marketing and the executive vice-president's office have one resignation each, and administrative services has two. The pilot project's projected saving is based on the assumption that three positions will be eliminated through attrition.

3. No additional clerical staff need be hired to implement this project. At least five present clerical employees have word processing experience, according to the personnel department. Four of these employees have requested transfer to the departments designated for implementing the pilot project.

4. Even though budgets will be cut, we anticipate little reduction in the amount of clerical work to be done. Only through increasing our efficiency by the addition of word processing systems will be be able to keep up with the work.

    I'd like to explain these points further and answer any questions you may have. May I please take 10 minutes during your September 21 meeting to do so?

Figure 2 A persuasive memo

Often, however, the action you request can't be taken immediately. If you ask readers to follow a certain shipping procedure the next time they return goods or to speak at your club next month, then their doing so right now is clearly inappropriate. You must figure out some action they can take right now that will symbolize their commitment to the desired later action. That's why you ask the warehouse chief to send a memo to his supervisors—today, while he's thinking about it—directing them to follow the new procedure. And that's why you ask the invited speaker to write you—right away!—agreeing to come speak. If you can get your readers to take such a symbolic step, then you've enormously increased the probability that they'll complete the main action later.

One final note before we discuss the planning of a persuasive message: when you're trying to persuade, remember that absolutely nothing you can do will guarantee success 100 percent of the time. No one's record is that good; certainly the record of Madison Avenue advertisers, our society's most accomplished persuaders, is far from perfect. The only reasonable way to approach persuasion is on a percentage basis: sometimes you'll succeed and sometimes you'll fail. But by doing the best job you can, you'll certainly improve your batting average. Therefore, don't be pessimistic even when you know your argument is weak and your chance of success is low. If you wait until you have a sure thing before you attempt to persuade people, then you'll miss many opportunities that might have paid off.

PLANNING AND WRITING PERSUASIVE MESSAGES

The general plan for a persuasive message is as follows. The opening sentences secure the reader's interest and present the basic motivational appeal—namely, the benefit to the reader. The body justifies in detail your argument that by acting as you wish, the reader will get the benefit you're promising. The ending calls for action.

The Opening: Securing Interest

The first three or four sentences of a persuasive message must try to accomplish several things at once. First, and most important, the opening should get the reader's attention and arouse interest. Business people tend to skim their mail, as we've seen; you want them to read your message carefully.

Second, the opening should present the benefit that the rest of the message is based on. This is the place to impress the reader with the most vivid image possible of the benefit he or she will receive. More often than not, this benefit can itself arouse interest. Remember, however, that the first job of the opening is to catch the reader's interest. Interest must be secured right at the beginning, even if you have to postpone stating the benefit for a sentence or two.

Third, to establish credibility, you must immediately indicate, at least in a general way, what the reader must do to receive the benefit. It's often wise to avoid detailing the action too much in the opening; that can wait until the body of the message. But do indicate the kind of action needed so the reader understands what the message is all about.

Every once in a while, an executive receives a letter that begins the way Figure 3 does. It's really boring! Besides displaying his ineptitude, the writer has completely wasted his reader's time with this opening, and he's hardly increased the probability that she'll put the meeting on her calendar. If the meeting proceeds at the same plodding pace as the invitation, attending it would hardly be pleasant.

Figure 3 also shows an alternative opening that's hardly earthshaking but would surely do a better job of persuading the reader. Such an opening secures interest very directly by immediately stressing the key benefits that the message will discuss in detail later: talking to and helping business students who are highly qualified prospective employees. In addition, the opening gives a general idea of what the reader is being asked to do, while leaving the details of scheduling until later. Notice that, in the third

---

Boring

Dear Ms. Verein:

    I am John Peroni, and I am writing to you for the Future Business Leaders Association here at Southern Michigan University. Our group has more than 35 members, and we meet on the second Tuesday of each month. Over the next few months we will be devoting our meetings to hearing from successful executives like yourself. The executive committee of FBLA has asked me to write you to inquire whether you would be interested in coming to talk to one of these meetings. . . .

Better

Dear Ms. Verein:

    How would you like to help 35 Future Business Leaders at Southern Michigan University gain a more accurate understanding of your business, and at the same time establish early contact with some of the same young men and women that your company will interview for jobs in the coming two or three years? If you can give us an evening of your time later this spring, we can promise you an attentive and interested audience of the top-ranking business majors in our school. . . .

Figure 3 Persuasive openings

sentence, attention immediately shifts back to the benefit once information about the desired action has been provided. The writer will discuss the details more fully—after he's persuaded the reader to come. Right now he wants to keep her attention on the benefits.

The question opening that this example illustrates is often an easy way to get the message started: "How would you like to . . .?" or "Would you be interested in . . .?" (see Figure 4). Of course, the reader's reaction to such a question may be negative, but in that case the approach you're thinking of would probably fail no matter what you say in the opening; the reader simply isn't interested in the benefit you offer. Normally, if the benefit is well chosen, the reader will be mentally nodding in agreement to your question. And in the process, the reader's interest and curiosity will have been aroused.

The Body: Justifying the Benefit and Explaining the Proposal

The body of a persuasive message must cover a lot of ground in vivid detail, so it's usually fairly lengthy. It must perform four major functions. First, the body must explain the benefit in glowing, but realistic, terms. Second, the body must fully clarify the connection between the proposed

```
        How would you like to be able to let the typists in your
office go home 30 minutes earlier every day--and still produce as
much work as they do now?  By saving those typists nearly a
minute on every single letter they type, the Simplified Letter
Form can help you do just that!
        Let me show you how they'll save that minute. . . .



        Wouldn't it be a good feeling to know that you'd helped 40
enthusiastic young people develop a more realistic picture of the
world of corporate accounting?  By spending two hours with our
Accounting Students Association here at Daley University, you can
have an interesting evening of give and take with students who
really need the information and guidance you can give them.



        Here's a way you can put $39.76 back in your pocket at the
end of every month--and get the bonus of not having to fight the
rush hour traffic every morning and evening.  If you're a typical
commuter employed at United Industries, that's exactly what
you'll save by joining a UI vanpool.
        According to a recent survey, as a typical UI commuter you
drive 32.4 miles roundtrip 20 work days per month. . . .
```

Figure 4 Persuasive openings

action and the benefit, so that even resisting readers will see it. Third, the body must deal with any objections. Fourth, the body must explain with perfect clarity what action you want; if readers finish the letter without knowing what you're asking them to do, then they can't do it even if they want to. The body must do all these things in vivid images that keep the readers' emotional reactions in key (see Figure 5 on pages 286–287).

In general, the body should progress from focusing mainly on the benefit at first to focusing mainly on the desired action near the end. In this way, as the reader becomes more and more fully persuaded, the attention shifts from the benefit to the proposal. Of course, just to make sense, you'll have to refer to the desired action early in the message, and even late in the message the reader will be thinking about that action in light of the expected benefit. Nevertheless, the principal focus of attention should shift from benefit to proposal.

At the same time, the phrasing can subtly shift from conditional at the beginning ("If you do it") to definite in the middle ("When you do it") as readers are becoming persuaded, and then to instrumental near the end ("Here's how to do it"). This shift shouldn't be obvious to readers, or they may feel you're being manipulative, but it's almost necessary in persuasion. If you're saying "When you do it" right at the beginning, it'll probably sound pushy. But if you're still saying "If you do it" at the end, you indicate that you yourself don't really believe readers will be persuaded. Figure 6, on pages 288–289, illustrates these shifts.

If you must deal with objections, normally the place to do so is about one-half or two-thirds of the way through the body. For instance, when you're selling a product and price is a possible negative factor, you normally get specific about price fairly late in the message. Sometimes, of course, an objection is so important to readers that it must be met early in the message, but unless there's a reason to do otherwise, deal with objections fairly late in the body. If you wait, be sure not to make even the slightest reference to an objection until you're ready to address with it. You don't want readers to think about a negative factor while you're trying to tell them about benefits.

The Close: Getting Action

In the last paragraph or so, your message should confidently press for action and remind readers of the benefit they can expect.

If the message succeeds, then as readers reach the end they'll be as persuaded as they'll ever be. Now is the time to get action. You've fully justified the action you're requesting. You've shown the readers that they'll benefit by acting. Now tell them to act. Figure 7 (page 290) shows examples of appeals for action.

This is no time to be wishy-washy; a fairly firm command to act makes sense at this point. Advertisers say "Act now!" or "Do it today!" Why shouldn't you be firm? If your readers are persuaded, they should accept a direct call for action. It they're not persuaded by now, then the message has already failed, and a direct call for action can do no further harm. Often, when a firm call for action might appear a bit strong, the word *please* may add the needed courteous touch. "Please let me know which date would be best so I can schedule our meeting" should seem reasonably courteous to most readers. It's far better than "If you can come, please let me know," which displays a lack of confidence that the reader may detect.

Besides firmly calling for action, the close should create an image of that action and attach it to the benefit. The reader's final impression should include both action and benefit. By this point, you've explained the benefit in vivid detail, so your reference should be brief but clear. The same kind of phrasing you used in the opening may be appropriate.

A little formula sentence that may help you remember what the close should say is: "Do it! And get the benefit!" The close should be a firm call for action and a reminder of the benefit.

ROUTINE AND NONROUTINE PERSUASIVE MESSAGES

It's hard to imagine a situation in which a persuasive letter or memo would be written as a routine message. Persuasion situations tend to be unique, and the message for each must be planned on its own. In many bad-news messages, as we've seen, certain sections can be written pretty much by formula, but such formulas don't apply to persuasion; the situations are too varied.

If you're forced to write a persuasive message in limited time, then here are some questions you should consider quickly in your planning: (1) What's the most valuable benefit I can offer this reader? (2) How can I make this reader feel the value of this benefit? (3) Exactly what do I want this reader to do (and what immediate action, if any, should I press for)? and (4) What major objections to the proposed action will this reader probably have, and how can I deal with them? After drafting the message, revise it by answering at least these questions:

1. Does the opening get attention and vividly portray the benefit?

2. Does the body emphasize the benefit near the beginning and the proposed action near the end?

3. Does the body explain clearly exactly what I want the reader to do?

4. Does the close firmly press for action and relate it to the benefit?

5. How could I make the images more vivid?

Unfortunately, the less time you spend planning a persuasive message, the more time you must spend drafting and revising it. Persuasion takes time and thought.

David Takigawa, Principal
Chester A. Arthur Elementary School
San Diego, CA 92112

Dear Mr. Takigawa:

How many times have you heard cynical people say, "Just
wait until there's a fatal accident at that intersection--then
the city will be out the next day to put up a traffic light." As
a public official, you must be saddened when you hear such
comments, because you know the problems other public officials
face. And yet there's exactly this kind of situation right in
your school district.

As you're aware, about forty of your Arthur Elementary
students come from the Whispering Oaks apartment complex at 58th
and Park Boulevard. Because of the peculiar configuration of
streets at this point, every one of these six- to ten-year-old
children must walk down one side of Park Boulevard, a major
thoroughfare carrying hundreds of cars an hour at forty to
forty-five miles an hour. Since the children don't walk across
Park Boulevard, we recognize that the school cannot justify an
adult guard or official safety patrol program. But when forty
normally playful elementary children are each walking several
blocks a few feet from heavy traffic, wouldn't it make sense to
do whatever we can to protect them?

Concerned parents in the apartment complex have met several
times on this problem, and we have a suggestion we'd like you to
consider. Since these children don't actually cross the street,
a formal safety-patrol program isn't needed. But we think an
informal program may be quite feasible. Responsible older
students--probably drawn from among the sixth graders who live
here in the apartment complex--could be assigned to positions
along this three-block area of Park Boulevard, say every two or
three hundred feet. They could be wearing bright orange
pullovers and carrying bright caution signs, rather than the stop
signs the regular safety patrols carry. Such an informal program
would accomplish two things. First, it would alert motorists to
the fact that small children are walking along that street. And
second, it would provide someone to remind the littler children
to stay away from the street in their walking-home games.

Because we are concerned, Mr. Takigawa, we have actually
tried to organize a program like this here in the complex. But
without the support of the school, the older children don't feel
they have the authority to remind the younger children to stay
out of the street and be careful. Then, too, the rewards of
serving as a safety patrol are fewer when the school isn't
involved in the program.

That's why we would like you to take over our program. We
wouldn't for a minute minimize the work it will involve for you
and your staff. It will indeed be a job. But I know you've
driven past this part of Park Boulevard when school was getting

Figure 5 A persuasive letter

out, and so I know you recognize the consequences of passing up this opportunity. How long will it be before a playful six-year-old darts into the street to catch a school paper that's blowing away? It's amazing that we haven't had a serious accident already!

Please ask one of your sixth-grade teachers to begin working on this plan, Mr. Takigawa. When you begin next fall's school term knowing that the Whispering Oaks children are safer, it will be one load off your mind. And the parents here in the complex will be tremendously relieved. But most important of all, that one little six-year-old who <u>doesn't</u> have to suffer through a broken leg--or worse--will make the extra work very much worthwhile.

Sincerely,

Figure 5 (continued)

American Association of Automated Office Managers

6315 Bridger Street, NW, Washington, D.C. 20009

October 19, 1983

Ms. Jane Froberg, Director
Administrative Services Division
The Greendale Clothing Corporation
738 Harding Avenue
New York, NY 10019

Dear Ms. Froberg:

What are the greatest benefits of office automation to
American organizations? The greatest costs? Which office
functions should be automated? How satisfied are automated
office managers with their present facilities? What changes do
they foresee in the next five years? These are questions your
organization has surely spent thousands of dollars to answer--in
consulting fees, research studies, and subscriptions to
high-priced newsletters.

But now there's a less expensive way to get even better
information. If you'll spend just twenty minutes time sharing
your knowledge, you can receive a report including the views of
more than 1000 of America's top specialists in this field: your
fellow members of the American Association of Automated Office
Managers.

You and the other 1067 members of AAAOM are the
acknowledged experts in office automation today--the managers who
are actually implementing automated systems. That's why we want
to know about your experience. We'll combine the information you
provide with your fellow members' responses to produce one of the
most detailed reports on the status of office automation ever
compiled. And all you have to do to receive a copy is to
complete the enclosed questionnaire. A summary of our report is
scheduled for publication in <u>The Automated Office Manager</u>, but
the full report, including detailed findings, will be mailed only
to those who participate by responding to the enclosed
questionnaire.

Take just a minute to peruse the questionnaire. Quite
frankly, responding won't be just a 3- or 4-minute task. The
results of such a "quicky" questionnaire wouldn't be very
valuable to you. We estimate that the average manager will need
about 20 minutes to give careful, thoughtful answers, the kind of
answers that will make the resulting report valuable in your
day-to-day work.

Figure 6 A persuasive letter

When you fill in the questionnaire, you'll answer most of the thirty questions simply by checking off all the listed responses that fit your organization's experience. But since no list can include all possible answers, plenty of space is provided to allow you to comment further. By all means do so. Such comments are often the most valuable data available, and they will be compiled right along with the check-off answers when we prepare our report.

To assure complete anonymity, the questionnaire does not ask for your name, your company's name, or any information that we think may identify you. If you believe your answer to any question would reveal your identity and you prefer to avoid doing so, please skip that question. When you have completed your answers, place the questionnaire in the enclosed envelope. Be sure to write your name and address on the envelope, so we'll know where to send the report. Our clerical staff will type mailing labels from the information on the envelope and pass on the questionnaires, unidentified, to our committee.

Right now, while you're thinking about it, schedule the 20 minutes you'll spend responding to this important questionnaire. The valuable information you'll receive in return will be well worth those few minutes.

Cordially,

Jerome V. Holz

Jerome V. Holz, Chairperson
Membership Survey Committee

Figure 6 (continued)

```
        Drop me a line--today, while you're thinking about it--and
I'll send your free examination copy of our Simplified Letter
Form Manual.  In fact, why not ask your secretary to use the
Simplified Letter Form in typing the letter--just the way this
letter is typed.  Then you'll see for yourself how much you'll
save when the whole company adopts the Simplified Letter Form.
It'll be substantial!



        Please write me soon that you'll be coming to speak to
these 40 eager young accounting students.  It'll be a rewarding
evening--to you and to us!



        To find out just how much $39.76 is really worth to you,
fill out the enclosed questionnaire and work schedule, and let us
show you exactly how a vanpool can serve you.  Send me the
questionnaire today, and I'll phone you within two days with the
full details.
```

Figure 7 Persuasive closings

FURTHER EXPLORATION

1. Give five or six specific examples of ways that money satisfies needs other than physiological and safety needs. How many kinds of needs motivate people to seek money?

2. Give five or six specific examples of behavior that benefits others and is motivated only by the good feelings it produces in the actor. Are such cases common?

3. If a job that you'd love to have was available, but you thought there was little chance you could get it, would you apply for it? Or would you concentrate on applying for jobs you thought you were more likely to get? People differ quite a bit in their willingness to take risks for high rewards. How do you compare with others in this respect? Are very good persuaders high, low, or average in their willingness to take risks?

4. Select six of the writing exercises at the end of this chapter and analyze each one to identify (1) the exact action(s) the writer wants the reader to take, including any immediate action that may be called for; (2) the major objections the reader will probably have; and (3) the benefit that should be the focus of the message.

WRITING PROBLEMS

1 At the end of the recent term, you and your roommates moved out of the rented house you shared. As informal treasurer of the group, you took care of paying the bills, and this morning you received the forwarded bill for an additional month's trash hauling. Apparently whoever was supposed to cancel the trash hauling forgot to do it. You paid the bill and canceled the service.

Checking your notes to see who was supposed to take care of this chore, you find that the culprit is Pat Mafnas. Pat now lives at 2119 Richley Court, Apartment No. 393, Binghamton, NY 13903. Write Pat a highly persuasive letter that will get your $11.45 back. After all, it was his fault that you were billed for the extra month.

2. As a first term senior, you recently attended an all-day session on how to land a job. High point of the day for you was the talk by Norman G. Levi, Marketing Vice-President, Combest Pharmaceuticals, Inc. (2300 Combest Avenue, your city). Levi was an animated, exciting speaker, and he had some terrific job ideas for marketing students. Just the person, you think, to fill the November place in your Student Marketing Association meeting calendar. As program chairperson, write an invitation sufficiently persuasive to get agreement from Levi. Students in your group are marketing juniors and seniors with high grade-point averages, and the meeting will give him a chance to meet them. Perhaps some of them will become interested in Combest. Attendance at meetings is good (on this topic probably 50 or so), and question sessions have been pretty lively recently. Unfortunately, there's no budget for an honorarium (or even for the speaker's dinner). The meeting is Thursday, November 18, at 7:30 P.M., 210 Student Center on campus.

3. Your rapidly growing digital electronics company will soon nearly double its administrative office space, and in the expansion it is planning to install an extensive word processing system. More than 85 word processing units will be installed over the coming 18 months. As Administrative Vice-President, you're in charge. You have narrowed the choice to three models that have the necessary capabilities—not only do they have full word processing capability and some computation capability, but they can communicate data from one word processor to another and to and from the company's other computers.

Write to each of the three vendors' representatives. Before committing yourself to any specific model, you want to test each to be sure that it provides all the features claimed and that it can work efficiently with the company's present data communications network. Word processing units, computers, and data communications networks are all very complex, and the only way to verify that they can be interconnected is to plug them together and test every type of anticipated transaction—a substantial task. Your engineers say that it will take about a week to test each of the three models and that assistance from the vendors' engineers probably will be required to interconnect the systems correctly.

You recognize that word processing manufacturers don't normally provide demonstration units for this purpose, and you're aware that it will be costly to deliver a unit, set it up, provide engineering help in connecting it, and then come back to pick it up a week later. At the same time, most purchasers of word processing equipment don't order 85 units at a time, as you plan to do. Once you're committed to a particular model, you'll presumably be ordering additional compatible units—about 40 to 50 a year if your company continues its present rate of expansion. Persuade each representative to meet your needs. Provide information that each can use in persuading his or her boss to authorize the test.

4. Over the past year your company's engineers have redesigned the four models of conveyors that you sell to the strip-mining industry. As Marketing Vice-President, you've been in charge of producing a series of instructional videotapes describing the technical specifications of these improved machines and the changes in the strip-mining process that must be implemented to achieve the substantial savings that their innovative design makes possible. To meet the March 1 introduction date, you've scheduled these videotapes for production by William Dean, a local independent video contractor, in late January. This morning you received a memo from your president asking whether the tapes can be completed in time for showing at the annual convention of the International Association of Strip-Mining Engineers in Kansas City beginning January 17. He says that the preliminary information that the company has released on these units has attracted a great deal of attention, and the convention organizers have invited the company to introduce the units there. Your videotapes, along with a presentation by your company's engineers, will be scheduled—if the tapes can be completed in time.

Write Mr. Dean. You need to move the production schedule up to late December, probably the week between Christmas and New Year's Day. You realize that most people, perhaps including him, prefer a light schedule during that week, and he may have difficulty hiring the necessary technical people then. On the other hand your company has given him a significant amount of business over the past few years and expects to do so in the future. Perhaps he'll make this schedule change as a favor.

Presentation of the tapes at the convention will guarantee a much wider audience than they'd normally have. All the convention attendees—about 1100—will see them. Not only would this enhance the value of the tapes to your company, but it also will provide a much larger audience for Mr. Dean's work. Of course, his business title will be prominently displayed on the screen during each tape. It could be excellent advertising for him.

5. Because so many students in your school are majoring in business, business courses have become overcrowded. As a result, your school is considering limiting the number of business majors it will accept and also limiting enrollment in business courses to business majors. If such a step is taken, the restrictions would be applied beginning next fall. As president of the Business Student Council, you sat in on school meetings where this possibility was discussed, and you believe that implementation of the new policy is likely. As you consider how this policy might affect the students, it occurs to you that many of your friends who are working on majors in business have not formally declared their majors at the Records office. You suspect that trying to declare a major after the new policy is in effect will be a real hassle, especially during the initial shakedown period while administrative procedures are being developed and refined. Many of these undeclared business majors expect to graduate in the next two or three semesters. If the policy passes, they could be in real trouble.

Enlisting the help of the executive committee of the Business Student Council, you decide to communicate with all students (or as many as you can reach) who are taking courses toward a business major but who have not declared their major. You will try to persuade them to go over to the Records office and formally declare their major, which simply involves filling out a short form. Since you don't have funds for a real mailing (and anyway there would be no way to get a list of names), you'll write a memo to be posted on the bulletin boards in the various business classrooms. Be as persuasive as you can.

6. You are Melinda Cruz, Director of Personnel. Here is a memo from your assistant, Bernard Selinger.

```
DATE: November 24, 1983
TO: Melinda Cruz
FROM: Bernard Selinger
SUBJECT: New Employee Data Forms
```

Here is the information you requested about the difficulties we have been having with the new employee data forms that we recently ordered from Wenright Office Forms Company.

Since Wenright told us that the forms would be delivered by November 18, we decided to discontinue using our old forms on October 1 and hold all filing until the new forms were available so we could get some concentrated experience in using them. This way everybody could find out how the forms were going to work out and how to use them.

The forms arrived only yesterday, and we can't use them. They didn't seem to get anything right. They left off four items that we specifically ordered, and about half the

space on the forms is for information we don't even collect
(and don't want). To put it simply, they didn't send us what
we ordered. They didn't even spell our name right (Gregary
instead of Gregory) at the top.

Fred Silberman, the salesperson from Wenright, promised
that all the specifications that we asked for would be met,
but they just weren't met. These forms are nearly the same as
the sample copies that we originally looked at.

I think that the Wenright forms would be a real
improvement over the forms we have been using, but only if
they can get them printed correctly. Could you drop them a
line and try to get the order reprinted. We need them right
away—the work is really piling up.

7. You are a marketing executive of the Medvale Furniture Corporation. Medvale issues portable tape recorders to all sales representatives when they are hired. These recorders, which are to be returned when a rep leaves the company, are used to record customer orders immediately after a sale is completed. Clerks in the regional sales offices then transcribe the tapes onto standard order forms. The use of these recorders has significantly increased the speed and accuracy of order processing.

One of your regional sales managers has recently "terminated" a rep. She plans to hire a replacement within three months. She feels that she should keep the recorder that was assigned to the former rep and give it to the new one she plans to hire. Your problem is convincing the sales manager that you must have the recorder back. It needs to be cleaned, checked for possible repairs, and replenished with new tape cassettes, instruction book, and so forth. You have found that many of these recorders have been abused and neglected. Wouldn't the new sales rep get a bad impression of the company if he or she were given a malfunctioning recorder?

The woman who is reluctant to release the recorder is a very successful, though opinionated, manager. She has been with the company for many years and sometimes feels that new methods and procedures are silly. Write a memo that will persuade her that there is a reason for the procedure.

8. As the program chairperson of an organization you belong to (or some organization you'd like to belong to), invite your business-communication instructor to address a meeting of the organization. Since such an address will be time-consuming for your instructor to prepare, assume that you'll have to write a more persuasive letter than just a plain invitation, and assume that you're not offering anything of value as payment for the talk (no money, no high-priced dinners, no trips, and the like). By this time in the term, you know your reader pretty well; base your persuasion on your own perceptions of this instructor's interests and values. What do you think would motivate this particular person to give up a free evening

(and the afternoon it would take to prepare the talk) to spend time with your group?

9. As Administrative Services Manager, you were responsible for the acquisition of a new offset duplicating machine last spring. You argued, successfully, that the machine should be purchased from a local vendor, even though you paid slightly more than the best price. The value, you argued, was that a local vendor would provide after-sale services, including quick repairs and help in training operators. Until recently, buying locally has paid off. Hendricks Office Products was extremely helpful in getting the machine in operation. They trained your first operator and continued to help when the operator ran into difficulties. They have also provided repairs within two hours each time your machine needed service. The value of these services has more than offset the difference in price your company paid.

Now there's a problem. First, your offset machine operator has suffered a major medical emergency and is off the job permanently. He had partly trained a backup operator, but that man is not yet fully qualified to use the machine.

Second, the manager of your local Hendricks store has been transferred to another store. The new manager, Elizabeth Strand, agrees to provide rapid repair service, but she believes your company should send the new operator to the manufacturer's training facility in Minneapolis for a two-week training course. You checked, and the next training course begins in three weeks. That means your machine would be out of operation for five weeks until the operator returned. You've come to depend on the machine, and you simply can't have it out of service that long. In addition, the cost of your operator's travel, lodging, and meals would would cancel out the benefits you counted on by buying locally.

Your agreement with Hendricks included training operators, and Hendricks did train all the operators you presented for initial training; it's your own fault that you only had them train one operator. On the other hand, there was no time limit in the agreement, and it could be read to cover your present request. See if you can persuade Ms. Strand to accept the following compromise. She will supply a trainer for perhaps two or three days, just long enough to allow the new operator to use and maintain the machine safely for straightforward jobs. In addition, her trainer will provide telephone consultation and brief in-plant visits to help the operator as he builds skill on the machine. You will pay a token fee, say $100 a day, for the full-day training, and she will absorb the cost of the further brief consultations.

Write the letter that will persuade her. And for heaven's sake start right now figuring out how you'll train a backup operator!

10. Now that you realize the advantages of dividing the writing process into the three steps of planning, writing, and revising, write a letter persuading a business associate to try this approach. Most people can easily understand the value of planning before writing, at least in principle. Few can immediately see the benefit of drafting and revising (until they've experienced it), so focus your persuasion on that point. Draw on your own writing experience in devising appeals.

11.   Your local Junior Chamber of Commerce group has undertaken a project to provide playground equipment for two new city parks in poorer parts of town. To raise money, your group is selling packages of a dozen long-life light bulbs to local residents. Comparative tests done under rigorously controlled conditions simulating household use demonstrate that these bulbs last, on the average, more than twice as long as standard bulbs. Although they produce slightly less light than a standard bulb, few users would notice the difference. They are especially useful for hard-to-get-at fixtures and difficult-to-replace bulbs. At a price differential of about 30 percent over (nondiscounted) standard bulbs, they are a good value.

But more important, every purchase is a donation toward the purchase of playground equipment for Robert E. Dolan Park at 9th and Delwin and another park, yet to be named, at 3800 Old Springfield Pike. City appropriations were used up in grading and landscaping, and no budgeted funds remain for equipment. Without your fund-raising project, these parks would remain bare at least until next year when they could be budgeted for completion by the city. That would mean no swings, slides, softball backstops, playing field equipment, and other essential items for the coming summer. Playgrounds in wealthier parts of the city are well supplied with equipment purchased under earlier city budgets. The city budget does include funds for playground supervision, equipment checkout, maintenance, etc., if equipment can be provided.

One of your city's large corporations will donate a mailing to city residents in support of your project. Letters will go out to residents of the city, section by section, with door-to-door canvassing by project members in each section two or three days later. Your job is to write the letter. Try to have residents sold on buying packages of bulbs before the canvassers call.

12.   Several years ago when your first child was a baby, you and your spouse eagerly joined a babysitting cooperative group formed to serve families of your company's younger managers. Coop members babysat for each other's children on an exchange basis. When you or your spouse babysat for another member, you received credit which you could use to "pay" other members to babysit for your family. No money changed hands, but even more important, everyone knew their children were under the care of competent parents like themselves. For a time the process worked well and everyone was enthusiastic. Recently, however, enthusiasm has fallen off. A number of members have dropped out completely, and many of the others babysit only seldom. Many weekends there will be half a dozen requests for babysitters and not a single member who is willing to sit. You estimate that active members are down to about a quarter the original number.

Now that your family is larger, you'd like to rejuvenate the baby-sitting coop. With that in mind, you plan a dinner party at your house the third Sunday afternoon of next month for all the original members. With several weeks' notice for a Sunday afternoon event (when most people have little else scheduled), you should get a pretty good turnout. Coop parties used to be great fun when the group first began. At the party, you hope to revive the group's old enthusiasm. Write a letter of invitation that will get the old members to come and that will get them started thinking about ways of rejuvenating the group. Supply realistic details from your imagination to make the situation come alive. (See also the following problem.)

13.   The babysitting coop party (see the preceding problem) was a great success. You discovered that a number of the other couples, especially those who, like you, have recent additions to their family, shared your eagerness to get the coop working well again. And even some of those whose children were beyond babysitting age came to the party for old time's sake. A great party!

What you found was that you can expect about eight or nine families to remain as active members. That is not a large enough group to make a really effective coop. Somebody pointed out that a new generation of younger managers and staff members has been hired at your company since the old coop was formed, and many of these surely would be interested in joining. In fact, new people are hired all the time, and everyone should have the opportunity to join. Somehow you got elected to carry the ball.

The plan is to get all the publicity you can for an organizing meeting for old and new prospective members at the home of Mr. and Mrs. Hilton Sundy, 1994 Roseclay Manor, at 4:00 P.M. on the last Sunday afternoon of next month.

This morning at work you checked with the offices responsible and got agreement to provide all the necessary publicity; now you must write the messages. Write whichever one(s) your instructor assigns. Note that similar points and even similar phrasing could be used in all three messages, with some adaptation.

A.   The editor of the company's management newsletter will be happy to run about 100 words about the coop in the next issue. Since that's very little space, concentrate on the benefits of the coop and invite interested persons to call you (company extension 439) for details of the meeting. Your boss has OK'd this arrangement.

B.   You have permission to mail a letter to the homes of all management and staff employees hired since the original formation of the coop. This should include most of the people who might want to join now. Do your best to persuade these people and their spouses to attend the organization meeting. Notice that this message is much more likely to reach spouses than the notice in the management newsletter, so make a pitch that is appropriate and effective.

C.   The Personnel Department has agreed to put a letter from your coop into the new employees' informational packet—the package of information provided to all new management and staff employees. Thus, people hired from now on will know that they can join the coop if they like. Here, your goal is to arouse interest in the coop and induce newly hired staff members and spouses with children to give you a call. Provide your home phone number. This letter is an opportunity to keep the coop on an even keel in the future and avoid slumps like the recent one, so make it persuasive enough to do that important job.

14.   As Shipping Supervisor at Avery Equipment Company, your responsibilities include management of both shipping and warehouse operations. You need projections of sales by type of product—weight and package size—to help you plan shipments and inventory storage. The marketing research department regularly makes sophisticated projections of sales of products manufactured by your company's five major divisions. Unfortunately, each division makes products in widely varying sizes and weights, so their projections are only barely useful in your planning. You imagine that in projecting sales by division they must compile figures based on specific product types—and that's just the information you need.

Ask for it. Some extra work will be involved for marketing research, so be persuasive. Better planning of shipping and warehouse operations would allow better service to customers, a marketing benefit. It would also substantially reduce shipping and warehousing costs, releasing funds to other departments. Probably the most important benefit, though, would be to make optimum use—from a company-wide viewpoint—of the work being done by the marketing research department.

Based on your observations of Geraldine Schlied, Director of Marketing Research, you anticipate her objection that the figures you need are not precise enough to be usable, since they're compiled for a very different purpose. Compared to the guesses you're now using in your planning, though, even imprecise figures would be a vast improvement. Perhaps you could agree to confer with a marketing research assistant before you submit plans based on their figures. This way, Schlied could be confident that your work is done with full respect for the limitations of their projections.

15.   Assume the post of office manager of the Steadfast Life Insurance Company, Indianapolis, Indiana. You and other members of management are quite concerned with the embarrassingly poor quality of the correspondence being sent through the mails by your company. And you've decided to do something about it. After considering the problem, you decide to write to Dr. Terry V. Shakley, who taught you business communication at Daley State University in Chicago. You consider him an authority in business writing and an outstanding teacher. Dr. Shakley does a great deal of consulting work—at $400 a day for away-from-town work. Although your company can't afford that price, you decide to try to get the professor-consultant to consent to fly to your office in Indianapolis once a week for six weeks to carry out your much-needed correspondence improvement program. You'll pay his air fare and $250 a trip—but that's all. See if you can persuade him to put on the program within your budget.

16. As in past years, your company will soon be welcoming groups of high school students who will tour your four main assembly plants. These tours, guided by trained staff members, are educational for the students, many of whom will become assembly employees of your company, and they are also excellent public relations. Many long-time local residents feel a special relationship to your company largely as a result of the tours they took in high school.

Every year the tours have been followed by a few complaints from high school teachers about coarse horseplay and strong language by assembly employees in the presence of students. Therefore, every year you, as Director of Public Relations, write a letter asking supervisors in assembly plants 3, 4, 7, and 10 to try to persuade employees to cut down on the profanity and obscenity and to behave themselves when students are nearby. In fact, the atmosphere of an assembly plant (in your experience) traditionally includes a great deal of coarse joking and strong language, and even when employees attempt to behave civilly, slips of the tongue frequently occur. At the same time, your obligation is to be as persuasive as you can, not only because you hope to improve the situation but also because you must go on record as disapproving of such behavior. In your replies to the inevitable complaints from teachers, you'll be quoting from this letter, so make it as persuasive as you possibly can. Use the principles of persuasion discussed in this chapter.

17. As office manager, you've noticed that the gradual stretching of coffee breaks that occurs in most offices has nearly gotten out of hand in your office. Your 7 staff assistants, 16 secretaries and typists, and 11 clerks have gradually stretched coffee-break time to a bit over 25 minutes, headed for 30. In addition, one clerk each day is selected to drive to a pastry shop to pick up the group's morning snack; the currently favored shop, you understand, is about 20 minutes' drive from your office—each way. Another clerk fetches afternoon snacks.

You've never been a stickler for the letter of the law in such cases— office morale is more important in getting the work done on time. But enough is enough. If you don't call a halt soon, your boss will be noting the problem in your performance reports.

To provide a clear record of your action, write a memo to all office employees calling attention to the official company policy on coffee breaks: employees are requested to take 15-minute coffee breaks morning and afternoon away from their desks but on the company premises. Official errands away from the office—to the post office, etc.—can often, but not always, be scheduled to allow a clerk to stop on the way for snacks near break time. Perhaps someone can be delegated each day to pick up snacks on the way to work. Actually, dieting is a staple topic of coffee-break conversation; perhaps a majority would prefer to forgo the snacks.

Your memo should firmly persuade employees to abide by the official rule, but it should do so tactfully and in a low-key way. Office morale is very high, and you want to keep it that way. Use the principles of persuasion discussed in this chapter.

18.   As administrative assistant to the president of McReady Fastener Corporation, help your boss handle this personnel problem.

James H. Melchior is Vice-President of Employee Relations. This is his twenty-second year with McReady. He started as a machinery maintenance worker, a job at which he quickly excelled. He seemed to know more about our equipment's operation than the manufacturers and could often get malfunctioning equipment back in operation faster than their engineers. He was well liked by his fellow workers, who often asked him to help with their cranky machines.

After a few very satisfactory years in this job, he took evening courses in a local university's management program and graduated with a bachelor's degree. He quickly showed unusual ability in solving personnel problems, often settling employee-management disputes quickly and happily for all concerned. He was assigned to the employee relations department, and his ability and training helped him achieve his present position. He is a very valuable executive.

But there's a problem. Several times when the president phoned Melchior's office, he was told that Melchior was out in the shop working on equipment problems. Routine work has been delayed several times because of such absences. Recently your boss called about an important memo for a major meeting and was told that it wasn't ready and that Melchior had been tied up for the past two days correcting a complicated machine problem in the shop. Later, Melchior explained that it was extremely important to keep production going, and his presence was desperately needed in the shop.

Draft a memo for your boss's signature tactfully pointing out that machinery maintenance is not part of Melchior's job any more, and that he should apply his talents more diligently to the office of vice-president of employee relations. Obviously you do not want to offend so valuable an employee, but at the same time you do want him to do what he's supposed to do, and nothing else.

19. When you, as a department director for a large corporation, hired Rich Harlington as your administrative assistant, you were impressed with his credentials, but not with his appearance. Your corporation places great value on the personal appearance of staff members, but Rich is one of those people who manage to look pretty dumpy most of the time. Before you hired him, Rich agreed to clean up his act by visiting a good hair stylist and a good tailor, whom you recommended. Now, six months later, Rich "hasn't had a chance" to do either. He's certainly paid well enough to afford good clothes and grooming, and each time you've reminded him, he's agreed to take care of it right away.

Rich's appearance has drawn many comments from other members of your staff, and yesterday your boss asked you to do something about it. Now you have no choice. Write a letter officially persuading Rich to take more care in grooming. If he doesn't, you'll be forced to let him go. The letter will go into Rich's personnel file to establish a basis for firing him, if necessary, so make it clear that this is a possibility, but emphasize a persuasive appeal rather than the threat.

You really don't want to fire him. As an assistant, he's been quite competent, and you enjoy working with him. Besides, firing anyone is extremely unpleasant. So be as persuasive as you can.

20. Write a memo to your business-communication teacher persuading him or her to make some specific change that you think would improve the business-communication course in future semesters.

The improvement you propose should be specific and serious, one that you actually believe would make the course more rewarding for future students. You should assume that your instructor is interested in improving the course and that he or she will not feel threatened or insulted by a serious proposal. You may also assume that certain kinds of proposals (for example, to replace the present instructor with a better one) may be viewed with some lack of enthusiasm, but that others (for example, changing the way certain material is presented or the way grades are earned) will be viewed as helpful criticism.

You have had several months now to learn how your instructor's mind works. On the basis of that knowledge, select an approach that you think will be persuasive. Don't forget to stress the benefit your instructor will receive from the proposed change.

15

Special Applications of Persuasion: Claim, Collection, and Sales Letters

We may pity, though not pardon thee.
Shakespeare (Comedy of Errors)

This pound of flesh which I demand of him
Is dearly bought, is mine, and I will have it.
Shakespeare (Merchant of Venice)

Although claim letters, collection letters, and sales letters do employ the principles of persuasion discussed in the previous chapter, sometimes the best applications of these principles aren't particularly obvious until you've written some messages of these types. Fortunately, you can draw upon the experience of other talented writers who've spent years perfecting approaches and techniques that work well in these fields. This chapter is based on that experience.

WRITING CLAIM LETTERS

Even in the best-run organization, mistakes sometimes occur. In the best of hotels, sometimes a room isn't thoroughly cleaned. In the best of universities, sometimes one student's registration record is fouled up. In the best of canning plants, sometimes one can is filled mostly with liquid instead of green beans. Whenever human beings take responsibility, mistakes can be expected.

If you're the person who buys the improperly filled can, then you've paid the full price but haven't received the full value. That's certainly not fair. But when the company refunds your money or replaces the can you bought, it spreads the cost of the mistake over all customers in the form of slightly higher prices, which is a much fairer arrangement. If too many mistakes occur, the company risks pricing itself right out of the market.

In a well-run organization, standard quality assurance procedures will catch most mistakes, but not all of them. As a manager, you'll find that a few errors creep through no matter how careful you are, and as a customer you realize that, once in a blue moon, you'll be a victim. When that happens, you write a claim letter.

Planning the Claim Letter

The first step in planning a claim letter is to decide what you want your reader to do. Do you want to return the product for a refund? Do you want a defective product replaced? Do you want part of your money back? Exactly what will make you satisfied? If you can tell the reader exactly what you want, then he or she can best satisfy you. If you can't, you make the reader's job very difficult.

The next step is to analyze your audience. The most important question is this: how much resistance will the audience feel toward your claim? Most businesses, from the smallest to the largest, have specific policies for handling claims. For example, many businesses normally refund a customer's money when a product is returned in saleable condition soon after being purchased. If you believe that the reader will consider your claim one that should clearly be granted, then your letter can simply provide the information to support that decision. Figure 1 shows an example.

In more complicated cases, a fair amount of judgment may be required to determine whether or not your claim fits any standard policy. In such

```
Rhode Center Publishing Company:

     Thank you for sending a copy of Modern Collection
Procedures, by George L. Seeger, which I'm returning.  As the
enclosed bill indicates, I'm returning it within the 10-day
examination period you allow.  Please return the $44.95 I paid.

Sincerely,
```

Figure 1 A simple claim letter

cases, and especially when the legitimacy of your claim is doubtful, your message should be more persuasive. Thus, your audience analysis should be more detailed and explicit.

It's important to recognize that organizations vary in their reactions to claims. Some organizations greatly emphasize quality and take pride in assuring customers' satisfaction. Others cut costs to the bone, with less attention to quality control. Usually, your previous contacts with the organization will help you determine its approach. Even when quality isn't emphasized, though, managers often feel great pride in the organization. Having the lowest prices in town can be a substantial achievement that's worthy of pride.

Therefore, claim letters work better when they're carefully phrased to avoid verbal attacks on the organization, its managers, and their motives. For example, consider how you'd feel toward the writer of the "claim" letter in Figure 2. Normally, your claim doesn't result from someone's intentional effort to cheat you, and even if you suspect such intentions, accusatory language may be a poor tactic. Strong language may make you feel better, but it certainly doesn't put your reader into a favorable frame of mind to make a judgment about your claim.

Similarly, legalistic language normally does little good. Claim writers tend to lapse into pseudolegal jargon to imply that they intend to take the matter to court unless the claim is granted. But most managers have some knowledge of the legal principles that apply to their line of business, and before making claim judgments they almost automatically consider the possibility of a lawsuit. Lawsuits are expensive enough that you probably won't take the reader to court over most claims, and the reader knows it. Thus, legalistic language is usually pure bluff, and it seldom fools the reader for a moment.

If you're actually contemplating legal action, even though you'll probably lose money, you should calmly tell the reader this. For the threat of a lawsuit to be effective, the reader must believe that you'll sue, so you

```
Dear Student:

     What kind of an idiot do you take me for, anyway?

     When I made this week's writing assignment on Monday, I
expected you to learn certain principles and to apply them in
your work.  Not only did you not bother to use the principles
discussed in the text and lectures, you even neglected to apply
principles you've been using correctly all through the term.
What a sleazy job!

     You couldn't possibly have spent more than five minutes on
this preposterous paper, including the terrible typing job.  If
you ate as sloppily as this, your shirt would be full of garbage.

     Work of this quality certainly doesn't meet the
requirements of the assignment, and I am certainly not going to
give you any credit for it.  You'll have to do it
again--seriously this time.

     Let's have no more of this junk!

Sincerely,



Stanley Powell
Instructor
```

Figure 2 Accusatory language in claim letters

should explain why you're ready to do so. The most believable explanations are ones showing that the failure of the reader's product or service has caused a loss far greater than the amount you paid. If you're thinking of bringing suit, you should get legal advice as early in the claim process as possible.

Organizing the Claim Letter

Use the following three steps to organize a claim letter, as illustrated in Figure 3. First, present the relevant facts. In the opening, simply explain what happened. Cite any documents (such as bills, receipts, or advertising materials) that substantiate your version of the event. Keep this section as uncomplicated as you can, both in content and phrasing, so the reader can clearly understand what happened. Remain factual, avoiding accusatory language.

Second, show how the facts support your claim. This is the stage in which you'll meet resistance, so carefully spell out why you believe your claim should be granted, even though you think the reasons are pretty

Dear Mr. Fong:

After seeing your ad in the <u>Morning News</u> last December, we asked you to install cable TV service, including the pay movie channel, in our house. The installer who ran the cable into our house on January 6 recognized that the signal was unusually weak, and she noted that fact on the work receipt, as you can see on the enclosed copy. She indicated that she'd request a check on the signal.

At that time, our cable reception of local channels was much worse than we'd been getting from an indoor antenna. The several channels not available locally did come in on the cable, but the picture was extremely snowy and unpleasant to watch. The pay movie channel didn't come in clearly enough to watch.

In the two months since installation, one of us has stayed home from work on four different occasions to admit your service people, but our reception hasn't improved at all. In that time, we've paid you $42.78 (including the original installation fee), and we haven't had acceptable viewing on the cable at any time. Not once during that time have we been able to watch a single movie on the pay channel. Our indoor antenna continues to provide very clear reception of local channels.

For the $42.78 we've paid you, we've received no value. Therefore, we believe we're entitled to a refund of that full amount.

If your company can provide good cable reception to our house, we'd be delighted to have it. We'd be willing to miss work one more time if your service people can get the installation working. And we'd be happy to pay the monthly fee of $16.36, beginning the very first day we actually receive a viewable picture on cable.

We'll be expecting your refund check for $42.78 in the next few days. And we're looking forward to your telephone call to arrange a time for your service person to come over to get our installation working correctly.

Sincerely,

Figure 3 A persuasive claim letter

obvious. For example, if the product didn't function as the advertisements or the seller's oral statements claimed it would, then say so explicitly. Or if your claim is based on a policy that you assume the reader adheres to, then spell out what you think that policy is (or why you think the reader should follow such a policy).

Third, indicate what you believe should be done. The close should briefly, but confidently, say what you expect the reader to do. If appropriate, say when you expect action and say—not threateningly, but factually—what you intend to do if your claim hasn't been granted by then.

Once you've had some experience with claim letters, writing them can be fairly quick and straightforward. And most people have plenty of opportunities to gain the necessary experience—if they take advantage of them. But many people don't pursue claims, and they automatically forfeit benefits they were entitled to. Perhaps more significantly, when really important situations arise, such people lack the needed experience to write effective claim letters. That's why it can be worth your while to write a claim letter every time the opportunity arises. The experience can really pay off in the future.

WRITING COLLECTION LETTERS

When someone owes you money and doesn't pay in response to your normal billing, then you begin the collection process. If payment were the only goal, collection would be a rather simple process. But the process has two goals: collecting the money and retaining the customer's future business. And the two must be balanced very precisely. Too much emphasis on one reduces the chance of achieving the other.

The collection process usually begins with the assumption that most people intend to pay their bills, that their failure to pay is due to an oversight or to temporary financial difficulties. Because of this assumption, collection is generally a four-stage process.

The notification stage Early in the process, the messages may take the form of repeated bills, perhaps rubber-stamped "Reminder" to indicate that the amount owed is past due. These bills are mailed at shorter and shorter intervals, perhaps reaching a minimum interval of one week.

The reminder stage If several such bills produce no response, then relatively mild form letters are sent. At first, these may be phrased as reminders, urging the recipient to give some attention to the bill. Later, they may say, in effect, "We realize that temporary circumstances may be delaying your payment. Please let us know when we can expect you to resume payments on schedule." Normally, such letters are obvious form letters, indicating that the matter has not yet warranted the management's personal attention. Figure 4 shows an example.

```
Dear Mr. Jung:

     When a payment on your account came due recently, I wrote
to remind you, just as I'd want you to remind me if our positions
were reversed.

     I felt sure your remittance would be here by now.  I'm
surprised that it hasn't arrived.  Won't you please send it by
return mail, to get back on the payment schedule you promised to
maintain?

     Another payment will be due very soon.  While you're at it,
why not send them both?  Then you'll be right up to date.

Sincerely,
```

Figure 4 A reminder collection letter

Under unusual circumstances, as illustrated by Figure 5, a company may jump directly to the reminder stage. When a customer sends a bad check, the company may justifiably feel special concern about the status of that account; it may be a symptom that the customer has serious financial problems. If the matter isn't cleared up quickly, then the company may proceed directly to the final-action stage with no further delay.

```
Dear Mr. Sondergard:

     Did you know that your check of January 28 for $37.50 has
been returned to us by your bank?

     They marked it "Refer to maker."  Usually this means the
writer doesn't have quite enough money in the account to cover
it.  Of course there may be other reasons, too.

     In any event, these things happen, and I know you'll want
to straighten the matter out at once.  Please don't feel
embarrassed about it.  You can send us another check or money
order, and as soon as we get it we'll mail the original check
back to you.  Or, if you authorize us, we'll destroy the
original.

Sincerely,
```

Figure 5 A collection letter for a special circumstance

The persuasion stage   In unusual cases, one or more reminder letters may still produce no acceptable response. Then persuasive collection letters, typed as personal letters from a company official, are sent. These are built around one of several possible appeals. One is the appeal to fairness: "You're enjoying and profiting from the product; it's basic fairness to pay for it." Another is the appeal of maintaining the customer's high self-esteem as someone who meets obligations and responsibilities (Figure 6). Another appeal, sometimes used after others produce no results, focuses on avoiding loss of property (through repossession) or loss of credit (through unfavorable credit reports), as illustrated in Figure 7. These messages still stress the benefits to the customer and are carefully drafted to retain as much goodwill as possible.

The final-action stage   In a few cases, all previous efforts fail and the company decides to take final action. Normally, two actions are possible: turning the account over to a collection agency or filing a lawsuit. Neither alternative is attractive, so a company won't turn to them until it's convinced that nothing else will work. Collection agencies return only

```
Dear Mr. Swayzee:

      You have every right to feel proud!

      When you applied for credit six years ago, we made our
usual routine credit check and found your credit rating to be
topnotch.  Until recently, your payment record fully justified
that rating.  Such a record was worthy of your pride.

      Every month Consolidated Equipment extends credit to
hundreds of its customers, and 98 percent of them justify our
policy by mailing a check to cover their obligation.  They
appreciate the convenience of our immediate shipment on credit
purchases, and they also value the flexibility that an
outstanding credit rating provides.  They're proud of their
record of responsibility, and they should be!  Fewer than 2
percent don't pay right on schedule.  Most of these have good
reasons, and they write or phone to explain.  Only a few allow
their accounts to fall into the poor-credit-risk category.

      We don't think you belong in that category.  Won't you
please mail a check today for the $753.28 that has been
outstanding for the past 45 days?  This would let us return your
account to the excellent rating it's always deserved.

Sincerely,
```

Figure 6 A persuasive collection letter

```
Dear Ms. Berstin:

     I'm shocked at your response to my last letter.  You say
you were only 17 years of age when you ordered the tape deck
about two months ago.  You also say you can't afford to pay for
it, and you can't return it because it fell out of your fishing
boat recently and was lost.

     Ms. Berstin, I'm very disappointed in you.  I checked your
order for this tape deck, and you very clearly marked your age as
21.  Had we known you were a minor, we would have asked that your
parents guarantee your account--something we ask of all our
customers who are minors.

     I talked this matter over with our attorney, and he agrees
with me that you probably didn't intend to defraud us by making a
false statement.  It's very easy to make a mistake in filling out
a form, and perhaps you were thinking of something else when you
wrote 21 instead of 17.

     Our attorney recommends that you talk this matter over
frankly and honestly with your parents and see if they'll help
you make these payments.  This will justify the faith we had in
you.

     I'm sure you'll agree that you have a duty here that you're
honor-bound to act upon.  Will you do this today?

Sincerely,
```

Figure 7 A persuasive collection letter

a portion of the amount owed, often half or less. And lawsuits are expensive to undertake.

But both alternatives are likely to be even less attractive to the customer. Collection agencies use much more insistent collection techniques than you do—after all, they have no interest in retaining the customer's future business. And a lawsuit not only forces the customer to bear the cost of defense, but it also alerts other creditors to the customer's possible financial difficulties. In both collection and litigation, the action will be noted in the customer's credit rating and may adversely affect other companies' future credit decisions about the customer.

There's little point in threatening final action unless you intend to carry out the threat. After all, if you threaten to sue and then don't do it, what's left to say to the customer? If you do intend final action, then it's worthwhile to tell the customer exactly what you plan to do and when, as in Figure 8. Not only is this a matter of basic fair play, but it also gives the customer one last opportunity to pay the amount owed.

Dear Mr. Sondergard:

    Frankly, I don't know what to make of your silence. But it does give me a very unpleasant sensation.

    You haven't yet sent a replacement for your $37.50 check that was returned to us by your bank three weeks ago. I'd have thought you'd be eager to make it good at once.

    If some emergency has caught you short of funds, we'll certainly grant you a reasonable extension. <u>But I must hear from you within five days!</u>

    Otherwise our company will have to turn your account over to a collection agency and submit an unfavorable credit report about your account. I hope you'll save me from such an unpleasant action by getting in touch with me at once.

    Write, telegraph, or telephone (315) 555-6767. And do it now.

Sincerely,

Figure 8 A final action collection letter

Even at this stage, letters should be written to retain the customer's goodwill and future business (probably for cash), if possible. After all, your final action is not motivated by any ill will toward the customer, but simply by good business practice. If the positions were reversed, the customer would be justified in taking similar action toward you. Therefore, while the news may be unpleasant, the tone should be informative and perhaps mildly sympathetic—certainly not accusatory or hostile. Figure 9 shows an example.

Except in the very smallest organizations, collections are supervised by professional collectors. Such people spend years developing sophisticated techniques for writing collection letters and other collection messages. And they draw on a highly developed professional literature—books and journals—in the field. The quality of their messages reflects this professionalism. If you find collection problems and collection messages interesting, you may want to consider a career in this field.

WRITING SALES LETTERS

Like collection letters, most sales letters are written by professionals who spend their careers perfecting skills in this field. Some of the most highly polished and tested writing in the world consists of direct mail sales letters. This certainly doesn't mean, though, that average business

Dear Mr. Limon:

    Years ago, in the Old West, the advice given by the tough old gunfighter to the young greenhorn was "Never pull your six-gun, Sonny, unless you figure to shoot somebody with it."

    Today (in our company, at least), the policy is "Never push the legal-action button unless you're going to sue somebody."

    Well, Mr. Limon, I know you've been a good customer for years, and we've always had the highest regard for your company. But we both know how often you've promised to pay this balance of $1138.45 and how often you've failed to keep your promise.

    Now my hand is on the button. I'm going to push it in just 48 hours unless you send us at least a partial good-faith payment and a written plan for clearing the balance.

    I can't make it any clearer than that, can I?

Sincerely,

Figure 9 A final action collection letter

people can't write sales letters. In fact, most business people do write sales letters at one time or another in their careers—if not to sell products, then to sell ideas or new procedures.

A large body of sample sales letters is readily available for you to learn from. The direct mail advertising letters you receive are virtually a textbook on the latest professional techniques in this field, and they're worth paying attention to. Once you have a basic understanding of sales letter writing, the best way to continue learning is to study these letters.

Planning the Sales Letter

The job of writing a sales letter is perhaps 70 percent planning, 10 percent writing, and 20 percent revising. The planning stage is certainly the most critical in determining the success of the letter.

Goal selection   Selecting the goal for a sales letter is often a major strategic decision. If your product or service is fairly inexpensive and you believe readers may buy after receiving a single letter, then your goal may simply be to make the sale. But when the price is higher or you think it may take more persuasion than a single letter to make the sale, then your goal may be much more complicated.

Often your goal may be to persuade the reader to request further information: additional advertising material or a personal sales call. By narrowing down your list of prospects to those who so respond to a first letter, you can limit your more expensive sales efforts to those who are likely to buy. In other cases, you may plan a series of sales letters in which you expect the second or third to be the most successful in producing sales. In such a series, the first letter or two probably does invite the reader to buy, but its real purpose is to arouse interest and get the reader thinking about buying. Figure 10 shows such a series.

Audience selection and analysis Sales letters are mailed to prospects who are carefully selected in advance. Often the prospects' names come from company records: former customers, people who've inquired about the product, referrals from the company's sales staff, and so on. You may also purchase a list of prospects from a commercial mailing list broker, other companies that sell their mailing lists, or government organizations. Such lists are often sorted to include only persons in certain age, income, occupational, consumer preference, or other categories. Lists are priced according to their "purity" with respect to the categorization of prospects and the proportion of "undeliverable" addresses included. An enormous variety of lists is available from commercial list brokers, who will make up lists to virtually any specifications you can devise.

Once you select the list, make a preliminary analysis of it. Begin by noting the known characteristics of the people on the list. Then itemize what these characteristics imply or suggest. For example, a list including homemakers aged 25–40 who've previously ordered items by mail probably has a high proportion of mothers of grade school and high school students. A list including information systems managers of the nation's 100 largest corporations probably has a high proportion of people who commute a good distance to work each day by car. Obviously, you can't draw such conclusions with certainty, but you can usually be mildly confident of them.

Your primary goal in audience analysis is to identify prospects' motivations that you can relate to your product. To do that, you must also analyze the product in detail.

Product analysis Even though you may be familiar with your product, a sales campaign calls for a fresh look. To sell your product to someone, you really have to know it. One aid is to compile a fact sheet that includes the factual details about every possible aspect of the product. This sheet will then provide plenty of raw material for the writing stage.

Final analysis At this point, you've defined your goals, selected your audience, analyzed your audience, and analyzed your product. You have all the facts you need. But facts don't make a sale; you must now turn all those facts into persuasion. In the previous chapter, you saw that persuasion often uses three main appeals: earning or saving money, saving time

First Letter to Potential Advertisers

<u>WE'D LIKE YOU TO MEET A VERY VALUABLE CUSTOMER</u> . . .

He--and often she--is a lawyer, with a net income of about $50,000.

This customer has had at least seven years of university education, and may hold a doctorate. He dresses well, drives a better-than-average car, and usually owns his own home. He enjoys good food, good living, good hostelries, and good restaurants. He invests prudently, travels considerably, and buys insurance, stocks, bonds, and investment real estate.

This customer probably spends his professional life in an offices--as 78 percent do. He and his associates buy office furniture, equipment, filing systems, books, copy machines, dictating machines, and stationery. He's rapidly moving into computerization. If not in general practice, he holds an important position in government, business, or industry. Or he may be an educator, editor, or writer.

What's more, this person holds important offices in state, county, and city government. You'll find him on boards of directors of hospitals, businesses, banks, charitable groups, foundations, and universities.

There are over 75,000 of these customers, investors, and opinion makers in this state. And every one of them receives the <u>State Bar Journal</u>. This is the largest--and we think the most enthusiastically read--state bar publication in the nation. The <u>Journal</u> is truly a best buy among high-income, prestige groups.

You can put your full page ad into the hands of all these 75,000 members at a cost of only about $ .009, less than a penny each. A rate card and insertion order are enclosed. Why not schedule your ad now--an ad that is guaranteed to reach this important, highly responsive market? Phone me for your space reservation.

Sincerely,

Figure 10 A direct mail campaign

Mailed to Advertising Agencies during the Same Period

Among your agency clients, there's at least one with special media requirements. That one may be a bank, a securities broker, or real estate syndicate. Or perhaps a title company, trust company, or office equipment company. Or even an airline, or a hotel.

Ask yourself if that client's interests wouldn't be best served by advertising in a magazine whose readers

*Make up one of the highest-income groups in the nation?
*Include <u>every one</u> of the state's 70,000-plus lawyers, plus about 1100 judges?
*Are highly influential in investments and management decisions?
*Can be reached at a cost of <u>less than a penny for each delivered full page advertisement</u>?

Since last January, the <u>State Bar Journal</u> has had a new, larger format; a larger professional editorial staff; more graphics; and better and more compelling articles. Our most recent issue, a symposium on the legal problems of the state's coastline, drew requests for almost 2000 extra copies. Yes, we're a strong magazine! We're a powerful advertising medium for the right advertisers. Which ones, among your clients, belong in the bimonthly <u>Journal</u>?

Those clients should be getting exposure in this distinguished, well-read publication now. Just complete the enclosed insertion order--or send along your own form--and mail it to us with your copy or repro and your check. Or we'll bill you later. And if you have any questions, please phone me.

Sincerely,

Figure 10 (continued)

Second Letter to Potential Advertisers

You're really a pretty special organization.

That's why we'd like to see your advertisements in the State Bar Journal. Because when we say you're special, that's not just some copywriter's hyperbole. We hand-picked you as a potential advertiser. In fact, you've probably never been on a smaller mailing list. Our list of banks, trust companies, equipment dealers, airlines, and a few others actually numbers less than 300.

It's small because there are a great many fine organizations that just wouldn't benefit greatly by advertising with us.

And--to put it bluntly--there are some others we'd rather not have in the Journal. We've turned down several full-page ads lately. Yes, we are picky, picky. And not a bit ashamed of it, either. For Heaven preserve us if we don't keep faith with our readers. Hell hath no fury like a barrister bilked!

So you see, we're really sincere when we say you're a pretty special Journal prospect! We believe the Journal will be good for you. And that you'll be good for our 75,000 readers. This can really be a beautiful relationship! And one that's quickly and easily available, because you need only phone me for your space reservation. Or complete and return the enclosed insertion order with your copy or repro. It'll be the best thing you did all day!

Sincerely,

Figure 10 (continued)

and effort, and having good feelings about oneself. Turn your creative imagination loose and think of the best ways to motivate the readers toward your goals by using product facts.

For example, suppose you're planning a regional convention of plumbing supplies dealers that will include over 30 talks by national experts in the field and over 110 displays by nearly every major manufacturer. Your promotional letters could emphasize that the convention goers will obtain the latest marketing tips and information about new products and techniques—information they can turn into higher profits, beginning next month! And they can also trade ideas with more than 400 other owners and managers who are expected to attend—ideas on solving problems that are common to the field.

Or suppose your company's two-day seminar on using homemade alcohol in automobile engines and home generators will describe methods of making alcohol and converting gasoline engines to use it. You could emphasize that this information will enable a family to save $400 a year or more in automobile fuel alone.

Or suppose the bus line your city agency operates provides service to within six blocks of over 70 percent of the city's households and over 90 percent of the businesses at least every 20 minutes during rush hours. You could emphasize that it provides most residents a convenient alternative to the tiring hassle of commuting and permits substantial cash savings.

In this final analysis, try to create as many persuasive approaches as you can. Don't quit after the first few good ideas. Although you may not use all your ideas in the message, often the discipline of looking past the first few ideas will help you come up with really useful ones. One idea leads to another, and pretty soon you have plenty of ammunition for persuasion. That's certainly better than having to make the best of the first four or five good ideas you could think of.

Organizing the Sales Letter

Even though your planning has generated quite a few persuasive appeals, carefully construct your letter around one appeal. Select the one pitch you think will be most effective, and thread that theme through the whole letter. Many of the other appeals can be worked in as supporting points. Concentrating on one main appeal gives unity and continuity to your letter. It also helps ensure that at least that one appeal will be fully explained and supported.

As in other persuasive messages described in the previous chapter, the sales letter begins by securing interest. Normally, you secure it by presenting your main sales appeal in its strongest form right at the beginning. Since people often have fairly high resistance to sales appeals, work especially hard to arouse interest in the opening. If you don't succeed, few readers will even read the rest of the letter.

In the body of the letter, present your product's benefits in full detail and show how they arise from your product. Note that the sales letters you receive don't skimp on this stage. Professional sales letter writers often spend two or three pages presenting and justifying benefits, and they do so in the most vivid, detailed way possible. Paragraph after paragraph, they coax the reader's imagination into perceiving the benefits they're describing. Their goal is to get the reader actually to feel the benefits, because feelings lead to purchases. Figure 11 shows a letter that takes plenty of time to explain benefits that are especially oriented to a bank president.

The ending of the sales letter describes in vivid detail how to purchase the product. If the letter's true goal is to obtain some action other than buying, the ending probably still focuses upon the purchase, but it proposes that action as an intermediate step. Your goals and audience analysis from the planning stage will shape the ending.

As in any persuasive message, the ending should firmly press for action. Anything less simply wouldn't fit the occasion. After two or three pages of vivid persuasion, your blunt insistence on action will seem entirely reasonable to the reader.

FURTHER EXPLORATION

1. How well do you think the concept of honesty would work as the basic theme of a claim or collection letter? A claim letter could, for instance, offer a reader the opportunity to demonstrate his or her honesty by complying with your claim. How would readers react to such a theme?

2. People frequently have the chance to write claim letters. List at least six chances that you've had. In how many of those cases did you actually write a claim letter?

3. Determine several organizations' policies toward claims and adjustments. What is the general pattern in these policies?

4. Find out the costs and procedures involved in bringing suit in your state's small claims court. After reviewing these facts, what circumstances would lead you to file suit in small claims court? Is your state's small claims court a reasonable threat to use in your claim and collection letters?

5. If you were a collection manager, what criteria would you use to decide how long to wait before taking final action in a given case? What factors would you consider? What's the soonest you'd take final action? The latest? If possible, ask a collection manager what criteria his or her organization uses and how much time is normally given before final action.

Ms. Anita Flammarion, President
Women's Bank of South San Francisco
7171 Mission Street
South San Francisco, CA 94230

Dear Ms. Flammarion:

I've been admiring your ad series on radio and in newspapers stressing your newness in the community. I'm sure the series has been productive for you.

Soon, however, you'll deplete all the sales arguments that newness makes possible.

To replace that appeal with an equally forceful and durable platform, Hedge Associates has developed an annual CONTROLLED ADVERTISING PROGRAM for Women's Bank that will

1. Attract new customers.
2. Increase the number of bank services that each current customer uses.
3. Establish you as South San Francisco's preferred bank by enhancing and expanding the friendly, helpful image with which you wish to be associated with.
4. Strengthen your competitive position by supplying future and present customers with a unique, useful free service no other area bank will be able to duplicate.

CONTROLLED ADVERTISING is especially equipped to achieve these four goals. In fact, no other promotional medium could begin to approach the effectiveness of a CONTROLLED ADVERTISING PROGRAM. Therefore, before detailing our proposal, I'd like to tell you something about the outstanding advantages of this distinctive medium.

Four qualities make CONTROLLED ADVERTISING particularly apt for the program Hedge Associates has developed for Women's Bank.

1. As the only <u>selective</u> advertising technique, CONTROLLED ADVERTISING is the perfect medium for reaching a broad but well-defined audience. This selectiveness means that your message will be directed to a <u>chosen</u> group. Thus, just those people who are <u>most able</u> to take advantage of your services will be viewing your ads. So you'll waste far less of your advertising dollar on nonprospects. Your budget will go further; you'll reach more truly potential customers for less money.
2. CONTROLLED ADVERTISING is <u>measurable</u>. Because of several devices our program features, you'll get concrete, <u>countable</u> reactions to your messages. Plus valuable, additional data that could benefit your outreach efforts in many ways.
3. CONTROLLED ADVERTISING is the most <u>personal</u> of any existing promotional medium. As part of the prospect's daily mail, the CONTROLLED ADVERTISING piece receives the prospect's <u>undivided attention</u>. Your message isn't rivaled by radio and television entertainment. Nor must

Figure 11 A sales letter

```
                your message compete with text, pictures, and other ads
                that appear on a typical magazine or newspaper page.
             4. Finally, CONTROLLED ADVERTISING is unusually enduring in
                its ability to maintain audience interest throughout a
                sustained promotional effort.  It establishes attention
                patterns that considerably extend your message's
                action-taking cycle.

                I'm confident, Ms. Flammarion, that our proposed program
        can do an excellent job for Women's Bank of South San Francisco.
        Its elements are distinctive, suited to a sustained promotion.

                And these techniques are an impressive replacement for the
        newness appeal that you are now using.

                I'll phone you in a few days to see what time would be
        convenient for you to meet with me for perhaps 30 minutes.

        Cordially,

        Harry Newman
        Account Executive
```

Figure 11 (continued)

6. See whether or not your school library has books of model collection letters—most libraries do. You may find the letters exemplifying the persuasive stage especially interesting. How many basic themes can you find in such letters?

7. Over three or four weeks, keep all the direct mail advertising you receive. (Supplement it by asking friends or parents to save theirs too.) Then read all the material you've collected. Are there common factors in most or all of these advertising pieces? How long are they? How do they treat the potentially negative factor of price? How are the closes phrased?

8. There are fads among direct mail advertisers, as among most groups. One year, for example, many advertisers will include little pencils in their mailings (for filling out the order blank), another year they'll use cartoons at the top of the letter, another year they'll include a separate letter stamped "To be opened only if you decide not to order" that often begins "Frankly, I'm puzzled about why you have decided not to order." What current advertising fads do you find in your mail?

9. What kinds of products can best be sold through direct mail advertising? Are certain price ranges especially suitable? Are there differences between what a local organization and a national advertiser can successfully market through direct mail?

WRITING PROBLEMS

Claims

1. Several weeks ago your company returned 12 cases of duplicating masters used in your offset printing operation to the manufacturer, American Business Machines Company. When your print shop attempted to use the first few of these masters, they discovered that it was impossible to get good output from them. A sampling from other cases confirmed that the entire shipment was defective.

Yesterday morning you received ABMC's reply. They refused to refund your money. There is no question that the masters were defective, they said, but that was only because they were extremely old. In fact, masters of that type had not even been manufactured in the last five years. The batch numbers printed on the cases indicated that these were manufactured in 1975. In addition, the condition of the packing cartons indicated that they had been exposed to high humidity, even though warnings were printed on each carton against storage in an excessively humid environment.

In a large company like yours, you philosophized, such things can happen, and you almost dropped the matter. But on a hunch, you phoned warehouse chief Ron Dulik to see whether his records would show when the cartons arrived and how they were stored.

Ron's reply this morning was enlightening. Because of a computerized warehouse inventory system installed early last year, he was able to trace every movement of those cartons.

The cartons were each clearly stamped with an ABMC batch number, and these are recorded on both the manufacturer's invoice and the incoming packing slip dated July 20, last year. Also available are copies of receipts from the shipper specifying the same numbers, same date.

The cartons remained on the receiving dock, a protected, air-conditioned area, until July 21, last year, when they were moved to the company archive area in warehouse 5. The cartons were stored there because at that time the warehouse areas that normally would have been used to house them were overstocked and because the newly completed archive area was not yet employed for its intended purpose. The archive area was designed by professional records-management consultants to provide safe storage of company records for century-long periods. It has full temperature and humidity controls, the ideal storage environment for paper products. A computerized control system produced hourly records of temperature, humidity, and certain other values throughout the period these cases were stored in the archives. Ron knows that no irregularities occurred during that period; he can supply a full printout if you need it.

On December 9, last year, the cartons were shifted approximately 25 feet to give access to some cartons of stationery stored nearby. They were not moved again until 43 days ago, when they were transferred to the print shop, also fully air conditioned and humidity controlled. Then 36 days ago, they were transferred back to the shipping department for return to ABMC. They remained on the shipping dock for 2 days, in an air-conditioned storage room, and were accepted by the shipper 34 days ago. The ABMC batch numbers noted on the shipper's receipt agree with those noted previously.

Ron agreed to mail a copy of the invoice, packing slip, and computer printout he was reading from to your office right away. When it arrives in the afternoon mail, include it with your claim letter to ABMC.

2. When Harvey Grindler and his partner set up a new North Park branch office, you (North Park Office Supply) outfitted the office with furniture, typewriters, dictation machines, copier, and everything else they'd need. The new office is located two doors down the street from your store, convenient for any necessary additions or repairs (you provide factory-authorized repair service for the brands you sell).

The day before Harvey's office was to open, a freak storm blew out the windows of the building and caused extensive water damage. Fortunately, he hadn't accepted delivery of any furnishings, so the damage was confined to broken windows and stained drapes, walls, and carpeting. After much discussion, Harvey, the landlord, and you agreed that he'd go ahead and take delivery of the furnishings, stacking them in their cartons in the undamaged storeroom of his new office while the landlord cleaned up the storm damage. This arrangement allowed you to move these items out of your overcrowded storage area and receive payment, Harvey to have everything in place as soon as his office suite was cleaned up, and the landlord to receive a small token rent payment on the suite in the meantime.

A little more than six weeks later, Harvey was finally able to return to the building, open the cartons, and get the office into operation. To be neighborly, you spent a Sunday afternoon helping him unpack all the cartons and get the machines working correctly.

Three weeks after that, one of the dictating machines went dead. He brought it in, and you repaired it and sent the $161 bill to the manufacturer for reimbursement under the 60-day warranty.

This morning you got the bad news. The manufacturer, it seems, insists that the 60-day warranty began the day Harvey accepted delivery of the unit; thus the repair bill is his to pay. Under the circumstances, you cannot ask him for payment; after all, Harvey accepted early delivery largely as a favor to you. At the same time, you shouldn't have to take this loss yourself. This ought to be a legitimate exception to the manufacturer's 60-day warranty limit, you believe. There's no question that the repair was caused by a defective component, and you can verify that the unit sat sealed in its carton for the first 47 days of the warranty period—you supervised delivery to the storeroom, and you carried it out and unpacked it yourself. Renew your claim for reimbursement from the manufacturer, American Business Machines Company, more persuasively this time.

3.   After you finished your bachelor's degree in accounting, you decided to stay at the university to work on a master's degree in the same field. After two semesters, during which you nearly completed your course work for the advanced degree, you decided that what you really wanted was a doctorate in international economics. Checking with several faculty members whose judgment you trusted, you found that the place to get that degree is Daley University in Chicago. Not only does Daley have an outstanding reputation in the field, but its program in international economics leads straight from the bachelor's degree to the Ph.D.; you don't have to write a master's thesis.

In a discussion last spring with Dr. Henry M. Grossland, director of the program in international economics, he indicated that you had quite a head start in his program because your credits towards a master's in accounting could easily be transferred to Daley to fulfill the requirement for a five-course minor area. Partly on the basis of that promise, you applied for admission to Daley and began working on the Ph.D. this past fall.

But when you stopped by to see an adviser in the School of Accountancy at Daley to straighten out the details of transferring your credits last week, you found that Dr. Grossland had misinformed you. The accounting adviser agreed to accept your credits, certainly, but he made it clear that you'd still have to meet the usual requirements for a minor in accounting at Daley—requirements that will take you nearly all of one semester to meet. He indicated that there was no possibility whatsoever that the accounting credits you already have will qualify as a completed minor. When you told him about Dr. Grossland's promise, he said that surely you had misunderstood, because Dr. Grossland had no authority to make commitments for the School of Accountancy.

You spent several days talking to everyone you could think of trying to get the situation straightened out, including Dr. Grossland and two other economics faculty members and another accounting adviser. And now it looks like you can plan to spend an extra semester at Daley working on your minor.

Even though it appears you're not very likely to change anyone's mind about accepting your credits as a minor, you're too irritated just to let the matter drop. In your own mind you've composed scathing letters to the campus newspaper, poison pen letters to Dr. Grossland, hate letters to the president of Daley University, even a letter to Ralph Nader. But now that you've gotten some of the irritation out of your system, select a person at Daley University who might actually be able to do something about the situation—perhaps the dean of the Graduate School or the university ombudsman—and write a letter that will persuade him or her to intervene.

4. The day you and your partner signed the contract giving you exclusive dealership for Huebner hydraulic presses in your state was one of the most important days in the history of your profitable business. Huebner presses almost immediately became the foundation of your business, and you have both worked nights and weekends ever since to exploit the value of the outstanding Huebner name. In the three years since that time, you've grossed more for Huebner than any previous dealer in this state, and you've profited handsomely. Huebner seems happy with you, and you are delighted to be with Huebner—until last Tuesday, that is.

Tuesday morning, you got a call from Spectner Plastics Company asking your help in getting needed repair parts for their Huebner press. "What Huebner press?" you asked. "Surely not the one we submitted a bid on last October? We didn't get the contract."

"Oh, no," replied Spectner, "another source underbid you."

"Who?"

"Huebner Corporation. They underbid you by nearly 20 percent."

What a mess! You're supposed to have an exclusive dealership, and you find yourself competing with the head office of your own company— and they're underbidding you. In fact, not only did they underbid you, but they actually sold the press to Spectner for less money than it costs you to buy one from the company (in effect), since your commission on press sales is only 17.5 percent.

You've spent the last three days talking your partner out of suing Huebner. Now that he's calmed down a bit—and has realized that once this situation is straightened out you could have a very profitable relationship with Huebner again—you're ready to approach Huebner.

Based on your rereading of your contract with Huebner, you're convinced that you should have a commission of 17.5 percent of the price Spectner paid for that press. You also want to know what other direct sales Huebner has made in your territory, and you want settlement for those. Finally, you want clear agreement from Huebner that they will make all future sales in your territory through you, as their contract appears to state very clearly. After all, you're the dealer who provided specifications and design help to Spectner engineers before sale, and now you're the dealer who will provide after-sale help to Spectner in keeping the press operating. That's what your commission is supposed to pay for.

To be sure you say exactly what you mean in this heated situation, communicate your claim in a letter to Huebner.

5. When you rented a two-bedroom apartment in Spring Valley Gardens last year, you paid the $100 damage deposit that the manager demanded. During the year you lived there you were delighted with your apartment, and you were very happy with the service that Mr. Skornia, the manager, provided. He made several necessary repairs to your unit quickly, and he went out of his way to be pleasant and to keep the residents reasonably quiet in the building.

However, when the lease ended and you indicated your intention to move, your relationship with Mr. Skornia changed completely. He stalled and stalled about refunding your $100 deposit. Finally, he gave you a form to fill out and return for him to relay to the corporation that owned the apartment complex. You waited for just over six months to get your refund—of $51.

Since you did not damage the apartment in any way, and since you spent three days cleaning the place from floor to ceiling before you left, you simply can't understand why the landlord charged you $49 for "damage." After several heated telephone conversations, Mr. Skornia finally told you that the $49 charge was for repainting the apartment after you left. You had noticed during your stay that the management always repainted apartments at the end of leases; you had assumed that this was simply normal maintenance of the buildings. You think you've been taken.

You made one final attempt to talk Mr. Skornia into refunding the rest of your deposit. During this telephone conversation, Mr. Skornia convinced you that he had no control over refunds and that you'd have to contact the landlord corporation about the matter. Based on your previous experience with Mr. Skornia, you conclude that he is telling the truth.

Write a letter to the Central Standard Corporation that will persuade them to return the $49 balance of your deposit. Can you do it without getting Mr. Skornia in trouble? (Assume that the legal status of damage deposits is unclear in your state.)

6. About 18 months ago, your insurance agency purchased a small computer system to be used in accounting and client record-keeping. Recently you added the software needed to do word processing on this system, and then you discovered that the video display terminal you own, the model 38 manufactured by Hoffman Data Products, Inc., can't be used with standard word processing software. In word processing, when your typist strikes a key on the terminal, under certain circumstances the terminal transmits the corresponding letter code two or more times, rather than just once. If this happened with every keystroke, the cause would be obvious to any competent technician, and repair would be easy. Unfortunately, it happens only under certain complex, but describable, conditions, and your repair technician is stumped.

Two months ago you attempted to call the customer service department at Hoffman Data Products, without success—the person you reached referred you to his supervisor, Thomas Germain, who was always away from his desk when you called (several times). So you wrote a letter to Mr. Germain describing the problem. You reported that your technician had suggested that the problem may be a design defect in the unit. You asked that the company either specify how to get the unit repaired if it is repairable or replace it if this problem cannot be eliminated.

You received no reply from Mr. Germain, so one month ago you wrote to the president of Hoffman Data Products enclosing a copy of your earlier letter and requesting a reply.

Now, you still haven't received a reply. Hoffman has your money, but you don't have a terminal that can be used for word processing—one of the standard functions for which such a terminal is sold. When you originally sought a terminal, Hoffman responded to your request for specifications in far less time than this. You believe this should have been a fairly routine inquiry, quickly answered with no irritation either to you or to Hoffman. You still want Hoffman either to tell you how to get the terminal repaired or, if your problem results from a design defect and the unit can't be repaired, to replace it with a unit that will perform successfully in your word processing application.

Collections

7. Today at Dolman Brothers Building Supplies Company you received a letter from your customer, Fence Posts Unlimited, enclosing a check for $500, partial payment for supplies charged to their account. They say they're aware of your policy regarding credit, but although they've completed their contract to build an industrial fence for a local electronics plant, they've not yet been paid. The electronics company tells them their check is being processed and will be mailed from the Chicago office. They say payment to them is already 10 days overdue, and if it's not received shortly, they intend to place a lien against the property.

You discussed this with your boss, the credit manager. "Well," he said, "we may have a problem here. But the fact that they sent $500 is a mark in their favor. We'll know if and when they file a lien through our credit information system. But whether they do or not, or whether they collect from their customer or not, this obligation is Fence Posts's and no one else's.

"Write and thank them for the check and say we'll look for the balance on the first of the month, as promised. You might say something to the effect that we appreciate their concern and hope the money will not be further delayed. Add whatever else you think appropriate."

Draft the letter. (See also the following problem.)

8. As assistant to the credit manager of Dolman Brothers, you note that Fence Posts Unlimited has not cleared its account within the required 30 days and is now in its forty-fifth day without full payment. (See the previous problem.) It is not now delinquent, but will become so in two weeks.

Write the partners a tactful, cordial letter pointing out that you have had to impose a 1.5 percent finance charge amounting to $44.45 on their $2963 outstanding balance, and as new customers they may not have realized this charge would be imposed. Say the full amount must be paid within two weeks, on the first of the month, but if they will send payment within five days you will, because this is the first time, waive the $44.45 finance charge. Add any other comments you think would be useful, such as offering the consultation services of your engineer or inviting them to come in and see a new line of copper alloy rivets that may be useful in their line of work (enclosing a brochure from the manufacturer).

9.   As Credit Manager of Central Glass and Paint, you are responsible for establishing the credit terms your store extends to commercial painting contractors. Many are contracting companies, but some are small shoestring operations—one person working part-time under a state contractor's license. Floyd Oersted is one of the latter. His 11-year account shows purchases of $200 to $300 worth of paint and supplies every two or three months, with his check arriving right on schedule, until recently. His present balance is $327.93, now 67 days past due. Last month you sent the standard bill with your usual past-due notation; no response. Because of Mr. Oersted's long record of prompt payment, this month you repeated the bill with the past-due notation, and several days later you received his check for full payment. This morning the bank returned it marked "Refer to maker," which normally means that insufficient funds were in the account to cover it.

A bad check from any customer is a credit danger signal. Often, though not always, it means the customer is in financial trouble. An account 67 days past due is another danger signal. The two put together force you to take immediate action.

This is a situation not covered by the set of form collection letters you've assembled over the years. You'll have to write a brand new letter to meet it. Central Glass and Paint must have immediate payment of the $327.93. You realize that in Mr. Oersted's work, he sometimes faces slow payment from his customers, but his account with you is his obligation, not theirs. If he has a problem in meeting this obligation, he must get in touch with you; you must hear from him within 5 days. You should make these points firmly, yet in a spirit of cooperation that allows Mr. Oersted to save face (by getting in touch right away) and feel comfortable continuing to patronize Central Glass and Paint in the future. It usually works better to persuade than to demand.

10.   Allenby's, a large discount department store, encourages charge accounts. It has two types of accounts, the 30-day and the deferred-payment. With the first, the customer gets a plastic credit card that allows him or her to charge items up to a limit of $250. The customer gets a statement of purchases soon after the first of each month and is expected to pay all charges within 30 days. There are no interest charges except on balances remaining unpaid 60 days or more.

Deferred-payment allows customers to buy items up to a $3000 limit (over that, with credit office approval), charge them, and pay not less than 10 percent of the balance each 30 days. There is a finance charge of 2 percent per month on unpaid balances. When a customer opens an account, he or she agrees to this and also agrees that if the account becomes delinquent, it may be declared fully due and payable. The customer also agrees to be liable for reasonable attorney fees if you must file suit. A provision is included that the merchandise will be considered on lease until the final payment is made, when the title passes to the customer and he or she becomes legal owner. Finally, the customer agrees to return merchandise on demand if the account is delinquent.

The store allows customers to change 30-day accounts into deferred-payment accounts if they wish. If a customer owes, say, $200 and can't or doesn't wish to pay within the 30 days, he or she may put it on a deferred-payment basis. That is, the customer may pay $24.00 the first month (10 percent of the balance plus 2 percent finance charge), $21.60 the second month (10 percent of $180 plus 2 percent), and so on. Allenby's encourages customers to take the deferred-payment plan because it makes a substantial profit on the finance charge and because customers tend to continue buying on that plan.

Most of Allenby's customers are in the lower economic strata, where unemployment and emergencies requiring cash are somewhat higher than in the population at large. Consequently, credit losses are higher than average, and so are repossessions of some types of household goods. Allenby's sets prices about 5 percent higher than other stores to compensate for these losses.

As a new assistant to the credit manager of Allenby's, you're asked to revise the first of the series of three collection letters now used. "For one thing," says your boss, "it's stuffy. And it uses big words. A lot of our customers are not well educated. For many, English is an acquired language. I'm convinced that some of our worst credit failures are people who simply can't read what we write them." He then describes the kind of situation that calls for sending the first collection letter:

"The customer hasn't responded to our monthly statement, and more than 30 days have gone by. Figure out the appeal you'll use, but keep it friendly and human. Suggest that if there's a problem, the customer should let us know right away, because it's our policy to cooperate in every possible way. And stress the value of a good credit record." (See also the following two problems.)

11. Your boss at Allenby's (see the previous problem) has asked you to revise the second letter in the store's collection series. "The next collection letter should go out about two weeks after the first one," he said. Here's where you've got to walk a fine line. Stay friendly, sound helpful, but be firm about the need for making up the missed payments. Allenby's is willing to help, but help depends on their getting in touch." (See also the following problem.)

12.   Your boss at Allenby's (see the previous two problems) has asked you to revise the final letter in the store's three-stage collection series. "If we don't get a response to the second letter in 10 days," he said, "then someone in the office will try to reach the customer by telephone either during the day or early evening hours. That might resolve the problem.

"If not, then we go on to the third letter. Use your discretion here. Point out that we've tried to reach them both by letter and by phone. Say the account is now seriously delinquent—60 days delinquent. Don't threaten, but let them know that we can't let this go on indefinitely. Indicate some kind of time limit on how long we can hold this. Don't be specific about what action we may take, since that'll depend on each situation, but make it clear that we will take action and when. And use whatever other strong appeals you think are appropriate."

13.   The Commonwealth Galleries furniture store is located in the most prestigious shopping area in the city. It provides the very highest quality home furnishings, including many unique items, to people who can afford the best. The showrooms (galleries) are plush and uncrowded, the sales people are talented interior designers, and the service is outstanding. Prices are high.

Although most credit purchases are made on bank credit cards, the store runs its own credit operation, begun some years before the wide availability of bank cards. Since successful credit applicants have incomes in the top 10 percent and impeccable credit histories—and can afford the merchandise—credit losses are low. And since the average credit buyer purchases more than $10,000 worth of goods annually, some many times that amount, you, as Director of Accounts, handle any credit difficulties with kid gloves. At the same time, since delinquent accounts often involve many thousands of dollars, you watch them very carefully. Even in this income range, personal and professional emergencies—for example, divorce and business failure—do lead to defaults.

Credit terms are the same as when the program began in the late 1940s: payment of 20 percent or more of the outstanding balance is accepted each month without interest. A charge of 1.5 percent per month on the unpaid balance is made when a monthly payment is overdue more than 60 days.

If any amount is overdue 30 to 60 days, a note to that effect is added to the regular monthly bill. At 60 days overdue, your department runs a standard credit check to determine whether other creditors are having difficulties and whether legal action—divorce, bankruptcy, or lawsuit—has been filed. Unless the result provides a reason for immediate action, the next step is a form letter signed by you, which is mailed when an amount is 75 days past due. Write a model draft of that letter.

The goal of the letter is to stimulate some response from the credit-holder. You'd prefer payment of the amount past due. If the credit-holder is withholding payment for some reason, you'd like to know why. If an emergency prevents payment at this time, you'd like to be able to cooperate in arranging alternative terms that will be met. In any case, you need to have some communication from the credit-holder. The letter should be low key and friendly, but firm in its request for a response.

As needed, individual letters based on your model will be typed and mailed. If you believe resale material suited to your store's image should be included, provide a model of such material; that section of the letter can be updated as needed each time such a letter is mailed.

If the credit-holder does not respond to this letter within 10 days, your next step is to attempt to reach the person by telephone during the daytime or early evening hours. Since many people would prefer to avoid such personal contact, you may wish to mention this next step in an extremely low-key, nonthreatening way.

Sales

14. Several years ago, Jackson-Feathers Insurance Agency wrote a policy providing $4000 of fire insurance on household goods to Mrs. Agnes Sutton, an elderly widow. You have inherited her file from a previous agent, and the policy expires soon. Since household goods cost considerably more to replace now than they did when the policy was first written, you think she should increase the value of the policy when she renews it. The premium on a three-year policy for $10,000 coverage is $121.38, whereas coverage for $4000 is $62.77. Moreover, the companies with whom you place insurance are becoming increasingly reluctant to issue policies on property that is obviously underinsured. Even the smallest of fires can quickly do $4000 worth of damage to household goods.

Write a letter that will persuade Mrs. Sutton to increase the coverage of her policy. Of course you'll make more commission on the larger coverage, but she won't find your proposal very persuasive if she gets the idea that this is the primary reason for your concern.

15. As Director of Marketing of Warm 'n' Snug Electric Heater Company, you're in charge of sales promotion for a new line of radiant quartz heaters now starting production. After testing your heaters and finding them especially efficient, your local utility company has agreed to include a slip with the next monthly billing telling about your products. They hope to encourage customers to save energy by using your heaters for spot heating during cool weather rather than turning on expensive furnace heat. A furnace heats the air, which then warms surfaces it contacts. A radiant heater, on the other hand, emits infrared light, which warms nearby people and objects without having to warm all the air in a room or house.

An assistant in another department suggested the following text for the slip, seemingly designed to anger the utility company, frighten potential customers, and provide work for the legal departments of your company and RayBeam. Write a version that will sell heaters.

NEW ELECTRIC HEATER

```
     Customers who are tired of paying big utility bills can
have their costs cut through the use of the newest Warm 'n'
Snug electric heater.
     They do not warm the air. People who stand or sit near
these heaters are warmed 10 degrees in five minutes. They
have wire grills at the front to keep from getting burned.
You can order them for $89.95 plus shipping from Warm 'n'
Snug, P.O. Box 234, your city, state, ZIP. The models are
three feet high and have a base that sits on the floor.
     There is another heater like this put out by another
company, RayBeam. Their model is more dangerous than ours.
Our tests show that if the RayBeam tips over on a hard floor,
the tubes often break. When set upright again, a wire shorted
and arced and threw out a chunk of molten wire. Also, after a
fall, there was a dangerous current leakage.
```

For the record, the dimensions of the unit at the base are 9 inches by 11 inches; weight 12 pounds, 8 ounces. Local shipping costs $2.41. A number of early radiant quartz heaters were found to have design defects such as the one cited. Most, including yours, are now designed to remove these dangers. Although the quartz heating elements are rather fragile, shock-absorbing mountings reduce the likelihood that tipping will result in breakage, and other safety measures ensure that breakage will not result in any hazard.

16.   You have just been promoted to administrative assistant in the headquarters of a nationwide supermarket chain. Your chain has contracted with a food packer for a line of convenience foods packaged in sealed pouches. The pouched food is neither frozen nor dehydrated. It can be eaten directly from the pouch or heated by immersing the pouch in boiling water.

Some background: During the 1950s new plastics and adhesives were developed that could withstand very high temperatures. The United States Army tested these materials for packaging food. Researchers packaged various kinds of food, stored them, cooked and tasted them, and had them analyzed by microbiologists. They dropped the pouches from heights of 14 feet, squeezed them in vices, slid them down inclines into walls, and vibrated them. Troops carried them through obstacle courses.

There were problems. The researchers discovered that traces of the adhesives used to seal the pouches were seeping into the food. In addition, some pouches leaked under mass-production methods. After several years of improvement and further testing, the Army settled on a pouch made of three-ply laminated material, with transparent polyester on the outside, aluminum foil in the middle, and polypropylene inside. More stable adhesives were also developed.

Consumer testing followed, using fruits, ready-to-eat meats and stews, and cookies. Army consumers rated these for taste, odor, texture, and appearance, finding them a vast improvement over the Army's traditional canned rations. As a result, the Army ordered 24 million meals in these pouches.

Pouches are already common in Europe and Japan. Customers are attracted by the taste of the products—better than canned goods; not quite as good as frozen. Pouches can be stored more or less indefinitely at room temperature and are lighter than equivalent cans or bottles. To heat, merely drop the sealed pouch into boiling water; to clean up, simply throw the empty pouch away. Energy savings are substantial, both in transportation to the local supermarket and in cooking.

Write a letter to all store managers encouraging them to order and stock pouched foods. Assume that they are unfamiliar with the packaging and do not care to handle items they do not know about. Tell them that there will be national and local advertising and that in-store informational materials—posters, display racks—will be available. Describe the packaging in detail to help overcome managers' feelings of unfamiliarity. Motivate orders, and persuade managers to feature this line prominently.

17. Louis Garvey, proprietor of Garvey's Auto Supply, prepares four mailings a year to customers and local residents. As a freelance advertising consultant, you propose to improve his results more than enough to pay for your services. Here's his draft of his next mailing. Show him what you'd say.

Dear Customer:

This week only you can get a Minerva Meter Master for only $14.95. It's selling around the country at a regular price of $19.95. You probably already know about the Minerva Meter Master; it's a magnetic device that fits easily on your carburetor and creates an ionic dispersal of gasoline. Many customers report several miles a gallon more with it.

Garvey's Auto Supply doesn't have many sales, but when we do have one, it's terrific! There are big discounts on practically every item in the store. For example, a rebuilt engine for your eight-cylinder Ford or Chevrolet, regularly $660, only $549 during this sale. Snow tires at only $60 the pair. A fine brand-name oil, any weight, is a giveaway at $2.98 per <u>gallon</u>.

The enclosed circular tells you about many more items you may want for your car. We've just about everything you need for either maintenance or repair. With new cars costing what they do these days, <u>it really pays to keep what you have in good mechanical condition</u>.

And what is really valuable about Garvey's: all our clerks are automotive specialists. Tell them what's wrong with your car, and they can often suggest what to do for it. And they'll carefully explain how you yourself can do it. Many a time they've saved motorists hefty auto repair bills.

This one week of specials starts tomorrow, April 8, and ends at close of business on the 15th. Don't miss this gala, gala sale!

Sincerely,

18.   Mooney Brothers Department Store is opening a new branch at Third and University in your city, two blocks from the main entrance of a major university campus. The store will cater to the student trade, featuring a book department, a youth-oriented men's wear department, and a young women's clothing department with the full gamut of styles from jeans to formal wear. It will also carry accessories (belts, purses, wallets, jewelry, makeup), and small appliances.

The grand opening is scheduled for September 15, just after the start of the fall term. Cookies and punch will be served. The store got a good buy on one thousand polyester backpacks in the school colors of blue and gold, and it will give these away free, one to a student, until the supply runs out. To get a backpack, a student must appear in person and present the letter you're about to write.

Mooney Brothers has turned over to you a list of the names and addresses of all preregistered students. Write a sales letter for mailing to them about a week before the grand opening.

19.   As a partner in the communications consulting firm of Wylde and Schulte, you have proposed to president Arthur B. Cormany of Intersystems Corporation that your firm develop a comprehensive plan to enhance the public image of Intersystems. In his office yesterday morning, Mr. Cormany listened with interest to your pitch and seemed to be leaning toward acceptance of your proposal. When you telephoned this morning, though, he indicated that he did not believe Intersystems needed an image-building plan. He said, "Our product communicates all the image we need." Obviously, he talked to his marketing people.

As far as it goes, his comment is correct. His products do have an excellent image among those who buy and use them. Marketing surveys confirm this high regard. But this image does not extend to other Intersystems publics, all of whom are important to the corporation. Although they are not buyers, their high regard can be crucial in the future. Examples: suppliers, business and trade organizations, senior officials in other companies, Intersystems stockholders, Intersystems employees, legislators, government officials, international political and economic agencies, banks, institutional investors, private investors, local community leaders, consumer organizations, environmental organizations, educators, and union officials.

Executives of many leading companies believe that although people are primarily interested in the quality of products, there are other areas they are concerned about. Examples: treatment of employees, strength of management, range of company activities, research and development efforts, financial strength, export performance, and concern for environment. These matters can be dealt with in advertisements, but they also should be addressed in other ways, including news releases, audio-visual presentations, newsletters, special publications, and speeches.

A coordinated and comprehensive plan is needed to tie all this activity together, to take advantage of special opportunities, and to maximize return on the time invested by many company officials. Wylde and Schulte has the knowledge and experience needed to develop that plan. Write a letter that will persuade Mr. Cormany.

20. The Everlast Sod Company is the third largest supplier of sod in Denver. (Sod is live lawn grass that is grown in a field, cut in strips along with a thin layer of soil, and then spread over bare dirt at a building site, where it roots and forms a finished lawn in a matter of weeks.) Largely through your vigorous efforts as Marketing Director, the company has nearly tripled its sales (currently $2.5 million annually) in the last two years. The largest market for sod in Denver is commercial development—office and industrial buildings, apartment complexes, and condominiums—and you have captured a substantial portion of that market.

The ideal variety of sod forms a dense growth of rich green, fine-bladed grass that requires little water and fertilizer, is tolerant of shade, and grows slowly and evenly to reduce mowing requirements. Denver's arid climate and strict regional watering restrictions limit the usefulness of traditional varieties that need heavy watering and fertilization to maintain the desired green color. These varieties also grow so quickly that they must be mowed weekly.

Last year your company tested Greensward, a new patented variety of sod developed in northern Arizona. It requires less than half the normal amount of water to maintain a pleasing appearance. It remains green under slow growth, requiring only about half the fertilization and mowing of traditional varieties. The three clients who laid test lawns last summer are happy with the results, finding that their lawns recovered from winter browning earlier in the spring and remained green later in the fall than normal for your area. Their labor and water savings in the first season alone more than paid for the extra cost of this variety. The test lawns show that this variety is ideal for large open areas with little foot traffic. It does poorly in heavy traffic areas and does not tolerate heavy shade at all. The majority of lawns in commercial developments meet these requirements.

As most commercial developers are aware, last summer the regional water authority debated a measure that would have totally banned the installation of new lawns in commercial developments in your area. If the measure had passed, Greensward would have qualified as an exception under the measure's provisions. Most developers you've talked to expect this measure to be proposed again.

You have many acres of sod bed seeded in Greensward for this season's sales. In preparation for the new season, draft a sales letter for mailing next month to all your present commercial customers and then to new commercial developers as you uncover them. Emphasize your proven record with traditional varieties and the advantages of Greensward, now available in Denver only through you. Persuade them to invite your bid on any future sod work.

16

Job Applications

*The advantage of doing one's praising for
oneself is that one can lay it on so thick and
exactly in the right places.*
Samuel Butler

*Do you wish people to think well of you?
Don't speak well of yourself.*
Pascal

L anding a good job is basically a communication task. Of course, your education, grades, work experience, and other qualifications are also important, but recruiter after recruiter reports that what companies are looking for is someone who "comes across well," someone who can communicate his or her qualifications effectively. The job-finding process is one instance in which the most careful analysis and planning will pay off. All you've learned about audience analysis will come into play.

This chapter, then, is for those who intend to put forth real effort in the job-finding process. There's no guarantee that the approaches we discuss will get you a better job than someone who just wanders into a personnel office unprepared for an interview; luck can play a part in any job search. But these approaches clearly put the odds in your favor. You'll be more likely to find an opening that no one else knows about, and when you find that opening, you'll know how to take advantage of it.

THE PRELIMINARY ANALYSIS

Before you can even begin planning intelligently for job-finding communication, you must make two analyses. First, you must determine what you want from your future job and employer, and second, you must determine what you can offer an employer.

Determine What You Want from Your Job

If you're in your early twenties, then between now and retirement you'll probably spend nearly as many hours at your job as the waking hours you've had in your whole life up to now. That's a lot of time! And the decisions you'll make in your job search are important ones. Thus, it's worth some effort to improve the quality of those decisions.

Recruiters and personnel people think so. They're continually appalled that people apply for a job with only the vaguest notions of what it involves. They find that person after person has chosen a career because he or she identified with some TV character or liked the instructor who happened to teach the introductory course in that field. The worst problem is that such people often find they're dissatisfied with their jobs, they aren't very productive, and they quit jobs rather quickly. No doubt this all sounds like an unpleasant future, one you'd like to avoid. And your prospective employers share your view. They normally expect to spend about $10,000 or more training you before you really begin carrying your weight in the organization. If you quit soon, then the organization gets little return on that investment. Prospective employers have just as big a stake in your self-knowledge as you do.

What kind of work do you want to do? By the time you seek a career, you've probably taken several courses that could lead to it. But that certainly doesn't mean you're stuck with that one field. It does mean that you have some information that'll help you evaluate that field. You may also have had some firsthand experience with the field through summer jobs or internships. If not, then it would be a lot cheaper to spend some time investigating the field now than to wait until you've been hired, especially if it turns out that you don't like the work. Do you know what people do all day in that job? If you don't, then you should find out.

If you have no opportunity to get firsthand experience, then there's nothing to stop you from marching into the offices of 10 or 12 persons in your field and asking them about their work. Some may be too busy to talk, but others will be very interested in helping, especially if your request clearly isn't just a ploy to get a job interview outside the normal channels.

How much time and energy will you devote? Some people spend nearly all their time and energy on their careers, with little left for other pursuits. Many such people are on the "fast track" in their organizations, headed for upper management positions. Others expect to divide their time and energy among a career, family, friends, and other activities; relatively few of these people will ever become vice presidents of substantial organizations. If you expect to succeed on the fast track, you must select a first job that rewards competitiveness. If you're not interested in the fast track, then you should be looking for a less competitive job that you can succeed in at a slower pace.

Incidentally, a good many researchers have studied how many hours executives work. The results are pretty consistent. The average manager, from president down to first-line supervisor, works about 10 hours a day in a five-day week. The 7- or 8-hour day is an unrealistic estimate of the managerial workday; managers frequently take work home and devote many out-of-office hours to company meetings, professional conferences, and so forth. Do you feel strongly about avoiding that? If you do, you should plan accordingly.

How much pay do you want? If you think realistically about your expected salary before you enter the job market, you can prevent a lot of anxiety during your search. You can also confidently reassure an interviewer, with facts and figures, that your expectations are realistic. Ideally, before you contact the first prospective employer, you'll know enough about the salaries in your field to evaluate specific offers.

When job offers start coming, you'd like to line them all up and decide which is best. But a job search hardly ever permits that. More likely, the first offer will come in before you even know whether any other organizations are interested in you. And you have to accept or reject it without knowing what else may come along. Such decisions are difficult at best, but they can be a little easier if you have some basis for evaluating the salary offer.

Knowing the approximate range of salaries in your field would be very useful. That is, what salary is so high that you could accept it immediately, knowing that there's little chance that anyone will offer more?

And what salary is so low that you'd harm your long-term prospects by accepting it? If you're willing to work for far less than your abilities are worth, you may later have difficulty persuading anyone that you're worth more. If you can realistically determine maximum and minimum figures for the salary range you expect, then you're much more able to make calm judgments about salary offers and nonsalary factors (which in the long run are usually far more important).

Where do you want to live? Where you live is one of the many nonsalary factors that may be important to you. If you're like many young people who are beginning careers, you can throw all your earthly possessions in the back of your VW and move anywhere in the world fairly easily. But remember that, in another 5 or 10 years, this will no longer be the case. When you have a spouse, two or three kids, a large dog, and a house, you're not very mobile any more. Therefore, if you think someday you'll want to live in New York City or California or Montana or someplace else, by all means try to go there right away, while you can still do so fairly easily.

If nonsalary factors are important to you, think them out before your job search. Try to determine how important they are and what you'd trade to get them. And if they're options that people don't get in their first jobs, then figure out what sort of first job will put you in position for them the quickest.

Analyze What You Can Offer

Your analysis of what you can offer a prospective employer is certainly a key step in the job-finding process. Take this step after you've identified the kind of job you'll apply for, because what you can offer may depend on the job. For most young people seeking a first job, considering the following questions may be a good way to start. Get out your pencil and paper and take notes on your thinking.

What parts of the job have you done? Break the job down into its component tasks to see which ones you've done before. Some of these tasks will be trivial and hardly worth attention, of course, but it's worthwhile to let your imagination roam in this area. By brainstorming, you'll probably make some good discoveries.

For example, most jobs involve some communication tasks. Which of those have you performed in this book's practice problems? Which tasks have you performed in other college courses? In past jobs? In social activities? In other settings?

Here we're looking at your experience in a fresh way by drawing as many parallels as possible between it and the job you're applying for. Many parallels probably involve coursework; others involve work experience and social activities. Also, be sure to include experiences that aren't part of such structured activities; often these are the very experiences that set you apart from other applicants.

In this analysis, you're interested not only in drawing parallels between your experience and the job's tasks, but also in characterizing the quality of that experience. For example, there's a big difference between your communication practice in this book and the task of being someone's secretary and drafting many letters and memos yourself. Certainly the latter is more persuasive evidence of communication skill. There's also a difference between writing practice that earned a C grade and practice that earned an A. Your notes should include such distinctions.

This analysis requires that you know in detail what people do in the job. Don't just guess—find out!

What needed character and personality traits do you have? Companies believe that, to succeed on the job, an employee should have initiative, a firm sense of responsibility, a strong commitment to success, and other old-fashioned sounding character traits. These character traits are almost always sought in job candidates. What have you done that demonstrates such traits?

In addition, certain jobs require special personality traits. For instance, accountants should be high in dependability and attentiveness to detail. Salespeople should be aggressive in meeting personal goals and adept in getting along with others. What personality traits are associated with the kind of job you're interested in? And how have you demonstrated them?

For most people, earthshaking examples from their backgrounds don't spring quickly to mind. Yet, with a little thought, you'll probably notice elements that might be worth adding to your notes. For example, in your parttime job in the produce department of a grocery store, were you responsible for accepting deliveries when the produce manager was out? When you worked at a gas station, were you responsible for opening or closing? Were you ever responsible for cash?

Certain kinds of experience demonstrate responsibility, initiative, and success orientation especially clearly. For example, in starting and operating a small business successfully you demonstrate all these traits, even if the business was very small or operated for only one summer. A sidewalk lemonade stand wouldn't be very impressive, but a summer house painting business that earned enough money to keep you in school for a year is quite impressive. A successful newspaper delivery route is impressive because it has so many of the characteristics of a small owner-operated business.

If you've already begun a career and can show traits like these through your work record, then concentrate on conveying that information effectively. But if you haven't begun a career, then make the most of the smaller-scale experiences you've had. Structured experiences like paid jobs and organized social activities are easier to explain than unstructured ones, but if unstructured ones are your best evidence, then note them.

How have you demonstrated leadership skills?   Within a year or two of being hired, if not immediately, you'll be placed in charge of other people. Managing others successfully requires leadership skills. The question here is: have you already begun acquiring those skills?

If you've ever been a full-fledged supervisor, then your notes should concentrate on that experience. If not, then search your experiences for times when, however briefly or informally, you were the leader. Did your supervisor ever put you in charge when he or she had to be away? Did you ever hold an office in an organized group? (No one will ever know that the Central High School French Club was a pretty ragtag outfit unless your tone reveals it.) Were you ever the team captain in a sport?

Make Notes on Your Conclusions

Take some time to complete this analysis before your job search begins. Complete it right now, even if your job search is two years away. Thinking and making brief notes take very little time, and these notes will give you a tremendous head start when you need them.

You do need written notes because the results of your analysis should be detailed and far too extensive to remember without them. You needn't make them particularly formal at this point. Jot down some notes every once in a while when you're thinking about your experience, and store them in a safe place. When the search begins, you'll be delighted to have them.

By the time you're ready to use these notes, they should be extensive; even someone with a tremendously boring, humdrum life has had millions of experiences. If you've managed only a page or two of notes, then you're surely not ready for a job search. You may never use all the notes you've made, but until they're lengthy you can't be reasonably confident that you've remembered the most useful points.

THE JOB SEARCH

Some people land good jobs after three or four interviews in the school placement office. You can improve your odds considerably, however, by approaching the job search in the spirit of a major sales campaign—one directed at selling you to prospective employers.

If you approach such employers rather than just waiting for them to find you, you may well turn up a number of openings that other people will never know about. Smaller organizations, for instance, can't afford to travel to campuses for interviews, and they often have attractive openings. And even large organizations have last-minute needs for people. In this kind of search, you must make the initial contact rather than waiting for interview announcements or help-wanted ads.

Locating Prospective Employers

The first step in your search is to assemble a list of prospects. If you can narrow down the kind of job you want and the geographical area you like, you should be able to identify many organizations you could work for. Many applicants aim for an initial list of about 100 prospects.

If you start early, assembling your list can be fairly easy. Keep your eyes and ears open, and you'll hear about many suitable companies. Supplement them by reading the trade journals in your field for a year or two, making notes on selected companies. Often, regional journals have news sections describing personnel changes and new products. This is just the information you need.

As you list prospects, keep notes on 3″ × 5″ cards. You'll want the company name and address, the name of an executive you can contact, and background information about the company; the latter demonstrates your interest in the company. All this information can be collected rather easily if you identify your target market early. If you start a year or two early, you can combine your search for prospects with your regular reading for class assignments.

Mailing Résumés and Letters

If you're sending a mailing to 50 or 100 prospects, you'll want to minimize the work involved without reducing the impact of your message. In a prospecting application package, most authorities suggest sending a résumé summarizing your experience and an application letter highlighting and elaborating on selected aspects of your experience.

The résumé   The résumés you mail can be identical reproductions. They can be reproduced from a very clear master by a photocopier at an instant printing company, but insist on especially clear copies, which you may have to pay extra to get. Résumés can also be reproduced by offset duplication, which yields much more impressive results. Masters for this process can be made by typewriter on special paper, and the copies look like extremely clear original typing. If you need 100 or more copies of your résumé, offset duplication may be economical.

The application letter   Reproducing your application letter may be a little more complicated. Although the body of the letter may be pretty much the same for each prospect, the inside address will certainly be different for each, and you'll probably want to customize the opening paragraph of each letter to integrate the information you have about the company.

A typing service that uses word processing equipment may be able to type such letters individually for you at a reasonable price. The typist will enter the inside addresses and opening paragraphs, but the rest of each letter will be typed automatically. As a last resort, you could consider typing each letter yourself, or hiring someone to do it. This would be pretty expensive, in money or time. But even worse, it's likely to be error-prone, which is a serious drawback because the letters should be perfectly typed. Letters with even one typographical error or smudged erasure shouldn't be sent. You wouldn't go to an interview in an old sweatshirt and gym socks, and your résumé shouldn't be sloppily dressed, either.

You must understand right from the beginning that a search like this will cost some money, perhaps about $250 or so to send letters to 100 prospects. And you're gambling that the search will pay off; on the average, you might expect 5 to 10 replies offering further contact. You must decide whether this gamble is likely to be worth it. Weighed against the value of a really good job, $250 isn't so much money. On the other hand, if you're confident you can get such a job less expensively, then the $250 might not be well spent. Much depends on the nature of your field and how well you can specify exactly what kind of job you want. The more selective you are, the more likely you'll want to invest in this kind of search.

Writing a Résumé

The employment résumé is one of the most important documents you will write in your lifetime; its potential to advance your fortunes is enormous. But at the same time, the résumé has a very limited function. It stands in for you on those occasions in the job-finding process when you can't appear in person. Your résumé represents you while the organization decides whether or not to grant you an interview. After the interview, your résumé represents you to other people the interviewer reports to. To these people, the résumé is you; it's the only information they have about you.

The reader's viewpoint As the reader looks at your résumé for the first time, he or she forms crucial impressions about you. Here's what the reader should find.

1. That your résumé is attractively laid out, neatly typed, and scrupulously "clean"—that is, tidy and error-free. Organizations hire expert secretarial help to make their own documents look good, and they're used to seeing accurate and attractive ones from other companies. Even against that professional backdrop, your résumé should look sharp.

2. That your résumé is phrased clearly with perfect grammar, spelling, and punctuation. Your ability to use the mechanics of English correctly represents, in many people's minds, your overall intelligence. Two or three muddled phrases suggest that maybe you yourself aren't so clear thinking. And a couple of misspellings or grammatical errors suggest that your résumé was not seriously executed—that it was just whipped out on the spur of the moment. After all, if you don't take your résumé seriously, then what do you take seriously?

3. That your résumé is persuasively written. You carefully analyzed particular employer's viewpoint and the requirements of the job, then you selected the facts that present you in the best possible light. You also employed all your persuasive skill in phrasing the résumé, emphasizing the positive points and dealing with any negatives deftly. Of course we realize that these are communication skills, but to your reader they very likely represent—much more than your grades—your potential management abilities. When your reader thinks of a very bright manager, he or she is thinking of someone who can write and persuade well.

4. That your résumé shows why you are the best candidate for the job. This is the last feature your reader will see, and by then he or she has already formed strong impressions about you. Top-notch qualifications—in terms of grades, work background, and social leadership—are important; it would be silly to say otherwise. But top-notch qualifications aren't the whole picture. In fact, they are not more than half the picture, and they may be less. The way you handle yourself in applying for the job is at least as important.

The most important question in your reader's mind is very simple: how are you a better prospective employee than the other applicants? Perhaps your educational background is unique, either in content or quality. But if you majored in business, then many other applicants probably studied the same business subjects you did, and some of them may have gotten better grades. Thus, other factors become important: your attitude toward the job, your desire to succeed in it, your special background in related areas, your strength of character and personality, and your leadership abilities.

You can't hope to communicate persuasively if the résumé merely lists the standard facts about you: where you went to school, what clubs you belonged to, what grades you got, what jobs you held. The reader wants to know why you're qualified for the opening he or she must fill. And while those standard facts do help, they probably don't indicate your most important qualifications. Your résumé should go beyond the standardized listing by concentrating on the evidence that will answer the real questions in the reader's mind.

The content The extensive notes you made in analyzing what you can offer an employer are the basis of your résumé. Writing the résumé is a matter of editing and reediting those notes.

To begin, go through your notes and rank the items. Some are extremely important and certainly must be worked in. Others may be less critical. Still others may be used if they happen to fit smoothly but aren't basic to the images you want to create.

After familiarizing yourself with your notes, list the key images you want to create. As a prospective employee, what are your most important qualifications? What are the 8 or 10 most important points the reader should know about you after reading your résumé? How are you a better candidate than all the others who took the same courses that you did?

Then sort your notes, grouping them around the key images. Since most résumés are organized according to education, work experience, social activities, and military service (if any), the reader probably expects to see those categories. And they may suit the information you want to communicate. But even if you use them, be sure to focus the attention on the key images; don't let your résumé degenerate into a mere fact sheet listing the standard names and dates. Figures 1 and 2 show persuasive résumés.

Certain names and dates should be provided, though. These include your name, address, and telephone number; the names of any degrees you've received since high school, what institution conferred them, and when; your most recent few employers, their cities, and your supervisors' names; and any military service. Beyond these few points, you should select only information that supports the key images.

A basic principle of résumé writing is this: don't insist on telling the reader anything he or she will already infer. For example, if you have an accounting degree from a major business school, a reasonably well informed recruiter will know most of the courses you took. Little is accomplished by listing the standard courses; call attention only to those that are special, either because few other accounting majors took them or because you accomplished something special in them. Or if you list a part-time library job, the reader will already assume that you sorted books, shelved them, and checked them in and out. That goes without saying. Instead, mention the parts of the job, even if they were small, that aren't predictable. For instance, you may have performed some unusual task or supervised others.

Because of recent civil rights laws and federal regulations, employers may not consider information about your age, sex, race, or marital status, even if you volunteer it. If you provide such information, many employers feel obligated to blank it off your résumé before circulating it, because you've put them in the embarrassing position of having information they may not legally consider.

Before they hire you, most organizations require the names of three to five people who can tell them about your background. The résumé may cite these references, typically near the end, or you may offer to provide them later. Some organizations contact references; others don't. Even when they do, the information received from references, unless it is negative, usually isn't weighed very heavily in the evaluation. Any negative comments from your references raise questions, since employers assume that you can find five people who'll say good things about you.

Your references should be mainly teachers or former employers. The opinions of clergy, doctors, lawyers, and friends are generally discounted unless they're relevant for some special reason. Organizations usually want the opinions of people who have been in professional contact with you. One absolute must: never, under any circumstances, cite someone

RESUME OF   William Robert Tryon, Jr.

Address until May 18, 1983:   Beginning May 19, 1983:
   319 Marshall Road, Apt. 5   1316 Winding Way
   Clearwater, MI 49001   Springfield, IN 46603
   Phone 616 555-4602   Phone 219 555-5041

EDUCATION

B.B.A. degree with concentration in Management, Southern Michigan
   University, May 1983. Minor in Information Systems, although
   no minor required for degree. Served as project team leader
   in senior management-decisions course to produce A-rated team
   presentation on critical-path scheduling. Interned in
   management at State Fireman Insurance Company, Fall 1982.
   Average grade in Management and Information Systems courses,
   3.69 on 4-point scale.

WORK EXPERIENCE

Summer 1982: Started own housepainting business with two
   employees, Springfield, Indiana. Earned enough to pay
   employees and cover full year's school expenses.
Summer 1981: Painter and laborer, Wilson Painting Contractors,
   South Bend, Indiana. By end of summer, was left in charge of
   other workers when supervisor had to leave job. Was asked to
   return following summer.
Winter 1980-81: Office assistant, School of Engineering,
   Southern Michigan University. Opened mail room in morning and
   was in charge of distributing mail to proper boxes.

Have earned my own spending money since age twelve, and have been
   fully self-supporting since 1978.

SOCIAL ACTIVITIES

Vice-President of Data Processing Management Association student
   chapter in junior year.
Events chairperson for Management Students Association in senior
   year.
Also active in intramural basketball. Enjoy flying radio-
   controlled miniature airplanes in spare time.

References available upon request.

Figure 1 A persuasive résumé

```
RESUME OF       ANITA JANE MERRITT    2307 Balboa Court, Apt. C
                                      Cucamonga, CA 91700
                                      (714) 555-3537
                                      (until June 9, 1983)

                                      39043 Sun Valley Parkway
                                      Doxon, CA 92204
                                      (714) 555-9844
                                      (after June 10, 1983)

PROFESSIONAL    Executive position in the Accounting Department
  OBJECTIVE       of a major American corporation.

EDUCATION       California State      B.S. degree in Business
                  University,           Administration, 1983,
                  Cucamonga             with honors.  Advanced
                  1979-1983             accounting courses
                                        included advanced tax
                                        accounting, advanced
                                        managerial accounting,
                                        and auditing.  Grade-
                                        point average, 3.47 on
                                        a four-point scale.

                                      Small Business Internship,
                                        Fall 1982.  Member of
                                        three-student team who
                                        performed management
                                        study of small towel supply
                                        company.

WORK            Accounting Dept.,     Senior assistant.  Tutored
  EXPERIENCE       CSUC                 introductory accounting
                  Spring, 1983         students.

                James Merritt,        Set up and operated
                  Attorney              accounting record system
                  Doxon, CA            for father's law practice,
                  1980-1983            summers and weekends.
                                        Increased collection rate
                                        by 12% in two years.

                Brown Construc-       Secretary to Lisa Aguilar,
                  tion Company          company accountant.
                  Pasadena, CA         Prepared and mailed
                  1977-1979            monthly billings; recorded
                                        routine transactions; was
                                        entirely responsible for
                                        many small-volume company
                                        purchases.
```

Figure 2 A persuasive résumé

```
SOCIAL           CSUC Ski Club        Treasurer.  Set up and
  ACTIVITIES     1981-1983              operated accounting
                                        system.  Trained new
                                        treasurer in accounting.

                 Future Business      Treasurer of high school
                   Leaders of           chapter.
                   America
                 1976-1977

                 Junior Achievement   Treasurer of New Era
                 1974-1975              Company.  Manufactured
                                        and marketed home fire
                                        extinguishers.

                                      Enjoy skiing and desert
                                        hiking

   REFERENCES    Ms. Lisa Aquilar, Accountant
                 Brown Construction Company
                 19345 River Road
                 Pasadena, CA  91105

                 Dr. Gerald Winston, Chair
                 Accounting Department
                 California State University, Cucamonga
                 Cucamonga, CA  91103

                 Dr. Gretchen Sommers, Director
                 Management Internship Program
                 School of Business Administration
                 California State University, Cucamonga
                 Cucamonga, CA  91103

                 Prof. James Bailey
                 Accounting Department
                 California State University, Cucamonga
                 Cucamonga, CA  91103
```

Figure 2 (continued)

as a reference until you've asked his or her permission. You don't want anyone serving as a reference who doesn't want to do it. Give him or her a chance to refuse, preferably by asking permission in person so you can detect any note of hesitancy and bow out gracefully. When you get a job, it would be courteous to drop a note to your references, thanking them for their help.

In converting your notes into a finished résumé, work on phrasing the content precisely and laying it out attractively on the page. Remember, though, that the real work of writing a persuasive résumé consists of editing your notes. The quality of the résumé depends on the quality of your analysis and editing. All you're going to do after that is pretty it up for public view.

The format For quick reference, most résumés begin by listing the applicant's name, address, and telephone number. If your address will change at the end of the term, provide a "before" and "after" address. Since prospective employers will probably call you and since you may be out during the normal workday, you may want to provide the telephone number of a friend or associate who's near a telephone all day and will take messages for you. Few prospective employers object to such an arrangement if you return their calls promptly.

After the opening section, résumés are normally divided into sections that have headings. The typical headings are education, work experience, and social activities, but you can devise others if you feel your material will be more clearly organized in another way. To communicate a lot of information very efficiently, most résumés are written in phrases rather than full sentences. Résumés usually look more like outlines than like standard text. Using phrases also helps you avoid the overuse of "I," helping to maintain an objective tone.

If you're just beginning your career, most readers expect your résumé to be a page or a page and a half long. Within that space, experiment to find a layout that gets maximum information into minimum space and still looks clean and easily readable. Study as many samples as possible and use their best features.

Writing an Application Letter
If you're mailing the résumé as a first contact with the organization, then introduce yourself as persuasively as you can. This calls for a full-blown application letter.

The selling points A letter of application is mailed along with a résumé, so the two pieces should support each other. The résumé supplies key facts about you—persuasively selected ones—in a very concentrated and efficient form. Therefore, in your application letter you're free to emphasize and develop your strongest selling points. The résumé's tone is objective and factual. But the letter can express opinions and evaluate experiences to whatever degree you think the reader will accept. To be persuasive, support these statements with evidence, but you needn't use the purely objective tone of the résumé. Figures 3 (following page) and 4 (page 354) show sample letters.

To plan the content, look at the list of key images you compiled in preparing your résumé. From that list, choose three or four basic selling points and build your letter around them. For example, if you almost completed a degree in music before majoring in management, your letter to a musical instrument manufacturer could emphasize how unusual that combination is. Or if you earned spending money since age 11 and put yourself through college by working in your parents' furniture store, your letter to a furniture manufacturer could emphasize that few people your age have such an intimate, grass-roots knowledge of the furniture business. What points in your résumé would be most persuasive if they were emphasized and elaborated? Those three or four selling points will be the basic ones in your letter.

If your letter is for a sizable mail campaign, select points that have general appeal. But if you can draft a custom letter to each reader, then carefully analyze each reader and select or modify your points accordingly. A letter is certainly more impressive if it realistically considers the reader's special needs.

The introductory paragraph The opening of an application letter should (1) clearly indicate that you're applying for a job; (2) identify the job; (3) tell how you learned about the opening; and (4) introduce the three or four points you'll discuss in the body. In addition, unless you can customize the entire letter, the opening should mention at least one fact about the organization to indicate your genuine interest. Otherwise, you imply that you want to spend many years of your career working for a company you know nothing about, which is hardly an impressive ambition.

Being very specific about the job you're applying for helps the reader, because there may be little in your background to suggest what kind of work you'd like to do. For example, a marketing major might want to go into sales, sales management, marketing research, customer relations, or even purchasing; these are very different jobs requiring different interests. Although you may worry that the organization won't have openings in exactly the field you name, recruiters promise that, if you indicate your preference, they'll still consider you for all related openings.

Here's a formula sentence that illustrates how to assemble the elements needed in an opening paragraph: "I believe I'm the person you're looking for to fill the position of _____that you advertised in _____, because of these important qualifications: my degree in marketing from Springfield University, my successful sales experience, and my unusual ability to work effectively on my own initiative." This sentence clearly asks for a job, specifies the job, mentions how the opening was discovered,

319 Marshall Road, Apt. 5
Clearwater, MI 49001
March 12, 1983

Ellen Fieldman, Director
Personnel Department
Creel Information Processing Company, Inc.
4454 Riverton Drive
Akron, Delaware 19704

Dear Ms. Fieldman:

I would like to apply for the position of management
trainee you have advertised through the placement office at
Southern Michigan University. I think I am especially well
qualified to fill that position because of my unusual educational
background, my own successful experience in business, and my
demonstrated ability to work on my own initiative and assume
leadership.

In the Management Department at Southern Michigan
University, I participated in a nationally recognized innovative
educational program combining theoretical principles with actual
practical experience in supervision. And at the same time, in my
information systems minor I was learning the basic principles of
systems design and programming. As a result of my experiences in
these two programs, I not only have a basic understanding of
managerial processes, but I also understand the terminology and
viewpoint of professionals in data processing.

There's an old saying that the only way to learn about
business is to meet your own payroll. I'm not sure this is
really the only way to learn about business, but I do know I
learned many important lessons from my summer as an entrepreneur
in the housepainting business. Getting jobs, purchasing
supplies, supervising two experienced housepainters on the job,
keeping my customers happy--and meeting my payroll at the end of
the week--provided learning experiences I couldn't have gotten
any other way. And I'm proud of the result, too. At the
summer's end, I had thirty-one satisfied customers and enough
profit to finance a whole year's schooling without the part-time
work I had always done.

I got my start in the painting business the previous
summer, beginning as a day laborer with Wilson Painting
Contractors and ending the summer as a full-time painter and
occasional supervisor of a paint crew when the regular supervisor
had to leave the job site. Although most of the other painters
on these jobs were older men, some with years of experience in
the field, my supervisor felt I had the qualities needed to keep
things operating when he was away.

Figure 3 An application letter

```
        In my work in the Management Department at school, I found
myself gravitating toward positions of leadership in the same
way.  On our management project teams, leaders were normally
elected by the members of the group after the first three or four
meetings.  I was elected leader in three of the five project
groups I worked in.

        If these are the qualifications you're looking for in your
management trainees, please let me know when I can talk to you
further about the position.  I'm looking forward to hearing from
you.

Cordially,


William R. Tryon, Jr.
```

Figure 3 (continued)

and states the points that the rest of the letter will develop. You should find more original and creative phrasing, of course, but this formula illustrates how an opening could be drafted.

The body   In the body, provide a paragraph documenting and elaborating each point. The structure for these three or four paragraphs is the same. First, connect the paragraph with the opening by stating the point very clearly in the first sentence of the paragraph. Then, in the remaining sentences, provide evidence that the point is valid and significant. Several lines of evidence supporting each point are more persuasive than just one, so try to show several ways you've demonstrated the quality you're discussing or several ways that the quality will be valuable to the reader. Multiple lines of evidence corroborate that the quality exists and isn't just a one-time occurrence. Incidentally, the first time you cite a fact from your résumé, you might say something like "as the enclosed résumé indicates," just to encourage the reader to read the résumé. You needn't do this every time you cite such a fact.

The close   Ordinarily, the goal of an application letter is to get an interview. Probably someone, somewhere, has landed a job entirely on the basis of a letter, but most people are hired through an interview. Therefore, your close should concentrate on getting an interview. Something like this might do: "After you've had a chance to look over the enclosed résumé, please let me know when I can come to talk to you about my qualifica-

2307 Balboa Court, Apt. C
Cucamonga, CA 91700
April 17, 1983

Mr. Gregory Mees
Accounting Department
Ingres-Balk Packing Corporation
31739 North George Avenue
Reno, Nevada 89506

Dear Mr. Mees:

    I'd like to be one of the 12 graduating seniors you'll
interview for a job in your accounting department during your
visit to the CSUC campus on May 5th. The reports I've read
recently in The Wall Street Journal and Business Week about
Ingres-Balk's innovative management techniques make me eager to
join such an organization. And I believe my practical experience
in accounting combined with my fascination with accounting theory
will make me a valuable asset to your company.

    My introduction to accounting came during my two years as
secretary to the company accountant of Brown Construction Company
in Pasadena. In our two-person office, I quickly assumed
responsibility for many routine accounting tasks, and I found
them very interesting. Within a year, I was given full
responsibility for purchasing the company's office supplies and
equipment. Soon after, my boss encouraged me to become a
professional accountant.

    In my four years at California State University, I took
every accounting course I could fit into my schedule. By taking
additional accounting courses beyond the required minimum, I
broadened my theoretical accounting knowledge to cover many of
the areas needed by corporate accountants. My work earned a 3.61
grade average in accounting courses, and as a result I was
selected as one of four senior assistants to tutor students in
the introductory accounting course this semester.

    At Brown Construction Company, I soon saw that an
accountant's technical accuracy must be combined with skill at
maintaining the understanding and goodwill of people in other
parts of the organization. This lesson served me well in setting
up an accounting system for my father's law practice, where my
ability to explain complex techniques in simple terms allowed the
development of a rather sophisticated legal accounting system
over a three-year period. This ability also helped me succeed in
developing an accounting system now used by a small towel-supply
company and another now used by the CSUC Ski Club. And it was
invaluable in tutoring beginning accounting students, most of
whom weren't accounting majors.

Figure 4 An application letter

```
        I'd like to continue my accounting education as a member of
your accounting department.  If you agree that my practical
accounting experience, my broad background in accounting theory,
and my communication skills could be useful to Ingres-Balk,
please add my name to your list of interviewees for May 5.  I'm
looking forward to talking with you.

Cordially,


Anita J. Merritt
```

Figure 4 (continued)

tions. You can reach me at (phone number, including area code)." As in any persuasive letter, the close is a place to speak positively and avoid saying "if." Instead of "If you want to talk further," say "When shall I come?"

Preparing for a Job Interview

Most companies make their final hiring decisions after interviewing prospective employees in person. Interviews give managers the clear perception of applicants that's necessary to make a hiring decision. Therefore, the job interview is a critical step in the job-finding process.

If your interview is successful, that's probably because you went into it fully prepared. By doing that homework, you relieved a great deal of the pressure an interview can create. And preparing for an interview takes some real work. When you think about it, though, an interview may be one of the most important half hours you'll spend in your career, and it's certainly worth preparing for.

If you prepare adequately, you'll have the following four kinds of information well in mind before you walk into the recruiter's office.

The company and the interviewer The more you know about the company, the more intelligently you and the interviewer can talk about the job. The interviewer can hardly be impressed if you're willing to spend your lifetime working for a company but don't even know what it does or where its major branches are. If the company has been in the news recently, an interested applicant would have noticed.

A great deal of information about large- and medium-sized companies is available even in smaller libraries, and your placement office may have useful sources. Once you locate sources, you can get quite a bit of information on most companies in 15 or 20 minutes of research.

You'll also need some information about the interviewer. Pronouncing his or her name correctly is common courtesy; the receptionist will be happy to check your pronunciation. While you're talking to the receptionist, get the interviewer's office address so you can write a personal follow-up letter the next day reminding him or her of your interview.

The job requirements   The more you know about the job's requirements, the better you can present your qualifications persuasively. Find out at least the name of the job, and, if any requirements are mentioned, write them down. If you aren't sure what the job entails, ask a professor in that field about it; perhaps he or she can help you ascertain the needed qualifications.

Your qualifications   From your earlier analysis of your qualifications, you should be reasonably well prepared. Review your notes carefully, looking especially for ways that your background fits the special requirements of the job. Be sure you can supply concrete evidence of your main qualifications; get names and dates firmly in mind.

In addition, be sure to think about your weak points and what you'll say about them if asked. If the interviewer doesn't bring them up, ignore deficiencies unless they're extremely important ones. After all, no one's qualifications will match the job requirements perfectly, and your deficiency in one area will be balanced by your strengths in others. Leave it to the interviewer to bring up deficiencies.

Once deficiencies are brought up, however, you must deal with them. The ideal approach is to try to think about every possible deficiency in your qualifications a week or two before the interview. Then, just before the interview, use every device you know to think positively about your value to the company. In that frame of mind, you'll find that you can see your deficiencies as being relatively minor obstacles, and you'll remember that almost everything else is in your favor.

Think about how you'll answer specific questions that may reveal deficiencies. Practice before the mirror, if you have to, until you can say, "Yes, I'd considered that, but it seemed much more important to me that I'm well prepared in such-and-such areas." And proceed to talk briefly about a more positive point. Or perhaps you can turn a deficiency into an advantage by saying, "Yes, that is an area I'll need further training in, and I learn such subjects quickly, as my college grades in related fields show." Thus you've largely deflected the issue of the deficiency and turned the conversation toward your ability to learn and grow in the job, which is an important attribute.

Your career goals   At the very least, you should have pretty specific ideas about how much you expect to earn, where you want to live, and what working conditions you prefer. Accepting a job involves a long-term commitment, and normal people do have preferences in these areas. Be prepared to show reasonable flexibility in your preferences, but do know your own mind. Flexibility is called on when a job's shortcoming in one area is balanced by a very strong advantage in another.

You should also be prepared to ask some questions about the nature of the job or its future. Interviewers say they're seldom asked a good question beyond the obvious issues of salary and benefits. Every interviewer will ask you if you have questions and will be delighted to find that you're interested enough in the job to ask a solid, knowledgeable question. It shows you've done your homework.

Interviewing

If you've prepared properly, the interview can be a very interesting and challenging session of give and take. Very likely, the interviewer will spend the first two or three minutes talking, partly to give you some information about the company and the job and partly to help you overcome your natural initial nervousness. After a short while, he or she will begin trying to turn the conversation over to you, and this is when you should be ready to start talking.

Commonly asked questions Very commonly, interviewers will ask questions like these: "Tell me about yourself. How did you become interested in this job? What sort of work do you want to do? What's important to you in your career? What do you see as your most important qualifications?" Since you'll be well prepared to talk about these points, you'll have little difficulty carrying the ball.

Pride tempered by realism As you discuss your accomplishments, the interviewer will hope that you view them with some sense of pride. At the very least, you should view them positively, and certainly without apology. It's perfectly natural to feel that you've done some very worthwhile things in your life. At the same time, you should view your accomplishments realistically. It's probably unrealistic to think that they qualify you to join that company and revolutionize its operations or cut its costs in half. But you can become a contributing member and learn to improve its operations. And your qualifications show that you're capable of doing that.

Unexpected questions At some point in the interview, aspects of the job will come up that you haven't thought about. For example, the interviewer might indicate that no openings exist in the line of work you're really interested in and ask you to consider another opening. It's tempting to try to tell the interviewer whatever he or she wants to hear, especially if you're a little concerned about finding a job at all. But there are dangers in stretching the truth. If you say you'd be willing to change your goals, then you may have to take a job you don't really want or break the rather embarrassing news to the company that you didn't mean what you said. Neither alternative is attractive.

One way to approach such questions is to tell the truth, phrased as positively as possible. As a beginning, if asked about something you've never thought about, say that you haven't thought about it. This puts further discussion in context and allows you to ask about this new development without feeling that you're committing yourself completely. Then, in your comments and questions, try to be as positive as possible, maintaining this sort of tone: "I haven't really thought about that, but my first reaction is that I might be willing to do it. I'd like to know more about it." After such a beginning, a later refusal isn't particularly awkward.

The interviewer probably has a pretty accurate picture of your situation. If you tell the truth, this reassures the interviewer, because he or she will hear your comments in context. If you fib, however, be forewarned that the interviewer probably has a fair feel for what's likely to be true and what isn't. Once doubts are raised, they're hard to erase. Telling the truth, though, doesn't mean being brutally honest and open about everything, especially not about your weaknesses. If you have doubts about your readiness to go out into the great world, then talk to someone else about it, not to the interviewer.

The next step   After the interview, you'll want to know where you stand with the company. Are you being considered further? If so, what will the next step be? Very likely, the interviewer will volunteer such information. If not, be sure to ask. Before you go out the door, be sure you know when you can expect to hear from the company and what the next step in the process will be.

Following Up

After an interview, it's important to follow up with a short letter to thank the interviewer for considering you and express continued interest in the job (Figure 5). Such a follow-up letter is common courtesy, and it gets the reader thinking about you again, which can't hurt.

More important, a follow-up letter gives you a chance to reemphasize one or two of your strongest points. But don't do this blatantly or at great length; the main goal of your letter is to establish goodwill by an act of courtesy. You might bring these points up as thoughts you had after the interview, subordinating them to positive comments about the interview or the company. Or instead of reemphasizing information, you could provide some further information about areas the interviewer seemed interested in. The letter gives you a chance to say some of the things you wish you'd thought of during the interview. Such a letter could be relatively short and to the point.

Interviewers receive relatively few follow-up letters, which is one reason why they're so impressed by them. By following up, you indicate an interest in the job, and you also indicate a familiarity with the elementary social graces you'll need after you're hired. Follow-ups don't take long, and they're a worthwhile investment.

Dear Mr. Girarde:

      Thank you very much for talking with me Wednesday about job opportunities with State Fireman Insurance Company. The program you told me about sounds very interesting, and I am eager to talk with the company further.

      After our talk, it occurred to me that the very first thing I ever earned, when I was about seven or eight, was a fishing rod. I got it by selling three cases of mail-order Wolverine Salve to family friends and neighbors. Of course it's quite a step up from Wolverine Salve to State Fireman Insurance, but I'll wager I'm one of the few applicants for the job who can honestly point to a successful career in sales spanning more than a decade.

      Once you've had a chance to evaluate the results of your campus interviews, I'll be looking forward to hearing from you again.

Cordially,

Figure 5 A follow-up letter

FURTHER EXPLORATION

   1. How does a fact-sheet-format résumé differ from a persuasive résumé? Are the differences apparent at first glance?

   2. What trade journals in your field are the appropriate sources of personnel and product news that you'd need to compile a list of prospects for a job search?

   3. Spend 90 minutes in your library finding out all you can about a company that interests you. Try to find its annual report, and check the *Wall Street Journal* index for recent articles about the company. Also, consult Standard and Poor's registers, Moody's manuals, and the Dow directories. Now that you know where the sources are, how much information could you gather in half an hour or so the next time?

WRITING PROBLEMS

1. Fill a file folder with notes about what you want from a career. Spend at least 30 minutes each day for at least four days thinking and making notes on the following questions and and any others that are relevant.

A. What kind of work do you want to do? Don't just say you want to be an accountnat or an industrial sales person. List the specific aspects of the job you think you'd do well in and enjoy. What specific first job do you want after graduation? What job do you want to have 20 years from now?

B. How much time, energy, and competitiveness do you want to invest in your job? Do you prefer relatively predictable, routine work, or do you feel uncomfortable unless each day brings unpredictable challenges? Most people fall somewhere between these two extremes.

C. How important to you is high pay?

D. What specific organization(s) would you like to work for? What characteristics attract you to that organization: size, structure, management philosophy, type of product or service, and so on?

E. How much travel do you want to do in your career? How many days a year do you want to spend away from your home city?

F. Where do you want to live?

G. What other characteristics are important to you in a first job after graduation? In a job you'll hold 20 years from now?

H. What do you think you'll enjoy most about your job? What do you think you'll enjoy least?

At the end of the fourth day of thinking and making notes, write yourself a memo describing your ideal first job after graduation and your ideal of the job you'd like to hold 20 years from now. List the five most important characteristics of each job and the five least important. If possible, name the specific jobs, by title and company, that meet your ideals most closely.

(Many people find this exercise mildly intimidating. Yet you have every right—in fact, you have an obligation—to explore your own feelings about your career and to think about what will make you happy in your work. When good jobs are hard to find, it's more important than ever to know your own mind. You may find a job that approaches your ideal, or you may not. Either way, completing this exercise can help you search wisely and confidently.)

2. Fill a file folder with notes about what you think you can offer a potential employer. Spend at least 30 minutes a day for at least seven days thinking and making notes on the following questions.

A. What tasks do people carry out in the type of job you want? If you don't know, spend some time finding out.

B. Of those tasks, which do you think you'll do best at? What specific, factual evidence can you present that you'll be good at these things? What similar things have you done before? Be sure to note the experiences you've had outside the formal settings of education and work as well as those that occurred in formal settings.

C.   Which of your character and personality traits will contribute to your ability to do this job?

D.   What experience in leadership have you had?

E.   What have you been most successful at in your life?

F.   What education have you had? Make or get a list of every college course you've ever completed. Add relevant high school courses and non-college training courses. What has each course contributed to your ability to do the job you want? Compile an exact chronology of your college and other educational experience: exact dates of attendance and degrees, names of institutions and programs, exact names of degrees you've earned, and so on.

G.   What work experience have you had? What has each job contributed to your ability to do well at your ideal job? Compile an exact chronology of your work experience: exact dates, names of companies and positions, names of supervisors, lists of duties, reasons for leaving, and so on.

H.   What formal social activities have you participated in? What has each activity contributed to your ability to do the job you want? Compile an exact list of every formal social activity at least since high school: exact dates, exact names of organizations, names of offices held or major activities, and so on.

I.   What other activities have contributed to your ability to do this job?

At the end of the seventh day of thinking and making notes, organize your notes into related groups and compile them into a single well-organized outline of your experience, abilities, and traits. Focus your outline on the skills, abilities, and traits that are needed in the job you want. Include all the specific names and dates from lists you've compiled earlier. As much as possible, relate each past experience to the requirements of your ideal first job after graduation. If your outline only covers one or two pages, spend some more time on it; surely your 20 years or more of experience takes more space than that to describe in detail.

3.   Spend 90 minutes or more in the library finding out all you can about the organization you'd ideally like to work for. If it is a large company, try to find its annual report, and check the *Wall Street Journal* index for recent articles about the company. Also, consult Standard and Poor's registers, Moody's manuals, and the Dow directories. If it is another kind of organization, explore other similar sources of information. Following your brief research, write a detailed report about the organization. Include at least the following: exact name and address of the organization's headquarters, names of major officers, locations of major branch sites, summary of major product and service lines or activities, summary of the organization's history, and summary of major current organizational issues and concerns.

4. After completing problems 1, 2, and 3 above, write a persuasive résumé that you could use in applying for your ideal first job after graduation. If graduation is one or two years away, project as accurately as you can the courses you'll probably take, the jobs you'll probably hold, and the other experiences you'll probably have before that time. Be very specific in your projection, and as realistic as you can.

5. After completing the first four writing problems above, write a persuasive letter of application for your ideal first job after graduation. If graduation is one or two years away, project as accurately as you can the courses you'll probably take, the jobs you'll probably hold, and the other experiences you'll probably have before that time. Be very specific in your projection, and as realistic as you can. Assume that you will mail the résumé you wrote for problem 4 along with this letter.

6. Assume that your letter of application and résumé have gotten you an interview for your ideal first job after graduation. Spend at least 30 minutes a day for at least three days thinking and making notes in preparation for that interview. Consider at least the following questions:

    A.   What do I know about this organization? If you know very little about it, find out more using problem 3 above as your guide.

    B.   What do I know about the interviewer? Determine at least the interviewer's name, exact title, and business address. Find out any other information you can about this person's background or job responsibilities.

    C.   What are the requirements of the job? Determine at least the minimum qualifications required and the additional qualifications a successful applicant might need to have. What does a holder of this job do in a typical day? What special or nonroutine tasks must the holder of this job complete successfully?

    D.   What are your qualifications for this job? What are your strong points? Your weak points? How will you answer if the interviewer asks you to tell about your strong points? How will you answer if the interviewer asks a question that requires you to reveal a weak point?

    E.   What are your career goals? Use the questions in problem 1 above as a guide. How will this first job contribute to achieving your career goals?

    F.   How will you answer if the interviewer begins by asking you to tell about yourself?

    At the end of the third day of thinking and making notes, write yourself a memo to use as a guide in last-minute preparation for the interview. Include the most important points that you should review in the few minutes before the interview begins.

If it is not practical to focus this assignment on your ideal first job after graduation, select an interview announced on the bulletin board of your school's placement office or another source and focus the assignment on your preparation for that interview.

7. Write a follow-up letter that you could mail to the interviewer after the interview you prepared for in the previous assignment. Assume that the interviewer has said or implied that you are being considered for the opening, and assume that you are still interested in landing the job. Imagine the things that may have been said during the interview, and base your letter on those details.

IV
Reports

Although reports come in a tremendous variety of types, their main goal nearly always is to provide information. Reports are successful when the reader obtains the information efficiently and understands it correctly.

The major difference between reports and the letters and memos discussed earlier in this book is that reports communicate more complex information. In fact, some letters and memos that present complex information are actually, for all practical purposes, short reports. They're planned, drafted, and revised in the same way that reports are. At the other end of the scale, some reports are extremely long, sometimes running into thousands of pages. In a long report, you must organize the information for maximum readability just to make it understandable.

The most common type of report is the computer printout providing information from some data processing task. Similar in many respects are the many standard-form routine reports prepared by employees in most organizations. These reports are typically completed by filling in the blanks on a form, just the same as answering a questionnaire. In this part of the book, however, you'll study the basic principles and techniques for composing the many types of reports that are individually planned to meet a special need. You'll learn how to adjust your writing style to meet the report reader's needs and how to organize complex information for maximum understanding. Finally, you'll learn how to adapt the techniques presented in this book to planning and delivering oral reports.

17

Basic Reporting Principles and Techniques

I do not understand; I pause; I examine.
Montaigne

*Make no little plans; they have no magic
to stir men's blood.*
Daniel Hudson Burnham

The reward of a thing well done, is to have done it.
Ralph Waldo Emerson

The basic principles and techniques of reporting are very similar to those used in composing many letters and memos whose main goal is to provide information. Therefore, the principles and techniques of writing discussed in Chapters 7 through 11 of this book apply to reporting as well as to other business messages. This would be a good time to review those chapters to refresh your memory.

Report writing extends those basic principles and techniques. In this chapter, we examine the report writing process, objective tone, and learning aids.

THE REPORT WRITING PROCESS

Since reports are bigger and more complicated than the average letter, approach the job in a thoughtful and well-planned way. Review the suggestions in Chapter 11 on the job of writing, because they certainly apply to report writing. In addition, though, report writing has some unique aspects, and we discuss several of them in the following sections. These sections suggest a basic working plan for writing a report.

Analyzing the Audience

Audience analysis is a vital step. In this step, you note the biases and preconceptions that your audience will bring to the report. What do they know about the subject? Are they interested in it? What do they believe they need to know? What do they expect the outcome of the report to be? The more firmly you can assess the audience's knowledge, needs, preconceptions, and expectations, the more easily you can write an effective final report. Make written notes of your analysis so you have something tangible to work with later.

Most reports have two major audiences. The primary audience consists of people who will read the report immediately and use the information: your boss, his or her boss, your client, and so on. The secondary audience consists of people who will use the report in the future: people investigating how a decision was made, writers of similar topics, new employees, and so on. Your report should be self-explanatory to all these people, and you should consider them from the outset in your planning. In fact, considering the secondary audience often helps you meet the primary readers' needs. If you write the report so clearly and understandably that even readers who are unfamiliar with the situation can follow it, then your primary readers should find it easy to understand.

Determining the Goals

For many letters, the communication goals are so direct and obvious that they almost need no thought. But for complex reports, defining goals can save a tremendous amount of time by focusing the work on the crucial parts and helping you avoid the tangents. Unless you set clear goals, you're almost certain to spend much time spinning your wheels in work that proves useless.

If reporting assignments came in very neat packages, their goals would be obvious. But in real life they never do. Here's how a report is typically assigned. Your boss will say, "We've got a problem with the Cincinnati project. The people there think we should do such and such, but no one here has any solid information on it. Will you please look into it and make us a detailed report?" This is hardly a clear definition of the report's goals, and it's no wonder. If your boss knew for sure what the problem was and what goals were appropriate, he or she surely wouldn't go to the expense of having a report written on it. All your boss knows is that something is wrong, and it ought to be set right. Reporting on that is your job.

To determine appropriate goals, you must define the problem very specifically, but doing so requires information that you don't have at the beginning. Thus, at the beginning of a reporting project, you (and every other report writer) must grope in the dark somewhat. That is, you must simply spend a little time living with the report's subject and learning all you can about it. Little of what you learn will be directly useful in the final report, but some knowledge is necessary just to see what information will be needed in the final report. As you begin setting goals after some initial investigating, make written notes on what the exact problem is that you're investigating and what criteria the readers will use to make a final decision about that problem.

Suppose, for example, that a new machine now being marketed could be used in your company. It costs many thousands of dollars, but the manufacturer's literature includes figures purporting to show that it'll save enough money to pay for itself many times over in the long run. You're then assigned to write a report recommending whether or not to invest in the machine. Here's the problem: would such an investment be worthwhile?

But what does "worthwhile" mean here? If you can determine the exact monetary costs and benefits for a given future period, then how much must the company earn or save to justify buying the machine? What if the company would be 11 percent ahead after a 10-year period? Is that worthwhile? Maybe if the company invested the money somewhere else, it would be even further ahead. What if the company doesn't fully use the machine's capabilities (and therefore doesn't save much money) but can handle rush orders faster? Is that worthwhile? What if the machine would offer substantial savings but would very likely cause labor problems by automating some present jobs? Is that worthwhile? What factors will ultimately determine the decision?

If you can say in a sentence, "This is the problem," and write down what will determine your readers' final decision, then your reporting can be fully focused, and you can be reasonably sure of minimizing wasted effort.

Targeting and Gathering the Information

As you gather information in earnest, you'll want to be very confident that it's exactly what you need. If you've carefully identified the key questions, then your information gathering will be on the right track.

For example, when your company considers buying a machine, some key questions are immediately obvious. Certainly, company decision makers will want to know the machine's cost, both its direct and indirect costs, and they'll want to know how much money it can earn or save. But these questions are still rather general, and you could spend a lot of time gathering information on them that proves useless. You could also miss information that might prove invaluable. Both on the cost and the benefit side, you must break the questions down into more specific ones.

In terms of costs, for example, you'll need to know the exact cost of the machine, including all accessories. What accessories will you need? How much will the installation cost? Will you need additional plant space for the machine? Can you put it in the space now occupied by the old machine, or must you keep the old machine until the new one is operational? What's the cost of power to run the machine? Must its operators be more highly skilled (and highly paid) than present operators? If fewer operators are required, how much will it cost to retrain and transfer the present workers?

The first time you confront it, the question of cost looks simple. Then, as you explore it, it begins to look depressingly complicated—how can you possibly identify all the relevant factors? But fortunately, the question doesn't keep getting more complicated; after a while you finally get a grip on all the factors. And you should try to reach that point in the planning stage—before you start seriously gathering information.

At this stage, many experienced report writers make a large worksheet that lists every item of information they'll need, with space to check off each item as it's acquired. If the information comes from many sources and may be hard to keep track of, this worksheet can save a lot of time. As the information comes in, you'll need to file it systematically. Note cards, discussed earlier, are a time-tested, easily used method that allows easy sorting and organizing. It's hard to imagine another filing method that has more advantages.

Planning the Organization

A good way to test your information-gathering plan is to outline the complete report while you're considering what information will be needed. Seriously try to draft a final, topic-by-topic outline that you'll use to write the report (but remember that some changes may be needed as the information comes in). As you experiment with organizing the desired information and visualize the report's development section by section, you'll find gaps and weak spots in your list of needed information. You'll also see more clearly which items of information are vital and which are not. If you later discover that some item will be extremely expensive to get, you're then better able to decide whether to get it, settle for the best available guess, or do without it.

In the planning stage, it's relatively simple to experiment with ways to organize the report; it's extremely time-consuming to shift items or sections around after the first draft is written. So decide for sure how you'll organize the report from beginning to end, section by section, before you do any writing—and preferably before you gather information. Knowing exactly how each item fits into its section and into the logic of the report makes it easier to gather the information in its most usable form.

In reporting, there's no substitute for a written outline. With an outline, you know what you're doing at each step of the reporting project. Without an outline, you're working blind and trusting to luck. Your outline needn't be a formal one with roman numerals and so forth, but it must be detailed enough to show exactly how the report's sections will fit together. And the outline must be written, or it won't do the job.

Constructing the Figures

Construct each graph or table as soon as complete information for it comes in. That way, you won't have to construct all the figures in one long session, and you'll be more likely to give full attention to planning each one. Graphs and tables will probably constitute most of your figures, or visual displays.

The first step in constructing a figure is to think about it and plan. Decide what its main goal is. Should it present specific numbers or show relationships among numbers? What pattern should the reader see in it? Will the reader recognize that pattern quickly and easily, or must it be emphasized to be clear?

The second step is to make a first draft or rough sketch of the figure. A graph should be sketched entirely freehand, and quickly, as Figure 1 was. That way, even after it's finished you wouldn't hesitate to tear it up and redo it if you thought of a better design. For this reason, set a time limit of 15 minutes to make a rough sketch. Although not as neat as the final version, this sketch should be as complete and accurate as you can make it by freehand drawing. Hand-letter all labels in roughly the same size as typewritten characters, and enter all wording that will appear in the final version. Draft the title and check it for completeness and clarity.

The final step is to do a preliminary revision of the figure. (You'll do the final revision when the whole section it belongs in is assembled.) This preliminary revision helps you ensure that the figure is clear and achieves its main goal. Use the "janitor test": if the janitor found this figure lying on the floor, could he or she see exactly what it means? If not, now is the time to fix it.

Drafting the Sections

Since all reports must be revised when transitional material is added, the sections of a report needn't be drafted in the order of their intended

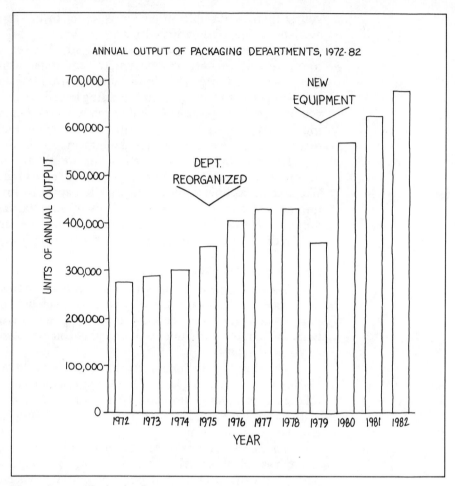

Figure 1 First draft of a figure

appearance. Your outline, written earlier, tells you what information goes in each section. So when the information for a given section is available and all the figures in it are constructed, you're ready to draft that section.

First, plan the section in detail. Reviewing your outline and audience analysis, determine what the section's main goals are. Then review its figures and the other information you've collected, and revise the outline for that section to ensure the clearest and most efficient order of presentation.

Second, draft the section. Begin by writing the body, being sure to connect each figure with the text by referring to it in the text and indicating what the reader should see in it. Then write an introductory summary for the section, referring to each of its main points in the order of their appearance. Finally, write a heading for the section that expresses its main point in relation to the full report.

Finally, do a preliminary revision of the section. In this revision, you're principally concerned with the section's internal clarity: does it clearly and effectively communicate the information necessary to achieve its main goal?

Revising the Body

Once all the body sections have been completed and revised for internal clarity, revise the entire body for coherence and continuity. At this stage, you're concerned with the interrelationships among sections. Ensure that each section provides the information necessary to understand the following ones and that no section repeats information that was fully explained earlier. Also, add transitional material to the beginning of each section to show the reader how you're shifting the subject. That is, add some words that clearly refer to the main point of the preceding section.

Drafting the Beginning and Ending Sections

A typical report consists of a beginning, a body, and an ending. The beginning has three purposes: it summarizes the report, explains the events that prompted the report, and indicates how the information was gathered. The body presents the gathered information. The ending typically has two purposes: it summarizes the information presented and explains the reasoning underlying the report's recommendations.

Since much of the content of the beginning and ending depends on information explained in the body, draft the body first. Then you can draft the beginning and ending confidently, knowing exactly what you're summarizing.

Revising the Whole Report

Since much of the report has already undergone preliminary revision, final revision is somewhat easier. But this is the last chance you'll have to ensure that the report is clear and logical, so approach it afresh and revise thoroughly. Let the draft cool as long as possible before revising.

As with any revision, the quickest way to get the best results is to go over and over the draft, each time checking for something specific. Begin by checking aspects that may lead to the farther-reaching changes, such as general logic and clarity. When all the material is in its final position, ensure that transitions exist to guide the reader. Finally, check for mechanical correctness.

Producing the Report

After revising is complete, you are ready to produce the final report. Calm your nerves, get out a ruler and a black ball-point pen, and draw the finished versions of your graphs. Type the numbers and letters and use a ruler and pen for the lines.

A figure will often appear on a page together with typed text, so you could draw the figure onto that page and then type the text around it. But if you make a major typing error on such a page, you'll not only have to retype the page, but you'll also have to redraw the figure. To avoid that, draw each figure on a blank sheet of paper, and type the text separately, leaving a blank space for the figure. To mount the figure in the blank space, use double-sided cellophane tape rather than paste or rubber cement, which tend to pucker the paper. If your instructor permits, turn in an extremely clear copy of your report and save the master for future reference. That way, your instructor won't have to worry about accidentally detaching your figures in handling.

Sometimes, you have to make a figure larger that it should be just to fit in the typewritten labels. Many of the bigger office photocopiers can reduce the figure—that is, make copies that are smaller than the original. You can usually reduce a figure to half its size with little loss in legibility if all its wording has been typed. The copying services in your area may also be able to do this for you.

Whether you type the report or a typist does, you will be responsible for the result, good or bad. Therefore, your job doesn't end until the report is completely typed and assembled and you've checked it for accuracy. When all is said and done, it's your report, not your typist's.

MAINTAINING AN OBJECTIVE TONE

As a report writer, you're actually representing your readers in observing or developing facts and making them available. You're the readers' eyes and ears in some situation that the readers can't investigate for themselves. The conclusions your report draws, therefore, should be the ones they'd have drawn if they'd conducted the investigation.

Thus, a report should first of all be totally objective; neither the selection nor the presentation of facts should be influenced by your personal biases and feelings. Very likely, you'll conduct your investigation impartially. The problem then is to convey this attitude to the readers so that they trust the objectivity of your reporting.

One way to assure readers of the report's objectivity is to describe your methods of gathering information; in your description, demonstrate that your biases didn't affect the conclusions.

You can also communicate your objectivity in the way you phrase your findings. Be very careful to phrase them in terms of the facts of the situation, and let the facts force you to any conclusions you reach.

To write in an objective style, focus on the facts. Any statement that isn't supported by facts is just a little suspect. Too many such statements begin to undermine the objectivity of the whole report. If you must base part of your conclusions on your (or someone else's) estimate of the situation rather than on hard facts, then do your best to support that estimate by quoting the experts who provided it or by showing the reasoning behind it.

Avoid any suggestion that your conclusions are based on your feelings and hopes. One way to undermine a conclusion is through a common phrase that you might use unintentionally: "I feel that such and such is true." A much better choice of words, and one that probably says what you really mean, is this: "The facts show that such and such is true." Above all, insinuations and snide remarks, as in the following example, have absolutely no place in an objective business report.

> The running noses and wheezing coughs that can be heard throughout the day in the administration building attest to the violent fluctuations of temperature in the building. Secretaries entering the building from the 90-degree heat outdoors may be observed shivering—and hardly with delight—as they slip on sweaters and jackets against the chill indoors. And those same young ladies will be seen perspiring several hours later in the heat of their offices. It's a well-known fact that clerical employees, like most females, complain constantly, but this time there's real evidence that their complaints are entirely valid.

Such comments can hardly inspire confidence in your report.

In many organizations, reports are conventionally written entirely in impersonal language, with no "I" or "you" appearing in the text. For example, the biased paragraph shown above can be revised to emphasize objectivity by focusing entirely on the facts of the situation:

> To determine the exact temperatures, accurate recording thermometers were placed in east-facing and west-facing offices during a period of 90-degree weather in July. The graphs produced by these automated instruments indicated that temperatures rose from a predawn level of 65 or 66 degrees to a high of 86 degrees in the west-facing office in the afternoon. At the same time, just across the hall, an east-facing office registered only 68 degrees. Interviews with building occupants confirm that this pattern is typical.

If your organization seems to feel that an impersonal style is essential in good business reports, then by all means use it.

Avoiding the use of "I" and "you," however, is not the key to an objective style, and it does raise two problems that may be worth considering. First, occasions will arise in which you must explain that you personally looked into a situation and are reporting what you saw. If you must avoid saying "I," then you'll have to use such awkward phrasing as "The author observed the following facts" and "The following facts were observed." A much simpler phrasing would be "Here's what I saw."

Second, when you use impersonal phrasing, not only do you lose the inherent interest value of sentences about people doing things, but you can also easily slip into a stuffy, bureaucratic style. Sentences that are full of people are more interesting, and they help you stick with the natural phrasing and direct sentences that make for interesting reading. The following revision creates such interest:

To determine the exact temperatures, I placed accurate recording thermometers in east-facing and west-facing offices during a period of 90-degree weather in July. Checking the graphs these automated instruments produced, I found that temperatures rose from a predawn level of 65 or 66 degrees to a high of 86 degrees in the west-facing office in the afternoon. At the same time, just across the hall, I found the east-facing office registering only 68 degrees. From occupants of offices in the building, I learned that this pattern is typical.

An objective style doesn't have to be impersonal, as the above paragraph illustrates. You can have lots of personal pronouns in your writing and still keep your focus on the facts that support your conclusions. And you can rigorously exclude "I" and "you" and still be obviously biased and subjective, as the initial version of the above paragraph illustrates. Unless your audience will object, increase clarity and interest by keeping people in the picture.

USING LEARNING AIDS

A report requires readers to learn complex facts and conclusions quickly. Typically, a 10-page report conveys information that took you a week or more to gather and master. And you expect readers to master that same information in just a few minutes (at an average reading speed of about one typewritten page per minute). The learning aids you provide in your report help compensate for that difference in learning time.

In an earlier chapter, we saw that a paragraph's structure provides learning aids of this kind. The main-idea sentence in the paragraph orients readers to the kind of information they'll encounter, and the sentence and paragraph transition help them follow the sequence of ideas. In reports, you expand on that system of learning aids. Headings and summaries are two additional aids that provide signposts for report readers.

Headings

Headings are the titles and subtitles that break a report's text into sections. For instance, the word *Headings* at the beginning of this section is a heading.

If they're well chosen, headings help readers in two ways. First, they indicate the kind of information that will appear in each section of the report. Thus, readers are prepared to receive that information intelligently and "file" it efficiently in their minds. Second, headings indicate where the major shifts in the subject occur and how the report is progressing through the contents that were summarized at the beginning. Readers can then see such things as the relative importance of various points and the logical relationships among them.

Report headings can do these jobs if they simply name the subject to be discussed. But they can do even more if they tell the main idea of the coming section, that is, if they're informative. Figure 2 shows some

Subject Heading	Informative Heading
Cash Flow	Cash Flow Position Has Improved by 27 Percent
Preferred Location	Keane Shopping Center Area Is Preferred Location
Quality of Fishing	Fishing Will Be Better in June
Plant Material Needed	Three Truckloads of Plant Material Will Be Required
Production Improvement	Tripling of Production Expected
Orders	Orders Reach $300,000 per Month
Resource Management	New Resource Management System Should Be Implemented

Figure 2 Informative headings

examples. In sections organized in the direct plan, the main idea can usually be stated in the heading so that the reader knows exactly what's coming. Knowing what the section will lead to, the reader can very easily sort out its details and quickly learn them. Whenever you can, use informative headings rather than mere subject headings.

If they did nothing else, headings would be worthwhile just for their value in breaking up dull-looking blocks of text into manageable-looking chunks. As an old hand at textbook reading, you can no doubt sympathize with the report reader who looks with a sinking heart at five pages of unbroken text; it certainly looks formidable! The same text broken up by several headings doesn't look so tough at all. For this reason, revise to be sure that your headings come at fairly short intervals.

Certainly, four or five pages of text without any break is going to look hard to read, and in fact it will probably be hard to read. Dividing it into sections usually makes the logic clearer, and breaking up that long block of text surely makes it look easier to read.

On the other hand, if a draft has three or four headings per typewritten page, you've probably gone too far with headings. For one thing, you're nearly devoting more space to headings than to the text. But more importantly, the flow of ideas is probably so interrupted by the headings that the material becomes harder, rather than easier, to learn.

Summaries

In very short messages, those shorter than a page or so, the main-idea sentence tells what the message is about and prepares the reader to understand it. But as messages get more complex, a single sentence can no longer do this job. You use summaries in reports the same way you use main-idea sentences in letters and memos.

Letters and memos usually have a single main point and some supporting points. But even a fairly short report usually has a general main point supported by three to six major supporting points, each of which is explained by still another layer of supporting points. Since the structure of the information is more elaborate in a report, the structure of its organizational plan must be more elaborate, too.

Thus, instead of having one main-idea sentence at the beginning, a report has an opening summary of all the major points in the text. And each section and subsection opens by summarizing the key points it contains, as in Figure 3. Often, the report also ends by summarizing all the information presented and recommending a course of action. Each of these summaries gives the reader a complete picture of what's coming, thus preparing the reader for the details when they appear. The amount of detail a summary includes depends on various circumstances, such as the reader's needs, but a summary should always mention points in their order of appearance in the text. This sequence not only tells the reader what will be discussed, but it also helps the reader keep track, throughout the text, of what's already been discussed.

To the writer, who's already familiar with the information to be presented, all this summarizing can seem pretty repetitive. But to the reader, who's trying to master complex new information in a matter of minutes, summaries are a welcome, effective aid. Without these signposts, most reports would be very difficult to follow.

Graphs and Tables

Graphs and tables are a tremendously important learning aid. Their major advantages are that they convey quantitative information quickly and clearly, and they show certain relationships better than any other format can.

Tables consist of rows and columns of data, which may include words, symbols, or numbers. They present precise quantities or relationships economically and efficiently. Graphs use lines, bars, circles, and other shapes to represent quantities. Their greatest value lies in showing the relationships between quantities quickly and clearly.

Many beginners resist using graphs and tables because they look hard to design. But compared with presenting a set of quantities in sentence form, the graphic approach is actually quicker, and it's almost always clearer. Consider, for example, the following paragraph:

Between 1972 and 1982, the output of the packaging department increased by almost two and one-half times. In 1972 the output was 278,156 units. In 1973 it had risen to 288,043, and in 1974 it was up to 305,994. In 1975, when the department was reorganized, the output climbed to 356,871. And in 1976, the first full year after the reorganization, it reached 412,217. In 1977 the output of the department was 431,537, and in 1978, 435,680. In 1979 the output of the department was curtailed by a major installation of new equip-

NEW SYSTEM WILL PROVIDE MORE COST-EFFECTIVE INVENTORY

(Opening Summary)

The proposed inventory control system will reduce high inventories of low-sales items, reduce the incidence of out-of-stock orders, and improve the accuracy of inventory planning.

(Body of Section)

By establishing a specific reorder quantity for each inventory item, we can reduce inventories of slow-moving items to a minimum, thus saving warehouse space and reducing our investment in low-turnover inventory. As Figure 2 indicates, the company's total investment in the 50 slowest-moving inventory items was over $17,500 last year. Our estimates indicate that the new system would allow us to reduce the necessary inventories of these items to less than $2600 total, which is a substantial savings.

In addition, the new system will reduce the incidence of out-of-stock orders by automatically reordering items when the quantity on hand falls below the preset reorder quantity. Thus, we'll no longer depend upon warehouse operators' observations to warn us of low inventories of items in the periods between our regular order dates. Figure 3 shows that, on the average, we processed just over 300 out-of-stock orders per month last year. Our estimates suggest that the new system could reduce this number by at least one-half.

But probably the most important source of savings from the new system will be our ability to plan our inventory needs in detail and implement the plan precisely and accurately. Our present system depends heavily upon the specialized skills of only a few employees--skills that can be developed only through years of experience in our warehouse. When these employees retire or leave the company, it'll take months or years for others to reach those employees' levels of expertise. The new system will gradually assume control of inventory operations, making intensive use of the expertise these few employees have developed. As a result, management will be able to plan inventory much more precisely and control implementation of that planning with high accuracy.

Figure 3 A section opening summary

ment, and in that year output was down to 361,807. But in 1980, the first full year with the new equipment, output skyrocketed to 577,991, and it has grown steadily since that time, with 630,784 in 1981 and 686,312 in 1982.

Such a paragraph is very difficult to write, requiring careful transitions and varied phrasing to avoid monotony. But even if well written, it places an almost intolerable load on the reader; it's nearly impossible to read with full comprehension. The skimmer won't even attempt it. Compare that paragraph with Figure 4. In effectiveness, there's hardly any contest between the two; even the skimmer might stop for a moment and inspect the graph. And without reading a word of the text, he or she will understand the idea the graph conveys.

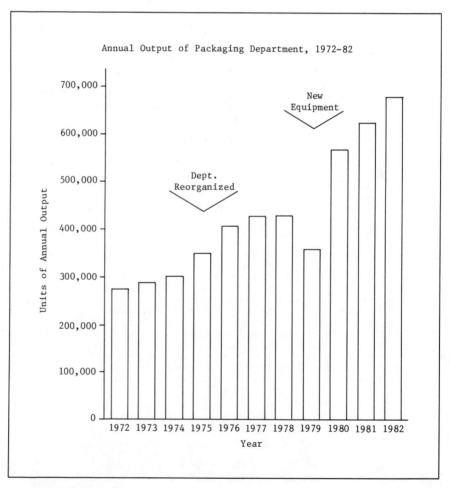

Figure 4 A bar graph

Tie graphs and tables into the text   Figure 4 illustrates two practices that help make graphs and tables useful as learning aids. First, always tie figures to the text by some reference in the text that tells readers what to look for. A comment in the text about the contents or significance of a figure not only alerts readers to its presence but also encourages them to look at it carefully, which they may not do otherwise.

Second, title figures clearly and fully and label their parts in suffi-cient detail so that anyone can tell at a glance what they represent. Extremely clear titles and labels communicate key points not only to skimmers, but also to careful readers who may survey the report by leafing through it quickly (often looking only at headings and figures) before a thorough reading.

Write clear titles and labels   The title of a table or graph should begin by naming the things that are counted in its body. If it's a table of production figures, then the title may begin with "Number of Units Pro-duced." If population figures, then with "Number of People" or "Number of Females under Age 25." If sales figures, then with "Sales, in Dollars." Then continue the title by indicating all further information that the reader needs to understand the table or graph without referring to the text. Who or what is being counted? When did the count take place? Where? As the titles of the sample tables and graphs in this chapter illustrate, this procedure produces rather long, but very clear, titles. Again, use the "jan-itor test."

Just as important, use great care in labeling each row and column in a table and each element in a graph. The ideal, not always completely feasible, is to make the figure pass the "janitor test," even if its title were torn off. But you can always give enough information in the labels so that the title is necessary only to provide the context. Then the reader can obtain information from either the title or the labels, whichever catches the reader's eye first.

Therefore, the labels repeat much of the information in the title. For example, in a table entitled "Number of Men and Women Aged 18 and over, by Age Group, in Provo, Utah, 1980," you'd expect to see at least such labels as "Number of Adult Men," "Number of Adult Women," and "Age Group." Figure 5 shows such a table. The repetition or near repetition helps the reader understand what's in the table and is rarely even noticed.

Labels in newspaper and magazine figures sometimes include the note that all values are to be multiplied by some number: "Population (in thousands)" or "Sales ($\times$ \$1,000,000)." This practice often leads to such ludicrous outcomes as quoting the number of males in a large city as 2.5, which is hard to believe until you notice the little note "(in millions)" down in the corner. Certainly 2.5 is harder to understand than 2,500,000. In unusual cases, you may have to omit the lower decimal places of num-bers simply to make the numbers fit into the available space. Normally,

Gross Sales of North Central District by Type of Equipment, 1982–83		
	Sales (in dollars)	
Type of Equipment	1982	1983
Typewriting	$1,363,182	$1,510,526
Dictation	693,549	741,013
Copying	191,324	456,008
Miscellaneous	143,493	142,502
Total	$2,391,548	$2,850,049

Figure 5 A table (The corresponding bar graph is shown in Figure 11.)

though, the figure can be read more quickly and easily when numbers are shown in full.

A graph or table that isn't clearly titled and labeled is nearly useless. Use the "janitor test" to be safe.

CONSTRUCTING TABLES

Tables are lists of data arranged into rows and columns and labeled clearly for quick reading. Some tables simply list numbers, and others compare certain numbers, such as numbers derived from two time periods or two similar cases. Sometimes tables contain rows or columns that sum to a total; in those cases, indicate the total.

If a table is to compare sets of numbers, construct it so that the main numbers to be compared are next to each other horizontally. For whatever reason, the human eye can more quickly and accurately compare two numbers that are adjacent horizontally than two that are adjacent vertically. Usually, you can simply exchange the positions of labels and cells so that a horizontal row becomes a vertical column and vice versa. Thus, it's easy to rearrange a table to get comparable numbers next to each other horizontally. Figure 6 shows how to do this.

CONSTRUCTING GRAPHS

A graph is a cartoon-like drawing of the relationships between numbers. Aside from absolutely clear labeling, which can't be emphasized too much, the most important principle of graph construction is to present an accurate image of the relationships. To do so, keep the graph clean and

Number of Men and Women Employed
as Accountants and Computer Programmers
in Anderson and Muncie, Indiana, 1980

Emphasis on Comparing Men and Women

	Accountants		Programmers	
	Men	Women	Men	Women
Anderson	226	220	153	142
Muncie	217	201	139	132

Emphasis on Comparing Accountants and Programmers

	Men		Women	
	Accountants	Programmers	Accountants	Programmers
Anderson	226	153	220	142
Muncie	217	139	201	132

Emphasis on Comparing Anderson and Muncie

	Men		Women	
	Anderson	Muncie	Anderson	Muncie
Accountants	226	217	220	201
Programmers	153	139	142	132

Figure 6 Changing the layout of a table

simple. Readers look at a graph because, provided it isn't cluttered and confusing, a graph is inherently interesting. Make your graphs large enough so that the necessary detail can be drawn and typed in without crowding.

Although there are many types of graphs, the ones most commonly used in business reports show three basic kinds of information: proportions of a whole, continuous variables, and discrete variables.

Showing Proportions of a Whole

The pie graph and the segmented bar graph are most often used to show the parts of a whole, often with each part labeled to show the percentage it accounts for.

The pie graph (Figure 7) is conventionally drawn with the largest part beginning at the "12 o'clock" position and progressively smaller parts appearing clockwise. The smallest or final part appears just before the 12

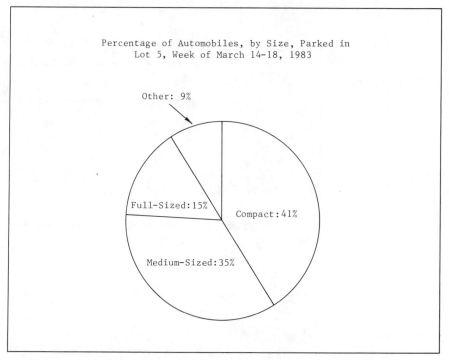

Figure 7 A pie graph

o'clock position. Often the final part sums up even smaller parts that are too small or insignificant to include and is labeled "Miscellaneous" or "Other." If the graph's information has some natural order, present the parts in that order. For instance, a graph showing the percentage of students by class will probably be easiest to read if it maintains the freshman-sophomore-junior-senior order.

Although the human eye can discern the proportions of a circle fairly well, you can assist it by labeling each sector of the circle to show the percentage or quantity it represents. If the graph is large enough, you can enter the percentages inside the larger sectors, but you'll probably have to enter them outside the smaller sectors and connect them to the proper sectors by lines.

The segmented bar graph (Figure 8) can be oriented vertically or horizontally on the page, as needed. Normally, the quantities represented are arranged from largest to smallest, beginning from the bottom or from the left. Labels for each segment should be typed to prevent crowding.

Showing Continuous Variables

Some variables are continuous. For example, if the temperature in your room rises from 72 degrees to 74 degrees, it passes continuously through all the values in between—73 degrees, 73.4 degrees, 73.4918 degrees, and so on. Thus, it is a continuous variable.

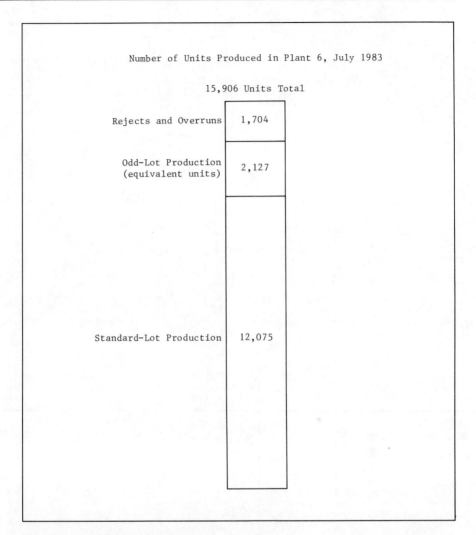

Figure 8 A segmented bar graph

The line graph is normally used to show a continuous variable (Figure 9). Usually it plots the values of some variable over time, with time as the horizontal axis and the earliest time at the extreme left. The variable to be plotted forms the vertical axis, which appears on the left side with the lowest value at the bottom.

Showing Discrete Variables

Other variables, such as hats, are discrete. If a store sold 23 hats on Friday and 28 hats on Saturday, that doesn't mean, as with temperature, that between those days the number of hats sold somehow passed through the values of 24, 25, 26, and 27. Rather, the number of hats sold is a discrete variable. It jumps directly from one value to another without passing through the range in between.

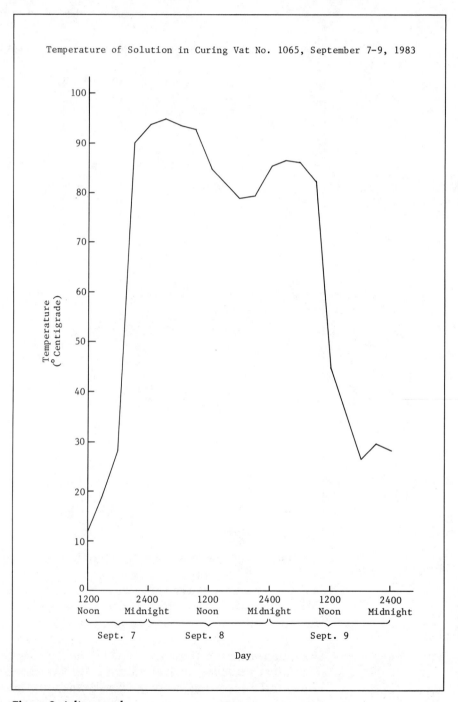

Figure 9 A line graph

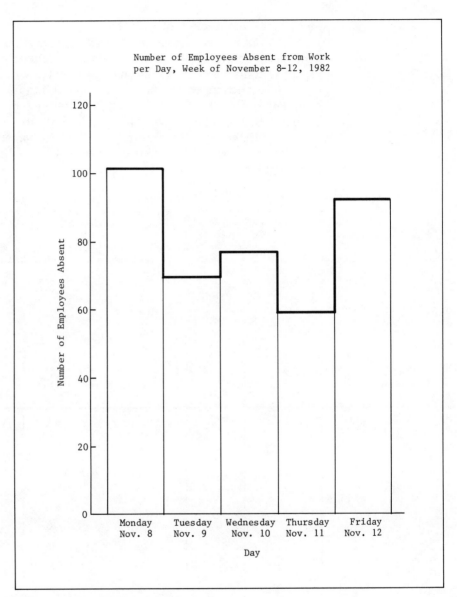

Figure 10 A multiple bar graph

The bar graph is usually used to show a discrete variable, with a separate bar to represent each value plotted. The bars normally touch one another so that the step-like broken line formed by their tops represents the jumps from one value to another (Figure 10). The bars can be oriented vertically or horizontally, with the lowest value at the bottom or the extreme left.

Showing a Combination of Variables

You can also construct graphs that show more than one set of relationships. For example, you can use two or more segmented bars, as in Figure 11. This graph shows the change in total production and in product types for each time period, with total production for each period represented by the whole bar and product types for each period represented by the bar's segments. Such a comparison is difficult to show with pie graphs, because differences in circle sizes are hard to perceive accurately. For instance, how do you draw one circle so that it looks 14 percent larger than another?

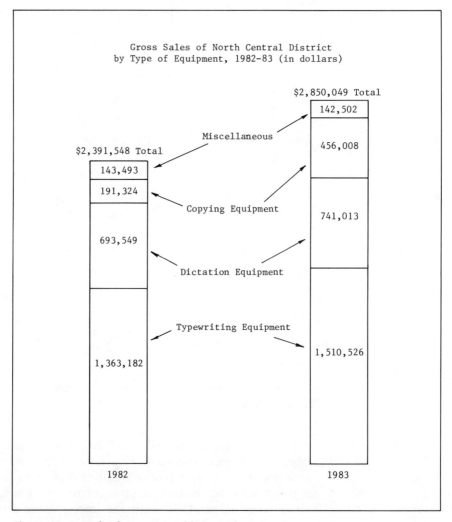

Figure 11 A multiple segmented bar graph

You can graph more than one value at a time on line graphs and bar graphs. Figures 12 and 13 show examples of this. But be very careful to prevent multiple-variable graphs from getting so cluttered that they're hard to read, and be especially careful about labeling when you're plotting more than one value. If possible, type labels directly on the graph, rather than using a key or legend to identify the quantities; such an arrangement makes the graph harder to read. Using both dotted and continuous lines can effectively indicate which line is which, but labels should still be typed on the graph whenever possible. Remember that, because most business reports will be duplicated on a black-and-white copier, color coding usually isn't useful.

Designing Scales

Like a cartoon, a graph represents an abstract idea through very simple lines and lettering. To accurately depict relationships and thus make its point clearly, the graph must have a properly designed scale.

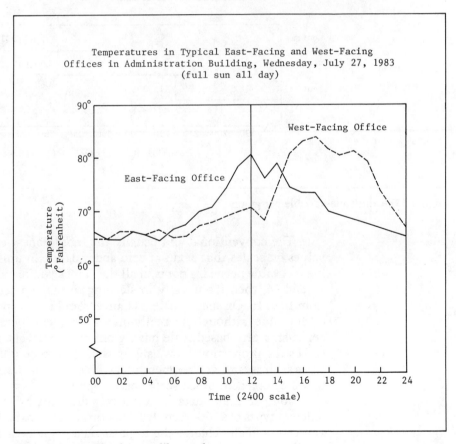

Figure 12 A multiple-variable graph

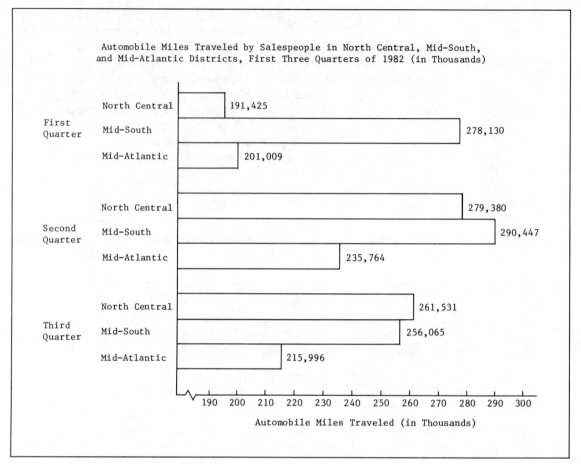

Figure 13 A multiple-variable bar graph

The conventional and usually the most honest approach is to plot values on scales that begin at zero and progress in uniform jumps to the highest value needed. That is, if all the values you're plotting fall between 11 and 14, then it's usually misleading to make a scale that runs only from 10 to 15. On such a scale, a change from 11 to 12 looks like a doubling of the value, although it's really only a 9 percent increase (Figure 14). In contrast, a zero-based scale having uniform intervals between units preserves the proportions you usually want to depict. (Of course, for quantities such as time and temperature, which don't normally have any meaningful zero, a zero-based scale doesn't apply.)

You can make data look entirely different by experimenting with different types of scales. Simply by making a scale spatially larger or smaller, you can radically change the impression a graph creates (Figure 15). You must ensure, though, that the scales you use help to represent reality fairly and clearly.

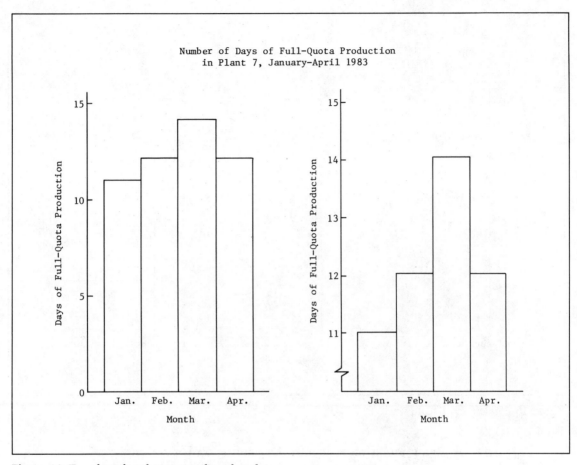

Figure 14 Zero-based and non-zero-based scales

With that in mind, you can intelligently use certain departures from the conventional zero-based scale. When you're absolutely sure that a departure won't create a distorted picture, you can use a scale that doesn't begin at zero. When you do so, indicate by a break in the scale that you've left out a segment of the values.

Another departure is to use nonlinear scales. In a logarithmic scale, each major step represents twice the value of the one before it (Figure 16). On this scale, a doubling of a value at any one level of the graph looks like the same amount of change as a doubling at any other level. If the number of management personnel in a company has increased from 25 to 50 and the number of employees has increased from 450 to 900 in the same period, then a logarithmic scale would emphasize that the two groups are increasing at the same rate. But a linear scale large enough to indicate the number 900 would show that, in absolute terms, the number of management personnel is rising slowly while the number of employees is

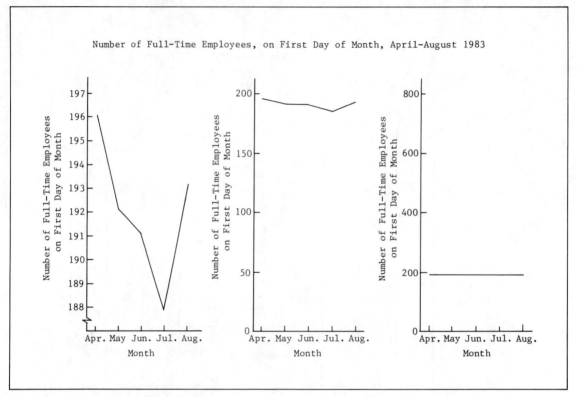

Number of Full-Time Employees, on First Day of Month, April-August 1983

Figure 15 The effect of scale size

rising much more rapidly. Depending on the writer's goal, either graph could be an accurate representation of these data.

In your planning, then, the first step is to determine what kind of relationship a graph is supposed to depict. Ascertain the true relationship in the situation being reported. Then devise scales that depict that relationship clearly and efficiently.

FURTHER EXPLORATION

1. The problem of achieving objectivity in business reports is similar to the problem of achieving it in news reports. What are some of the devices news reporters use to create an objective tone?

2. What kinds of learning aids do your college textbooks use? Could these aids be improved to help you learn more efficiently? Are such techniques applicable to business reports?

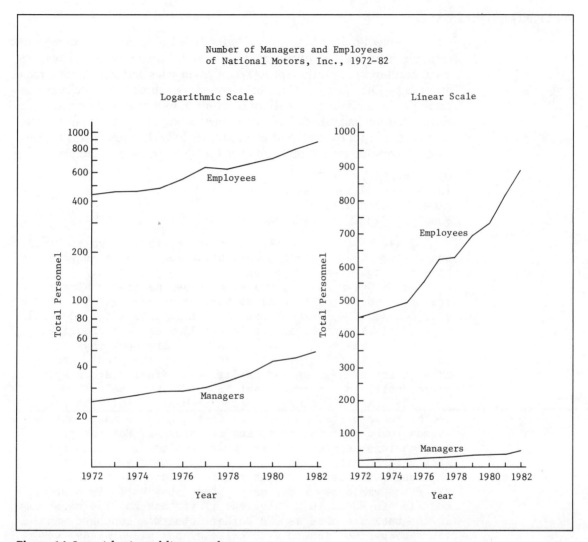

Figure 16 Logarithmic and linear scales

3. Find parallels between the heading-summary-text structure of business reports and the structure of newspaper stories.

4. Analyze the next 10 or 12 graphs and tables you see. Do the graphs correctly represent continuous and discrete variables? Do the tables position the main comparable numbers so they're horizontally adjacent? Are titles and labels as clear as they should be in business reports? Try the "janitor test."

WRITING PROBLEMS

1.   As New Product Manager of Better Tool Company, you are responsible for ensuring that your company's new 3/8-inch power drill reaches
the market in time for this spring's handyman sales. Subcontractor Green
and Seales Die Casting, Decatur, Georgia, is scheduled to deliver test
castings of the pistol-grip shell for this unit in four weeks. Your assistant,
Roger Stafford, had scheduled a trip to visit relatives in Atlanta this week,
so you asked him to stop in Decatur and see how the project was coming
along. Here's his report, dictated over the phone to your secretary.

```
DATE: March 12, 1983
TO: Glenda Guidon, New Product Manager
FROM: Roger Stafford
SUBJECT: Visit to Green and Seales
```

I never saw such a nervous bunch as those guys at Green
and Seales, boss. It's a spooky situation, and we're going to
have to watch them like a hawk!

James Green and Ray Seales both met me at the airport
yesterday morning and insisted that we go straight to the
golf course. They seemed jumpy as all getout. After 18 holes
of golf (I shot an 81 and collected $13) and a four-drink
lunch, they wanted to show me a new fishing spot they had
found. I sort of insisted that we stop by the plant, and
after a lot of hemming and hawing, they finally drove by
there, still in a hurry to get to the fishing hole.

The plant was like a morgue—probably about five people
in the whole place. One guy was in the machine shop, but he
seemed to be just puttering and cleaning up. Not one press
was running, and the smelting pots were cold. I doubt if
they'd run a single casting in at least several days, from
the looks of things. They nervously explained that they'd
given the employees a few days' break, but March is a pretty
odd time to schedule a vacation, if you ask me. The warehouse
in the back was bare as Old Mother Hubbard's cupboard, and
you remember how jammed with pallets that place always was.

After prodding, Ray Seales showed me the drawings for
the shell, but he said the dies were "out for hardening
treatment." I can't say they aren't, but I also can't say
that they even exist. I can say that I never saw two guys so
determined not to talk about something as Green and Seales
were about this contract. They brightened considerably as I
let them steer me out the door to go fishing. Had fun, drank
too much beer, and caught more catfish than I've ever seen
before. The next morning about 9:30, I drove by the plant on
the way to the airport, and there were four cars in the
parking lot.

Green and Seales are nice guys, as you remember, and
they've done great work for us. But if I had to make a guess,

```
I'd say they'll be belly-up before those castings ever get
delivered. If not, then only our job will save them. We'd
better stay alert!
```

You must alert your boss, Vice-President Aaron Pryor, to this development right away. Normally, you'd just pass Roger's memo along to him, but this time you conclude that its tone isn't suitable. Use its facts to write your own more objective report to your boss.

    2.   As a manager in Fuhrman and Coster, a CPA firm, you are responsible for writing the final report of your company's audit of the Armwood County Bank. The first part of the report, the formal audit report, is finished. Now you are working on the accompanying "management letter," in which your firm evaluates the accounting procedures and controls in use at the bank. During the course of your audit, all members of the audit team have been making notes about procedures and events they happened to witness. Among the notes and draft paragraphs submitted to you was this one.

```
    In the course of our examination, we observed two
failures of the customary controls that normally govern a
bank computer installation. (1) Failure to enforce existing
rules with respect to computer-room security. We observed
frequent violations of the rule requiring no smoking in the
computer room, violations which could lead to serious
consequences in the event such smoking resulted in a fire in
the bank's computer. In addition, computer-room personnel
often neglected to lock the doors, leaving access to this
sensitive area uncontrolled. Such violations often occurred
when personnel stepped out of the room briefly and returned,
a factor that cannot mitigate the seriousness of the
violation. (2) Inadequate control over access to the computer
area. Although management policy requires the doors to the
computer room to be locked, it has not adequately controlled
access to adjacent areas. Allowing full access to these areas
leaves the bank vulnerable, especially when the rule
requiring a locked computer room is laxly enforced. It is our
recommendation that the existing rules be enforced more
vigorously, and that access to areas adjacent to the computer
room be controlled, at least to the extent that visitors are
allowed into these areas only on a sign-in basis.
```

In reading the paragraph, notice these things:

- A lot of words with bad connotations are being applied to your client (failure, violation, neglected, inadequate, lax).
- The emphasis is on the negative side (the problem) rather than on the positive side (the solution).

- As a result, the tone of this paragraph is not very objective; it may appear to the client that you're being intentionally negative and hostile.

Revise this paragraph as a section in your report, including a heading or headings as necessary.

3. The management consulting firm where you work has performed some experiments for a client on the effect of varying the speed of an assembly line. One part of the experiment determined the effect of speed variation on the number of finished assemblies rejected by quality control. Here are the results:

At an assembly line speed of 1 foot per minute, 63 units were assembled per hour with a 4.8 percent reject rate, giving a net production rate of 60 units. At 1.5 feet per minute, 94 units were assembled per hour with a 5.3 percent reject rate, giving a net production rate of 89 units. At 2 feet per minute, 126 units were assembled per hour with a 7.1 percent reject rate, giving a net production rate of 117 units. At 2.5 feet per minute, 157 units were assembled with a reject rate of 8.3 percent, giving a net production rate of 144 units. At 3 feet per minute, 189 units were assembled with a reject rate of 13.2 percent, giving a net production rate of 164 units. At 3.5 feet per minute, 220 units were assembled with a reject rate of 20.0 percent, giving a net production rate of 176 units. At 4 feet per minute, 252 units were assembled with a reject rate of 27.8 percent, giving a net production rate of 182 units.

You've been assigned the job of designing the table or graph that will be included in the consulting report to show these results. Include a title and all the labels that should be provided.

4. For your city's Chamber of Commerce, prepare an effective graph or table summarizing your city's retail trade statistics. The following figures are taken from table 4 of the *1977 Census of Retail Trade, Geographic Area Series, [your state]*, which was published in 1980 in Washington, D.C., by the Government Printing Office. The author is United States Bureau of the Census.

Total 1977 sales in the 3147 retail trade establishments in your city were $1,295,066,000; the 2287 establishments with payroll employed 22,734 paid workers for the survey week of March 12. Total sales of the 140 retail establishments in the building materials, hardware, garden supply, and mobile home dealers category were $81,895,000; the 99 establishments with payroll employed 857 paid workers. Total sales of the 74 retail establishments in the general merchandise group stores category were $138,953,000; the 61 establishments with payroll employed an undisclosed number of paid workers. Total sales of the 399 retail establishments in the food stores category were $294,509,000; the 311 establishments with payroll employed 3162 paid workers. Total sales of the 262 retail establishments in the automotive dealers category were $260,853,000; the 189 establishments with payroll employed 2024 paid workers. Total sales of the 330 retail establishments in the gasoline service stations category were $128,164,000; the 292 establishments with payroll employed 1435 paid workers. Total sales of the 207 retail establishments in the apparel and accessory stores category were undisclosed; the 170 establishments with payroll employed an undisclosed number of paid workers. Total sales of the 227 retail establishments in the furniture, home furnishings, and equipment stores were $65,496; the 138 establishments with payroll employed 907 paid workers. Total sales in the 686 retail establishments in the eating and drinking places category were $117,959,000; the 569 establishments with payroll employed 7353 paid workers. Total sales of the 70 retail establishments in the drug and proprietary stores category were undisclosed; the 69 establishments with payroll employed 932 paid workers. Total sales in the 752 retail establishments in the miscellaneous retail stores category were $107,536,000; the 389 establishments with payroll employed 1874 paid workers.

Note that these figures apply to your city's Standard Metropolitan Statistical Area (SMSA), a census area including the city and its surrounding market area. Total sales figures are accurate to the nearest $1000. The Census Bureau does not disclose certain figures when it determines that the figures could be analyzed to determine the sales of a particular establishment.

5. As part of your company's Share-a-Ride program, the Plant Security Department surveyed the cars arriving in the parking lots at the beginning of the main shift last Thursday according to the number of occupants. Here are their results: the number of cars with one occupant was 1621; 2 occupants, 432; 3 occupants, 121; 4 occupants, 57; more than 4 occupants, 108. Format these figures in the most effective way for presentation to the Share-a-Ride steering committee members.

6. For planning purposes, on one day of each month the operator of your company's timesharing computer system records the number of jobs running on the system each hour. Here are the results for Thursday of last week: 1:00 A.M., 13 jobs; 2:00 A.M., 11 jobs; 3:00 A.M., 14 jobs; 4:00 A.M., 15 jobs; 5:00 A.M., 11 jobs; 6:00 A.M., 16 jobs; 7:00 A.M., 22 jobs; 8:00 A.M., 46 jobs; 9:00 A.M., 74 jobs; 10:00 A.M., 79 jobs; 11:00 A.M., 78 jobs; 12:00 noon, 83 jobs; 1:00 P.M., 71 jobs; 2:00 P.M., 84 jobs; 3:00 P.M., 91 jobs; 4:00 P.M., 94 jobs; 5:00 P.M., 95 jobs; 6:00 P.M., 38 jobs; 7:00 P.M., 43 jobs; 8:00 P.M., 47 jobs; 9:00 P.M., 34 jobs; 10:00 P.M., 28 jobs; 11:00 P.M., 33 jobs; 12:00 midnight, 23 jobs. Format these figures in the most effective way, with title and labels, for inclusion in your Information Systems Department monthly report.

7. To help in justifying the addition of a staff member in your legislative liaison section, your boss, the Director of Legal Affairs, has asked you to prepare figures showing the number of bills introduced in your state legislature each year that would directly affect some aspect of your company's operation. Since some interpretation is required to determine whether a given bill would directly affect your company's operations, your figures are only approximate, but you used consistent standards in compiling each one. Here they are:

In 1975, 217 such bills were introduced. In 1976, 184. In 1977, 203. In 1978, 246. In 1979, 210. In 1980, 293. In 1981, 268. In 1982, 297.

Format the figures in the most effective way and present them to your boss in a short report.

8. In some companies, monthly sales figures and other values may fluctuate wildly. For example, monthly sales may be artificially high for the month of April simply because several large sales contracts negotiated over the previous several months all happened to be signed during April. In fact, because salespeople were concentrating on these large-sale negotiations, sales for March may be artificially low. When you summarize changes in such a variable, it is important to reduce the misleading effects of such random variations.

To reduce the misleading effects of such changes, sales figures and other such variables are sometimes reported as 3-month moving averages. Using this method, average sales for months 1-3 are calculated, then average sales for months 2-4, and so on. The result is a graph or table showing these moving averages rather than the specific monthly figures.

Assume your company's monthly sales last year were: January, $44,600,000; February, $39,300,000; March, $28,200,000; April, $61,500,000; May, $43,700,000; June, $45,000,000; July, $33,800,000; August, $97,400,000; September, $84,500,000; October, $131,300,000; November, $51,400,000; December, $89,200,000. Format these figures as moving averages in the most effective way for publication in your company's annual report. Include a title and all needed labels. Assume that your readers understand the concept of moving averages.

9. As assistant to the Comptroller, you have received the following figures from the manager of the retail store your company operates to sell steel-toe shoes and other safety equipment at cost to employees. In 1973, an average of 136 items were sold per week in 51 separate transactions for average weekly gross receipts of $2271.23. In 1974, the weekly averages were 151 items, 56 transactions, $2823.95 gross receipts. In 1975, 151 items, 58 transactions, $3561.67 gross receipts. In 1976, 167 items, 62 transactions, $4061.39 gross receipts. In 1977, 164 items, 62 transactions, $4713.11 gross receipts. In 1978, 171 items, 65 transactions, $5331.83 gross receipts. In 1979, 185 items, 69 transactions, $5781.69 gross receipts. In 1980, 199 items, 73 transactions, $6591.27 gross receipts. In 1981, 203 items, 77 transactions, $7183.05 gross receipts. In 1982, 216 items, 81 transactions, $7974.83 gross receipts.

The manager's memo says that receipts have increased 350 percent during these 10 years, yet the store's sales staff has been increased only from two to three salespeople.

He requests authorization to hire two additional salespeople. You checked his facts against those maintained by Accounting and Personnel and found them correct. Looking them over, you note that while the dollar amount of sales has increased dramatically, the number of trans-actions and the number of items sold have increased at a much lower rate. Your argument is that the increase in sales staff has just kept pace with the increase in work and that no further staff increase is necessary. The great increase in dollar sales volume may be due largely to inflation.

Format the manager's figures in the best way to contrast his argu-ment for two additional salespeople and your argument against them. Present the results in a short report to your boss recommending against the additional positions.

10.   Warehouse 3 is used mainly for long-term storage of bulk production materials. As manager, you keep informal, but accurate, records of the number of materials-handling requests processed by your workers, and you've noticed that your records always include substantially more trans-actions than the monthly computerized materials-handling report indi-cates. (Materials-handling requests are transactions requiring the move-ment of materials into and out of the warehouse, as when materials are received from their manufacturers and put into storage, and when mate-rials are moved from storage to the production plant.) Your figures for last year show January transactions, 3986; February, 3729; March, 4670; April, 5156; May, 5175; June, 4857; July, 5077; August, 5598; September, 7139; October, 7258; November, 7210; and December, 5014. The mate-rials-handling report shows January transactions, 3241; February, 3187; March, 3892; April, 4147; May, 4329; June, 3944; July, 4236; August, 4557; September, 6163; October, 6320; November, 5803; and December, 4144.

In a memo to systems analyst Fred McCortney, Information Systems Department, contrast the two sets of figures and ask for an explanation of the differences.

11.   As Assistant Physical Plant Director, one of your responsibilities is the maintenance of company parking lots, which are heavily over-crowded. At a meeting yesterday on this problem, the Chief of Security pointed out that the present pattern of spaces in the lots was laid out back in 1975 and that the proportion of spaces of each size was determined by a survey of the cars parked in the lot on a typical day according to their size. He brought a copy of the results of that survey showing these figures: of the 2423 motor vehicles parked in the lots on October 10, 1975, 117 were motorcycles; 486 were subcompact cars; 644 were compact cars and trucks; 1107 were full-sized cars, trucks, and vans; and 69 were trucks and campers larger than full-sized. He also brought a copy of the most recent such survey showing these figures: of the 2758 motor vehicles parked in the lots on April 14, 1983, 277 were motorcycles; 943 were subcompact cars; 844 were compact cars and trucks; 595 were full-sized cars, trucks, and vans; and 99 were trucks and campers larger than full-sized. He suggested that more vehicles could probably be accommodated if the pattern of spaces in the lots were changed to reflect the larger number of motorcycles and small cars now parked.

It seems clear from these figures that redesigning and repainting markings in the lots would permit additional spaces. It would require a full study of each lot to determine exactly how many spaces would be gained, and you'd prefer not to do that until the repainting (estimated cost about $4000) is authorized. Format the results of the two surveys in the most effective way for presentation to your boss when you propose this expenditure.

12.   The Thayer Corporation builds large metal cabinets to house radar equipment. Each cabinet, consisting of 40 to 80 precisely machined parts, is built to order to fit a specific electronic assembly manufactured by other companies. Thayer makes a tidy profit on the production of about 100 such cabinets annually. It operates three shops to fabricate the parts.

Hoping to increase production and reduce the rate of rejected parts, the company renovated the main shop in 1978 and the Plant B shop in 1979. Now management is considering renovating the north shop. To help in making the decision, you have gathered figures on total production and number of parts rejected by year from 1973 to 1982 in each shop. (Note that 1978 was the year of the long strike that reduced production and raised the reject rate in all parts of the company.)

In the north shop, 1973 total production was 2423 parts, and quality control inspectors rejected 601 of them. In 1974, total production was 2380 parts with 621 rejects. In 1975, total production was 2516 parts with 546 rejects. In 1976, total production was 2329 parts with 673 rejects. In 1977, total production was 2184 parts with 457 rejects. In 1978, total production was 1319 parts with 386 rejects. In 1979, total production was 2558 parts with 578 rejects. In 1980, total production was 1979 parts with 517 rejects. In 1981, total production was 2368 parts with 526 rejects. In 1982, total production was 2127 parts with 536 rejects.

In the main shop, 1973 total production was 2814 parts, and quality control inspectors rejected 825 of them. In 1974, total production was 2821 parts with 882 rejects. In 1975, total production was 2663 parts with 719 rejects. In 1976, total production was 2903 parts with 810 rejects. In 1977, total production was 2820 parts with 823 rejects. In 1978, total production was 1792 parts with 590 rejects. In 1979, total production was 2870 parts with 548 rejects. In 1980, total production was 2838 parts with

652 rejects. In 1981, total production was 3004 parts with 634 rejects. In 1982, total production was 2776 parts with 660 rejects.

In the Plant B shop, 1973 total production was 1676 parts, and quality control inspectors rejected 349 of them. In 1974, total production was 1785 parts with 409 rejects. In 1975, total production was 1699 parts with 352 rejects. In 1976, total production was 1843 parts with 422 rejects. In 1977, total production was 1727 parts with 361 rejects. In 1978, total production was 935 parts with 231 rejects. In 1979, total production was 1864 parts with 356 rejects. In 1980, total production was 1677 parts with 280 rejects. In 1981, total production was 1725 parts with 278 rejects. In 1982, total production was 1778 parts with 307 rejects.

Present these figures and summarize their implications in a short report. Do not make recommendations, but only present the facts and call attention to their significance.

18

Short Reports

Ther nys no werkman, whatsoevere he be,
That may bothe werke wel and hastily.
Chaucer

To err is human, but when the eraser wears
out before the pencil, you're overdoing it.
J. Jenkins

Learn, compare, collect the facts.
Pavlov

S hort reports are the most common application of the reporting techniques discussed in the previous chapter. In a typical organization, for every long analytical report written, there are scores or even hundreds of short reports. In this chapter, we look at some examples of short reports and consider how to make them as effective as possible.

Your ability to write good short reports will be a valuable asset in your career. Their quality is commonly assumed to represent the quality of your work as a whole. Although your boss will soon become familiar with all aspects of your work, your boss's boss will see your reports much more often than he or she will see you personally. And your boss's boss is the one who must be convinced when the time comes for your raises and promotions.

There's no standard line of demarcation between short and long reports. Typically, reports having fewer than five or six pages are considered short reports. The main difference is that a long report is typically more important than a short one. Reporting projects large enough to uncover and present a great deal of information are usually important, often vital, to the organization. Otherwise, readers (especially, very busy executives) will probably be happier with a short summary-type report, trusting to the writer's intelligence and integrity for accurate condensation.

SHORT REPORT FORMAT

Although short reports sometimes use the formal report format (described in the following chapter), they more often use the letter or memo format. Letter reports are usually intended for audiences outside the organization, and memo reports are usually intended for those inside the organization. Typing a formal title page for a short report can suggest that it's an unusually important message worthy of the attention usually given to a formal report.

A short report differs in purpose from other kinds of letters and memos: It provides complex factual information in an efficient form. Thus letter and memo reports are written in an objective, factual tone, and they use the full range of learning aids discussed in the previous chapter. Headings and summaries are used to help the reader through the complexity of the information, and graphs and tables are used to communicate statistical data quickly and clearly.

Enumeration

In addition, short reports often use enumeration to show how points are related. For example, if a memo-report makes three major points, as in Figure 1, then numbering or lettering them helps the reader to follow and remember them. Often a short report consists almost entirely of a series of numbered paragraphs, similar to military style, sometimes with a few sentences of introduction before the first point. In other cases, enumeration can be used for shorter items that occur within sections.

Date: July 28, 1983

TO: Guenther Tschauner, Director of Information Systems

FROM: LaNelle Billings, ALLOT Project Chief Analyst

SUBJECT: Steps taken at July 27 project meeting

The following actions were taken at Monday's coordination meeting for the ALLOT project:

1. Aline Probst's preliminary draft of the functional specifications was approved in principle by both user and management representatives. A number of revisions were suggested, and Aline will work these into a final draft for approval at the August 10 meeting. It looks like we're finally going to get this document cleared and be able to get on with the design work. Aline deserves commendation for steering this work through the difficulties of the past three months.

2. Ray Hjalmarson's mock-up of the data entry screen displays was demonstrated, and comments were generally positive. Demos should be scheduled now with the order entry and warehouse people. Ray will be checking with you on scheduling.

3. There was some discussion of the target project completion date. At this point we've had three delays, all caused by conflicts between users and management representatives, with our people just watching. But if we don't get the target date set back, we're going to get the blame. Any lobbying you can do at your level to help get this date changed would be appreciated.

Figure 1 A short report with enumerated points

For lists of items, major or minor, enumeration is a good way to increase understanding and retention.

Organization

Most short reports can be organized in the direct plan. In the direct plan, the report's focus is at the beginning, where the main point is stated and the major supporting points are summarized. Usually, the sections of short reports can be organized in the same way, with each section's main point and summary of supporting points at the beginning. A direct-plan short report ends with the last informational section; there's no closing summary or other ending material.

Infrequently, a report's material may not be well suited to the direct plan. Figure 3 in Chapter 10 is an example. If readers will have consider-

August 4, 1983

TO: Harold Thornbee, Plant Director

FROM: Sheila Vargas, Administrative Services

SUBJECT: Air Conditioning System Allows Wide Swings
         of Temperature in Administration Building

The temperatures of offices in the administration building
vary as much as 19 degrees from daytime to nighttime, and as much
as 12 degrees from office to office at the same hour.

To determine the exact temperatures, I placed accurate
recording thermometers in east-facing and west-facing offices
during a period of 90-degree weather in July. Checking the
graphs these automated instruments produced, I found that
temperatures rose from a predawn level of 65 or 66 degrees to a
high of 86 degrees in the west-facing offices in the afternoon.
At the same time, just across the hall, I found the east-facing
office registering only 68 degrees.

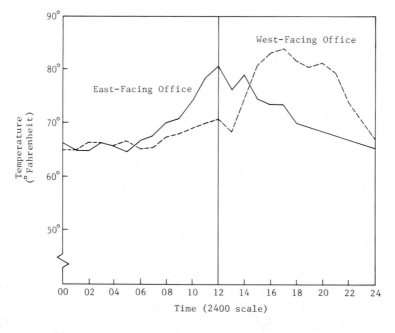

Figure 2 A short analytical report

When I talked to occupants of the building, I found that
the pattern shown in the attached graph is typical. Offices are
typically quite chilly the first thing in the morning, then the
east-facing offices, which get morning sun, begin warming up
quite rapidly, reaching a high of 80 degrees or so just before
noon. The west-facing offices, which are still in shade, warm up
more slowly, reaching only 70 degrees by noon. At noon as people
leave their offices and heat-producing machines are turned off,
temperatures in all offices drop two to four degrees. In the
early afternoon, east-facing offices quickly cool to moderate
temperatures, but west-facing offices, which are now getting full
sun, begin to heat up. Typical afternoon temperatures on sunny
days in these offices reach 82 to 84 degrees; in some cases they
are even higher.

Now that specific information is available about the
seriousness of the problem, I am looking forward to action from
your department to provide a remedy.

Figure 2 (continued)

able emotional resistance to the report's main conclusion or won't understand the subject until it's explained, then consider the indirect plan, even though it's less efficient. In the indirect plan, the opening simply introduces the subject and is followed immediately by the body sections. These sections explain the main idea or present evidence designed to remove emotional resistance through persuasive facts and figures. Then the general summary and conclusions come at the end. Short indirect-plan reports can seem a bit cryptic and hard to follow, since you're asking readers to digest details without giving them the usual introductory learning aids. Even though a report as a whole is organized in the indirect plan, usually most sections can still be organized in the direct plan. As you organize each section, determine whether or not the direct plan would impair clarity. If not, use the direct plan.

In unusual circumstances, one of the less common organizational plans, such as chronological order or the alternative-elimination plan, may fit your material better than the direct or indirect plan. Once in a while, such nonstandard plans are useful, but because they provide fewer learning aids than standard plans do, use nonstandard plans sparingly and carefully.

SHORT ANALYTICAL REPORTS

A short analytical report presents facts and analyzes what they mean to the organization. Sometimes the report recommends that some action be taken in response to these facts. Figure 2 shows a short analytical report.

Planning

Short analytical reports are planned and written in the same way as long analytical reports, which will be discussed in the following chapter. Obviously, the fact gathering, writing, and revising tasks will be simpler for a short report. Unfortunately, the planning stage isn't very much simpler. Analyzing the audience, defining and refining the problem and goal statements, specifying the audience's decision criteria, and determining the major points take almost as much time whether the report is long or short. In short reports, you'll often be sorely tempted to skimp on the planning, but that's false economy. A hastily planned report isn't likely to be effective.

Since the direct plan is the most efficient organizational plan, use it unless there are compelling reasons not to. Begin planning your organization by determining what your report's main point is. Your key recommendation, if any, is often the main point. If the report doesn't include recommendations, then your most central factual conclusion is usually the main point. In either case, consider the readers' needs and interests, since they see the situation differently than you do.

Next, plan the rest of the report around the main point. Identify the three or four most important points that support it and make those the major subdivisions, then identify the key supporting points for each of those subdivisions, and so on until you've fitted all your material together.

Even though the report may only be two or three pages long, use the full range of learning aids to help the reader understand it. Since it's short, the reader will assume it's simple and straightforward, but even two or three pages will provide a lot of material to master. The better your learning aids, the better the reader's understanding will be.

The Beginning

Ironically, one of the most important results of your careful direct-plan organization and learning aids is that the readers probably won't have to read the whole report. This comes as a shock to the beginning report writer, but it does make sense. Once readers discover your key ideas at the beginning of the report, they can quit reading if they feel satisfied. The rest is only supporting material. Therefore, they'll read further only if they want more details or specific evidence for certain points.

As a result, the opening summary and the graphs and tables are the places to concentrate your greatest time and attention. Those parts must reflect the remaining content accurately. Since typical readers read the first page or so and then look at the figures, those parts must quickly convey the same information readers would get if they read every word in the report.

That requires careful planning. And it also requires that the body be written first, so that you're completely sure of what you're summarizing when you write the opening summary. No matter how carefully you plan, often you'll still see new ideas and relationships in the material as you write the first draft. Thus, wait and see exactly what the body says before you summarize it.

A good agenda for the writing stage is as follows. First, construct all the graphs and tables, since the body will probably be organized around them. Then draft the body sections, one at a time; first draft the text of a section, then its opening summary, then its heading. Finally, draft the opening summary of the whole report and then the title. If you can, construct a title that communicates the report's central point in just a few words.

PROPOSALS AND JUSTIFICATION REPORTS

A proposal recommends a certain action and offers reasons for it, as illustrated in Figure 3. A justification report, as in Figure 4, offers reasons for an action that's already been proposed. These two types of reports are therefore very similar. In both, the writer is assumed to favor the recommended action, and the report's purpose is assumed to be persuasive, although a special kind of persuasion is involved. As with a job application résumé, readers realize that the writer is advocating an action, but instead of emotional arguments they expect objective ones based on facts and figures.

Planning

Therefore, a key question in the planning stage is what kind of evidence will be persuasive. For instance, objective analysis that shows cost savings is often persuasive and relatively easy to explain. Analysis that shows improved organizational performance is also likely to be persuasive.

In thinking about kinds of evidence, consider the reader's prior knowledge and preconceptions. Often, the readers already believe the action should be taken, and the purpose of the proposal or justification is to explain exactly how the action should be undertaken and document its rationale in facts and figures. In such cases, the report's main goal is to provide a paper record of how and why an action should be taken. It's important, even in these cases, to be sure that evidence is planned carefully, if only to forestall last-minute doubts and objections among readers.

In other cases, proposals and justification reports must persuade readers to act by overcoming their resistance and objections. For example, sometimes two or three competing proposals are written or action is recommended that readers may not initially agree with. Here the need for careful audience analysis and planning of evidence is obvious. The planning is the critical stage.

September 15, 1983

TO: Ms. Elva Haskins, Director of Personnel

FROM: Ernest Crawford, Public Affairs Officer

SUBJECT: Recommendations for Action Concerning Proposed
        Health Benefits Law

The concerns you expressed in the Executive Committee
meeting last Friday about the potential adverse effects of
Assembly Bill 482 on our present staff health-maintenance program
appear well founded. If this bill is passed into law in its
present form, we will be forced to discontinue our effective
program of preventive health care. Although the legislative
sponsors of the bill apparently did not intend this result, we
should take action to encourage the necessary changes in the bill
before final passage. I recommend three courses of action:

1. We should encourage employees and their families and
   friends to write to the involved legislators about this
   problem. A list of those legislators is attached. To
   assist the writers, we should furnish a low-key summary
   of the facts, pointing out the value of our program and
   the problem posed by Assembly Bill 482. Space for this
   purpose can be reserved in next week's staff newsletter.

2. We should send a representative to the capitol to testify
   and file a written statement concerning this issue. A
   hearing on Assembly Bill 482 will be held at 10:00 a.m.
   on Monday, October 4.

3. We should issue a press release, including a copy of our
   statement before the hearing panel, for publication
   following the hearing. The press is often interested in
   health matters and may help in disseminating information
   about the problem.

The legislative statement and the press release should be a
joint effort of the public affairs office and the legal
department, using facts provided by your office. Once the facts
are assembled, I will be glad to draft a summary for the staff
newsletter.

I believe that immediate action on this problem is
essential. Can you provide the necessary factual information
early next week?

Figure 3 A proposal

July 11, 1983

TO: Purchasing Department

FROM: Neil Townsend, Training Department

SUBJECT: Justification for Purchase of Stanton Roller Tables

The Stanton Roller Tables we requisitioned June 17 will provide a significant improvement in the Training Department's use of audio-visual equipment in our training programs.

Many of our presentations involve the use of several pieces of electronic equipment, including multiple slide projectors and audio equipment. In some cases, as many as six or seven different units must be plugged together, tested, and synchronized before the presentation begins. With the Stanton Roller Tables, instructors will be able to assemble and test their presentation equipment in their offices and then wheel it into a conference room for ready use. Preparing equipment away from the conference room eliminates the need for hurried setup in front of an assembling audience, with the attendant danger of mistakes and delays. It also frees the instructor to confer informally with members of the training group before session, a valuable opportunity.

The Stanton tables appear to meet our needs quite adequately at a moderate cost. Trials by our staff show that their two 18-inch by 24-inch shelves are sufficient to carry all the equipment we normally use, and the 25-inch height of the top shelf is ideal for audio speakers for a seated audience and for transparency projection equipment. The 4-inch wheels on these tables will make them much more stable and less subject to tipping--with loss of expensive equipment--than standard roller tables with smaller wheels. In addition, the fiberglass construction provides greater strength and less weight than comparable metal units. If the Stanton tables are not available, an alternative with these qualities should be sought.

Figure 4 A justification report

Organizing

In proposals and justifications, the benefits of the recommended action should be emphasized. The main arguments should be arranged with the most persuasive one first, so that additional arguments further secure the reader's growing agreement.

Unless your audience analysis indicates an actively hostile audience or one that won't understand what you're talking about, organize the report in the direct plan. This means putting the recommendation and the summary of evidence at the beginning. Even at that point, try to focus on the benefits of the action, possibly with an opening like this: "To (obtain such-and-such benefit), I recommend that we (take such-and-such action)." After this opening, continue focusing on the benefits. Leave further discussion of the proposed action until somewhat later in the report.

In many proposals and justifications, a major part of the content is a detailed description of how the action should be taken. Often, for example, anticipated problems could be avoided if the action is performed in a certain way. In fact, sometimes this material is even more important than the facts and figures supporting the recommendation, as in a proposal that must describe the proposed project's scope and methods in great detail. Unless such descriptive material is very lengthy and detailed, it can often be integrated into sections that are organized around benefits. But if necessary, the sections could be organized around the descriptive material.

There should be little or no ending material in most direct-plan proposals or justifications. Unless the rest of the report has grown so long (more than 10–12 pages) that a closing summary is needed as a learning aid, all the summary material should come at the beginning. When you reach the end of the final body section, simply stop there.

Writing Research Proposals

When a proposed research project will require a long report, it's common for the researcher to write a short proposal early, after a preliminary investigation. This short report describes why the proposed research should be undertaken, what its scope and goals will be, and how much it will cost. The main goals of the proposal are to justify the required time and money and the project's goals to the decision makers who will use the resulting long report. If the proposal is approved, then the project can proceed.

Commonly, the project's benefits are so clearly understood that the proposal subordinates them to the descriptive material. Often the title provides the main direct reference to benefits; in the proposal itself, benefits are so closely identified with the project's goals that they require little space.

Although the exact format for such a proposal may vary across organizations, it's typically a memo with the subject line "Proposal for a Study of [such-and-such problem]." The sections used in Figure 5 are typical.

Background of the problem   The background section discusses the conditions that gave rise to the problem and provided the context for your research. A good technique is to imagine that the reader is generally knowledgeable about business but has no previous knowledge of your organization or this problem. If you can then explain the problem's background clearly and briefly, you're sure to include the information the reader needs to assess your understanding of the problem.

In doing this, you'll certainly be mentioning some things that the reader already knows. The purpose of the background section, though, is to show how you perceive the context of the present problem, and this section often draws comments from the reader that clarify the problem and help focus your work. In addition, this section is useful to those who will come across your project report later, when the context is no longer clearly remembered.

Statement of the problem The statement of the problem formally defines the problem. Very often, the problem is that the organization lacks the information needed to make a decision or lacks the plan needed to take effective action. The problem statement, then, describes the needed information or plan.

Project goal The goal section describes the project's outcome as clearly as possible. You're reporting after only a quick preliminary investigation, so you shouldn't even hint at what the findings may be, but you should be able to describe their nature—what topics the findings will cover. In addition, this section should include one key sentence specifying the kind of major recommendations, if any, that the final report will make. For example, if the project's goal is to recommend whether or not to purchase a new machine, then this sentence would indicate that such a recommendation will be made.

Research plan The research plan section describes how you plan to gather information. It's sometimes entitled "Scope," since the research plan describes the scope of the research and its limitations. Unless you're specifically asked to detail the research plan, keep it general. If you're going to consult several experts, visit several prospective locations, or survey 2000 local residents by mail, that's about all the detail most readers will want. More detail would only burden them.

In the planning stage, consider information-gathering methods that would occur to any intelligent reader. In a location study, for instance, nearly anyone would think of visiting the prospective sites. If you don't intend to take such obvious steps, then your research plan should say so, and it should probably briefly explain why.

Project cost The cost section estimates the project's cost, most of which will often be the researchers' salaries. Estimate the number of hours each step in the research plan will require and add the cost of clerical help and other dollar costs. Also break the costs down somewhat to show how the total cost was derived and why that total is justified.

PROGRESS REPORTS

In most organizations, periodic project reports are required for activities organized as special projects. Such projects often include new product development, government contracts, system development, and major

January 4, 1983

TO: Ms. Wanda Wise, Director of Corporate Development
    Black Shoe Company

FROM: Thomas Winston, Project Manager
      Baxter and Burstein, Management Consultants, Inc.

SUBJECT: Proposal for a Study of Fresno SMSA and Bakersfield SMSA
         as Possible Locations for a New Black Shoe Store

Background

    The Black Shoe Company manufactures and markets men's dress
shoes in the 70-100 dollar price range. Styles are generally
conservative. The shoes are very well made and are entirely
repairable, making them unique in today's men's shoe market.

    The Black Shoe Company operates its own retail outlets, an
unusual phenomenon in the shoe industry. Most of the stores are
located in the East and Midwest, but the company is interested in
further expansion in the state of California. Present California
stores are located in Los Angeles, San Francisco, San Diego, and
Sacramento, the four largest market areas in the state.

    The company would like to open a new store in one of the
state's smaller market areas. Such a store would not only
increase the company's sales, but it would also serve as a test
case to help determine the feasibility of further expansion into
other smaller California market areas. The cities of Fresno and
Bakersfield have been selected by the company as alternative
locations for the new store.

Statement of the Problem

    The problem is that the company lacks the information
necessary to make a comparison between Fresno and Bakersfield as
potential market areas. Although the populations of the Fresno
and Bakersfield SMSAs are comparable, at 515,013 and 403,089,
respectively, little is known about the specific market
potentials of the two areas for Black Shoes. (The SMSA, or
Standard Metropolitan Statistical Area, is a geographical unit
used by the Census Bureau and others in market studies. The
Fresno SMSA includes all of Fresno County, and the Bakersfield
SMSA includes all of Kern County, where Bakersfield is located.)

    Information is needed to compare the relative potential of
the markets in Fresno and Bakersfield for conservative men's
dress shoes in a relatively high price range. Information is
also needed about the present level of competition in the men's
shoe business in the two markets. Finally, since this new store
will serve as a test of the market for Black Shoes in
medium-sized California SMSAs, information is needed to make

Figure 5 A research proposal

comparisons between Fresno and Bakersfield and other smaller California market areas.

Goal of the Project

The goal of this study is to provide a recommendation, supported by statistical information, of either Fresno or Bakersfield as the better location for a new Black Shoe store. Information in support of this recommendation will be drawn from published statistics and other sources available locally. Following an evaluation of the material in this study, the company may wish to arrange for an on-site investigation of the two cities, but such an investigation will not be included in this study.

Research Plan

The information presented in this report will be gathered entirely from publications of the United States Census Bureau, the Department of Commerce, and other sources that may be located during the course of the investigation. Since only preliminary reports of the 1980 Census of the Population are now available, most Census information will be taken from earlier reports.

Such information will support a preliminary recommendation of the better location for the new store and will serve as an excellent background to any subsequent on-site investigation of the two cities that may be commissioned. Since local libraries have excellent collections of governmental publications and other reference materials, no travel will be necessary in this study.

The Cost of the Project

Because of the nature of this problem, the only item of cost is the hourly billing for the researcher's time. The following rough estimates will indicate tentatively the cost of the project:

Preliminary planning and interviews with Black Shoe Company personnel	5 hours
Investigation of Census Bureau sources of information	10 hours
Investigation of other published sources of information	10 hours
Preparation of graphic materials	5 hours
Preparation of final report	10 hours
Presentation of report to Black Shoe Company	5 hours
Total	45 hours

At an average billing rate of $75.00 an hour, the total cost of this project is estimated at $3375.00.

Figure 5 (continued)

12 January 1983

TO: Elizabeth Linnington
    Vice-President for Information Systems

FROM: Luis Mendoza, Project Coordinator
      Cyber Installation Project

SUBJECT: Progress of Cyber Installation

In the fourth quarter of 1982, phase one of the installation of the new Control Data Corporation Cyber 174 computer was completed on schedule. The installation team expects the installation to be completed by April 1, as planned.

All wiring, flooring, and ductwork is now completed in the new computer room, and the water cooling system has been installed. Site preparation for the Remote Job Entry terminals in the Engineering Building and in Plant Four is completed, and several pieces of equipment have been delivered to these sites slightly ahead of schedule.

According to the Expediting Department, Control Data Corporation indicates that delivery of the computer and major peripheral equipment may be anticipated on schedule. The supplier of our power conditioning unit has indicated that delivery will be about two weeks behind schedule, but installation of that unit on schedule is not a critical requirement, and we anticipate no delay in phase two because of it.

Figure 6 A progress report

written reports. In a progress report, the project director is expected to discuss progress in relation to the official schedule, special problems that may affect deadlines or goals, and any other special events that should be officially recorded. Figure 6 shows an example. The project proposal, its acceptance, the progress reports, and the final project report constitute the official project history. Together, these documents provide all project information necessary for future reference.

The reader's first question about a progress report is usually whether the project is on or behind schedule, and if behind, how much delay will occur in meeting the schedule checkpoints. Thus, the opening normally centers on this question and briefly summarizes the remaining material in the report. If the project is on schedule and no special problems have arisen, then the progress report may be fairly brief and to the point. For the record, even if the project is on schedule, the progress report usually confirms by title each major schedule checkpoint that's been met since the previous progress report.

If the project is behind schedule or special problems have arisen (as usually happens), the progress report should briefly discuss what has happened. Discussion of delays and special problems forms the body of most progress reports. If current problems may have future implications for the project, then the progress report should discuss these implications and provide a revised schedule if necessary. In progress reports, it's very tempting to paint a rosy picture of events in hopes that an endangered schedule can be rescued before anyone finds out that it's endangered. In fact this is so tempting that the mythical "Progress Report for Those with No Progress to Report" (Figure 7) gets a chuckle from managers the world over. However, if you can earn a reputation for truthful progress reports, it will help your career.

```
        During the report period that ended [fill in date]
significant progress was made in the preliminary phase of work
directed toward the establishment of the initial activities.
[Meaning:  We are getting ready to start, but we haven't done
anything yet.]  The relevant background literature has been
surveyed, and the functional structure of the component parts of
the cognizant organization has been clarified.  [We looked at the
assignment and decided that Harold should do it.]

        A number of questions have arisen concerning the
optimization of materials and methodologies in the implementation
phase, but this problem is being attacked vigorously, and we
expect that the design phase will proceed satisfactorily.
[Harold is looking through the manual.]  In order to assemble
critical data concerning previous efforts in the same field, it
was necessary to establish a survey team which conducted a rather
extensive tour through various facilities in the immediate
vicinity of the vendor's alpha and beta test sites.  [Harold and
George had a nice time in New York last week.]

        At its regular meeting, the Steering Committee considered
vital policy matters pertaining to the overall organizational
levels of the line and staff responsibilities that devolve on the
personnel associated with the specific assignments resulting from
the broad functional specifications.  [Untranslatable--sorry.]
It is believed that the rate of progress will continue to
accelerate as necessary personnel are recruited to fill vacant
billets.  [We'll get some work done as soon as we find someone
who knows something.]
```

Figure 7 A progress report for those with no progress to report

PERIODIC ADMINISTRATIVE STATUS REPORTS

In many organizations, managers and supervisors must describe developments in their areas in monthly or quarterly status reports to their bosses (Figure 8). Although these reports contain little that their writers haven't already discussed with their bosses, such reports do provide a written record of that material. In this way, ideas for change and development become more official and likely to be binding. And over time, the series of status reports becomes a written history of the area each manager is responsible for. Most managers have continuing responsibility for routine tasks, but they're also expected to take initiative in developing and improving their areas, setting up new systems, recruiting new subordinates and helping them to become promotable, and generally creating more effective and efficient operations. Status reports concentrate on these nonroutine responsibilities.

If you must write status reports, you'll soon develop a set of standard topics corresponding to areas of continuing development you're responsible for. Each time you write a status report, in the planning stage you'll mentally review these topics. In addition, you should recall what you've spent the most time on during the current reporting period; some of those tasks will be worth adding to your list of topics. Before long, throughout each reporting period you'll be making notes of items that your status reports should mention, and then planning these reports will be relatively easy.

STATISTICAL REPORTS

Many reports—such as financial reports and inventory reports—consist simply of large tables of numbers. If you ever design the layout of a statistical report, remember that many of the organizational principles discussed here can be applied to them.

For example, most statistical reports consist of many detailed statistics and a few summary values. To organize such reports in the direct plan, present the summary values at the beginning of the report and the detailed statistics later. In the beginning, present the most general or widely used figures first, and then the less widely used ones. And in each section of the statistics, place the summary material at the beginning.

Of course, certain kinds of accounting and other statistical reports have been presented in a certain way for so long that readers are completely accustomed to that manner of presentation. But when you design new reports, plan them carefully for efficient reading.

                                                    April 11, 1983

TO: Terrence X. Danaher, Administrative Vice-President

FROM: Reba C. Czerny, Expediting Manager

SUBJECT: Expediting Status Report, First Quarter, 1983

        The following major developments took place in the
Expediting Department in the first quarter of 1983:

Staff

        The department has been returned to full staff with the
hiring of Expediter Trainees Esther McFean and Rex Schlosser.
Harold Farland was promoted to Senior Expediter in February.

Revision of Expediting Procedures Manual

        The revised Expediting Procedures Manual is nearly
complete. The final revision should be ready for review by the
Executive Committee at the June meeting. Testing of new
procedures was completed in early March, and staff suggestions
are now being incorporated into the final draft. Special credit
should go to Senior Expediters Mike Jarrett, Roxanna Dunn, and
John Washalosky for their valuable suggestions and criticisms
during this stage of the project.

Changes in Daily Expediting Status Report

        Changes in the format of the Daily Expediting Status Report
required by the new procedures have been made by the Information
Systems Department. The new report structure incorporates
several helpful improvements, and we appreciate the cooperation
of Info Systems in implementing these changes ahead of schedule
to allow us time to test the new form before our revision
deadline.

Future Developments

        During the next quarter, the Expediting Department
anticipates final approval and full implementation of the revised
procedures. In addition, we will be completing the first stage
of planning for the move to the fourth floor planned for the
first quarter of next year.

Figure 8 A periodic status report

FURTHER EXPLORATION

1.   What are the differences between short reports and the usual kinds of correspondence? Specify at least six kinds of differences.

2.   Obtain copies of several short business reports for analysis. In each, go through and underline each specific fact the first time it's presented. Most of the remaining material in the report (the part not underlined) should consist of learning aids. What kinds of learning aids did the authors use? Can these aids be adapted to your writing?

3.   What are the differences between persuasive reports (proposals, justifications, and résumés) and the persuasive letters discussed in earlier chapters? Specify at least six kinds of differences.

4.   Do you know of other folklore examples of business writing such as the "Progress Report for Those with No Progress to Report"? Often such humorous materials are reproduced by office copier and passed from person to person, and they sometimes achieve national circulation. What can you learn from the examples you've seen?

WRITING PROBLEMS

1.   Sit in for Professor A. Louis Solof, Chemistry Department. Recently, hijinks in the lab above your office led to leakage of a colorful (but harmless) fluid through your ceiling and down the wall. As part of the cleaning up, painters came and repainted the wall, but the fluid has proven more powerful—the stain shows through all too clearly.

What you need is something to cover up the spot; you don't like looking at it. A map of the United States would be nice. It would need to be at least 60 inches wide and 38 inches tall to cover the spot. These are minimum dimensions; the map may need to be bigger in one of the dimensions to be big enough in the other, depending on the sizes of maps available.

Write a memo to your dean justifying the cost of the map. You have already tried justifying it simply as a way of covering the spot, unsuccessfully. Your current government grant involves evaluation of a chemical process used in an industry with plants all over the United States. No doubt the research could be carried out successfully without the map, but mapping the distribution of industrial application would make a colorful display. Whatever your justification is, it should be presented as a serious (if not earthshaking) argument.

2.   The "honor" of writing up the minutes of meetings of the city Chamber of Commerce Program Committee rotates among members from meeting to meeting. It was your turn at last evening's meeting. Your notes:

- Meeting called to order 7:32 P.M. in Chamber Council Room.
- Present: John Alksne, Sharon Nicochea, Jess Viray, R. Duarte Mateus, Susan Garfin, Chairperson Mary E. Annable, Lincoln Kershaw, Reva L. Comer, and me. Ervan Clegg was excused (notified chairperson in advance); Marlene J. Irion absent without excuse. Dr. J. Oscar Herrero, Unified Community College District, seated as guest by consent of members present.
- Minutes of last month's meeting accepted.
- Viray reported plans for next month's Chamber meeting program. County Planning Board Staff Director Bruce Jaeschke will discuss growth trends in area and answer questions. Current Planning Board recommendations as reported in press may stimulate many questions.
- To allow him to meet another scheduled commitment, Dr. Herrero next discussed District's faculty speaker's bureau, a list of instructors who volunteered to speak on areas of expertise. List changes from time to time with personnel changes and faculty interests. As issues arise, Dr. Herrero attempts to locate speakers. Urged those present to contact him for Chamber meetings and any others. He left meeting.
- Alksne reported negotiations for meeting two months hence with State Senator Alexander "Steve" Krooskos, heading Senate subcommittee holding hearings on budgets for state universities, including local U. Tentative speaker's fee of $100 plus expenses of about $150 for Krooskos moved, seconded, and approved.
- Annable listed assigned meeting responsibilities for next 5 months: 2 months away, Nicochea; then following months in order, Comer, me, Clegg. List moved, seconded, approved.
- Lengthy discussion of arrangements for annual Chamber banquet. Kershaw accepted position of chairperson, with Mateus and Clegg to serve as nucleus of banquet committee; others to be recruited from Chamber membership. Moved, seconded, approved. Kershaw will report tentative banquet date and full committee membership at next meeting.
- No further items of business. Adjourned 8:54 P.M.

Use the current calendar to name months mentioned. Many minutes are unnecessarily stiff and formal. State actions clearly and precisely, and keep it readable.

3. Your company belongs to a trade association that tries to arbitrate disputes between business people and the public. Executives of various companies are asked to sit on three-person panels from time to time. Usually your boss serves as representative of your company, but this time he must send you instead. This evening's dispute involves James Froscher, a customer, against Welber's Sound Store.

Mr. Froscher claims that Welber's overcharged him for a Suhatsu model 367 stereo system. "I heard that the Suhatsu system had a lot of special features. So I went to Welber's and asked about it. The clerk demonstrated it. It sounded great, so I bought it. The price was $1480, and I paid $290 down and signed a contract to pay $85 a month.

"Two days later I passed another stereo store and saw this very same model of Suhatsu priced at only $1160. So I went around to a couple of other stores. One had it for $1120, another for $1175. Then I went back to Welber's and told them I wanted a refund. They refused. I don't think it's right for them to charge about $300 more than other stores in the same part of town are asking. They should reduce their price by $300.

Mr. Welber disagreed. "Our price for the system Mr. Froscher bought is based on a percentage markup over cost that we have used for years. In some cases our prices are higher than our competition, in some cases lower. Our store has a right to charge whatever it chooses. Mr. Froscher is an adult; he wasn't forced or coerced in any way. He could easily have shopped around. It's his own fault that he failed to compare prices and shop where he felt he could get the best deal. After all, you don't quarrel with one supermarket if you pay 99 cents for an eggplant and later find the same item selling at another store for only 64 cents."

Following the hearing, each panel member writes a brief report summarizing the facts of the situation and proposing a solution to the problem. Several days later, the panel members meet, discuss the three reports, and agree on a joint proposal. Write your report. You may propose accepting Mr. Froscher's proposal or Mr. Welber's, or you may propose a compromise.

4.   Central Professional Publishers, Inc., is one of the best-known publishers of books for lawyers, having established a solid regional reputation for accuracy and authority. Their publications include tape recordings, and they run seminars for lawyers in all regions of the country. They have been very successful in these activities, with gross annual revenues of about 10 million dollars—quite exceptional in this type of publishing.

For the last two years, the company has been feeling the impact of increased competition, and they have retained your advertising firm to recommend methods of increasing the impact of their advertising. They send dozens of mailings—leaflets, catalogs, and letters—a year to about 125,000 lawyers in the region. Your review of last year's mailings reveals that the language is pretty stodgy, lifeless, and unexciting. The material is written by a Central Professional editor who has no particular background in advertising copywriting. In addition, the graphics and design lack sparkle and zing. Therefore, you recommend that they engage a professional advertising person to prepare final copy and aid in design and graphics.

While Central Professional is very active in advertising to the 125,000 present lawyers in the region, most of the 50,000 students in the region's law schools have never heard of the company since it publishes no textbooks. These students are the future buyers. Basic advertising principles suggest that the company should be building recognition and confidence among them. You recommend:

- Establishing an annual award in each regional law school for moot court excellence, an outstanding law journal article, or some other distinguished achievement; multiple winners should be awarded plaques at a well-publicized annual dinner attended by Central Professional executives.
- Publishing a Central Law Student Reporter, an 8 to 10 page newsletter of book information and articles of interest to law students (interviews with major law firms on the regional job market and what qualities they're looking for, opportunities in small towns, student letters, and so on), and distributing copies in bulk to each regional law school.

Write your final report. Your agency can provide professional services in copy preparation and design, if Central Professional prefers, but your recommendation is that they hire a full-time person in this area.

5. When you submitted a requisition to the Purchasing Department for a $330 program for your Investment Section's microcomputer, you expected the purchase to be routinely processed. Today you got a memo saying that all software must be approved by the Information Systems Department, probably a leftover regulation from the days when all software was for use on that department's large computer and cost many thousands of dollars. In any case, you must write a justification for your purchase.

- The program is named Wizard Spread Planner.
- It is an automated spread-sheet system used in financial planning.
- It is one of the most widely used programs available for microcomputers.
- You'll use it for various kinds of planning and projections in your department's investment programs.
- You have already obtained a user's manual for the program.
- You have ordered the version that runs on your Digiproc 3200 microcomputer (company ID#3822403).
- The version you ordered is compatible with the ConPro/Micro operating system that you now use.
- Two staff members have experience with this program where they previously worked, and they recommend it highly.

- You have already arranged to send one staff member to a seminar in Seattle early next month to develop enough expertise with the program to operate it effectively.
- Data files created and used by the program are compatible with those of your present word processing, graphics, and data communications software.
- You believe this program's purchase is very important to your department's operation.
- You understand that no further software is needed to make effective use of this program.
- As far as you could determine, no other department in your company is now using this program.

Address your justification to the Purchasing Department; they will pass it on to the Director of Information Systems for approval of the purchase.

6.   Prepare a monthly progress report for a new product under development, the "Cavalry" project, which is your responsibility.

- The first stage of consumer testing showed that the fasteners were not strong enough.
- New fasteners have been devised.
- The fastener attachments have been redesigned to be stronger.
- The changes will add 3/10 of a cent to the production unit cost.
- The redesign delayed the project one week.
- The project was three weeks behind schedule at start of period, and is now four weeks behind schedule.
- There is apparently no way to make up this time.
- No other problems surfaced in the first stage of consumer testing.
- Stage two of consumer testing is scheduled to begin late next week.

7.   As a management trainee for a chain of fast-food restaurants, you're assigned to assist Frank Fletcher, Customer Relations Manager, whose main responsibility is to encourage restaurant managers to become more customer-oriented. To help identify problem areas, Mr. Fletcher has asked you to visit certain of the chain's restaurants as a customer and to report your observations in three areas:

- The overall cleanliness of the customer areas of the restaurant and the kitchen areas visible to customers
- The cleanliness of the rest rooms
- The pleasantness and helpfulness of the staff

Mr. Fletcher wants you to report both positive and negative observations.

*For this assignment, spend at least 20 minutes in a fast-food res-
taurant observing the three areas noted above. Make at least one out-
of-the-ordinary request, such as asking a counter person to change a
dollar bill or to give you directions to some place. Also observe the staff's
interactions with other customers. Report your observations.*

8. As a management trainee in the regional distribution center of a
large supermarket chain, you're assigned to assist Marketing Director
Lorinda Holmes. One of your jobs is to maintain records of competitors'
pricing practices. Each week you are given a list of at least twelve specific
items, and by visiting competitor's stores and checking the shelves you
determine each competitor's prices for those items. Your report provides
the results in a format that allows efficient comparison. The items selected
always include at least:

- One produce item (lettuce, apples, tomatoes)
- One bulk meat item (hamburger, pork roast, chicken parts)
- One packaged meat item (bacon, luncheon meat, sausage)
- One canned fruit or fruit juice item (orange juice, applesauce)
- One canned vegetable (red beans, tomatoes, beets)
- One fresh bread item (bread, rolls, buns)
- One paper product (paper towels, napkins)
- One kitchen cleaning item (dishwasher detergent, copper cleaning
  pads)
- One laundry item (detergent, bleach, fabric softener)
- One breakfast cereal item (oatmeal, dry cereal)

*For this assignment, select at least 12 items including all 10 cate-
gories listed above. Select specific brand-name items, where applicable,
and specify exact package sizes. Determine ahead of time what to do if
a store doesn't carry the brand or package size you have listed. Compare
prices in at least three local supermarkets. Report the results.*

9. In the last three months, your personnel department processed 931
applications for hourly-paid jobs and 615 applications for salaried jobs. In
that time 143 hourly-paid workers were hired, and 22 salaried employees
were hired. You processed 210 resignations and terminations. The company gained one tenth of one percent toward its equal opportunity and
affirmative action goals for hourly-paid workers, and remained even with
the previous figure for salaried employees. Of the 51 employees whose
jobs were eliminated in the current cost-reduction program, you arranged
relocation for 33 but could not arrange relocation for the remaining 18,
who have been given rehire priority A.

Since this is the first quarter of the cost-reduction program, you
developed procedures for relocation of employees whose jobs are elimi-

nated. John Verderosa worked very effectively with all four unions to negotiate an acceptable procedure; all appear satisfied, and there have been no grievances from the 18 employees laid off in this quarter.

In the cost reduction, the personnel department lost one secretarial position. Two secretarial employees resigned during the quarter; one clerk-typist was promoted to secretary, and her former position was quickly filled. The other vacated secretarial position was eliminated.

A review of the effects of the current cost-reduction program is being conducted by Art Frias and Claudia Noel. Their report, which will propose major changes in personnel information systems, should be presented early next month. Art and Claudia mentioned that the Information Systems Department obviously wants to minimize such changes, and there may be some conflict about this.

As Director of Personnel, write your quarterly administrative status report to your boss, Administrative Vice-President Roberta Duran. The figures on applications, new hires, resignations and terminations, progress toward equal opportunity and affirmative action goals, and relocation of employees in eliminated positions are included in every quarterly report you write, and until now you've always presented them in sentence form. Devise a more efficient way of formatting those figures that you could continue to use in future quarterly status reports.

10. Revise the following report.

```
DATE: May 3, 1983
TO: Evelyn M. Faurote, Comptroller's Office
FROM: Loren Kathol, Vehicle Maintenance
SUBJECT: REPLY TO MEMO OF 3/19/83
```

This is in reply to your memo of 19 March in which you stated an inquiry regarding total miles traveled by company vehicles per month during the latter quarter of the last year. Upon receipt of your memo, Vehicle Maintenance instituted a fact-gathering program in this area. Because exact records of vehicle mileage are produced only at maintenance times, it is not possible to provide definitive exact figures. It is, however, possible to provide estimated figures at a fairly high degree of reliability of perhaps plus or minus between 3 to 4 percent for street vehicles. Most mileage may be extrapolated from maintenance records, assuming relatively steady accretion of miles between maintenance intervals. All auto mileage, except for rare cases when odometers are broken (none in this period), can be estimated to a high degree of accuracy this way. Street truck mileage can be estimated in the same way to the same standards of accuracy. Mileage of workyard vehicles is somewhat more difficult to estimate. Few of these vehicles have odometers; some have timeclocks for recording operating hours. Estimates were made for each of the 31 tractors, forklifts, yard vans, and motorized cranes by logging hours of operation for each vehicle for 30 days and taking five samples of 60 minutes of operation for each during that 30 days and measuring distance traveled by hand. It should be borne in mind that this procedure, though time-consuming, provides only a rough guide to actual mileage. I would reckon accuracy at plus or minus 20 percent. Vehicles remaining are small motorcycles and motor scooters. Mileage for these units may be estimated at a rather high degree of accuracy by interpolation from maintenance records.

Auto mileage, fourth quarter last year, is estimated at 274,991 miles. Street truck mileage is estimated at 177,590 miles. Yard vehicle mileage is estimated at 6052 miles. Motorcycle/motor-scooter mileage is estimated at 13,883 miles.

Total miles traveled by company motor vehicles during the final quarter of last year was 472,516 miles.

Consideration was given to breaking this total down by month as you requested. Since maintenance provides firm data at intervals that are normally longer time intervals than one calendar month, the most accurate estimates that could be made of vehicle mileages per month would be drawn by dividing the quarterly mileage by three, for a total of 157,505.33 miles per month. Wide tolerance should be allowed this figure if quoted on a month-by-month basis, since there appear to be fluctuations in vehicle mileage of substantial magnitude from month to month. Refining the present mileage estimate to provide a high degree of accuracy month by month would require new data collection procedures, probably a substantial financial investment.

It should be noted that none of the above includes mileage of nonmotorized company vehicles: bicycles, tool carts, carryall wagons, two-wheel hand trucks, etc. All of these were assumed to be outside the scope of the present request for figures.

Consider this office at your disposal should requirement for additional figures or further elaboration of the present figures arise.

11.   Your boss, Administrative Vice-President Ruth H. Kinsig, has been concerned that people in purchasing, expediting, engineering, and other departments who use long-distance communications services aren't really aware of the relative costs of the various means of communication. She has asked you to look into costs of sending written messages by the various means of transmission and to prepare for her signature a report to all employees who use these services.

After some investigation you have noted that while the actual costs of sending messages on these systems increases from time to time, relative costs tend to remain fairly stable, so you have decided to provide information as of August 1979, for which you happen to have a convenient source of figures. In addition, to keep the comparison simple, you have decided to compare costs from San Diego (your company headquarters) to New York City, a typical destination. You will want to note these points in your memo.

- A first class letter costs 15 cents to mail if it is of normal letter length. Delivery to NYC normally takes about a week.
- TWX to TWX is, for all practical purposes, instant communication. (TWX is teletypewriter transmission by telephone line, so the transmission itself is instant, but it takes a short time to prepare a TWX message for TWX transmission.) Transmission to NYC costs 75 cents for a message of 50 words, $1.50 for 200 words, and $3.75 for 500 words. TWX to TWX transmission is possible only when the destination company also has TWX service. A directory lists eligible recipients.
- Telex to Telex communication is also instant, working like TWX. It costs 55 cents to transmit 50 words to NYC, $1.80 for 200 words, and $4.50 for 500 words. Available only when recipient has Telex service; check the directory.
- Mailgram service uses TWX or Telex facilities to transmit messages electronically to the city of delivery, where they are printed and delivered in the next day's business mail. Rates are the TWX or Telex rates to the city of delivery plus 95 cents per message for handling and mail delivery.
- A telegram is delivered in about two hours during a business day to a business address. Fifty words are transmitted for $9.15, 200 words for $21.15, and 500 words for $45.15.

The goal of your memo is simply to provide information to readers who have probably never thought much about the relative costs of sending messages. It will probably be most effective to let each reader draw his or her own conclusions. Notice that it is fairly difficult to make comparisons when the information is presented in normal paragraph form. Devise the most efficient way of presenting your findings.

12. Analyze the five replies you received from advertisers when you wrote them for further information in Problem 3, following Chapter 11. Consider at least these questions.

- Did the reply answer your questions completely and adequately?
- If sales materials were enclosed, did you find them persuasive or not? Why?

- Do you now have the information you need to decide whether to buy the product?
- Did the reply convey an appropriate image of the company and its products? Consider grammar, English mechanics, and typing format in addition to other areas here.

Submit your analysis in a report to your instructor, attaching copies of your original inquiries and the replies you received.

13.   Arrange to interview an executive in a medium-sized or large organization about the value of communication in that organization and about the communication problems he or she faces as an executive. Be prepared to ask questions about the specific communication skills he or she thinks young people in business should have and about the ways he or she solves organizational communication problems. Before the interview, assemble a list of good questions, phrasing them to avoid simple Yes or No answers; you want to encourage the executive to do the talking.

As part of the interview, ask the executive to give you at least three samples of letters his or her company has sent or received. Try to get business correspondence other than advertising or routine billing letters. (Invite him or her to remove any identifying marks.) And ask the executive to describe the situation in which each letter was written.

In a short report to your instructor, report on the interview. Provide a clear summary of what your interviewee said and the attitudes he or she revealed during the interview. Structure your report around the major points of interest; a chronological account of the meeting will probably be neither informative nor interesting. As part of your report, present and discuss the letters the executive gave you, evaluating them in terms of the principles you have learned in this book. Be specific in your evaluation; go well beyond an overall good or bad evaluation to discuss specific good points and bad points.

Your instructor may ask you to work with one or two other students on this assignment. If so, your group will conduct a joint interview with an executive and then work together to produce a single report incorporating the ideas of all the members of your group. In evaluating your report, the instructor will assign equal credit to each group member, so make sure each member contributes to the project.

14.   The Dempsey Brothers Discount Store operates in a leased one-story building. It pays a rental fee of $3000 a month, and this cost is prorated among the various sales departments on the basis of floor space.

The department handling garden supplies and equipment has been put under scrutiny by the sales manager. A typical monthly operating statement of this department shows the following:

Sales			$1335
Less cost of merchandise			780
			$ 555

Direct Expenses:			
Salesperson's wages	$390		
Advertising	45		
		$435	

Indirect Expenses:			
Rent	$225		
Misc. overhead	40		
		265	
		$700	700
Net Loss			($ 145)

Also there is a storage problem in the pet department, which is adjacent to the garden department. If the latter were eliminated, sacks of dog food and fish tanks could be stored conveniently out of the way of customer traffic.

Mr. Jerome Dempsey, owner of Dempsey Brothers, has asked you, his accountant, to verify the wisdom of this supposition. Your interpretation of the facts is this: As long as the garden department produces enough income to cover all its direct expenses and some of the overhead on the space it occupies (rent and miscellaneous) it is much wiser to keep it in operation than to covert the area to dead storage that won't produce income or pay any overhead at all.

Remember as you write your report to Mr. Dempsey that he has prided himself on his ability to develop a store in which every single department worked on a pay-as-you-go basis. In fact, decisions to fire or demote personnel have often been based on the ability of a department manager to show a profit in his department. Your analysis of the pet department is based on a somewhat different set of suppositions than Mr. Dempsey has followed in the past. Would indirect order help?

15. You were recently hired as an administrative assistant in a small insurance brokerage office. One evening at a party, you ran into Charles Welcome and Bill Li, old college friends who were top students in chemistry and electronics. They said that they are now working for an electronics firm but intend to quit soon and start their own business. They have invented a medical diagnostic device, which they have tested, patented, and now have a backlog of orders for. The device is expensive—$11,000 for the central unit, plus a number of accessories.

They next day they stopped in at your office to talk further about the new business. "We'll be buying most of the components from other manufacturers," they told you. "But the key module is a small unit we'll put together ourselves, partly because no one else makes just what we need, partly so we can ensure secrecy. We'll employ 12 people to start and have worked out a system so that no one of those 12 people will have access to the complete design. As each machine is completed, it will be crated and delivered to the carrier at our shipping door. One of us will travel to the hospital or clinic site and supervise the setting up of the equipment where it will be used. That way we'll be sure it's in good operating condition.

"Since you're now in the insurance business, we thought you might tell us what business risks you see here and what kinds of insurance you think we ought to have. We don't have an insurance broker yet, and there's a chance we can do business together."

You are certainly interested. Though you are not yet in the sales end of the business, you know it will be a feather in your cap if you can bring in a new, aggressive company as an insurance client. You explained to your friends that you are not an expert on their type of insurance situation, but that you would be happy to check your sources and offer suggestions in writing in a few days.

You talked to your boss, who had a number of suggestions, and you read several manuals he mentioned. Here are your notes.

- Many things are insurable, but not everything.
- The famous French actress Mistinguette insured her legs for one million dollars. (You saw the old publicity photos, and her legs definitely weren't overvalued!)
- You can insure that it won't rain on your picnic, if you want.
- Insurance is a method of spreading a risk around a group of people or firms who have risks similar to yours.
- Risk may be the possibility of damage, loss, or injury: a delivery man trips on a cracked driveway on your property and breaks a leg, a customer who owes you money fails in business, your safe is burgled, your employee is injured working on a machine, your partner has a stroke and can't continue working.
- Some risks are not insurable: losing money in your business instead of making a profit, customers switching their business to a competitor.
- The general rules about insurability vary from company to company; most companies (but not all) refuse speculative risks.
- *Rule*: the loss must be one that can be accurately measured.
- *Rule*: the probability of loss must be predictable.
- *Rule*: the loss must be accidental, beyond the insured person's control.
- *Rule*: there must (usually) be others who wish to insure against the same kind of risk, spread over a wide geographical area.

- *Rule*: major catastrophes, such as war, riot, nuclear attack, or insurrection are not usually covered.

- Charles and Bill do face certain risks that meet these tests.

- *Risk*: death or disability of one of the principals.
- *Risk*: liability for accidental personal injuries or property damage incurred in the course of doing business; this is generally divided between automobile-related liability and nonautomotive liability.
- *Risk*: fire loss.
- *Risk*: theft loss.
- *Risk*: injury or illness to workers through some job-related activity.
- *Risk*: health-care expenses of partners and employees.
- *Risk*: loss of merchandise in transit (called "inland marine" loss in land shipment and "ocean marine" loss in water shipment).
- *Risk*: credit losses over the normal rate.
- *Risk*: miscellaneous other possibilities, such as machinery breakdown, boiler explosion, and power interruption.

- Each of these risks has an insurance remedy.
- If a partner must be replaced, the survivor must hire one or more people who can provide comparable services, which is expensive.
- *Cross-insuring* is when each partner buys life and disability insurance payable to the other which provides enough money to replace the lost services of the partner.
- *Key-man insurance* pays money to the business itself if either partner dies or is disabled.
- *Partnership insurance*, along with a purchase-and-sale agreement, would allow the survivor to buy the partner's interest from his estate at an agreed-upon price, with the insurance providing the money to do it.
- *Group health insurance* for partners and employees could reduce time off for illness and improve efficiency on the job by ensuring that those affected will seek (and be able to afford) competent medical care.
- *Liability insurance* protects against nonautomotive liability claims.
- *Fire insurance* provides the money to rebuild after a fire; it also should cover probable loss of business while getting back into production, cost of renting temporary quarters while rebuilding, any mortgage payments that must be made during rebuilding, loss of profits during rebuilding, and so on—limited only by the willingness to pay for further protection.

- *Theft insurance* will involve an expert review of the company's internal security, a secondary benefit.
- *Auto insurance* covers use of company-owned cars and the operation of partners' own cars on business (when the company might be liable).
- *Workers' compensation insurance* is mandatory state-operated insurance on which the company pays part and employees pay part by payroll deduction.
- *Marine insurance* protects against losses of merchandise in shipment.
- Sales and shipping documents should be carefully worked out with the advice of an attorney and the insurance company's representative to clarify when title is transferred to the buyer in shipping. Is property damaged in shipping yours or the buyers?
- *Credit insurance* is especially useful for a small, starting business, where failure of one big account could mean disaster.
- Comprehensive policies can cover many additional minor risks.

Organize your notes carefully and report in a letter to Charles and Bill. Your report should offer an objective analysis of such high quality that they will want further service from your company. Needless to say (but you ought to say it loud and clear!) your boss will be glad to meet with them to discuss specifics.

16. Mr. George Clemson, a wealthy investor, has asked you, an investment counselor, to provide information about high-yield second trust deeds as possible investments. These are second mortgages on (usually) single-family houses with values in today's market of $150,000 and up. High-yield second trust deeds are said to yield returns of 25 percent or more. Standard second trust deeds now yield 18 to 19 percent, with a possibility of higher return if the borrower prepays the loan.

What is a second mortgage and what are the rewards and risks for an investor? Suppose, for example, that the Jones family bought a house 10 years ago for $60,000, paying $7500 down and taking out a 20-year mortgage for the balance. During the 10 years, the Joneses have paid off $11,500 of the principal, reducing their indebtedness to $41,000. Meanwhile, house values have risen dramatically, and the house is worth $150,000. If they sold it, they could receive $109,000 cash (less selling costs) after paying off the mortgage; the $109,000 is their equity in the house.

Suppose Mr. Jones needs $50,000 to start a small business. Since he has a steady job and good credit, he is able to borrow that much as a second mortgage against his house. The lender is protected by the substantial equity Mr. Jones has.

But Mr. Jones doesn't have to pay 25 percent interest on this second mortgage, at today's rates. The prevailing rates are significantly lower. And if he feels the prevailing interest rates for second mortgages are too high, he can probably refinance his first mortgage at a more attractive rate of interest to get the money he needs. The more likely customer for the 25 percent second mortgage has a poor credit history or unsteady income. Someone who will pay 25 percent or more for money in today's market is either financially incompetent or has a record of defaulting on payments. People usually accept loans at that rate only out of desperation.

Your client is probably already aware of the typical situation in which second mortgages are taken, but you feel you should remind him of the risks of the high-yield type. If he wants to invest in second mortgages, you recommend a conservative approach, working with brokers who do not offer yields over the prevailing market rates.

Selection of a mortgage broker is important; his banker may be able to recommend someone. When considering a second trust deed investment, Mr. Clemson should:

- Get a sound, realistic appraisal of the property to be sure there is enough equity to cover him in case of foreclosure. (Typically, he should probably ensure that his mortgage will not create an encumbrance of more than 75 percent of the appraised value, allowing for a downswing in property values.)
- Review the potential borrower's credit history, verifying income and employment.
- Verify that the title is clear.
- Require title insurance in case the title turns out not to be clear.
- Require fire insurance to the amount of the investment.
- Include a "power of sale" clause in the mortgage allowing him to take over the property without court action if there is a default.
- Have at least one face-to-face meeting with the broker or the broker's representative.
- Check the broker's bank, professional, and customer references before doing business, no matter who recommended the broker to him.

If Mr. Clemson takes these precautions in investing in normal-yield second trust deeds, he may still face defaults and have to foreclose occasionally, but the chance of a loss is relatively small.

Your report should make your recommendations and support them.

17. Naturally Good is a restaurant in your city specializing in unprocessed, organic foods. Although its menu is not entirely vegetarian, most customers do not order meat items. The main clientele consists of business people at noontime, family and small social groups in the evening.

Believing that its clientele is especially health-conscious, the management is considering a total ban on smoking inside the restaurant. They are concerned, though, about alienating any sizable group of customers. Therefore, they asked your small consulting firm to conduct a survey of customers about their attitudes toward such a change. Your brief questionnaire was given to each customer when each was seated and picked up when the order was taken. After asking the customers to identify themselves as smokers (141) or nonsmokers (2915), you asked them to answer the three questions listed below. Only positive (yes) responses are given. (Some customers did not answer all questions.)

	Smokers	Nonsmokers
1. The management of Naturally Good is considering a ban on tobacco use in the restaurant. If smoking is banned:		
I would probably patronize Naturally Good more often.	23	2146
I would probably patronize Naturally Good less often.	102	588
2. If smoking is banned:		
I would be more likely to join business associates at Naturally Good.	12	1970
I would be less likely to join business associates at Naturally Good.	113	694
3. If tobacco use were banned:		
I would be more likely to join family and friends at Naturally Good.	24	2141
I would be less likely to join family and friends at Naturally Good.	98	485

In your report to Naturally Good's management, present and analyze your findings. Discuss the major implications you see. You were not asked for a recommendation.

18. Your company has traditionally asked employees to take vacation time from June 15 to August 15, a slack time in your business. Employees have been permitted to schedule vacation time as they pleased during that period, and often the company has been forced to hire temporary replacements to ensure that essential services are maintained. In recent years, a broadening of product lines has decreased fluctuations in work load throughout the year. Now, necessary cost reductions have forced a reevaluation of this policy.

A new policy has been proposed that would allow employees to request vacation time anytime during the year, but would require that departments refuse requests when granting them would interfere with maintenance of essential services. According to the proposal, when too many requests are made for any one period, priority would be given to those employees (1) whose absence would not interfere with the essential services of each department and (2) who have seniority.

As Director of Personnel, you have been asked to determine what patterns of requests may arise if employees are permitted to request vacation time in any month of the year. You have surveyed all employees. Here are the results:

1. If you were permitted to schedule vacation time during any month of the year, which month do you think you would normally select? Please mark first, second, and third choices.

	First	Second	Third
January	27	44	1
February	114	134	86
March	129	163	131
April	28	15	39
May	71	26	65
June	232	278	187
July	304	204	159
August	282	190	111
September	99	70	55
October	20	3	17
November	47	13	0
December	154	249	286

2. Would you usually prefer to take all your vacation time in one unbroken period, or would you usually prefer to break up your vacation into two or more periods separated by work time?
One unbroken period   1015
Two or more periods   360

3. How important is it that your vacation time be scheduled during the public school vacation period?
Very important   928
Mildly important   164
Not important   374

Present and discuss the implications of these findings in a report to the company Executive Committee. A recommendation to adopt or reject the proposed policy wouldn't be appropriate, but you should discuss the likely results of adoption in light of your findings.

19. As Director of Purchasing in charge of the acquisition of more than $25 million in tools and raw materials for your company each year, you have had a growing concern about the strain on the integrity of your staff.

When a single purchase decision by one of your buyers may involve revenues of as much as a quarter of a million dollars to a vendor, there is an obvious opportunity for the vendor to attempt to exercise illegitimate influence. It is common practice for vendors to send small gifts to buyers at holiday time, and rumors of large "gifts" (bribes?) are heard. Propose a specific policy on conflict of interest among employees including the following points in a report to your company's top-level Operating Committee.

- Employees are to be prohibited from accepting gifts or gratuities from vendors or competitors in the form of cash or gift certificates.
- Gifts of nominal value, including payment for meals, are OK, but gifts of substantial or lasting value are not OK under any circumstances. (Business relationships often include an element of personal friendship, and exchange of small gifts among friends should not be precluded.)
- The offer of gifts of substantial value under circumstances in which the refusal of such gifts might be perceived as offensive by the giver (as in the case of dealings with foreign nationals where such transactions may be commonplace) must be reported immediately to the appropriate officer of the company (vice-president level), who will specify action to be taken.
- Activities of employees, including outside work activities, before or after working hours, are their own business and are not properly the concern of the company. When employees moonlight, however, by working for vendors or competitors, possible conflicts of interest arise in which decisions may be influenced by such outside work. Outside work is prohibited only under such circumstances.

In your proposal, state the policy the way you think it should read. It will be ticklish to make these points without suggesting that violations are suspected (not the case) and without impugning the motives of honest employees. Reasons for the proposed policy should be clearly stated as part of the policy itself.

20. The Graduate Student Advising Office at one university has maintained the university's normal office hours of 8:30 A.M. to 4:30 P.M. Because the majority of graduate students attend classes in late afternoon and evening, the office has remained open until 7 P.M. (the typical starting time for the last scheduled class) during the first two weeks of each term. Recently, the Graduate Students' Association passed a resolution requesting that the office remain open until 7 P.M. every day; students express willingness to have the office open at 11 A.M. if that will allow the later closing.

Preliminary investigation reveals the following factors: The change cannot be implemented immediately (as the students ask), since work schedules of an associate dean, eight staff advisers, an office manager, and five clerical employees would have to be shifted; these people are long accustomed to the traditional schedule and would have to shift their own personal schedules (child care, teaching assignments, etc.) to suit. Many feel their jobs would be less attractive under the proposed schedule. It appears impractical to delay opening until 11 A.M., because other university offices (working on the standard schedule) must be able to contact graduate advising personnel and check records stored in this office. Similarly, advisors often must check with personnel in other university offices in the course of their work, and the new schedule would preclude such contacts after 4:30 P.M. Providing full service in the office on an 8:30 A.M. to 7 P.M. schedule would involve a staffing increase of about 25 percent, and budgeting limitations rule that out. Determining a suitable pattern of partial service on this schedule will be a complicated undertaking that will require some study before implementation. Other potential problem areas need to be explored fully before any possible plan is devised, so that unexpected problems (possibly more serious than the present one) don't arise.

The Graduate Dean has established a Task Force on Extended Office Hours to investigate the possibility of implementing the change; the group will have its first in a series of weekly meetings this week. The Dean has asked for a full report by the end of the present term.

In summary, the proposal is receiving a careful hearing. Nothing at this point appears to rule out a change of schedule, but careful study will be required before a specific plan of implementation is developed. No change of schedule should be expected during the present term.

Your job is to put this information into a report to the Graduate Students' Association for the signature of the Graduate Dean. Frame your message to take into account the reactions of GSA members who pass many resolutions and see relatively few changes in university procedures. Remember that students' time-frames tend to be short (many present graduate students will complete their programs and leave the university in one or two terms), and the usual time orientation of administrators is much longer. State the situation as positively as possible, but don't imply promises that may not be delivered.

21. As an independent business consultant, you have done considerable work over the years for John Robert Barron, Jr. Mr. Barron is a son of a wealthy family (originally silver, more recently department stores and real estate); his major activity is managing his family's estate. In that connection he sometimes invests in small business ventures, and over the last decade or so you have provided considerable research information in support of various ventures he's held interests in.

Although his small business ventures have usually involved backing would-be entrepreneurs, he has now become interested in initiating a small business venture himself. He has determined the nature of the business, and he has narrowed down possible geographic locations to two. Now he needs information about which of the two cities would make a better location for his business.

As a preliminary step in his project, Mr. Barron has asked you to make a quick investigation of the two cities he has in mind and, on the basis of information in various publications, provide a preliminary recommendation of which of the two would make a better location for the new business. At this stage, neither you nor Mr. Barron will be traveling to either of the cities; you will rely instead on published material available in the library. In previous projects of this kind, you have found the United States Census information to be extremely useful.

To justify spending your time (and Mr. Barron's money), you submit a proposal to him. Your proposal should include at least this information: (1) background of the problem, giving any information needed to understand the material that follows; (2) a statement of the goal of the project; (3) a description of what you plan to do in researching the problem and writing the report; (4) an estimate of the number of work-hours it will take to complete the job, including writing and typing time. Your time estimate should be in the form of an itemized list of activities, with the time estimated for each activity.

For this assignment, you will specify: (1) the nature of the small business Mr. Barron is interested in, (2) the two cities that Mr. Barron is considering as possible locations for this business. The business itself should be in the field of retail trade or service directly to the consumer. It should be a business that can be operated on a small scale, say, with one to eight employees, a business in which the owner-manager is the principal operator. Ideally, it will be a business you know something about or are interested in personally. You may not chose the shoe business.

The two potential cities you choose must be located outside California. They should be medium-size SMSAs roughly between 250,000 and 750,000 in population, and the two populations should be within 10 percent of each other.

The SMSA is a geographical unit used by the Census Bureau and others in market studies. As a rough definition, an SMSA is a geographic unit within which people living in that area tend to do most of their shopping. As you can see, city limits aren't very useful for the purpose of market studies, because often city limits are quite arbitrary from a marketing point of view. In a large urban-suburban area, people living in one suburb are as likely to shop in a shopping center in the next town as not, and the two towns should be considered as one marketing unit; in fact, the whole area should be treated as one unit, and that's just what the SMSA allows you to do. In using census data, use the tables that provide information by SMSA rather than other geographical units. (See also problem 1 in Chapter 19.)

22.   As Supervisor of Data Entry, you must recommend termination of Jeffrey Clayton, a data entry clerk. Jeffrey was hired 11 months ago, and his job performance was excellent during the three-month probation period. Beginning about three months ago, though, his performance deteriorated markedly, and it has remained at an unacceptable level since then. You have three areas of complaint:

- An unacceptable number of absences, totaling 4, 5, and 7 for the last three months
- An unacceptable number of days arriving late for work, totaling 5, 3, and 9 for the last three months
- An unacceptably high error rate in data entry, with errors affecting 12, 11, and 17 percent of the transactions he processed for the last three months (the acceptable rate would be 1 or 2 percent)

Jeffrey is a full-time college student who also must support a family. You sympathize with the difficulties that must bring, but the work must be done, and done accurately.

After the first month of problems, you discussed the situation with him and indicated that his current performance was not acceptable. He agreed that his performance was not up to its previous high level and earnestly promised improvement. He implied that he was having some personal problems but declined to say what they were. You offered any help that you or the company could provide, but he said he'd take care of it. Your notes of that interview are in Jeffrey's personnel file.

A month ago, after continued problems, you wrote Jeffrey a letter (with a copy to his personnel file) pointing to the continuing problems and indicating that further poor performance would force his dismissal. He immediately came in to see you after receiving your letter and again promised that he could take care of the problem and get his performance back to normal.

Write a report to your boss, Anthony Ayala, Director of Information Systems, recommending Jeffrey's dismissal and documenting your reasons.

19

Formal
Analytical Reports

*It is a capital mistake to theorize before one
has data.*
Sherlock Holmes

*Now, what I want is, Facts. . .Facts alone are
wanted in life.*
Dickens

*Oh that my words were now written!
Oh that they were printed in a book!*
Job 7:16

Although business people write fewer long analytical reports than letters, memos, and short reports, when they do write them they take them very seriously. A long report is often a turning point in the writer's career, since it offers very special opportunities to demonstrate the kinds of analytical and communication skills that upper management highly values. Long reports are normally read by people two or three levels above the writer. Therefore, they give the writer an opportunity to show very influential readers what he or she can do.

PLANNING THE REPORT

The quality of a long report depends on the quality of the planning that went into it. If the report is poorly or hastily planned, then no amount of care in the information-gathering or writing stages can rescue it.

Experienced report writers spend at least half the total reporting time on the planning stage, and they plan on paper, not just in their heads. After the planning stage, they have comprehensive notes covering every aspect of the reporting project. These notes keep the project on track by preventing time-wasting tangents, and they also provide a firm basis for writing the final report. With good notes, you know exactly what you did at each stage and why, and you can also see clearly what your writing goals are.

You've already studied the report planning stage extensively in an earlier chapter. As you begin a long reporting project, review that material. In addition, here are some suggestions on applying that material to longer reports.

Audience Analysis

To help focus your writing, write down the names, positions, and addresses of the report's primary readers. In addition, make some notes on each of these important readers: what do they already know about the subject, and how do they feel about it? Such notes are extremely useful when you're ready to write.

Goal Setting

Although goal setting doesn't seem very difficult at first, it's actually one of the most difficult parts of the reporting process. But it's essential. It's difficult because it requires that you consider the project's basic aims—which initially look obvious—and define them quite precisely. But goal setting is important because without it the whole project can get so far off track that the resulting report is no good to anyone. If you're fortunate, you'll learn this lesson from other people's experiences; if not, you'll certainly learn it from your own unpleasant experience. The feedback from a long and expensive project that didn't accomplish what was expected is very unpleasant indeed!

Three specific written statements should result from goal setting. The first is a statement of the problem that the project is to solve. The second is a statement of the project's goal. These two statements are related, of course, but they're sufficiently different that each is useful. The third is a statement (probably more than one sentence long) of the criteria that decision makers will apply to the information presented in the report. Once they're written, these three statements are available to help guide the project to its completion. If, as is often the case, you've cleared these statements with the project sponsor, then you can test all your further planning against them. Activities that directly aim at accomplishing these goals should be useful; other activities may lead the project away from its goals.

Once goals are drafted and work is begun, it may turn out that the goals can't be achieved or that achieving them would be too expensive. In that case, either the project is ended or new, more realistic, goals are drafted and cleared with the sponsor. To be useful, goals should be flexible when the need for change arises, but any changes in them should be made with all the seriousness that was applied to setting the original goals.

GATHERING THE INFORMATION

The situations in which analytical reports are written are so varied that it's nearly impossible to discuss specifically how to plan the information gathering. It's useful, though, to discuss the four basic strategies for gathering information: (1) direct personal observation, (2) consultation with experts either directly or by reading material they've written, (3) survey research, and (4) experimental research. All your information will come through one or more of these methods.

Direct Personal Observation

Probably the most common source of information for business reports is knowledge obtained directly from the report writer's observations. In fact, the earliest known historical reports are reports of battles by on-the-scene observers. The whole value of their reports lay in their firsthand observation of events. In a wide variety of business situations, you'll be asked to do exactly the same thing—describe events to a manager who couldn't witness them personally.

In the course of your job, you become the most knowledgeable person in the whole organization on some subjects. You become the expert on your little part of the organization. Since you'll have unique knowledge, you'll be asked to share it with managers who will use it to make decisions.

In other cases, you may be able to find a piece of information you need for a report simply by going out and looking for it. For instance, if you're considering where to locate a new machine, the easiest approach may be simply to walk around the plant and look for a place that fits your requirements. If you must determine whether or not the lighting in a given area is adequate, you can probably get a pretty good idea simply by turning on the lights and checking for yourself.

One important advantage of direct personal observation is that it gives you much more information about a subject than reading or listening does. For instance, if you were thinking of buying a house, you could read about it and look at photographs, but you wouldn't feel you really knew about that house until you'd visited it yourself. And if you did visit it, you'd find out more in just a few minutes than you had from all the second-hand information you'd gathered. Direct personal observation gives you a feel for a subject that you can't get in any other way.

At the same time, there's one problem that you must guard against. Your personal observation of an event gives you very clear and vivid perceptions of it, but those perceptions are influenced by your map of the world. Your selective perceptions give you somewhat biased information about the observed event, and your own peculiar mapping system is sure to distort that information in some way. Of course, when the observed event is very simple and easy to understand, you may be able to disregard this source of error. But if the event is very subtle or capable of many interpretations, your firsthand observations may be highly distorted, yet so vivid to you that they're hard to ignore. In such cases, observations by experts who have observed the event over a long period may be much more valid than yours, even though the information they provide is less vivid and rich in detail.

Consultation with Experts

If you need an item of information and know someone who has it, the easiest way to obtain it is to ask that person for it. If that person is, furthermore, an acknowledged expert on that subject, then his or her answer may be the best—and most credible—information available anywhere. And such information is often available at the cost of a quick phone call or letter.

Direct consultation   Experts are all around you. In school, you have access not only to professors but also to students who are experts on all sorts of subjects. To be an expert, a person needn't have a whole string of diplomas on the wall; he or she just has to know the answer to your question. For many questions, you can get expert answers from very average people. For instance, if you want to know when the next bus arrives at the corner near your house, you ask someone who takes the bus.

Some questions, though, can be answered only by someone who has specialized information. If you want to know whether or not a certain contract provision will hold up, you ask a lawyer. Some people who aren't lawyers may know the answer, but information from them won't be as convincing to your reader as information from a lawyer. In the same way, you consult engineers for technical information, acknowledged management experts for management information, manufacturers' representatives for product information, psychologists for information about attitudes, and so on. The need for expert credentials in these cases is twofold. First, you'll probably have more confidence in the information these people provide. Second, and more important, the reader will have more confidence in it, too.

Library research If no expert is available to consult, you can go to the library and read what experts have written on the subject. University and city libraries are absolutely crammed with information on almost every likely subject.

Finding information in a library can be extremely frustrating, though. You know that, somewhere among the million or so books, magazines, and pamphlets is exactly the fact you need, but you don't even know where to begin looking. Fortunately, there are three sources of help.

The first source of help is the card catalog. Every book in the library is represented in the card catalog by at least three alphabetically filed cards. One card is filed according to the author's name, another is filed according to the title, and a third is filed according to the subject. When you're looking for an item of information that a book might contain, begin by looking in the card catalog under the various subject headings that relate to that item. Remember that almost anything can go by a number of different names, so before you give up on this approach, try looking under every subject heading that might apply to the desired item. Be sure to check the index as well as the table of contents in each likely book.

If this approach fails, all is not lost. Use the card catalog to locate textbooks or other general books on a subject that's related to, but broader than, the desired item. Then check the bibliographies or end-of-chapter references in these books for a book or journal article more directly related to your subject. Often you can slowly zero in on the item you're looking for in this way—sometimes after tracking through a whole series of books that come closer and closer to it.

A second source of help is the indexes to magazines and journals. If the needed item of information concerns recent developments in some field, the best information may be in periodicals. And most are indexed in one of the periodical indexes in the library's reference room. The *Readers' Guide to Periodical Literature* lists articles from general-circulation magazines by author, title, and subject. Other indexes cover more specific fields in greater depth and are useful for finding specialized information. If you find a reference to an article that your library doesn't have, the librarian can probably arrange to get a copy of that article from another library through interlibrary loan.

A third source of help is the librarians themselves. Most university and large city libraries employ research librarians whose job is to help you find information. If you've made an honest but unsuccessful effort to find an item by yourself, then feel free to ask the research librarians' advice. They know all the tricks of the trade; if you can tell them specifically what you want, and if it's in the library, they'll show you how to find it. Don't hesitate to ask—after you've looked for yourself.

In using information that you've gathered from experts, either directly or through their writings, remember that experts are subject to the same perceptual distortions that everyone else is. Experts probably do have more accurate perceptions of events in their fields than other people do, but they also have their own biases. Be as alert as you can to such biases.

In using material from books and magazines, look for some evidence that the writer is actually an expert. The fact that writers convince someone to publish their work certainly isn't completely persuasive evidence that they have expert knowledge. Actually, getting published proves only that some publisher believed that people would pay money to read a writer's work. A lot of malarkey gets published, so insist on evidence of the writer's expertise. If you don't know enough about the field to tell whether or not the writer is an expert, ask someone who does know the field to help you decide.

Survey Research

When a question must be answered, many people's automatic advice is: "Do a survey." And, in fact, a great many questions can be answered by survey research. It's important to realize, however, that a valid survey, even a small one, is an extremely complicated and time-consuming way to gather information. Survey research is a method of finding out what a group of people thinks about a certain subject. Usually, surveys are used to sample people's feelings or attitudes, but they're also used to discover what people are doing or what facts they believe.

Planning a survey begins with two questions. First, what group of people are you interested in? Second, exactly what do you want to know from them? The more specifically you can answer these questions, the more easily you can design a valid survey. Once you've defined the target group, sample its members, questioning some of them and assuming that they represent the whole group. (Unless the target group is very small, you needn't question every member of it.)

Choosing a sample   There are two methods of sampling, or selecting respondents. In the first method, called random sampling, you select respondents systematically at random from the target group, or population. For instance, you might select every tenth name on an alphabetical list of that population or select every twentieth person who walks past a certain place, if all population members walk past it about equally often.

In the second method, called stratified sampling, you select respondents who represent major subdivisions of the target population. For this purpose, you must figure out what variables might affect people's answers to your questions and then select respondents who represent the target population in those respects. For example, if the target population consists of 25 percent men and 75 percent women and you think sex may affect people's answers, then you'll want 25 percent of your respondents to be men and 75 percent to be women.

The important thing in selecting respondents is to ensure that they truly represent the target population you're studying. Be extremely careful that your particular selection procedure doesn't bias the answers you get. For example, if you select respondents by walking down the hallway and collaring the first 20 people you meet, they're quite unlikely to represent a given larger population. There are no easy rules for determining whether or not your selection procedure will bias the answers, but if you think carefully you can probably find a procedure that at least doesn't introduce any obvious bias.

Planning the questions Having defined your sample, you're now ready to determine how you'll ask the questions. If you want answers that can be compared with one another, ask them the same way each time. Thus, you'll probably want to write them in a more or less detailed script, or questionnaire. The key decision about the questionnaire is whether you'll ask questions and let respondents answer in any way they wish (open-ended questions) or give respondents a list of answers to choose from (closed questions). Open-ended questions, because they let respondents answer as they wish, may give you considerably more information than closed questions. However, open-ended answers may be rather difficult to summarize. Answers to closed questions are relatively easy to summarize, but they may represent the respondents' ideas less accurately.

The key problem in writing a questionnaire is to avoid phrasing that will bias the answers. Some people tend to give you the answers they think you want to hear. Therefore, scrupulously keep your feelings out of the questions. This is difficult to do, and you'll want to get help from someone who's experienced in writing questionnaires. One of your college instructors or someone in your company's marketing research department may be very helpful.

Planning the administration of the questionnaire As you're thinking about the questionnaire, consider how you'll administer it. The three usual methods are personal interviews, telephone interviews, and mail questionnaires. You get the most information in personal interviews, because they almost always yield a lot of comments and discussion along with the respondents' answers. Often you can explore side issues in depth by following up respondents' comments with further unscheduled questions, or probes. But personal interviews are extremely time-consuming; you may, of course, enlist the help of other interviewers, but you can never be sure that they are following exactly the same procedure that you are.

Telephone interviews save time, and if your questions are brief and simple, you may get good answers. Since a telephone call will interrupt something the respondent was doing, however, carefully limit your questionnaire so it can be completed in three or four minutes at the most. If you take longer, the respondent may get irritated and give any old answer just to get rid of you, and you don't want that.

Mail questionnaires avoid many of these problems and are relatively cheap to administer. Unfortunately, they have two drawbacks. First, seldom are more than about 25 percent of mail questionnaires completed and returned. Second, you can never be quite sure that respondents really understood the questions, because of the lack of oral feedback. If you're asking one thing but the respondent thinks you're asking something else, then the answers won't be very useful.

When your survey is finished, summarize the results in some form that can be reported easily and understandably. Very often, percentages make the most sense; you can report that a certain percentage of the respondents said this and a certain percentage said that. To accompany these statistical findings, you may wish to quote some of the respondents' comments verbatim, since these usually give more of a feeling of reality than the statistics do. If you expect to do this, be sure to record the respondents' comments as you administer the questionnaires.

Experimentation

In experimentation, you systematically introduce changes into a situation to see how they affect the outcome. For example, to experiment with a machine, you might set the controls one way and see how it operates, then change the controls and see what effect it has. To experiment with a group of people, you might carefully vary certain factors in their environment and see how these factors affect their behavior.

The ideal of experimentation is to keep all factors constant except the one you're testing and test only one factor at a time. The key postulate of experimentation is ceteris paribus, which can be loosely translated as "everything else remaining the same"; that is, every factor other than the one you're systematically varying should be constant. Before you can make any meaningful statements about the results of your experiment, this condition of constancy must be maintained as fully as possible.

It's usually difficult or impossible, though, to keep all factors that might affect the outcome absolutely constant. A thousand factors might affect the performance of a machine: temperature, air pressure, voltage fluctuations, stray electromagnetic fields, dust particles, and so on. But controlling mechanical factors is simple compared with controlling all the factors that might affect human behavior. All sorts of factors affect people at work: family problems at home, rumors of good or bad news in the plant, new work rules, bad feelings between friends, and so on.

To reduce this problem, experimenters usually use two samples of the target population—a control group and an experimental group. The control group is selected from the same population that the experimental group is selected from, but the members of the control group aren't subjected to any changes or experimental techniques at all; they're simply left alone during the experiment. After the experiment, the control group's performance is used as a baseline for evaluating the experimental group's performance. In this way, the experimenter can identify and discount the effects of extraneous factors that affect the performance of the entire target population.

Because of the vital need to control all extraneous factors that could conceivably affect the outcome, experimentation depends even more critically on the quality of planning than other information-gathering methods do. To apply experimental results, you use the outcome of a small test situation to estimate the outcome of a larger real situation. This is very much like measuring the height of a tall tree by sighting past a ruler at arm's length and then extrapolating that measurement to the entire tree; even the slightest inaccuracy in your measurement will result in a great inaccuracy in your estimate. Very careful planning may reduce the inaccuracies to a minimum.

DOCUMENTING THE INFORMATION SOURCES

Right from the beginning, even in the planning stage, be aware that the final report must state where your information came from. Thus, as you gather information, also record the source citations that you'll need to document it. The section on research methodology will document the sources of information gathered through direct personal observation, survey research, and experimentation. But the source of any oral or written information from experts will be documented wherever the information is used in the text.

Citation Information

The information needed to document a source depends on the kind of source it is. For the most common kinds of sources, here's what you'll need:

Personal interviews: cite the name and title (if appropriate) of the expert you interviewed, a brief statement of his or her credentials (if necessary), and the date of the interview.

Letters: cite the expert's name and title, a brief statement of his or her credentials (if necessary), the name of the person the letter was addressed to, and the date on the letter.

Articles: cite the name of the author(s), the title of the article, the name of the periodical, the publication date, the page(s) that the whole article appeared on (not just the single item of information you're using), and the page(s) that the item appeared on.

Books: cite the name of the author(s), the name of the book, the city the book was published in, the publisher's name, the year the book was published, and the page(s) that the item appeared on.

Other sources: use one of the above formats that's closest in type to the source you must cite. For example, to cite an unpublished dissertation, use the format for a book citation, replacing the city of publication and the publisher's name with "unpublished doctoral dissertation, University of (name)."

Be sure to record source citations as you collect information for the report. If you wait until later, you'll have to reexamine all your sources to track down the citation. And you'll very likely have forgotten what (and where) some of those sources are. It's a lot easier in the long run to record the source citation on the same sheet or note card you use for the other information you gather from that source.

Citation Methods

Three basic methods of citing information sources are widely used in business reports. The first method is to place the citation in parentheses in the text. An example is "In his book, Language in Thought and Action (3d ed., New York: Harcourt Brace Jovanovich, 1972, p. 82), S. I. Hayakawa describes such symbols." If the report cites only a few sources, this kind of citation may not be too distracting. But if there are a fair number of citations, use another citation method.

The second method is to footnote the citation. An example is "S. I. Hayakawa has described such symbols.[1]" In the text, type a footnote number slightly above the typing line at the end of the information you gathered from the source. At the bottom of the page, type the full footnote as you see it here. As an alternative, you can put all the footnotes together at the end of the report, which makes the report a little easier to type.

The third method is to make a bibliography of all the sources you used to write the report. The bibliography entries are alphabetized by the first author's last name and then numbered. (If two or more sources have the same author, then arrange them by publication date, putting the earliest source first.) Parenthetical notes in the text refer to these numbers. An example is "S. I. Hayakawa (15:82) has described such symbols." The number 15 indicates that this source is labeled number 15 in the bibliography; the number 82 indicates that the information came from page 82 of that source. If this citation method is generally understood and approved in your company, it's probably the easiest method. Just in case some reader may not understand this method, you should briefly explain it, perhaps in an explanatory footnote keyed to the first such citation in the text.

---

1. S. I. Hayakawa, Language in Thought and Action, 3d ed. (New York: Harcourt Brace Jovanovich, 1972), p. 82. [Note: Book titles are underscored in manuscript; in print, of course, they are set in italic type.]

Footnote and Bibliography Styles

A number of styles for ordering and punctuating the elements in footnotes and bibliographies are acceptable. If your organization uses a standard style, then by all means follow it. The following examples, which illustrate one accepted bibliographic style, are the kinds of entries you'd use in the footnote citation method that was described above. The first time you cite a source, give all the necessary information. After that, you don't have to repeat the full citation. The short-form footnotes *ibid.* and *op. cit.* are used to cite a source after the first full citation. *Ibid.* is the abbreviation of *ibidem*, which is Latin for "in the same place". *Op. cit.* is the abbreviation of *opere citato*, Latin for "in the work cited."

1. Joan D. Palma, Director of Purchasing, Acme Castings, Inc., Fort Wayne, Indiana, interview June 9, 1983. (*An interview citation*)

2. John W. Maltzer, Partner, Jenson and Walters, Certified Public Accountants, Oceanside, California, letter to George X. Hennesey, President, American Business Machines Company, dated July 29, 1983. (*A letter citation*)

3. Helen Smith, "A Study of Employee Turnover in the Production Control Department," report to Personnel Department, American Business Machines Company, February, 1983, pp. 7–9, 12. (*A report citation*)

4. "General Tire's Aerojet Unit Names Nichols to New Post," The Wall Street Journal, 24 August 1972, p. 6. (*A newspaper article citation. If the author's name is listed in the article, include that as the first item in the footnote.*)

5. Herbert W. Hildebrandt, "Cultural Communication Problems of Foreign Business Personnel in the United States," The Journal of Business Communication (Fall 1975): 14–15. (*A journal article citation. In a footnote, indicate the page(s) that the information appeared on; in a bibliography entry, indicate the page(s) that the whole article appeared on.*)

6. Earl Selby and Miriam Selby, "Can This Law Stop the Trashing of America?" Reader's Digest (March 1976): 72. (*A magazine article citation*)

7. Alfred Korzybski, Science and Sanity, 4th ed. (Lakeville, Connecticut: The Institute of General Semantics, 1958), pp. 194–198. (*A book citation*)

8. Claude E. Shannon and Warren Weaver, The Mathematical Theory of Communication (Urbana: University of Illinois Press, 1964), pp. 22–24, 87–91.

9. Ibid. (*Ibid. means that the source for a footnote—in this case, footnote 9—is exactly the same as that cited in the preceding footnote, namely, Shannon and Weaver's book, pp. 22–24, 87–91.*)

10. Ibid., p. 88. (*Once again we're referring to Shannon and Weaver's book, but this time the information is on page 88. Then, if footnote 11 were merely Ibid., it would mean that page 88 is again being referred to.*)

11. Palmer interview, op. cit. *(Op. cit. means that the source for the footnote is exactly the same as that cited in an earlier footnote, but not the immediately preceding one. To clarify which earlier citation is meant, such a footnote consists of an abbreviated title or name of the earlier source, together with the words op. cit. Footnote 11 refers to the Palmer interview, cited in footnote 1, where the full citation appears.)*

12. Korzybski, op. cit., pp. 196–197. (Here the source is the same as in the earlier footnote for Korzybski, except that the page numbers are different. If two or more works by this author had been cited earlier, then this footnote would include the title of the relevant work as well as the author's name.)

ORGANIZING THE REPORT

Since the information in a long report is especially complex, the direct plan offers the reader considerable learning efficiency. Most long reports should use the direct plan for their general organization.

The sections of a direct-plan long report, however, may be organized in other ways, as needed. Often, a direct-plan report contains one or more indirect-plan sections presenting information that the reader may have resistance to. Chronological order may occasionally be useful for a section, but seldom as the organizing plan for a whole long report.

Learning Aids

The complexity of the report's information makes the learning aids discussed in earlier chapters especially important. Heavy use is made of summarization. Since the report is long, summaries are placed at the end of the report in addition to the beginning of the report and the beginning of each section. Thus, a long report is usually extremely repetitive. Major points are repeated several times in it, and the main conclusion or recommendation is repeated quite often.

There are two reasons for all this repetition. First, repeating major points in several different forms throughout the report helps focus the readers' attention on those points as they plow through a considerable amount of detail. Second, repetition helps readers understand the main thrust without having to read the whole report. Some readers need to know only the major points.

To be as helpful as possible, repetition must be carefully structured; it isn't simply a matter of repeating the same material over and over again at random intervals. Here's how it's done in a standard direct-plan long report.

1. The informative title states the report's main conclusion or recommendation.

2. The table of contents lists the section headings and the beginning page number for each. Since the headings of body sections are all informative, the table of contents can be read as a brief summary of the report; it states the report's major points.

3. The synopsis is a brief introductory summary of the report. It boils all the material down to a level of detail that can usually be presented on one page. It includes the report's major conclusions and recommendations and a summary of the supporting evidence and reasoning.

4. The informative headings throughout the body state the key findings and factual conclusions, one by one. Readers who accept some conclusions but question others can leaf through the report, skipping the sections whose conclusions they accept and reading those whose conclusions they question.

5. The two or three opening sentences of each section repeat the point made in the heading and elaborate it by indicating the main supporting evidence or reasoning. These opening summaries provide an overview of the section just as the synopsis provides an overview of the whole report.

6. The conclusions section near the end of the report summarizes all the factual findings.

7. The recommendations section at the end indicates what should be done in light of the findings summarized in the conclusions section.

As your report travels up your organization's hierarchy to the level where decisions are finally approved, readers will be less and less interested in knowing details. They'll want to know only the key facts, and this system of repetition makes these facts easy to find; in fact, it makes them almost impossible to miss, no matter where the reader looks first. Such readers don't want to know all the facts, but they do want to feel confident that some responsible person in the organization has carefully looked at all the facts and drawn reasoned conclusions from them. The sheer bulk of the report should convey the care with which you investigated the situation, and the systematic repetition makes your logic clear. For this reason, the report can simply be duplicated and passed directly to higher levels of management without having to be further summarized or rewritten.

Formal Elements

Most organizations have either a standard or a customary format for formal reports that's been established by long usage. The following formal elements, which are also illustrated in Figure 1, are often included in such formats.

Title page The title page should follow your organization's preferred format. It should include at least the report's title, your name, the name of the person or organization the report was written for, and the date that the report will be submitted. Unless the report is organized in the indirect plan, use an informative title, one that states the main conclusion or recommendation.

Letter of transmittal   A letter of transmittal is written to the person who will formally receive the report. In the letter, simply indicate that this is the report that you and that person agreed you'd provide and refer to the terms of the assignment, if any. In addition, you'll normally indicate that working on the report was an interesting experience and you hope to have an opportunity to do such work again.

Sometimes a letter of transmittal also serves as a brief summary of the report's major conclusions or recommendations. More commonly, though, a separate synopsis is provided, which is easier for the reader to find because it's labeled more clearly.

Synopsis   The synopsis is a complete, self-explanatory summary of the whole report and is usually single-spaced on one page. It certainly shouldn't be longer than one page for every ten pages of the report's body. All the significant conclusions should be summarized in the synopsis, and all the recommendations should appear here unless they're so detailed that the synopsis would be prohibitively long.

The synopsis is a particularly important part of the report, because in many cases the people who will make the final decision about the recommendations will see only the synopsis; they won't take time to read the full report. Therefore, the synopsis should include everything they must know to make intelligent decisions. For this reason, write the synopsis last. You can most accurately summarize the report after every word you're summarizing has already been written.

Table of contents   The table of contents is simply a list of the report's headings and the page on which each appears. Sometimes figures (tables and graphs) are also listed after the headings. Since the preliminary parts of the report come before the table of contents, it normally doesn't list them. If it does, their page numbers are designated by small roman numerals (i, ii, and so on), since the first page of the introduction is normally considered to be page 1 of the report.

Introduction   Since the introduction must cover roughly the same ground that your earlier proposal (if any) did, you may be able to use the proposal almost word for word as an introduction. Doing so may require only minor revisions in phrasing, such as changing from the future tense, ("Here's what I will do") to the past tense ("Here's what I did") and revisions in content elements that have changed since the proposal was written. The proposal sections entitled "Background," "Statement of Problem," "Project Goal," and "Research Plan" cover what needs to be said. If you haven't written a proposal, review the material on proposals in the previous chapter.

The introduction begins the regular text of the report, thus it normally begins about a third of the way down on page 1. From there to the end of the report, the text is normally typed continuously; each new section begins right after the previous one without skipping to a new page.

Body The body sections of the report follow the introduction. Besides text, these sections also include the report's figures.

Conclusions The conclusions section summarizes the report's factual findings. It's written both as a review for the reader who has been reading the whole report and as a self-explanatory summary for the skimmer who may flip to the end to read this section first, as many readers do. The conclusions section covers much the same ground as the opening summaries of the body sections, and you may be able to construct it by copying those summaries in order and adding transitional material. If those summaries accurately represent their sections, then the resulting conclusions section should accurately represent the report. In any case, this section should be written after the body sections are fully drafted, so you can be sure of the material you're summarizing.

Recommendations Whereas the conclusions section summarizes the facts of the situation you're reporting on, the recommendations section indicates what you'd recommend doing about the situation. In some cases, the recommendations can be summarized in a sentence or two, with perhaps a brief discussion of your reasoning as well, and this section can be quite brief. In other cases, the recommendations may involve several options or a whole series of actions, and a detailed explanation will be needed.

If you were asked to recommend a course of action, then you must do it. It isn't fair to your boss or client to beg the question and refuse to recommend an action. If you have a good reason for not making specific recommendations for action, then check with your boss or client to see what he or she wants you to do.

In writing recommendations, remember that you only recommend action; someone else will decide whether or not to accept your recommendation. Thus, it's tactful to phrase your recommendation in that vein, avoiding phrases like "I decided" and "my decision," which suggest that you think you're making the final decision. The decision maker, not you, is the one who accepts final responsibility for the result.

Appendixes Lengthy detailed data or bulky exhibits that would interfere with the reader's comprehension of main points are often presented in separate sections at the end called appendixes. Often, such material is not duplicated for all readers, but exists only in a single master copy that readers may consult if they're interested.

BLACK SHOE COMPANY SHOULD LOCATE NEW STORE

IN FRESNO RATHER THAN BAKERSFIELD

Prepared for
Wanda Wise
Director of Corporate Development
Black Shoe Company

January 19, 1983

By Thomas Winston
Project Manager
Baxter and Burstein, Management Consultants, Inc.
January 19, 1982

Figure 1 A formal analytical report

BAXTER & BURSTEIN

Management Consultants, Inc.

11895 Park Dr. • Newton, MA 02100 • Tel (617) 555-6500

January 19, 1983

Wanda Wise
Director of Corporate Development
Black Shoe Company
41 L Street, N.W.
Lowell, MA 01800

Dear Ms. Wise:

Here is the report you requested on January 8 comparing the SMSAs of Fresno and Bakersfield as possible locations of a new Black Shoe store. As the report indicates, the statistical information points to Fresno as the better choice. No doubt your own on-site investigation will provide more precise information.

It has been a pleasure to provide this information to you, and I sincerely hope I will have the opportunity to serve you again in the future.

Cordially,

Thomas Winston
Project Manager

Figure 1 (continued)

Synopsis

I recommend that the Black Shoe Company tentatively select the Fresno SMSA rather than the Bakersfield SMSA as the location for a new California store. This recommendation is supported by three kinds of statistical information gathered from local libraries during the course of this study.

First, the Fresno SMSA has more potential customers for a Black Shoe store. The Fresno SMSA has just over 20 percent more men between the ages of 35 and 69 with 1969 incomes over $15,000 a year, and 28 percent more men employed in the categories of white-collar and professional occupational categories in which conservatively styled dress shoes might be worn.

Second, the economic climate for shoe stores is more favorable in the Fresno SMSA. The Fresno SMSA has 26.3 percent more people, and it has 71.0 percent more shoe stores with total sales 31.0 percent higher. The Fresno SMSA has four times as many men's shoe stores and employs 136.6 percent more shoe repair personnel.

Third, since the company intends this new store to test potential markets in medium-sized California SMSAs, it is significant that the Fresno SMSA is more typical than the Bakersfield SMSA of the dozen medium-sized SMSAs in the state. Of the twelve largest California SMSAs other than the four where Black Shoe stores are already located, the Fresno SMSA is closer to the mean values for population, retail sales in apparel/accessory stores, retail sales in shoe stores, number of shoe stores, and number of men's shoe stores. Although the Fresno SMSA is the lowest of the twelve in median income and the Bakersfield SMSA is second lowest, the Fresno SMSA is higher than the Bakersfield SMSA in number of men who can be considered customers for Black Shoes by age and income level.

As the next step in the planning for this new store, I recommend an on-site investigation of the Fresno and the Bakersfield SMSAs.

Figure 1 (continued)

Contents

Figure 1 (continued)

BLACK SHOE COMPANY SHOULD LOCATE NEW STORE

IN FRESNO RATHER THAN BAKERSFIELD

Introduction

Background

The Black Shoe Company manufactures and markets men's dress shoes in the 70 to 100 dollar price range. Styles are generally conservative. The shoes are very well made and are entirely repairable, making them unique in today's men's shoe market.

The Black Shoe Company operates its own retail outlets, an unusual phenomenon in the shoe industry. Most of the stores are located in the East and Midwest, but the company is interested in further expansion in the state of California. Present California stores are located in Los Angeles, San Francisco, San Diego, and Sacramento, the four largest market areas in the state.

The company would like to locate an additional California store in one of the state's smaller market areas. Such a store would not only increase the company's sales, but it would also serve as a test case to help determine the feasibility of further expansion into other smaller California market areas. The cities of Fresno and Bakersfield have been selected by the company as alternative locations for the new store.

Statement of the Problem

The problem was that the company lacked the information necessary to make a comparison between Fresno and Bakersfield as potential market areas. Although the populations of the Fresno and Bakersfield SMSAs are comparable, at 515,013 and 403,089, respectively, little was known about the specific market potentials of the two areas for Black Shoes.[1]

(The SMSA, or Standard Metropolitan Statistical Area, is a geographical unit used by the Census Bureau and others in market studies. The Fresno SMSA includes all of Fresno County, and the Bakersfield SMSA includes all of Kern County, where Bakersfield is located.)

1

Figure 1 (continued)

Information was needed to compare the potential sizes of the markets in Fresno and Bakersfield for conservative men's dress shoes in a relatively high price range. Information was also needed about the present levels of competition in the men's shoe business in the two markets. Finally, since this new store will serve as a test of the market for Black Shoes in medium-sized California SMSAs, information was needed to make comparisons between Fresno and Bakersfield and other smaller California market areas.

Goal of the Project

The goal of this study was to provide a recommendation, supported by statistical information, of either Fresno or Bakersfield as the better location for a new Black Shoe store. Information in support of this recommendation was drawn from published statistics and other sources available locally. Following an evaluation of this report, the company may wish to arrange for an on-site investigation of the two cities, but such an investigation was not included in this study.

Research Plan

The information presented in this report was gathered entirely from published sources, including publications of the United States Census Bureau and the Department of Commerce, and other sources that were located during the course of the investigation. Since only preliminary reports of the 1980 Census of the Population were available, most Census information was taken from earlier reports.

Such information supports a preliminary recommendation of the better location for the new store and serves as an excellent background to the subsequent on-site investigation of the two cities that may be commissioned. Since local libraries have excellent collections of governmental publications and other reference materials, no travel was necessary in this study.

The Fresno SMSA Has More Potential Buyers
of Black Shoes

The most recent statistics available indicate that the Fresno SMSA has just over 20 percent more men between the ages of 35 and 69 with incomes over $15,000 a year (in 1969 dollars) and 28 percent more men in selected white-collar and service occupations. (The most recent statistics on population by age, income, and employment are taken from the 1970 Census of the Population; all income figures reported here are in 1969 dollars.)

2

Figure 1 (continued)

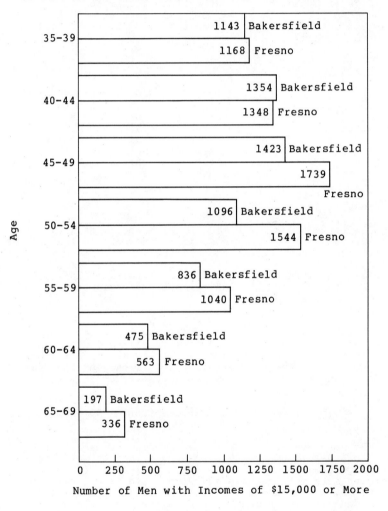

Figure 1
Number of Men Aged 35-69 with 1969 Incomes of $15,000
or More in the Bakersfield SMSA and the Fresno SMSA, 1969[2]

Figure 1 (continued)

More Buying Power Among Potential Purchasers
in the Fresno SMSA

A comparison of potential buyers of Black Shoes, men aged
35-69 years with relatively high incomes, indicates that there is
20.45 percent more buying power in the Fresno SMSA than in the
Bakersfield SMSA. I have assumed that the major market for
conservatively styled men's dress shoes is middle-aged men who
would wear them to work and to the kinds of social events that
people in that age range tend to participate in. I have also
assumed that the major market for these shoes is men whose
incomes allow them to invest in shoes of higher-than-average
quality. Even though the median family income is $315 higher in
the Bakersfield SMSA than in the Fresno SMSA ($8937 versus
$8622), Fresno still has the larger population in the age and
income ranges that are the most likely market for Black Shoes.[3]

As Figure 1 indicates, the Bakersfield SMSA includes 6424
men between the ages of 35 and 69 with incomes of $15,000 or
more, and the Fresno SMSA includes 7738, a difference of 1314
men. In the upper age ranges, the difference is even more
pronounced. Considering only men in the age range from 45
through 69, Fresno has 29.7 percent more potential customers.

More Men Working in White-Collar, Service, and
Professional Occupations in the Fresno SMSA

Compared with the Bakersfield SMSA, the Fresno SMSA has
28.0 percent more men in the occupational categories of retail
trade, finance, insurance, real estate, business services,
professional and related services, and public administration.
These, I have assumed, are the occupational categories in which
conservatively styled dress shoes might be appropriate workday
footwear.

Figure 2
Number of Men Employed
in Selected White-Collar Occupational Categories.
in the Bakersfield SMSA and the Fresno SMSA, 1969[4]

Occupational Category	Number of Men Employed	
	Bakersfield SMSA	Fresno SMSA
Retail trade	10,798	14,858
Finance, insurance, real estate	2,128	3,500
Business services	2,740	3,674
Professional and related services	6,108	10,478
Public administration	7,506	4,980
Total	29,280	37,490

4

Figure 1 (continued)

Of the Fresno SMSA's work force, including men and women, 48.0 percent is employed in white-collar occupations, and another 18.2 percent is employed in government. The Bakersfield SMSA's work force, including men and women, has 44.7 percent employed in white-collar occupations and another 20.9 percent employed in government. The total percentages are 66.2 percent for the Fresno SMSA and 65.6 percent for the Bakersfield SMSA.[5]

As Figure 2 shows, the Bakersfield SMSA has a total of 29,280 men in selected white-collar occupational categories in which Black Shoes might be appropriate workday footwear, whereas the Fresno SMSA has a total of 37,490, which is 28.0 percent larger. In the public administration category, the Bakersfield SMSA has approximately 2500 more employed men than the Fresno SMSA, and this difference is largely the result of a major federal government complex located in the Bakersfield SMSA. I have learned, however, that a federal government installation of similar size has been opened in Fresno since these figures were gathered, and this difference has been roughly eliminated.

Shoe Business Is Healthier in the Fresno SMSA

The population of the Fresno SMSA is 26.3 percent larger than that of the Bakersfield SMSA, and the Fresno SMSA's total sales in shoe stores are 31.0 percent higher, indicating a somewhat healthier climate for the shoe business.

As Figure 3 shows, the Fresno SMSA has 71.0 percent more shoe stores and 31.0 percent higher shoe-store sales revenue than the Bakersfield SMSA. Although average sales per shoe store in

Figure 3
Comparison of Shoe Store Trade
in the Bakersfield SMSA and the Fresno SMSA, 1977[6]

	Bakersfield SMSA	Fresno SMSA
Number of shoe stores with payroll	31 stores	53 stores
Total sales of shoe stores with payroll	$8,777,000	$11,496,000
Average sales per store	$283,129	$216,906
Shoe-store sales per capita	$21.77	$22.32
Number of men's shoe stores	2 stores	8 stores
Total retail sales, all types	$1,295,066,000	$1,788,817,000
Increase in total retail sales, 1972–1977	82.2%	88.9%
Increase in shoe-store sales, 1972–1977	57.7%	55.0%

5

Figure 1 (continued)

the Fresno SMSA are 23.4 percent lower, shoe-store sales per capita are somewhat higher, by 2.5 percent. The number of men's shoe stores in the Fresno SMSA increased from 0 in 1967 to 4 in 1972 to 8 in 1977, whereas the number in the Bakersfield SMSA remained constant at 2 throughout this 10-year period.[7]

The rapid increase in number of men's shoe stores over the past 10 years and the lower sales per shoe store in the Fresno SMSA may raise the question whether or not the Fresno SMSA may already have as many men's shoe stores as it can support. Since family shoe stores and department stores also sell men's shoes, however, these findings may not represent significant differences between the Fresno and the Bakersfield SMSAs in levels of competition in the men's shoe business. An on-site investigation may provide further information on this point.

Because Black shoes are repairable, I was curious to know how many shoe repair personnel there were in the two cities. According to the 1970 census, 41 people were employed in shoe repair in the Bakersfield SMSA and 97 people, or 136.6 percent more, were so employed in the Fresno SMSA.[8]

In the early 1970s, local experts expected the Fresno SMSA to grow more quickly than the Bakersfield SMSA during the 1970s, but recent reports show very similar rates of growth. A 1973 study by a California bank, for example, evaluated the economic prospects of the entire Central Valley, in which both Fresno and Bakersfield are located. The study found Fresno ahead of Bakersfield not only in most economic indicators in the early 1970s but also in prospects for continued growth. The study projected a significantly greater population growth rate and a greater increase in taxable sales in retail stores in the Fresno SMSA.[9] These projections, however, are not supported by more recent census figures. A comparison of 1970 and 1980 census reports shows a population growth of 22.8 percent in the Fresno SMSA and 22.2 percent in the Bakersfield SMSA population during the 1970s. A comparison of 1972 and 1977 retail trade census reports shows a growth in total retail trade of 88.9 percent in the Fresno SMSA and 82.2 percent in the Bakersfield SMSA in that five-year period.[10]

The Fresno SMSA Is More Typical
of Medium-Sized California SMSAs

Compared with the Bakersfield SMSA, in a number of key indicators the Fresno SMSA is closer to the average of the twelve medium-sized California SMSAs. These are the next twelve SMSAs after Los Angeles, San Francisco, San Diego, and Sacramento, where Black Shoe stores are already located. The Fresno SMSA is closer to the mean in population, retail sales in apparel/accessory stores, retail sales in shoe stores, number of

6

Figure 1 (continued)

Figure 4
Comparison of Population, Clothing Sales,
Shoe Sales, and Number of Shoe Stores in
Twelve Medium-Sized California SMSAs[11]

SMSA	Population	Retail Sales (in $1000's)		Number of Shoe Stores	
		Apparel Accessory Stores	Shoe Stores	Total	Men's
Anaheim-Santa Ana-Garden Grove	1,925,840	295,916	51,173	204	39
San Bernadino-Riverside-Ontario	1,583,066	173,204	33,001	132	15
San Jose	1,290,487	224,644	41,840	140	29
Oxnard-Ventura	529,425	53,304	10,908	44	4
Fresno	507,005	74,173	11,740	53	8
Bakersfield	401,540	NA	8,946	31	2
Stockton	347,312	NA	8,572	27	4
Vallejo Fairfield-Napa	325,640	28,122	5,817	26	2
Santa Barbara	297,722	NA	9,181	38	4
Santa Rosa	292,275	34,442	NA	24	2
Salinas-Monterey	283,086	58,809	8,816	37	8
Modesto	265,671	NA	7,544	35	5
Mean value for twelve SMSAs	670,756	117,827	17,958	66	10

shoe stores, and number of men's shoe stores (Figure 4). Since the prospective store will serve as a test market for Black Shoes in these SMSAs, these findings are very important.

In some other indicators, both the Fresno and the Bakersfield SMSAs ranked lower. In median income, for instance, the Fresno SMSA was the lowest of the twelve SMSAs at $8622 in 1969. The Bakersfield SMSA was second lowest at $8937. The average for the twelve SMSAs was $10,087.

Conclusions

This study comparing the Bakersfield and the Fresno SMSAs as possible locations for a new Black Shoe store on the basis of statistical information available in the local library has found that the Fresno SMSA may be more favorable than the Bakersfield SMSA in a number of respects.

7

Figure 1 (continued)

The Fresno SMSA has more potential customers for a Black Shoe store. The Fresno SMSA has just over 20 percent more men between the ages of 35 and 69 with 1969 incomes over $15,000 a year, and 28 percent more men in the white-collar and professional occupational categories in which conservatively styled dress shoes might be worn.

Although the Fresno SMSA is only 26.3 percent larger in population, it has 71.0 percent more shoe stores with total sales 31.0 percent higher. The Fresno SMSA has four times as many men's shoe stores and employs 136.6 percent more shoe repair personnel.

Predictions of significantly greater growth in the Fresno SMSA than in the Bakersfield SMSA during the 1970s have not been supported by recent census reports. Both SMSAs experienced just over 20 percent population growth during the decade, and the Fresno SMSA's rate of 1972-77 growth in total retail sales is just 8.3 percent higher than the Bakersfield SMSA's rate.

Finally, of the twelve largest SMSAs in California, other than the four where Black Shoe stores are already located, the Fresno SMSA is closer to the mean values for population, retail sales in apparel/accessory stores, retail sales in shoe stores, number of shoe stores, and number of men's shoe stores. Although the Fresno SMSA is the lowest of the twelve in median income and the Bakersfield SMSA is second lowest, the Fresno SMSA is higher in number of men who can be considered customers for Black Shoes by age and income level.

Recommendations

On the basis of these findings, I recommend that the Fresno SMSA be tentatively selected as the location of the new Black Shoe store, pending an on-site study of the two cities. If the full reports of the 1980 Census of the Population become available before a final decision is made, then I recommend that the conclusions of this study be reviewed in light of the newer information. In addition, I recommend that an on-site study consider the rapid recent increase in number of men's shoe stores in the Fresno SMSA and the possibility that the optimum number of men's shoe stores may already have been exceeded in this market area. Except for this question, the statistics point almost unanimously to the Fresno SMSA as the better location.

8

Figure 1 (continued)

Notes

1. United States Bureau of the Census, <u>1980 Census of Population and Housing, Final Population and Housing Unit Counts, California</u> (Washington: Government Printing Office, 1982), Table 1.

2. United States Bureau of the Census, <u>1970 Census of the Population, Vol. I, Characteristics of the Population, Part 6, California</u> (Washington: Government Printing Office, 1973), Table 193.

3. Ibid., Table 89.

4. Ibid., Table 184.

5. Ibid., Table 41.

6. United States Bureau of the Census, <u>1977 Census of Retail Trade, Geographic Area Series, California</u> (Washington: Government Printing Office, 1980), Table 4; United States Bureau of the Census, <u>1972 Census of Retail Trade, Area Statistics, California</u> (Washington: Government Printing Office, 1975), Table 2.

7. United States Bureau of the Census, <u>1977 Census</u>, op. cit.; United States Bureau of the Census, <u>1972 Census</u>, op. cit.; and United States Bureau of the Census, <u>1967 Census of Business, Vol. II, Retail Trade Area Statistics, Part I, California</u> (Washington: Government Printing Office, 1970), Table 4.

8. United States Bureau of the Census, <u>1970 Census</u>, op. cit.

9. Economic Research Division, Security Pacific National Bank, <u>The Central Valley Report: A Study of the Growth and Economic Structure of the San Joaquin and Sacramento Regions</u>, (Security Pacific National Bank, 1973), pp. 9, 19, 45, 83, 91.

10. United States Bureau of the Census, <u>1972 Census</u>, op. cit.; United States Bureau of the Census, <u>1977 Census</u>, op. cit.

11. United States Bureau of the Census, <u>1980 Census of Population and Housing, Preliminary Population and Housing Unit Counts, California</u> (Washington: Government Printing Office, 1982), Table 3; United States Bureau of the Census, <u>1977 Census</u>, op. cit.

9

Figure 1 (continued)

FURTHER EXPLORATION

1. On what occasions might managers need a formal analytical report written?

2. Many formal analytical reports are written by companies to satisfy government requirements. List several examples.

WRITING PROBLEMS

1. Mr. Barron has approved the project you proposed for problem 21 in Chapter 18. Now write the report. In planning your report, you may find it useful to organize your information-gathering around three key questions.

- How do the two SMSAs compare in numbers of potential customers? If you can reasonably conclude that there is some tendency (even if not 100 percent) for the customers of this business to cluster in age, sex, income, and categories of employment, then you'll be able to make some fairly concrete comparisons using detailed census statistics. In addition, if you can find other products or services that customers of this business also tend to buy, then you may be able to find information on sales or number of people employed in those lines of business.

- How do the two cities compare in the level of competition in this line of business? Although census figures aren't extremely specific, if you can determine that similar businesses, or businesses in the larger category to which this business belongs, are prospering more in one city than the other, this information will help in reaching a decision. You may wish to calculate for this line of business the average sales per establishment and the sales per capita for each city. In addition, you may wish to go back to the previous census reports and determine the rate of growth in this line of business over the last five or ten years in each city.

- What are the overall economic prospects for the two cities over the next few years? Using census materials, you may want to make simple projections of present growth patterns in such areas as population, employment, income, and retail sales. In addition, you may be able to find more specific information in your library about economic prospects in those communities other than census materials.

As a result of your findings in these three areas and others you think are relevant, you'll recommend to Mr. Barron which of the cities he should start his business in. This is a preliminary recommendation, of course, and he'll follow up this study by visiting the cities himself. But he wants to see your recommendation so he can be sure which course of action you think should be taken; you have a much more detailed grasp of the comparison from your research that he'll get from reading your report.

The final report should have at least the following parts.

- Title page
- Letter of transmittal
- Table of contents
- Synopsis
- Introduction
    Background
    Statement of goal
    Research plan
- Text
- Conclusions
- Recommendations
- Footnotes

When it would be useful, provide information in graphs and tables. Always be sure to mention the key information from graphs and tables in the text itself ("as figure 2 indicates . . .").

2.   A steady client of your consulting firm is a wealthy investor who turns to you for background research when she is considering an investment. She has just called to ask you to prepare a background report on a large American corporation.

From your college or local library, get a copy of the corporation's annual report, check the *Wall Street Journal* index, Standard and Poor's registers, Moody's manuals, and the Dow directories, and find recent information on stock performance.

Your report should provide background on the company (history, major products and services, major subsidiaries, major locations, and so on), present financial structure (balance sheet, recent stock performance, current product and market developments, current problems, and so on), and future prospects (long-range prospects for the corporation's major products and services, long-range prospects for this corporation's continued success in its major markets, current developments affecting the corporation's long-term prospects, and so on).

Present a formal report of the length specified by your instructor. Include graphs and tables to present and illustrate your facts when possible. Use the full range of learning aids discussed in this book.

For this assignment, select a corporation that is listed on the New York Stock Exchange or the American Stock Exchange. If possible, be sure you can locate a recent annual report of the corporation before you make your final choice.

3. The Cragmont Corporation, "the world's largest home remodeling company," sells franchises to local remodeling firms who agree to operate within certain guidelines and who benefit from Cragmont's extensive national and regional advertising. In its 10-year history, the company has grown by adding existing local remodeling companies to its chain, but it now has built enough resources to begin an aggressive campaign of establishing new Cragmont outlets in cities where no existing company has joined the chain.

Mr. Conrad Cherney, Development Director of Cragmont, has commissioned you, a business consultant, to provide a background report on one such city. He wants general background on the population of the city (population, number of family units, and patterns of income, education, employment, and so on), information about housing patterns in the city (number, age, size, and value of housing units of various types, and so on), and future economic trends for the city (prospects for future economic growth, industrial development, income trends, and so on).

Publications of the United States Census Bureau provide much of the information you need. You may locate additional sources of information. You are not asked to travel to the city to gather information.

Present a formal report of the length specified by your instructor. Include graphs and tables to present and illustrate your facts when possible. Use the full range of learning aids discussed in this book.

For this assignment, select a standard metropolitan statistical area of at least 250,000 population to investigate. The SMSA is a geographical unit used by the Census Bureau and others in market studies. As a rough definition, an SMSA is a geographic unit within which people living in that area tend to do most of their shopping. As you can see, city limits aren't very useful for the purpose of market studies, because often city limits are quite arbitrary from a marketing point of view. In a large urban-suburban area, people living in one suburb are as likely to contract with a remodeler in the next town as not, and the two towns should be considered as one marketing unit; in fact, the whole area should be treated as one unit, and that's just what the SMSA allows you to do. In using census data, use the tables that provide information by SMSA rather than other geographical units.

4. Select a specific question that some business manager needs to have answered, do the research necessary to gather information supporting a recommendation, and write an analytical report presenting your findings.

The question you select must be one that some particular business manager needs answered. You should be able to name the manager who needs this answer or name his or her position and organization. It is easier to gather useful information about a very specific question than about a general topic, so spend some time narrowing down the question your report will answer until it is quite specific and clearly defined. Examples:

Should the XYZ Company switch to a certain manufacturing process?

Should the XYZ Company change its personnel procedures in a certain way?

Should the XYZ Company locate a new branch in a certain city?

Should the XYZ Company develop a certain type of new product?

Should the XYZ Company purchase a certain new production machine or computer?

Topics that would be suitable for standard term papers and topics of textbook chapters are very poorly suited to this assignment. If you have access to information about a small, local company, you may be able to research an area that would provide useful recommendations to it.

The topic you select should be stated as a choice between alternatives: should the company make such-and-such change or not; should it select plan A or plan B? Since you're asked to write an analytical report and make a recommendation, topics calling merely for background information aren't suitable.

Your instructor may place some additional restrictions on the topics you may select from and will help you find a suitable one.

As the first step in your project, write a research proposal (as described in the previous chapter) addressed to the person who needs your question answered.

Be prepared at any time during the project to write a progress report describing the current state of your research, what remains to be done, and your prospects for completing the job on schedule.

Present a formal report of the length specified by your instructor. Include graphs and tables to present and illustrate your facts when possible. Use the full range of learning aids discussed in this book.

20

Oral Presentations

For I have neither wit, nor words, nor worth,
Action, nor utterance, nor the power of speech,
To stir men's blood: I only speak right on.
Shakespeare (Julius Caesar)

V ery often the final step in reporting is an oral presentation of the report to the people who will make the final decision. The oral presentation gives the decision makers an opportunity to focus on the report and discuss the findings, with the advantage of having you there to contribute your expertise. Often, most of the audience won't have looked at the report; in fact, in many organizations it's customary for the report writer to deliver copies of the report at the time of the oral presentation. An oral report before a group of top managers is a tremendous opportunity to impress influential people in the organization with your abilities. It's worth taking seriously.

PLANNING THE PRESENTATION

Even though your careful planning of the written report will be valuable in preparing the oral presentation, further planning especially for the oral presentation will be necessary.

Analyzing the Audience

Since an oral presentation is normally given at a scheduled meeting, you can usually get a list of the people who will attend. This allows you to make a detailed audience analysis based on your personal knowledge of these people and to tailor your material just for them.

At the minimum, you should learn something about each audience member you don't know personally. The company grapevine usually provides ample information about personalities and dispositions. Since your audience will probably consist of 6 to 12 people representing various areas of the organization, analyze how your conclusions and recommendations will affect each area represented. How could each listener construe your findings as positive, and how could each construe them as negative? Your notes from this analysis will help you adapt your findings to each listener's viewpoint.

If you're presenting a proposal or justification whose purpose is to persuade the audience to act, then make some notes on the benefits that each audience member may see and the objections that each may raise. In fact, during the planning stage of the written report, it's often worthwhile to visit each audience member's office to get his or her thoughts about your subject. Their comments and suggestions may be very helpful in planning the written report and certainly in tailoring the oral presentation to their particular viewpoints.

During the presentation, many experienced communicators make a point of somehow addressing each listener personally on some matter of special interest to that listener or to his or her department. And in the question period, your knowledge of each listener's background and thinking on your subject will help you consider a given questioner's special viewpoint and thus formulate answers that the questioner can benefit from.

Setting Goals

Why are you giving this presentation? If you know, then you can probably focus the presentation more specifically on its goal and thus increase your chance of success. If you're presenting a proposal, then clearly your goal is to get action. Can you reasonably ask for immediate action at the end of the presentation? Presumably, your listeners will be as persuaded then as they'll ever be. If you're presenting an analysis of a situation and perhaps some recommendations for action, then for your own use try to distill your main argument down to a few sentences, or even one sentence. If you can reduce it to one or two sentences you can understand, then your goal is to provide your listeners the information they need to understand it, too.

Organizing

The direct plan is just as efficient for listeners as for readers. By telling the listeners right at the beginning what the major points of the presentation will be, you give them an outline that they can very easily and efficiently fit the details into as they hear them. Use the direct plan unless you face significant emotional resistance from listeners or unless they won't know what you're talking about until it's explained. Even when you use the direct plan, though, endings are very important in oral presentations. Therefore, plan the ending as carefully as the beginning.

Typically, an oral presentation begins by summarizing the report's major points, most important first. Then it provides selected details, item by item (though probably far fewer details than in the written report, since time is limited). Finally, it summarizes the major points in reverse order, building up to the most important one at the end. If a call for action would be appropriate, it should come at the very end.

If you must organize the report in the indirect plan, then the opening summary simply names the topics you'll discuss, but not the major points themselves. Otherwise, this plan is very similar to the direct plan.

Preparing and Using Visual Aids

To hold the listeners' full attention, it's a good idea to give them something to look at while they're listening. People learn faster when they can both see and hear information. Therefore, plan some visual aids.

If you'll be presenting information that could be shown graphically, you might make large graphs or tables to display behind you as you talk. If your information isn't suitable for that, you could simply make outline-like notes containing the key phrases the listeners should remember, print them on large cards, and display these behind you as you talk. When you construct these visuals, be sure you make them large enough to be fully visible from anywhere in the room. Use large block printing on heavy card stock. And practice handling your visuals so you can confidently flash the right one at the right time without fumbling.

Be sure the material to be displayed is directly and obviously connected to what you'll be saying while it's displayed. If you put too much information on a visual, then it gives away the content of the next several minutes of your talk, and listeners spend all their time trying to guess what's coming next. If you want to conclude with a visual showing all the major points of your talk, find some way to build up the visual from smaller parts as you talk, or perhaps progressively uncover it part by part (being sure the covered parts are really invisible).

If a particularly important table is too detailed to reproduce for display, you might make a copy of it for each listener. You could either place a copy at each seat before the presentation, running the risk that listeners will read it during the first few minutes of your talk, or you could hand copies out when the table's information comes up in your talk. If you plan to hand out sheets during your talk, find a way to do it without distraction; perhaps you can ask an assistant to hand them out on cue. If you have to stop and fumble with handouts, that may be more distracting than having them in front of listeners throughout the talk.

Some experienced communicators like to pass out copies of the whole report and ask listeners to look at certain pages containing graphs or tables as their content is being discussed. If listeners won't have copies beforehand, this is a good way to build their interest in eventually reading the whole report. But it runs the risk that listeners may read the report right then and stop listening. Some particularly dynamic speakers can still hold listeners' interest, but most speakers run a substantial risk of losing many listeners through this approach. When the audience will see the report for the first time at the presentation, most communicators prefer to hand out copies right after the presentation, thus allowing listeners a few minutes to study the report at the beginning of the question period.

Preparing the Delivery

An oral presentation is a formal occasion, and the audience expects you to be fully prepared. If you try to compose and deliver a presentation off the top of your head, you'll quickly develop a reputation as a poor communicator. Few people have the skill and experience to present complex ideas effectively without preparation.

As odd as it sounds, it's also quite possible to overprepare for an oral presentation. Some beginners assume that they'll be most comfortable if they write the talk out completely; then, they think, they'll know exactly what they're going to say and how they're going to say it. There are two serious problems with this approach. First, written language isn't really like spoken language; even the relatively formal spoken language used in oral presentations is much less formal than standard writing. Therefore, what you write when you write a presentation will clearly sound like writing and not like talking.

Second, if you've written a complete text of your presentation, it's awfully difficult to resist the temptation to read it, or even worse, to memorize it. To maintain the audience's interest, your formal speaking style should very much resemble your normal speaking style. And very few people can read a text in a way that sounds natural. When expert TV newscasters read the news, it's obvious to everyone that they're reading, not talking. In addition, while you're reading it's very difficult to maintain eye contact with the audience. Eye contact personalizes your message and helps to keep your own perspective personal. When you lose eye contact, you lose a very important link with the audience.

Memorizing a talk has one pitfall so frightening as to rule it out as a way of preparing: what if you lose your place or forget part of the talk? Everyone who has given a talk knows what it feels like to search frantically for a word or to try to remember what should be said next. That's not really much of a problem if you can get back on track after a few seconds. Every listener has had the same problem and feels sympathetic during a brief pause. But in a memorized talk, it's possible to get stuck so completely that you can't continue at all, and listeners aren't so sympathetic about that. Memorizing is a very risky way to prepare.

If writing out a talk is a poor way to prepare your delivery, then what's a better way? Experienced communicators organize their presentations carefully and make very brief notes to use during the delivery. Notes can keep you on track and even provide key phrases for the beginning, ending, and other important parts of the talk. If you get stuck, your notes will remind you of what comes next. More importantly, using brief notes helps keep your attention and your eyes on the audience, where they belong. Using notes rather than a written text, you'll automatically speak in a natural-sounding way, which will help keep the audience's attention. If your notes are too detailed, though, they have almost all the disadvantages of a written text: you may find it hard to avoid looking at your notes rather than at the audience, and you may find yourself almost reading the notes to the audience. Very brief notes, written in phrases rather than sentences, help you resist these temptations.

DELIVERING THE PRESENTATION

Immediately before the presentation, you must prepare in two ways. First, prepare the room. Look at the room from a communicator's viewpoint for a minute and ask yourself what potential distractions could be removed. Is the room reasonably neat, or could a bit of straightening up help keep attention on your talk? Are the chairs arranged to direct attention toward you and help the audience see the visuals? Is there an appropriate place for you and your materials, including a convenient place to display your visuals without fumbling?

Second, prepare your own mind. Mentally review the goals you've set for this presentation. And quickly run through your outline or notes, recalling any key phrases you've been trying to remember. Be sure your mind is completely focused on the task at hand.

You can focus your mind best if you're reasonably calm. It's normal to feel a little keyed up just before a presentation; a certain amount of tension keeps your mind sharp and helps you think more clearly. But too much anxiety can dull your mind and make it difficult to think at all. Remember that you're simply going to talk to some people, telling them some things you've found out and sharing ideas with them. They won't be sitting there just waiting for you to foul up; in fact, they'll probably be very interested in what you're going to say. They want to know. If they didn't, they certainly wouldn't have authorized the expenditure for your report in the first place. You're completely prepared, so just relax and tell them about the report.

Answering Questions

At the end of your presentation, it'll probably be appropriate to ask for questions from the audience. This period can be awkward; therefore, prepare carefully for it. If you're not prepared, you could be standing in front of the audience not knowing quite what to say: "Uh, well, uh, I guess that's about all I have to say. Uh, uh, if you have any questions, uh. . . ." Very unprofessional. You should know exactly how you're going to make the transition into the question period. Plan that as part of your presentation.

Another source of awkwardness is that you'll be keyed up during the presentation, especially if it's your first, and your sense of time will be distorted. It may take the listeners some time to get their thoughts in order and begin asking questions. It might be a minute or two before anyone asks a question, and that will seem like an interminable time to you. If you're prepared for this feeling, you'll just stand as gracefully as you can and wait for the questions to begin.

Once the questions begin, you'll probably find that the question period is fun. After all the time you've spent with the subject, you're a real expert on it, and you'll be eager to explain things to the audience. If you get some really challenging questions, you'll be able to answer them confidently, and you'll find the exercise stimulating. Remember, if you don't know the answer to a question, there's nothing wrong with saying so; "I don't know" is often the best answer. If appropriate, offer to find out the answer and relay it later.

Following Up

After the presentation, while you're still keyed up, go back to your office or a quiet place and write some notes on your experience for future reference. What worked? What didn't work? What should you do next time to prepare better or deliver the presentation more effectively? Right after you finish a talk, you're the world's greatest expert on your presentation techniques, full of ideas for improvement in the future. Very soon all these ideas will fade from your mind, so write them down quickly. It would be a shame to waste these lessons just because you didn't take five minutes to record them.

Then, the next time you prepare a presentation, be sure to take advantage of those notes. That way, you can at least be sure that you're making progress in the areas you're aware of, and each time you deliver a presentation you can do it better than the last time. It's worth your while to be good at this.

FURTHER EXPLORATION

1. Which of the techniques you've learned about writing are also applicable to oral presentations? Can readability, tone, and organization techniques be adapted? What aspects of oral presentations are different from writing?

2. Assuming that chairs are movable, think of several ways to arrange them for an oral presentation in a classroom. Analyze the effects of each arrangement. Which ensures that the audience can see visual aids and best focuses attention on the speaker?

3. Analyze your experience with public speaking and determine two or three aspects that you need improvement in. Devise a plan for getting the necessary practice for this improvement.

4. As a student, you hear many oral presentations by instructors. Recall some that were effectively presented and some that weren't. Analyze the differences between the two. What conclusions can you draw for improving your own presentation skills?

PRESENTATION PROBLEMS

1. See problem 3 following Chapter 11 and problem 12 in Chapter 18. Present the results of your analysis of these problems to the other members of your class in a three- or four-minute oral presentation. Illustrate your presentation by showing your audience the companies' replies.

2. See problem 11 in Chapter 17. Present the results of your analysis to the Physical Plant Director and his advisory committee in a two- or three-minute oral presentation. Use one or more visual aids.

3. See problem 12 in Chapter 17. Present the results of your analysis to the top management Executive Committee in a three- or four-minute oral presentation. Use one or more visual aids.

4. See problem 4 in Chapter 18. Present the results of your analysis to the Executive Committee of Central Professional Publishers, Inc., in a five- to six-minute oral presentation.

5. See problem 10 in Chapter 18. Present the results of your analysis to the Finance Committee, consisting of the Comptroller and four other accounting department executives in a three- to four-minute oral presentation. Use one or more visual aids.

6. See problem 13 in Chapter 18. Present the results of your analysis to the members of your class in a two- to three-minute oral presentation. Illustrate your presentation by showing your audience the letters you collected.

7. See problem 14 in Chapter 18. Present the results of your analysis to Mr. Dempsey and three of the store's managers in a five- to seven-minute presentation. Use one or more visual aids.

8. See problem 15 in Chapter 18. Present the results of your analysis to Charles Welcome and Bill Li in a four- to five-minute oral presentation.

9. See problem 16 in Chapter 18. Present the results of your analysis to Mr. Clemson and several of his associates in a two- to three-minute oral presentation.

10. See problem 17 in Chapter 18. Present the results of your analysis to the management of Naturally Good restaurant in a five- to seven-minute oral presentation. Use visual aids.

11. See problem 18 in Chapter 18. Present the results of your analysis to the Executive Committee in a five- to seven-minute oral presentation. Use visual aids.

12. See problem 19 in Chapter 18. Present the results of your analysis to the Operating Committee in a three- to four-minute oral presentation.

13. See problem 1 in Chapter 19. Present the results of your analysis to Mr. Barron and a group of his business associates in a six- to eight-minute oral presentation. Use visual aids.

14. See problem 2 in Chapter 19. Present the results of your analysis to your client and associates in a six- to eight-minute oral presentation. Use visual aids.

15.   See problem 3 in Chapter 19. Present the results of your analysis to the executives of Cragmont Corporation in a six- to eight-minute oral presentation. Use visual aids.

16.   See problem 4 in Chapter 19. Present the results of your analysis to the intended audience in a six- to eight-minute oral presentation. Use visual aids.

Appendix A
How to Type a Letter

This appendix is aimed at the person who has never learned to type a letter in correct form. For that reason we will concentrate on the basics. If you are an accomplished typist, you may be aware of techniques and variations that will not be considered here. If you are a beginner, you will find that the material in this section will help you learn to style basic business letters. The forms presented here are not the only acceptable letter formats, but they are commonly used ones.

These forms are "correct" in the sense that everybody accepts them as correct. To be quite honest, some of the forms we use are entirely archaic in purpose and function; in a completely rational world they probably would be changed. They are correct for the same reason that a business suit is correct attire for business wear. And you accomplish the same goal when you type a letter in an accepted format that you do when you wear conventional clothing on the job. Odd or eccentric clothing takes attention away from the quality of work you're doing; odd or eccentric letter formats take attention away from your message.

THE FORMAL PARTS OF A BUSINESS LETTER

A business letter has six formal parts, as Figure 1 indicates. These are the parts that you'll generally find in business letters; as a beginner you should plan your letter layout to include these parts.

Letterhead

Goodfield Recap Tire Co., 23 Lawrence Rd., Creswell, KA 66000

September 5, 1983   Dateline

Mr. Rick Anaya   Inside Address
1925 Sunny Way
Rochester, Kansas   67200

Dear Mr. Anaya: Salutation

        From the information in your letter, I think you will be   Body
very happy with the Goodfield Mud and Snow Tread Recap, size
8.75-16.5, 8-ply rating, for your camper. The tread on this
model has been designed to provide excellent traction on slippery
surfaces with a minimum of hum on dry pavement. Owners report
outstanding durability of this tire on rough terrain.

        MacLaughlin's Auto Service, 151 Main Street in Rochester,
carries this model in stock. I'm sure you will be impressed by
the value you receive at the price he'll offer you.

Cordially,

                                                               Signature Block

Gerald Cresap
Sales Manager

Figure 1 The six formal parts of a business letter

The Printed Letterhead

The letterhead is printed at the top of the sheet of paper your company will supply for typing letters on. It almost always includes the full name of the company, the full address of the company, the telephone number, and possibly other information including the company logo or motto. Sometimes the letterhead will also identify your department or section of the company by name. Because all this information is already printed on the letterhead, you won't need to repeat it in the information you type on that sheet.

The Dateline

The dateline identifies the date on which the letter was mailed. Unless you know there will be some delay, you or your typist should type today's date here.

The Inside Address

This is the address of the person or company you're writing to, the same address that you'll type on the front of the envelope for mailing. Normally it will include the name of the person you're writing to, the name of the company he or she works for, the company's street address, the company's city, state, and ZIP code. (Figure 2 lists abbreviations of state names used by the Postal Service.)

AL	Alabama	LA	Louisiana	OH	Ohio
AK	Alaska	ME	Maine	OK	Oklahoma
AZ	Arizona	MD	Maryland	OR	Oregon
AR	Arkansas	MA	Massachusetts	PA	Pennsylvania
CA	California	MI	Michigan	RI	Rhode Island
CO	Colorado	MN	Minnesota	SC	South Carolina
CT	Connecticut	MS	Mississippi	SD	South Dakota
DE	Delaware	MO	Missouri	TN	Tennessee
FL	Florida	MT	Montana	TX	Texas
GA	Georgia	NE	Nebraska	UT	Utah
HI	Hawaii	NV	Nevada	VT	Vermont
ID	Idaho	NH	New Hampshire	VA	Virginia
IL	Illinois	NJ	New Jersey	WA	Washington
IN	Indiana	NM	New Mexico	WV	West Virginia
IA	Iowa	NY	New York	WI	Wisconsin
KS	Kansas	NC	North Carolina	WY	Wyoming
KY	Kentucky	ND	North Dakota		

Figure 2 Accepted two-letter abbreviations of state names

The Salutation

The salutation is the line that says something like "Dear Mr. Smith:". It introduces the letter in a pleasant way by addressing the reader by name. Normally the salutation begins with "Dear," then names the recipient by Mr., Ms., Mrs., Dr., Professor, or other title, and last name. This line ends in a colon (:).

When you do not know the name of the person who will read your letter, obviously you need an alternative form for this line. Until recently "Gentlemen:" (definitely not "Dear Sir:") was accepted. However, it has become obvious that "Gentlemen" has sexist overtones which make it unacceptable to many people, and at the time of this writing no other alternative has emerged as an accepted form. If you wish to avoid "Gentlemen," perhaps the best alternative is to leave this line out of your letter completely; most readers will not notice the omission, and many will be distracted by "Gentlemen."

The Body

The body of the letter is the actual message you're writing to the reader.

The Signature Block

The signature block is the formal closing of the letter. It consists of "Cordially," "Sincerely," or some other closing, then three empty spaces in which you'll sign your name in ink, then your typed signature and your company title.

THE ACCEPTED VARIATIONS IN LAYOUT

Although nearly all letters contain these six formal parts, there is some range of acceptable variation in the way the parts can be laid out on the page. Three items may vary: (1) The dateline may be typed at the left margin, or it may be typed toward the right side of the page, usually beginning roughly at the center or just right of the center of the page. (2) The first line of each paragraph in the body may be indented five to seven spaces, or it may be typed flush with the left margin just like other lines. (3) The signature block may be typed at the left margin, or it may be typed toward the right side of the page, usually in line with the dateline above.

Two combinations of these possible variations are commonly accepted.

Conservative Letter Style

One combination has the dateline and signature block aligned and positioned just to the right of the center of the page. In addition, the body of the letter has indented paragraphs. This style is generally viewed as a relatively conservative style, partly because it retains more of the flavor of the historical letter form. This format is illustrated in Figure 3.

Thompson Electronics Corporation

1125 WOODWARD ST. • POINT JENNINGS, CA 93100 • TEL (805) 555-1298

January 18, 1983

Mr. Al Howard
JZ Products, Inc.
12185 Industrial Park
Springfield, Texas 77300

Dear Mr. Howard:

The 365 oscillator-mixer circuit-board assemblies you're interested in could be delivered as early as March 25 at a cost of $26.72 per unit. These units would meet the specifications listed in your bulletin no. 4955 dated December 28, 1982.

If we are notified of acceptance of this offer by January 28, will be able to provide prototypes for testing February 18. Then unless there are major changes that require ordering of new materials, initial deliveries of completed units could begin as early as March 11, allowing normal shipping time. Our ability to provide prototypes for testing and completed assemblies on such short notice may be very helpful to your production people.

We will begin processing your order as soon as we have your go-ahead on this project.

Cordially,

Robert Juscik
President

Figure 3 Conservative letter style

Progressive Letter Style

The other accepted combination has every single line in the letter beginning flush with the left margin. Dateline and signature block begin at the left margin and paragraphs are not indented. This approach may save the typist a few seconds on each letter since there's no need to space over for the beginnings of paragraphs. This style produces an asymmetrical visual image on the page, and is generally considered a more progressive and modern style. It is illustrated in Figure 4.

Other combinations of variations in placement of the dateline, paragraph indentation, and signature-block style are sometimes seen, and actually all possible combinations are considered reasonably correct, especially if the format is selected with an eye to matching the geometrical shape of the printed letterhead.

SPACING THE LETTER

Because the length of the body varies so much from letter to letter, it is quite impossible to give simple rules for letter spacing that will work every time. A considerable amount of variation is accepted within certain basic limitations.

The most important guideline in spacing a letter is that the letter should be surrounded on all four sides of the page by a good wide band of white space, normally at least an inch to an inch and a half. If your letter is short, you'll have even wider margins at top and bottom.

The second principle is that the visual center of your typing should be located just above center page. That is, as you look at the typed material on the page, the center of the typed message (including dateline, inside address, and signature block) should be just above the physical center of the page. The most common fault in beginners' letters is that they're crammed up against the top of the page, with the bottom half of the page completely empty. If you're typing a short letter, you'll want to use extra wide margins and space the formal parts out to avoid this.

The third basic principle of spacing is: Single-space within elements of the letter and double-space between elements. This means that within the inside address and within body paragraphs you'll single-space between lines. Between formal parts and between paragraphs in the body, double-space. (In other words, leave one blank space between the two typed lines.) Sometimes you may use extra space to center a very short letter, but normally there are only two exceptions to the spacing rule. The first exception is the extra space between the dateline and the inside address. You'll usually space about an inch (six lines), although you'll vary this spacing in response to the length of your letter after you get some practice estimating this. The other exception is the spacing within the signature block. You normally leave three blank lines in which to sign your name between the "Cordially" and your typed signature in the signature block.

califano — kentucky land company, inc.

409 College Center Bldg. • P.O. Box 811 • Portland, KY 42100

August 2, 1983

Mrs. Roberta Morganstern
596 Second Street, No. 8
Part Henry, Maine 04100

Dear Mrs. Morganstern:

Here is your lease for apartment no. 2056 in the College Towers complex beginning October 2, 1983. Please sign the top copy of the lease and return it as soon as possible.

I have applied your $920 check to your account as follows:

First month's rent	$360.00
Last month's rent	360.00
Security deposit	200.00
Total	$920.00

I will make arrangements to be sure your apartment is fully cleaned and ready for occupancy when you arrive in Portland on October 2.

Cordially,

James McPherson
Manager

Figure 4 Progressive letter style

(Space down four lines and type your name on the fourth line, leaving three blank lines.)

In an average-length letter of three or four paragraphs, then, you'll single-space within elements (including paragraphs), double-space between elements, space six spaces between the dateline and the inside address, and space four spaces in the signature block to leave room for your signature. Once you get the spacing visualized, it's pretty easy to remember.

ADDITIONAL FORMAL PARTS

The six formal parts we discussed earlier are found in nearly all business letters. In addition to these, there are several parts that are sometimes used for special purposes.

Typed Letterhead

When you're writing a personal business letter and you don't have printed letterhead stationery, you'll need to type your return address someplace on the letter so that your reader will have it. The conventional place to type your return address is on the two lines directly above the dateline, single-spaced. Since your typed signature appears in the signature block, all you need at the top is your street address, followed by city, state, and ZIP code. See Figure 5 for an example.

Attention-Line Inside Address

Sometimes it is useful to make it clear that your letter is intended to be directed to a company, not to the individual (acting as an individual) who will read it. A legal offer to sell or a legal acceptance of an offer that forms part of a contract might be such a case. In such cases you may wish to address the letter to the company and include an attention line ("Attention: R. G. Brown") so the letter will be delivered to the right person. See Figure 6 for an example of this and the remaining special parts discussed below.

Subject Line

Subject lines just like those used in memos can be used in letters, although it's not common. If you wish to use a subject line, type it in all caps below the salutation. You can preface it by the word "Subject:" if you wish.

Company Signature

In a letter that has legal standing such as an offer or an acceptance of an offer, you may wish to indicate clearly that you are writing as a representative of your company rather than on your own behalf as an individual. To do that, you can type the company name in all caps two spaces below the "Cordially" in the signature block. Then below the company name you leave the three blank spaces for your signature followed

38491 S. 19th Street
Washington, Alabama 36100
July 11, 1983

Futura Imported Products
P. O. Box 843
Selma, Minnesota 55100

I would like to have more information about the silver and
turquoise watch band that you advertised in <u>Leisure</u> magazine.
Will the band fit all watches, or do I have to specify what type
of watch I have? If I have to specify, exactly what do you need
to know?

Since I have always thought both silver and turquoise were quite
expensive, how can you possibly sell a band like this for only
$14.95? Do you guarantee that the silver and turquoise are real?

I hope you can answer these questions, because the band looked
very attractive in the ad.

Cordially,

Cynthia Crighton

Figure 5 Letter form with no letterhead

by the typed signature. The first name that appears following "Cordially" or "Sincerely" is the name legally responsible for the contents of the letter, and this procedure clearly assigns responsibility to the company and not to you personally.

Your Title

If you wish to indicate your title (the name of your job), you do that in the line immediately below your typed signature. If you need to indicate both your title and the name of your department or sub-unit of the company, then you type your signature, a comma, your title, then the name of the department on the following line.

George C. Harlan   or   George C. Harlan, Director
Director   Sales Division

Initials of Dictator and Typist

To establish responsibility for the contents of the letter, many companies follow the procedure of typing at the bottom of the letter both the initials of the person who dictated or composed the letter and the initials of the person who typed the letter. Conventionally the dictator's initials are typed first in caps, with the typist's initials following in lower case. (See Figure 6.) Sometimes a colon separates the two.

Carbon Copy Notation

If you are sending a carbon copy of the letter to some third person, it is considered courteous to the recipient to indicate so. Usually this is done by the notation "cc:" or "copy:", followed by the name of the person who is receiving the copy.

Enclosure

If something is supposed to be in the envelope in addition to the letter, sometimes the notation "Encl." or "Enclosure(s)" is placed at the bottom. This serves as notice both to your own mail room and to the recipient's mail room that something else is supposed to be there.

Postscript

The "P.S." is seldom used in normal business correspondence, on the principle that anything worth saying should have been said in the letter. (If you have afterthoughts you should rewrite the letter to cover them.) A P.S. is sometimes used to emphasize a quick comment, which it does very well, or to add a handwritten personal note to the bottom of a letter that is otherwise about business.

JZ PRODUCTS, INC.
12185 Industrial Park
Springfield, TX 77300

January 24, 1983

Thompson Electronics Corporation
1125 Woodward Street
Point Jennings, California 93110

Attention: Robert Juscik

Dear Mr. Juscik:

ACCEPTANCE OF YOUR OFFER TO SUPPLY OSCILLATOR-MIXER ASSEMBLIES

Please go ahead with the development of the oscillator-mixer
circuit-board assemblies at $26.72 each according to the
specifications in bulletin no. 4955 (copy enclosed). We will
accept delivery of prototypes for testing by February 18, and we
will be expecting initial partial shipments of completed
assemblies beginning March 11, as you offered. Shipment of the
full 365 units will be completed by March 25.

Cordially,
JZ PRODUCTS, INC.

Al J. Howard
Director of Purchasing

AJHeb
cc: Roger Garold, Comptroller
Encl.

P.S. We very much appreciate your quick reply to our inquiry,
and we are looking forward to working with you again if this
contract is completed successfully.

Figure 6 Optional special parts found in some letters

Appendix B

How to Type a Memo

A memo consists of a heading and a body. The heading consists of four pieces of information typed at the top of the page: (1) the name of the person to whom the message is addressed, (2) the name of the writer of the message, (3) the subject of the message, and (4) the date on which the message was sent. These pieces of information are usually labeled "To," "From," "Subject," and "Date." Figure 1 shows how these parts are typically typed at the top of the page.

The subject line is sometimes typed in all caps; sometimes just the initial letters of the words are capitalized. The body—the message itself—is usually typed single-spaced, with double-spacing between paragraphs. Paragraphs may be indented or not indented, whichever is the usual practice in your organization. If paragraphs are not indented, then you must remember to double-space between paragraphs for clarity.

Memos are often typed on sheets of paper smaller than the usual 8 1/2 x 11 inch typing paper. Half-size paper (8 1/2 x 5 1/2 inches) is standard in many organizations. Some companies provide printed memo sheets with spaces for filling in the heading information above the body.

In most organizations, memos are signed simply with the writer's initials, as in Figure 1, if they are signed at all. Full signatures are seldom used. Often, in fact, the writer's typed name in the heading constitutes the only signature.

```
                                         January 28, 1983

TO: Vic Michaels, Engineering Manager
    Cynthia van de Wetering, Vice-President for Production

FROM: Robert Juscik, President

SUBJECT: JZ Products Contract


Congratulations on the fine work you did preparing the bid on the
JZ Products contract.

Bob Rinhardt in marketing thinks this could be the first of many
JZ Products jobs, and I believe that we should go all out to make
the dates we agreed to.  I'm counting on you to deliver.
```

Figure 1 Typical memo format

Appendix C

Review of English Fundamentals

INTRODUCTION

Words are merely tools that are used by writers and speakers to communicate thoughts and ideas. Too often, the listener or reader cannot interpret or understand those thoughts and ideas because the message is not clearly stated. In this section of the text, you will review some of the basic guidelines for making your own written ideas and thoughts more easily understood.

When you write, you assemble words into sentences, sentences into paragraphs, and paragraphs into a memo, letter, or report. A review of the basic parts of speech (functions of words) and the basic segments of sentences will help you understand and use words more effectively.

The basic functions of words in sentences are shown in the diagram on the next page. A sentence is the basis of all effective written communication. A sentence is a group of related words that asks a question, makes a statement, expresses strong feelings, or gives a command. The sentence is a complete thought and makes sense to the reader. The main elements of a sentence are the subject and the predicate. The subject of a sentence contains a noun or pronoun and adjectives. The predicate of a sentence contains a verb, or verbs, modifiers (adverbs and prepositional phrases), and sometimes a complement. Other parts of speech used in a sentence are interjections and conjunctions.

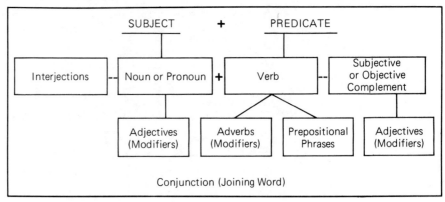

Figure 1 A basic sentence

NOUNS

A noun is a person, place, thing, concept, or quality.

Common and Proper Nouns

Common (general)	*Proper (specific: usually capitalized)*
author	Ian Fleming
city	Boston
ocean	Pacific Ocean
family	the Smiths
faith	Catholicism

Forming the Plural of Nouns

To form the plural of most nouns:

	Singular	*Plural*
1. Add *s* to the singular.	typewriter	typewriters
2. Change a final *f* or *fe* to *v* or *ve*, then add *s*. However, in some cases this rule does not apply. Merely add *s*.	knife half proof belief	knives halves proofs beliefs
3. Change a final *y* to *i* and add *es* if the letter preceding *y* is a consonant. However, if the letter preceding *y* is a vowel, do not change *y*, just add *s*.	laboratory attorney	laboratories attorneys

4. Add *es* to nouns ending in:

s	loss	losses
x	box	boxes
ch	lunch	lunches
sh	dish	dishes
z	buzz	buzzes

5. Change inside vowel(s) in some nouns that have irregular plurals.

man	men
foot	feet
woman	women

6. Learn these nouns with irregular plurals that are frequently used in business.

datum	data
analysis	analyses
crisis	crises
basis	bases
appendix	appendices
medium	media

Forming Possessive Nouns to Show Ownership or Source

1. To form the possessive of most nouns, add *'s* to the singular:

a typewriter belonging to Shauna   Shauna's typewriter

2. To form the possessive of plural nouns not ending in *s*, add *'s*:

coat department for women   women's coat department

3. Add *'* to plural nouns ending in *s*.

handbooks for secretaries   secretaries' handbooks

PRONOUNS

A pronoun is a substitute for a noun, a person, place, or thing.

Personal pronouns indicate:	*Singular*	*Plural*
First person (speaker)	I	we
	me	us
Second person (person spoken to)	you	you
	you/yours	you/yours
Third person (one spoken about)	he/she	they
	him/her	them
	it	they

Demonstrative pronouns (point out a specific person or thing)

this   that   these   those

Indefinite pronouns (generally refer to persons or things)

all	either	much	other
another	everybody	neither	several
any	everyone	no	some
anybody	everything	nobody	somebody
anyone	few	none	someone
anything	least	nothing	something
both	many	one	
each	more	one another	
each other	most	oneself	

Relative pronouns (used to connect parts of sentences)

who, whose, whom	refer to	people
which	refers to	things or animals
that	refers to	people, things or animals

Interrogative pronouns (ask questions)

who   which   what

Numerical pronouns (cite numbers)

cardinal: *one, two, three, . . .*
ordinal: *first, second, third, . . .*

Reflexive pronouns

myself	yourself	himself, herself, itself
ourselves	yourselves	themselves

Pronouns That Are Easily Confused with Other Words

1. *its/it's* Remember—*it's* is a shortened form of two words: *it is.* To determine which word to use, mentally substitute *it is* for *it's* to see if it makes sense in context.

   Example: The dog had hurt *its* paw. (Could you use *it is* paw? No.)
   Example: *It's* a shame you fell on the ice. (Could you use *it is*? Yes.)

2. *whose/who's* Remember—*who's* is a shortened form of two words: *who is.* Use the mental substitution test.

   Example: *Whose* coat was left on the ground? (Could you use *who is* coat? No.)
   Example: *Who's* going to the office today? (Could you use *who is* going? Yes.)

Pronouns and Antecedents Agree in Number, Gender, and Person

An antecedent is a word or phrase for which a pronoun has been substituted.

Example: <u>Marybeth</u> sighed as <u>she</u> started the letter again.

1. Try to achieve continuity in "person." A sentence or paragraph should be written in the first, second, or third person. Do not change from first person to second person to third person. Most business writing is done in the third person.

> Incorrect: Most *writers* are concerned with spelling and grammar. *I* always try to punctuate correctly also.
>
> Correct: Most *writers* are concerned with spelling and grammar. *They* always try to punctuate correctly also.

2. A singular pronoun should be used with:

    a. A singular antecedent
    Example: *Ben* dropped *his* eraser.

    b. Two singular nouns joined by *or* (or *nor*)
    Example: Either *Ed or Marvin* forgot to turn in *his* report.

    c. An indefinite singular pronoun: anyone, each, everything, somebody, neither, nothing, anybody, each one, every, something, no one, one, anything, everyone, someone, either, nobody, another.
    Example: Each man is responsible for *his* own actions.

3. A plural pronoun should be used with:

    a. A plural antecedent
    Example: The *secretaries* did *their* work efficiently.

    b. Two or more antecedents joined by *and*
    Example: *Ben and Joan* said *they* would attend the convention.

    c. Singular and a plural antecedent joined by *or* (or *nor*). Try to place the plural antecedent closer to the pronoun.
    Example: Neither Jones nor the *salespersons* have reached *their* goals.

    d. An indefinite plural pronoun: many, others, few, several, both.
    Examples: A *few* secretaries have finished *their* reports.
                 Both of the accountants have completed *their* work.

Pronouns Without Clear Antecedents

Avoid using pronouns rather than nouns when the pronoun does not have a clear antecedent.

> Vague: The secretary made four errors yesterday. *This* made her supervisor unhappy. (*This* has no specific antecedent—only an implied idea.)
>
> Better: After the secretary made four errors yesterday, her supervisor became unhappy.

Vague: The judge intended to excuse the jury early. She knew *it* would please them.

Better: She knew that such a move would please the jury.

Or: The judge knew that excusing the jury early would please them.

Vague: The office was the scene of a quiet routine; the secretaries seemed to appreciate it. (The routine or the office?)

Better: The secretaries seemed to appreciate the quiet routine of the office.

It is correct to say: *This* is the way we do our work. (*This* refers to a way.) It is also correct to say: *That* is a good idea. (*That* refers to an idea.) It is acceptable to use *you* in expressions such as: if you can type, you can get a good job.

Pronoun Case—Nominative and Objective

1. Use the nominative case (*I, we, she, he, they, who*) for:

a. Subject of a verb
Example: *She* walked to the store. (*She* is the subject of the verb *walked.*)

b. Subjective complement (describes or is the same person as the subject)
Example: The owner is *he.* (he-owner)

2. Use the objective case (*me, us, him, her, them, whom*) for:

a. Object of a verb (answers *who* or *what* after the verb)
Example: The personnel manager chose *her.* (Chose who?)

b. Object of a preposition
Example: Between you and *me,* I think Marlys should win.

c. Indirect object of a verb
Example: She gave *him* a package.

3. Sometimes it is difficult to decide which pronoun to use, as there are two or more pronouns (compound pronouns) used in a sentence.

Example: Mom gave the flowers to my sister and (*me/I*). (Reread the sentence and mentally leave out *my sister and.* It is easy to see that the correct pronoun is *me: Mom gave the flowers to me.*)

Example: (*We/us*) secretaries go to work at eight each day. (Reread the sentence and mentally omit *secretaries: We go to work at eight each day.*)

Example: Mary types much faster than (*he/him*). (Mentally add the logical word to the pronoun: *Mary types faster than he does.*)

Special Problems with Who and Whom

If you have trouble remembering whether to use *who* or *whom*, try substituting *he* for *who* and *him* for *whom*.

Example: Who/Whom is speaking? (He is speaking. Use *who*.)

To who/whom is John speaking? (John in speaking to him. Use *whom*.)

Whom were you talking about? (You were talking about him. Use *whom*.)

Placement of Pronouns

1. Avoid placing a pronoun in a position that makes it impossible for the reader to determine which antecedent is referred to.

Vague: Pat asked Martha if her report could safely be stored in her desk.
Does it mean: Pat's report in Pat's desk? Pat's report in Martha's desk? Martha's report in Pat's desk? Martha's report in Martha's desk?

Better: Pat asked Martha, "Could my report be safely stored in your desk?"

2. Avoid placing a pronoun too far away from its antecedent.

Vague: The engineers belonged to the best firm in the city. The buildings were beautiful, and the construction was solid. They were quite creative and innovative.

Better: The creative and innovative engineers who built the beautiful and solidly constructed buildings belonged to the best firm in town.

ADJECTIVES

An adjective describes, limits, or restricts a noun.

Avoiding Overused Adjectives

Avoid adjectives that are overused: *good, fine, wonderful,* and so on. For instance, a *good* friend could be an *understanding* friend or an *old* friend.

The Use of Commas with Two Adjectives

You may wish to use more than one adjective. You will have to decide whether or not to use a comma between the two adjectives. If you can say *and* between the two adjectives, put a comma between them.

Example: an old elm tree (You cannot say *an old and elm tree.* Do not use a comma.)

an old, battered boat (You can say *an old and battered boat.* Use a comma.)

A or An?

Use *a* or *an* for general references to persons, places, or things.

1. Use *a* before words beginning with a consonant.
Examples: a house   a car   a book

2. Use *an* before words beginning with a vowel.
Examples: an apple   an exciting book

3. Use *a* before words beginning with *h* or *u* if the *h* or *u* is sounded.
Examples: a high hill   a usual sort of day

4. Use *an* if the *h* or *u* is silent.
Examples: an hour   an unusual sort of day

5. Do not use *a* after *sort of* or *kind of.*
Examples: sort of day (*not* sort of a day)
kind of book (*not* kind of a book)

Comparison of Adjectives

Adjectives are used to compare two or more things according to degree.

1. The comparative of many adjectives is formed by adding *er.* The superlative is formed by adding *est.*

Simple	Comparative	Superlative
high	higher	highest
low	lower	lowest

Example: high hill (Simple form—simple)
higher hill of the two (Comparing two—comparative)
highest hill in the state (Comparing more than two—superlative)
happy person (Simple form—simple)
happier person (Moderate degree—comparative)
happiest person (Greatest degree—superlative)

2. The comparative of many other adjectives is formed by using *more.* The superlative is formed by using *most.*

Simple	Comparative	Superlative
likely	more likely	most likely
beautiful	more beautiful	most beautiful
expensive	more expensive	most expensive

3. Some adjectives change forms.

Simple	Comparative	Superlative
good	better	best
bad	worse	worst

VERBS

The main ingredient of the predicate portion of a sentence is a verb. The verb states something about the subject—an action, a condition, or a state of being.

Kinds of Verbs

1. Intransitive verbs need no complement.
Examples: Luke sleeps.   Pat walks.

2. Transitive verbs need a complement (called the object of a verb) to make a complete thought.
Example: The typist adjusted . . . . (The typist adjusted *what?*)
The typist adjusted the paper.

3. Linking verbs link the subject to a noun, pronoun or adjective (called subjective complements) and describe the subject or establish an identity or equality between the subject and the subjective complement.
Examples: John is tired. (*Tired*, an adjective, describes *John*, the subject.)
John is the secretary. (*Secretary*, a noun, establishes the identity of *John*, the subject.)

4. Auxiliary verbs are placed before a principal or main verb. Examples of auxiliary verbs are: *has, have, had, is, was, were, am, be, being, been, do, does, shall, will, would, should, may, might, must, can, could.*
Examples: Jane *is* (auxiliary) *typing* (main verb) the manuscript.
Mark *has* (auxiliary) *walked* (main verb) many miles.

Note: The main verb is usually an *ing* or *ed* word with auxiliary verb. Also, some auxiliary verbs can also be a main verb as in *I have a cold* or *Mr. Sparks is a teacher.*

Verb Tense

A verb indicates when an action takes place.

Present—fact or action takes place at the moment	I am watching the secretary type the report
Future—fact or action will take place in the future. (Use shall or will.)	The secretary will type the report tomorrow.
Past—fact or action that has already taken place. (Add an *ed* to verb.)	The secretary typed the report yesterday.
Special—use an auxiliary verb, *ed* form.	The secretary has already typed the report.
Special—use an auxiliary verb, *ing* form.	The secretary is typing the report right now.

Some verbs change form rather than adding *ed* or *ing*.

Present/future tense	Past tense	Special form (past participle)
begin	began	begun
drink	drank	drunk
sing	sang	sung
swim	swam	swum
do	did	done
see	saw	seen
go	went	gone
choose	chose	chosen
ring	rang	rung
find	found	found
take	took	taken
write	wrote	written

Remember—Always use an auxiliary (helping) verb with the special form verbs.

There are many more verbs that change form. If you have any doubts, consult a dictionary or a handbook.

Verbs That Are Easily Confused

1. *can (could)/may (might)*

    a. *can/could:* implies ability
        Examples: Can you type fast? (Are you able to type fast?)
        Could he really have lifted that huge box? (Was he able?)

    b. *may/might:* denotes permission or a possibility.
        Examples: I may not come to school tomorrow. (possibility)
        May I please see your notes? (permission)
        He might forget to call Mr. Barnes. (possibility)

2. *lie/lay*

    a. *lie, lay, lain,* and *lying:* mean to recline, rest, stay, or take a position of rest and do not require an object.
        Examples: Will Mr. Sloan lie on the sofa or the floor?
        She lay on the couch moaning her sad fate.
        The dog has lain on the porch since morning.
        He is lying on the grass.

    b. *lay, laid, laying:* mean to put something down or place or deposit something somewhere and always requires an object. (Hint: if you can substitute the words *place, placed,* or *placing* for *lay, laid,* or *laying* you have chosen the correct form.)

Examples: Please lay (place) the report on the table.
The student laid (placed) the report on the desk.
Have you laid (placed) the report on the table?
The workers are laying (placing) the carpet today.

Note: Lay can be used in each form of *lie* or *lay. Lay*—to put something or place something—is in the present. (*Lay the book on the table.*) *Lay*—to recline or rest—is used only in the past tense. (*She lay on the couch for an hour.*) Never: I will lay down for an hour.

3. *sit/set*

a. *sit, sat, sitting:* mean to rest in a chair or other place. *Sit* does not require an object.
Examples: John sits in the green chair every day.
Fran sat on the bench for an hour.
Is Greta sitting in the back row?

b. *sit, set, setting:* mean to put or place something somewhere. It always takes an object. (Hint: try substituting *put* or *place* for *set* or *setting.* If it makes sense, you have chosen the correct form.)
Examples: Please set (place) the typewriter beside the calculator.
Mary is setting (placing) the plant by the window.

4. *learn/teach*

a. *learn:* means to acquire knowledge or information.
Example: A good student can learn the keyboard in two weeks.

b. *teach:* means to impart or give knowledge or information.
Example: The teacher will probably teach the number keys in the next lesson.

5. *rise/raise*

a. *rise, rose, risen:* mean to move upward by itself, or go in an upward direction—self-movement.
Examples: Phillip rises early each morning.
The graceful bird rose into the sky.
Has the bread dough risen yet?

b. *raise, raised, raising:* mean to lift something or to move something in an upward direction. *Raise* needs an object.
Examples: Please raise the window.
The boy slowly raised his hand.
The clerk has been raising the flag each day at daybreak.

Agreement Between Subject and Verb
The verb in a sentence or clause should always agree with its subject in number—singular or plural.

1. A singular subject requires a singular verb.

Examples: The *typist was* tired.
The *book has* several torn pages.

2. A plural subject requires a plural verb.

Examples: The *secretaries were* tired.
The *books have* many torn pages.

3. Two subjects joined by *and* usually take a plural verb.

Examples: *Joseph and Karen are* good typists.

Note: If the two subjects refer to the same person or thing, however, use a singular verb.

Example: My good *friend and neighbor is* Mr. Windom.

4. Two subjects joined by *or* or *nor.*

If singular, use a singular verb: Either *John or Jill is* typing the report.

If plural, use a plural verb: Neither the *ribbons nor the books were* delivered.

If mixed (singular and plural subject), refer to the nearest one: The book and all the *papers were* damaged in the fire.

5. A collective noun (a noun that represents a group) takes a singular verb.

Examples: The *family likes* the new city.
The *class went* on a field trip.
Ten *hours is* a long time to type.

6. When the verbs are separated from the subjects, it may be difficult to determine whether to use singular or plural.

Examples: The typewriter which is surrounded by books and papers (is, are) for sale.
There (is, are) too many errors in this report.

Hint: Mentally eliminate the words between the subject and verb or rephrase. (The typewriter . . . is for sale. Too many errors are in this report.)

ADVERBS

An adverb modifies a verb, an adjective, or another adverb. An adverb tells *how, when, where,* or *how much.*

Forming Adverbs

1. Some adverbs are formed by adding *-ly* to the adjectives.

Adjective	*Adverb*
different	differently
distant	distantly
slow	slowly
solemn	solemnly

2. Some adverbs are the same as adjectives: *fast, far,* and *well* are examples.

Using Adverbs Correctly

1. An adverb can modify a verb.

Example: The typist worked *rapidly.* (*Rapidly* tells how the typist worked.)

2. An adverb can modify an adjective.

Example: The *very* efficient worker sorted the cards. (*Very* tells how efficient the worker was.)

3. An adverb can modify another adverb.

Example: The beginning typist worked *too* slowly. (*Too* tells how slowly the typist worked.)

Comparison of Adverbs

Adverbs, like adjectives, are compared in two ways, comparative and superlative.

1. Comparisons of adverbs are usually formed by adding *more* or *most* or *less* or *least.*

Adverb	Comparative	Superlative
rapidly	more rapidly	most rapidly
often	less often	least often

Examples: That car is moving slowly.
The car is moving more slowly than the truck.
The blue car is moving the most slowly.

2. Some adverb comparisons are formed by adding *er* or *est.*

Adverb	Comparative	Superlative
close	closer	closest
hard	harder	hardest
soon	sooner	soonest

Examples: The storm hit Des Moines *hard.*
The storm hit Chicago *harder* than Peoria.
Of the three cities, Milwaukee was hit *hardest* by the storm.

3. Some adverbs change form when forming comparisons.

Adverb	Comparative	Superlative
badly	worse	worst
little	less	least
much	more	most
near	nearer	nearest (next)
late	later	latest (last)
well	better	best

Examples: Mary writes *well*.
Karen writes *better* than Leona.
Of the entire class, Carl writes the *best*.

Adverbs and Adjectives That Are Often Misused

It is sometimes difficult to decide whether to use an adjective or its corresponding adverb.

1. *bad* (adjective)/*badly* (adverb
   Use *bad* to describe how a person feels.
   Use *badly* to show something is done poorly.

   Examples: I feel *bad* about the accident.
   Marion types *badly*.

2. *different* (adjective)/*differently* (adverb)

   Examples: The method is *different*. (describes method)
   She certainly drives *differently* since the accident. (in a different manner)

When you can substitute "in a different manner," use the *-ly* form. (This will also work for other words: *easy, careful, quick, safe*, etc.)

3. *good* (adjective)/*well* (adverb)

   Examples: Stacy read a *good* book. (what kind of book: adjective)
   Stacy reads *well*. (how Stacy reads: adverb)

4. *real* (adjective)/*really* (adverb)

   Examples: The ring has a *real* ruby for a center stone.
   He was *really* excited about the play.

5. *sure* (adjective)/*surely* (adverb)

   Examples: Tim was a *sure* winner.
   Vera was *surely* glad to leave early.

Avoiding Double Negatives

1. Incorrect: I couldn't find a ribbon *nowhere*.
   Correct: I couldn't find a ribbon anywhere.

2. Incorrect: Jerry *couldn't* hardly see the faded printing.
   Correct: Jerry could hardly see the faded printing.

PREPOSITIONS

A preposition connects a noun or pronoun to another word or words. Common prepositions are: *at, by, far, from, in, of, on, to, with,* and *over.*

Prepositional Phrases

A phrase has neither a subject nor a verb. The prepositional phrase contains the preposition plus a noun or pronoun and sometimes adjectives, articles, or adverbs.

Examples: John ate lunch *in the park.*
The trash basket is a receptacle *for unwanted paper.*
The clumsy clerk fell *over the chair.*

Unnecessary Prepositions

Do not add the word *up* to verbs such as *call, divide, eat, drink,* and so on. Do not add *of* or *from* to *off.* It is better not to end a sentence with a preposition.

Incorrect: Where is my book at?
Correct: Where is my book?

Incorrect: Which party are you going to?
Correct: To which party are you going?

CONJUNCTIONS

A conjunction is a word used either to connect words, phrases, clauses, or sentences or to show how one sentence is related to another.

Using Conjunctions Correctly

1. *Coordinating conjunctions* connect two nouns, two phrases, or two independent clauses. Examples of coordinating conjunctions are: *and, but, or, nor, for,* and *yet.*

Two nouns: My favorite foods are tacos *and* pizzas.

Two phrases: He walked around the park *and* through the forest.

Two independent clauses: The typewriter was delivered, *and* she began to work.

2. *Subordinating conjunctions* indicate that one sentence element, or clause, is subordinate to another.

Examples: *After* the letter was typed, Marvin went home.
If my machine stops one more time, I will be very tempted to quit for the day.
Ivan wants him to type the income statement *before* it is too late.

3. *Correlative conjunctions* are used in pairs or series. Examples of correlative conjunctions are: *neither . . . nor, either . . . or, both . . . and, whether . . . or, if . . . then.*

Examples: Edna finished *neither* the manuscript *nor* the report.
I can't decide *whether* I should go to the office *or* work at home.

4. *As* or *as if.* Do not confuse *like* (a preposition) for *as* or *as if* (conjunctions).

Incorrect: John acted like he had never seen a typewriter.
Correct: John acted as if he had never seen a typewriter.

INTERJECTIONS

An interjection is a word or group of words used to voice an exclamation or strong emotion. Often, an interjection is used as an introductory word and is immediately followed by an exclamation point.

Examples: Oh! I knew he was going to fall!
Edna! Is that really you, after all these years?
What! You mean to tell me that you wrecked it?

EFFECTIVE SENTENCES

An effective sentence expresses a complete thought clearly and precisely. A good writer has learned to construct sentences and paragraphs in such a way that the reader can quickly understand and comprehend the exact meaning or thought implied. By choosing precise words, writing effective sentences, and mastering the art of building paragraphs, you will be able to write so that your meaning is clearly understood. The following material gives some helpful guidelines about choosing words carefully and writing effective sentences, paragraphs, and compositions.

Choosing the Right Word

One of the most common problems a writer faces is how to choose the exact word to convey a certain thought or idea directly to the reader. Writing must be precise; vague words or unacceptable usage of words may obscure the author's meaning.

1. Use concrete nouns and descriptive adjectives, adverbs, and phrases. Some words are vague; they can mean many different things. Words such as *nice, good, bad, thing, work,* and so forth, do not give the reader much information.

Vague: The lecture was good and I learned a lot.
Better: The lecture solved two problems for me; I learned how to balance a checkbook and how to calculate interest.

Vague: a nice color
Better: an emerald green, a vivid scarlet, a dull black

2. Use the correct word; some words are often misused.

accept to take or receive	*except* to leave out; aside from
advice an opinion	*advise* to recommend
biannual twice a year	*biennial* once every two years
council a governing body	*counsel* to give advice
fewer Use with items that can be counted: fewer apples.	*less* Use with nouns that cannot be counted: less noise.
good Modifies a noun or pronoun.	*well* Modifies a verb or adverb.

3. Use English idioms correctly. An idiom is an expression peculiar to a language and is perfectly acceptable if used correctly.

Correct	*Incorrect*
acquitted of	acquitted from
aim to prove	aim at proving
can't help feeling	can't help but feel
comply with	comply to
independent of	independent from
in search of	in search for
kind of (+ noun)	kind of a (+ noun)
aloud	out loud
try to	try and

Simple Sentences

1. A simple sentence consists of a single independent clause. An independent clause is a group of related words that expresses a complete thought and can stand alone as a sentence.

 a. *Subject + verb:* Shauna arrived. (a complete thought)

 b. *Subject + verb + direct object:* Shauna opened the door. (*door*, a direct object, completes *opened*, the verb.)

 c. *Subject + verb + subjective complement: Shauna* is a *secretary*. (*Secretary*, the subjective complement, is the same person as *Shauna*, the subject.) Shauna is efficient. (*Efficient*, the subjective complement, describes *Shauna*, the subject.)

2. Modifiers (adjectives, adverbs, and phrases) can make a sentence more interesting and precise.

 a. *Phrases* A phrase is a group of related words that does not have a subject or a predicate.

 Prepositional phrase (preposition + object)

 Examples: *During the storm* the lights went out.
 I found the books *under the desk*.

 Infinitive phrase (to + verb + object)

 Examples: She tried *to complete the report*.
 To fly to the moon is Will's only ambition.

 -ing phrase:

 Examples: *Typing the detailed report* was difficult.
 Looking very sheepish, the clerk turned toward Mr. Jones.
 My favorite hobby is *running a mile a day*.

b. Look at the following sentences and see how each is made more interesting or precise.

Shauna arrived. (This sentence is dull and uninteresting.)

Poor, forlorn Shauna arrived at the office two hours late. (This sentence is more interesting and gives the reader more precise information—Shauna is poor and forlorn, and she arrived at the office two hours late.)

Smiling and whistling, Shauna breezed into the office two hours early. (The reader's image of Shauna would be changed entirely, simply by changing a few adjectives and adverbs.)

Shauna opened the door. (dull and not precise)

Shauna timidly opened the creaking door. (much more interesting)

Shauna threw the door open with a loud bang.

Shauna is a secretary.

Shauna certainly is a lazy and inefficient secretary. (Do you get a better picture in your mind?) or . . .

Shauna, without a doubt, is the most efficient secretary in the office.

Compound Sentences

A compound sentence consists of two related independent clauses joined together by a conjunction, a semicolon, or a dash.

1. A *conjunction* (*and, or, but, nor, neither . . . nor, either . . . or*) may be used to join two independent clauses. Always place a comma before the conjunction unless the two clauses are quite short.

2. A *semicolon* is also used to join two independent clauses.

3. A *dash* can also join two independent clauses; it often indicates a change in thought, abruptness, or greater emphasis. Use the dash sparingly.

Examples: The blue typewriter has a broken paper bail. The black typewriter has a frayed cord.
The blue typewriter has a broken paper bail, and the black one has a frayed cord.

The new production method was quite successful. The secretaries were all able to complete more work during the day.
The new production method was successful; the secretaries were able to complete more work during the day.

Jerry typed the paper very fast. But he made too many errors.
Jerry typed the paper very fast—but he made too many errors.

Complex Sentences

A complex sentence consists of an independent clause (which expresses the main idea) and one or more dependent clauses (which support the main idea).

> Example: Before we can type the reports, we must find a new typewriter ribbon.

The main clause is *we must find a new typewriter ribbon,* and *before we can type the reports* is the dependent clause (it cannot stand alone).

1. If a dependent clause is placed before the main clause, use a comma after the dependent one. Words such as *after, although, because, if, since, unless,* and *when* are frequently used to introduce dependent clauses.

> Example: *After they debated behind closed doors,* the committee members published the report.

2. If the dependent clause is placed after the main clause, a comma is not used.

> Example: The committee members published the report *after they debated behind closed doors.*

3. If the dependent clause is within the main or independent clause, determine whether the clause is restrictive or nonrestrictive.

> a. A restrictive clause is essential to the meaning of a sentence and cannot be eliminated. Do not enclose restrictive clauses with commas.
>
> Example: All employees *who arrive over thirty minutes late on Monday* will be required to work all day Saturday. Can you eliminate the clause? No. (The sentence would not retain the original meaning if you simply wrote: *All employees will be required to work all day Saturday.*) Do you need commas? No.
>
> b. A nonrestrictive clause adds information but is not essential to the meaning of the sentence. Always enclose nonrestrictive or nonessential clauses with commas.
>
> Example: Ms. Stewart, *who is my teacher,* will address the secretarial seminar. Can you eliminate the clause? Yes. The reader would still know who was addressing the seminar—the fact that she is the writer's teacher is additional information not essential to the thought. Do you need commas? Yes.

Note: *That* is usually used to introduce restrictive clauses. *Which* is usually used to introduce nonrestrictive clauses. Use *that* or *which* to refer to animals, places or objects. *Who* refers to individual persons. *That* is usually used to refer to a class, species, or person. Use *that* or *who* to refer to people.

Problems to Avoid in Sentence Construction— Misplaced Modifiers

1. *Dangling participles.* Place modifying phrases as close as possible to the word(s) they modify, to avoid confusion.

Incorrect: *Having completed the lengthy report,* the typewriter was covered by Phil. (Did the typewriter complete the report?)

Correct: Phil covered the typewriter after he completed the lengthy report.

Incorrect: *Muttering loudly,* the duplicator was totally jammed. (Did the duplicator mutter loudly?)

Correct: Muttering loudly, he (or she) saw that the duplicator was jammed.

2. *Misplaced modifiers*

Incorrect: To type *rapidly,* concentration is important. (Does the contentration type rapidly?)

Correct: To type rapidly, a typist must concentrate. Be careful with words such as *only, nearly, almost, hardly, scarcely, just, even,* and *quite.* Be certain that there is no doubt as to which word is modified. Consider, for example, the use of *only:*

My sister bought the typewriter last week.
My *only* sister bought the typewriter last week.
My sister *only* bought the typewriter last week.
My sister bought the *only* typewriter last week.
My sister bought the typewriter *only* last week.

Can you see why it is important to place words carefully in a sentence?

A General Reminder

Be careful where you place a phrase or clause in a sentence. Misplaced modifiers can be quite amusing.

Incorrect: Walking in the snow, the lights were barely visible. (Were the lights walking?)

Correct: Walking in the snow, he could barely see the lights.

Incorrect: I paid one hundred dollars for the typewriter at the store that was only worth ten dollars. (Was the store only worth ten dollars?)

Correct: At the store, I paid one hundred dollars for a typewriter that was worth only ten.

Index

B